MW01016516

TOWARDS THE NEXT ORBIT

The National HRD Network

www.nationalhrd.org

About NHRD

The National HRD Network is the largest association of industry professionals, academia, and students in India. It is committed to promoting the HRD movement in India and developing the capability of human resource professionals through the means of education, training, research, and experience sharing. Its overarching purpose is to enable HR professionals to contribute profoundly in enhancing the competitiveness of their organizations and in creating value for the society. A not-for-profit organization which was founded in 1985, NHRD has as of no more than 8,500 members spread across 30 chapters in India.

TOWARDS THE NEXT ORBIT

A Corporate Odyssey

Edited by

SUBIR VERMA

Response
Business books from SAGE
Los Angeles ▪ London ▪ New Delhi ▪ Singapore ▪ Washington DC
www.sagepublications.com

Jointly published in 2010 by

Response Books
Business books from SAGE
B1/I-1 Mohan Cooperative Industrial Area
Mathura Road, New Delhi 110 044, India

SAGE Publications Inc
2455 Teller Road
Thousand Oaks, California 91320, USA

SAGE Publications Ltd
1 Oliver's Yard, 55 City Road
London EC1Y 1SP, United Kingdom

SAGE Publications Asia-Pacific Pte Ltd
33 Pekin Street
#02-01 Far East Square
Singapore 048763

National HRD Network
National Secretariat
C-81C, DLF Super Mart I
DLF City, Phase IV
Gurgaon 122 002
www.nationalhrd.org

Published by Vivek Mehra for SAGE Publications India Pvt Ltd, typeset in 10/12pt Adobe Caslon Regular by Star Compugraphics Private Limited, Delhi and printed at Chaman Enterprises, New Delhi.

Library of Congress Cataloging-in-Publication Data Available

ISBN: 978-81-321-0631-9 (HB)

The SAGE Team: Rekha Natarajan, Sonalika Rellan, Rajib Chatterjee and Deepti Saxena

Dedicated

to

Dr Pritam Singh
Padam Shri and Professor of Eminence

My coach and mentor who taught me the virtue
of the ageless wisdom:

"Satyameva Jayate"

CONTENTS

Part II
Dialogs with Change Masters

LIST OF TABLES

LIST OF FIGURES

PREFACE

Towards the Next Orbit is a book on hope and optimism. It talks about what we need to have and what all we need to do in our journey towards a new dawn. This book could not have been more opportune—in terms of time, in terms of relevance, and in terms of faith. For, it was just a few years ago that the bubble had burst. The global meltdown, reminiscent of the economic depression in the inter-world war period, had exploded the initial optimism that the bounty of unlimited treasure would shower its riches on anybody and everybody who had the capabilities to seize opportunities, participate in, and be included in the inexorable march of globalization. This had been followed by the scourge of an approaching apocalypse due to climate change which underscored with remarkable urgency the need to protect the world from the rapacity and pillage of unbridled industrialization. All at once the dialog on the business land-scape became rife with the themes of regulated corporate behavior, sustainable business models, inclusive growth strategy, and localization as a significant driver of the globalization thesis. Amidst all this, in the flat, but an uneven world, marked by asymmetric relations at all levels of dualities (global vs. local, core vs. periphery, developed vs. underdeveloped, industrial vs. agricultural, and urban vs. rural, and so on and so forth), the balance started shifting. The rapidly developing economies of BRIC countries along with the effulgent economies of Central Eastern Europe, the South and East Asia began their march towards being the epicenter of global commerce. These rapidly emerging economies providing significant cost and capital advantages and having a huge and growing internal market in a world integrated by the internationalization of the production process, financial markets and corporate strategies, the diffusion of technology and related R&D and knowledge, the emergence of global media and communication mechanism and a global political economy—are now the engine of hope and recovery for economies all over the world. This book brings forth the ideas, the experiences, the studies and the insights, and suggestions from both the theoreticians and the practitioners towards rebuilding a new world.

The book has a unique architecture. It is divided into two parts. The first part has rich conceptual papers and research based empirical papers written primarily by thought leaders from all over the world. The second part has dialogs with persons who dot the business landscape as change masters.

The theoretical papers have been grouped around certain core issues on which the survival, excellence, and sustainability of organizations is posited in the next orbit.

The first and primeval theme relates to the Strategy for Aligning Organizations with the Business Landscape in the next orbit. There are three contributions on this. Asha Bhandarker and Pritam Singh's "Routes to Peaks for Building Corporate Renaissance," Arun Kumar Jain and Ajay Singal's "Strategic Positioning Choices for Indian Business: Beyond *Jugaad* into the Next Orbit," and John Pisapia's "Finding the Future and Making It Happen."

The next theme is Managing Performance which is the core of business survival. Here there are three contributions. The first is from Shivganesh Bhargava: "Managing Performance: Beyond Value-based Leadership." Then is from Subir Verma: "Empowerment Practices and Corporate Effectiveness." The third contribution is from Soumendu Biswas: "Antecedents of Employee Performance."

The third theme is that of Shaping Talents which is all about preparing generals for creating winning organizations. Under this rubric are four papers. They are Jyotsna Bhatnagar's "Managing Talent through Employee Engagement Strategies," S. Mohan's "Bharat Petroleum Building Capabilities through Competency Modeling," Asha Bhandarker, Ashita Goswami, and Kshipra Rustogi's "CEO Leadership, Organizational Culture, and Employee Affect Responses at the Workplace," and Deepa Mazumdar's "Managerial Work Values in Public Sector Banks in India."

Entrepreneurship and innovation are the key mantras for growth and excellence. While the former is an orientation and the latter relates to the outcome in terms of a product or service that is considered new or novel, both are poised on the ability to sense opportunities and to create wealth. Thus, are the articles by Shubhabrata Basu's "Architectural Innovation and SAIL's Strategic Response" and Sumati Verma's "Emergence of the Born Global Entrepreneur."

Orchestrating change is difficult. The challenge is because of the need to realign structure, strategy, systems, and processes in the organization. Davide Sola, Marie Taillerd, and Giovanni Scarso Borioli's "Orchestrating Change: Shared Intentions is the Key Factor Enabling Change to Happen" is a fine article on the theme.

In order to bring about change, organizations need muscles which can develop only when there are capable leaders in the organization. The theme, Leadership: A Kaleidoscope, highlights the criticality and importance of leadership, not only for bringing change and for managing perform-ance, but also and more importantly for success and excellence of the organization in the next orbit. Meena Surie Wilson and Ellen Van Velsor's "A New Terrain of Leadership Development: An Indian Perspective," Alfredo Behrens and James Wright's "American Human Resource Management Techniques Fit Poorly in Latin America," and Armen Petrosyanvs "Twin-born Antipodes: Leadership and Management as Methods of Organizational Rule" are illuminating contributions in that genre.

The second part of the book contains incisive, intense, and illuminating reflections by seven change masters on five themes: *(a)* what is the emerging features of the business landscape; *(b)* what interventions are required from the country, organization, and HR professionals; *(c)* what role do the HR professionals need to play in order to facilitate this transition; *(d)* what competencies are required from HR professionals, in order to perform and succeed in the journey to the next orbit; and *(e)* how can the young HR professional become better and succeed in their endeavors within the organization.

These change masters are Manoj Kohli (CEO International and Jt. MD, Bharti Airtel), K.R. Kamath (CMD, Punjab National Bank), Dr Santrupt Misra (CEO, Carbon Black and Director, Group HR, Aditya Birla Group), S.Y. Siddiqui MEO—Administration (HR, Finance, Company Law and Legal, Maruti Suzuki), Arvind Agrawal (President, Corporate Development and Group HR, RPG), Dr Yasho Verma (COO, LG Electronics, India) and Dr Pritam Singh (Padamshree and Professor of Eminence, MDI).

The choice of these change masters was made on the basis of their eminence and contribution to the business and HR function. Hence, the choice of Dr Santrupt Misra, Arvind Agrawal, Dr Yasho Verma, and S.Y. Siddiqui. These reasons apart, the reasons of convenience and accessibility, in terms of the fact that both were Delhi based, weighed overwhelmingly in favor of Manoj Kohli and K.R. Kamath. Then we had wanted an academic who was as much known for his thought leadership as for his administrative acumen. The choice could not go beyond that of Dr Pritam Singh.

The dialogs have then been used to develop the perspective, a cognitive framework, behavioral repertoire, and portfolio of practices for the transition to and success in the next orbit. These gleanings for HR managers have been captured in Subir Verma's article, "Towards the Next Orbit: Wisdom for HR Professionals."

Towards the Next Orbit is therefore not just a compendium of academic papers. Nor is the book about pompous sermons based upon ritualistic conversations with change maestros. Instead, this book encapsulates the journey from despair to hope, survival to sustainable, ordinary to exceptional, mediocrity to excellence, and ephemeral to transcendental. The book is an odyssey. It describes, it analyzes, and it prescribes.

ACKNOWLEDGEMENTS

This book is the brain child of Dr Pritam Singh, Padam Shri and Professor of Eminence at MDI, Gurgaon. It was he who conceived the idea that there should be a book which should come out on the occasion of the 14th National Conference of the National HRD Network. There could be no words to ever and completely thank the one who has been the moving spirit behind this book. The book owes itself to Dr Pritam Singh.

This book has a unique architecture. In one form it is a collection of research articles that were invited from some of the most reputed international and national thinkers and writers on management. We thank each one of them for contributing their papers on the theme of the conference.

In another form, this book is for the practitioners of HR. Therefore, we thought the studies done by the management thinkers be complemented by dialogs with some of the renowned practitioners of management and HR function. We thank Mr Manoj Kohli, CEO (International) and Jt. MD, Bharti Airtel; Mr K.R. Kamath, CMD, Punjab National Bank; Mr S.Y. Siddiqui, MEO—Administration, HR, Finance, IT, Company Law & Legal, Maruti Suzuki India Limited; Santrupt B. Misra, Director, Group HR & CEO, Carbon Black Business, Aditya Birla Group; Arvind N. Agrawal, President, Corporate Development and Group HR, RPG

Group; Yasho V. Verma, COO, LG Electronics India; and Dr Pritam Singh for giving us the opportunity and the time at the shortest of notice to record their views on some of the issue and challenges that besets corporate world and the HR professionals both in this orbit and the next.

I am grateful to Mr N.S. Rajan, National President, NHRDN, Mr S.Y. Siddiqui, Regional President, NHRDN, and Mr Suresh Tripathi, President Delhi Chapter of NHRDN and other colleagues in the organizing committee of the conference for their encouragement and support.

I wish to thank Dr Asha Bhandarker, my colleague and friend in MDI for being a constant source of support and assistance. A word of thanks is due to my colleagues Dr Metri, Dr S.K. Rai, and Dr Sumita Rai who provided the initial thrust for this book. I also acknowledge the help received from Ms Anjana Rai and Ms Nidhi for their research support. The credit for the fact that I was able to meet the strict deadlines of our publisher, goes to Ms Tara Shankar Basu, our doctoral student. Her contribution in the final moments actually bailed me out.

Dr Sugata Ghosh of SAGE Publications has been more than a friend. He has been patient, tolerant, and at times furious with me for missing the deadlines. And if this book is seeing the light of the day, then it is only because of his perseverance and commitment to take it out.

Finally, I would like to thank my wife, Surekha and my daughter, Shaurya for bearing with me during this pursuit. I am grateful to them for most of the good things in my life and now I can add this book to that list.

Part I

PAPERS

1

Routes to Peaks for Building Corporate Renaissance[1]

Asha Bhandarker and Pritam Singh

[1] Revised version of a book chapter from, "Winning the Corporate Olympiad: Renaissance Paradigm" (2002, Vikas).

Indian corporates clearly are in need of a drastic reorientation in tune with the massive paradigm shifts taking place in the business and social contexts. Synchronizing the mindset and style of businesses in line with these requirements is probably one of the biggest challenges facing the Indian industry. While the first decade of the 21st century has thrown up many outstanding Indian organizations—Tatas, Airtel, L&T, Reliance, Aditya Birla Group, and ICICI Bank—which successfully met the challenges of transformation and took advantage of the opportunities, there are many Indian companies still struggling to get their act together. This paper deals with routes to achieve and sustain cost leadership, quality leadership, market leadership, innovation and change and low time to market, the levers that ultimately determine the winners and losers at the global level.

At the end of the first decade of the 21st century it is clear that a large number of companies need to build corporate renaissance through sustained strategic and collective efforts. The 1990s have seen the use of a variety of structural approaches—downsizing, mergers, acquisitions, takeovers, and strategic alliances—for building a competitive edge. But worldwide experiences have indicated that these approaches by themselves could not help corporations build the competitive edge. The champions of business process re-engineering Hammer and Champy have observed that 70 percent of the re-engineering projects worldwide have been unsuccessful. Studies have shown that 50 percent of acquisitions have failed; 60 percent to 70 percent has been the failure rate of strategic alliances. The failures have taken place for two key reasons:

- Companies focused more on short-term and quick gains rather than creating a sustainable competitive advantage.
- Softer organizational issues like work culture, leadership and human side of enterprise were under-emphasized.

By and large, Indian organizations have also had similar experiences. Companies have sought to embrace new techniques and systems for building competitive excellence only to find that they did not deliver the expected results. A closer look at the modus operandi brings out some of the implementation-related problems faced in the Indian context. People in many organizations have in fact expressed that, the management is always in a hurry to get the results and if some approach does not deliver immediately, then it is discarded for something new and promising, something which is the flavor of the season. In the first place they did not spend enough time and effort to make the new intervention a success—neither was the approach adopted fully, nor was it given enough backing to make it successful.

Another reason for the indifferent outcomes of implementing various techniques has been an imitation of new systems and techniques, without suitable adaptation to the Indian context. Such artificial layers, like the ungrafted tissue, are rejected by the system. Many others have shared that these new techniques could have worked, provided the softer issues were also equally emphasized. In other words, the shift has only had a partial impact on companies, and anything deeper would require a vastly different approach. For instance, Indian companies trying to implement Japanese management systems, could not get outstanding results because the basic value systems and assumptions underlying the Japanese approach (such as working together and showing respect for each other) were not internalized. Therefore the changes became merely cosmetic and the old styles reasserted themselves.

Organizations, therefore, have to aim for deeper change—change on multiple dimensions of the organization—in fact, a corporate renaissance. Corporate renaissance is deeper than corporate transformation. Corporate transformation focuses more on bringing changes on various organizational dimensions, whereas, corporate renaissance seeks to bring a drastic shift in some of the deeply embedded company mindsets: for example, the company must discard its approach of making exploitative gains at the cost of the stakeholder and move to wealth creation; the company must move from the mindset of imitation (technology, services, etc.) to innovation; the company must realize that its biggest source of strength in terms of creative ideas and speed of achievement are its own people. Such shifts in mindset would be revolutionary in the context of Indian organizations. These will enable the organization to work on a radically different paradigm, release the creative potential of the people, and create the capacity to be self-determining, continuously learning, forever youthful and highly inspired. Thus, in corporate renaissance, the focus is not only on renewal and transformation, but also on a new creation which is different from the existing one. It is such corporate renaissance which Indian organizations need today in order to acquire the fitness to become winners.

The routes on which organizations have to work to bring about corporate renaissance have been discussed here:

- Winning Vision
- Creating New Business Models
- Customer at the Center
- Nurturing Intellectual Capital
- Soul of a Startup, Heart of a Colossus
- Preparing Today for Tomorrow
- Creative Destruction
- Teamwork
- Ethical Governance

The write-up on each route is followed by a checklist aimed at helping leaders critically assess the positioning of their companies on these dimensions.

WINNING VISION

Winning visions create excitement, capture the imagination of people, and provide them with a sense of meaning and purpose to move collective energies in the needed direction. The winning aspect is being emphasized here because in today's scenario, companies need to win even to stay in the race. Focus on a winning vision will create a sense of urgency in the organization, help build strategy and clarify the action priorities for building the organizational road map.

Great organizations like Sony, Motorola, Canon, 3M, National, GE, and ABB have successfully influenced organizational members through the power of passionate vision. In National Corporation, the vision was to "make electrical goods available as cheaply as water"; at Canon "living and working for the common good" was the future vision; in GE one of the earliest visions was for the businesses to "be no. 1 no. 2 or out"; expression of the Sony spirit clearly captured the company vision—"we shall welcome technical difficulties and focus on highly sophisticated technical products that have great usefulness for society regardless of the quantity involved."

People of these companies accepted these visions because of the inspirational content as well as the actualization of these visions by the management. Such visions provide meaning, direction, and focus. The importance of building a shared vision in today's context is aptly brought out by Mads Ovlisen, the CEO of Novo Nordisk:

> We are living in a world where all things that used to give business a competitive advantage are disappearing. The only thing left is our people. Our work on shared visions, values and fundamentals is aimed at unlocking that potential. . . the only thing that sets us apart, perhaps the only sustainable advantage we have as a company, is the ability of our people to learn and act faster than the competition.

The process of vision building can be initiated by first involving the opinion leaders, people with ideas, and those occupying key positions and later replicated at other levels in the company. Organizational members need to dwell on questions like—"what unique purpose is key to our existence as a company?" and "Where are we going and where should we be going as a company?" Answers to such questions will indicate the direction which the company needs to take.

The relevance of setting the section has been clearly highlighted by Ovlisen: "Vision 21 (Novo Nordisk's blueprint for the future) tells us where we are going, how we are going to get there, and Novo Nordisk's fundamentals outline our tactics and responsibilities." Further, such direction setting through active involvement of organizational members is critical in building a sense of ownership and commitment to reach the destination.

As mentioned earlier, the experience of vision building exercises in most of the Indian companies has shown that they begin and end with the top management. There is hardly any percolation of vision, sharing and exchange of reactions and contribution on the vision by the employees across the organization. In some Indian companies, vision building has been consultant-centric. Such visions become mere paper statements for dissplay in board rooms, holding no meaning for the majority of the organizational members. There is neither passion, nor commitment, nor any ownership. Creating such passion in people is the key to mobilize the collective towards the future. As Fisher (CEO, Kodak) puts it, "You don't have anything in the end, unless you have people who believe in the future. It's as simple as that."

Companies like GE have made the vision and purpose accessible to the people. In fact, in GE the vision has been widely shared, capsulated in catchy ways and proselytized till it became a part of the mindset of the people, influencing the way they look at situations (e.g., Will it enable us to win? Will it help us reach the goals?); the way people make decisions and solve problems; speed of response to customers, etc.

Despite being repeated, the vision may still not touch people unless it has an emotional appeal. Such emotional appeal can be built in only when the vision promotes certain higher values which make a difference to human societies or stir people's passion for work, and make them feel part of the challenge and excitement of it, as brought out in the vision statements given below:

- 3M—"To solve unsolved problems innovatively"
- Merck—"To preserve and improve human life"
- ABB—"To make economic growth and improved living standards a reality for all nations throughout the world"

Such visions reverberate in the hearts and minds of people, uplifting them personally, making them feel a part of something great and enhance their self-esteem and self-worth. Ultimately, visions derive credibility, acceptance and power when they are not only espoused but also guide the actions of the organization, the strategy, and the processes. At Canon, the vision of "living and working for the common good" has been translated into the business strategy of the company and also guides relations with people of the company, with outside stakeholders, as well as assuming global social responsibility and being active globally. In the Indian context, the vision articulated and actualized by Airtel, Biocon, L&T, Aditya Birla Group, ICICI Bank have immensely inspired employees to move forward collectively to actualize the vision.

Checklist 1.1: Winning Vision

- Does my company have a dream?
- Has this dream been converted into a clearly articulated vision?
- What is the distinctive "winning" characteristic of the vision?
- Is the vision pitched at a higher level, touching on the larger issues for humanity?
- Does the vision have global reach and depth? Is it a shared vision?
- Does the company vision have emotive content to inspire people?
- Are the strategy, structure, systems and styles aligned with the vision?
- Is the vision formulated through collective consensus or is it imposed?

- Do the organizational members passionately believe in actualizing the vision?
- What efforts do organizational members have to make to implement the vision?
- How often is the vision discussed, deliberated and talked about in the company?

CREATING NEW BUSINESS MODELS

The phenomenon of global markets, information technology, pace of technological change and the use of new competitors have together created a chaotic, disruptive business environment. Such complexities endanger the very survival of business organizations. Those companies which sailed along quite smoothly in placid business waters and made their tidy, assured profits suddenly find the waters turning choppy. Today, everything seems topsy-turvy, unpredictable, and basically out of control. The fortunes of highly successful giant corporations hailed for their outstanding performance till recently, are increasingly on the downswing.

Bill Gates' statement "We are always 2 years away from failure" simply and powerfully illustrates the precarious conditions even of a high performer like Microsoft. His statement makes the point about having to continuously move and create a new business model in order for the company to stay ahead in the race.

Today organizations need new business models and strategies with focus on the following:

- Building a world class organization
- Developing a wealth creating organization
- Evolving a customer-centric organization
- Creating cost leadership
- Building product innovation
- Running faster than competitors

(a) Building a World-class Organization

The emphasis here is clearly on world class and not on mere global presence. The vision of creating a world-class company ensures constant striving to reach the top through *(i)* benchmarking, *(ii)* acquiring best talent, *(iii)* learning, and *(iv)* restructuring the mode of functioning. When ICICI, Aditya Birla Group, and L&T decided to go global they first prepared themselves by becoming world class organizations.

(b) Developing a Wealth Creating Organization

Survival centric organizations are preoccupied with wealth extracting models and use approaches like BPR, restructuring, and incremental improvements. However, in the current business scenario, organizations will have to move from the preponderantly wealth extracting mode to wealth creating mode. They have to continuously move and operate in the zones of new opportunity. It is only such a strategy which will facilitate reaching the peaks of excellence and build sustaining power to stay there.

Companies will have to develop alert antenna as well as telescopic and binocular vision to spot new zones of opportunity. A highly structured business model will constrain organizational ability to see beyond the frame. No doubt the frame is needed to simplify the situation to aid action; but the frame itself can however become a blinker and restrict perception of new opportunities.

In order to continuously create wealth, organizations need to explore other powerful and important routes such as competitive-collaborative co-partnership, strategic alliances, mergers, acquisitions, etc. There is a lot which companies like Airtel and Aditya Birla Group have to teach in the creation of wealth creating organizations. In their quest for wealth creation by capitalizing on new opportunities and diversification, the company will have to constantly align its wealth creation strategy and its core competencies. Completely ignoring core competencies and aggressively pursuing wealth creation will not be in the interest of the organization. If at all the company pursues such an approach, special efforts must be made to create core competencies in that area—acquiring new talent, new technology, new work-processes, and building an appropriate culture.

(c) Evolving a Customer-centric Organization

The thrust of the new business model should be customer driven and begin with the end in mind. Employees must have the firm mindset that they are "paid by the customers." This will influence their entire perspective, attitude, and behavior on every aspect having impact on the customer. It will ensure capitalizing on new business opportunities driven by changing customer needs and styles. This will (i) facilitate new product development, (ii) help create a niche market, and also (iii) enable vacating unprofitable businesses. Further the market centric approach will force companies to be highly quality conscious, cost conscious as well as time and delivery conscious.

(d) Creating Cost Leadership

The fundamental paradigm of business is to minimize input costs and maximize profits through optimal utilization of organizational resources. Although this has been a perennial truism, relevance of this paradigm will only get further enhanced. Worldwide business is moving to cost competitive destinations. All companies must shape up to operate in and deal with the current market forces and systematically increase productivity.

(e) Building Product Innovation

The objective of every business is to create wealth and its main function is to create products and services to meet customer needs. While this has been the conventional paradigm followed by survival centric organizations, the front runners have always sought to create new customer needs and satisfy them through constant product and service innovation. In fact, winners have a policy of aiming to earn 30 percent to 40 percent of revenue annually through such innovation.

Technical innovation is the mother of product innovation. In order to have continued product innovation, companies will have to give significant thrust to their R&D efforts. Companies can no longer put off investing capital on R&D. Any company which ignores this cardinal principle will be doomed. In the emerging knowledge society, companies will have to accelerate their R&D efforts and also nurture intellectual capital for continued product and service innovation. The earlier practice of buying ready-made technology can create only laggards not leaders. This holds true for the nation and for the organization. The Tatas as well as Biocon have shown their prowess in technical innovation.

(f) Running Faster Than Competitors

The basic definer of the emerging high tech era is the heightened pace of change in corporates and those who do not keep pace will be outrun in the corporate Olympiad. To be winners, companies will have learn to run faster than the competitor, since in today's scenario, if one does not run ahead one is likely to fall behind. Companies will therefore need to build a sense of urgency, immediacy, and ability to quickly confront issues, rather than postponing them for the future.

Checklist 1.2:   Creating New Business Models

- Identify three key attributes of a world class organization
- To what extent do these key factors exist in your company?
- What percentage of your revenue is derived from wealth creation mode as compared to a wealth extraction mode?
- What are the two opportunities which can be used for wealth creation, which your company has not capitalized upon?
- What is the cost positioning of your product vis-à-vis the top three in your industry?
- How do you compare on product and service innovation vis-à-vis three top companies in your industry segment?
- What is the percentage of revenue accrued from new products?
- What is the speed of response of your company vis-à-vis your competitors?
- Give three reasons which can prove that your company is customer centric.
- Find out the areas where your company is weak and identify three reasons for this.
- Identify an action plan to enhance competitive positioning of the company in these areas.

CUSTOMER AT THE CENTER

In the era of break-neck competition, organizations must clarify the *raison d'être* for their existence. In today's scenario, one exists because of and for the customer. The spirit of this orientation is brought out vividly in the views expressed by Gandhi who said that the customer is God. Companies must put the customer at the center and reorient their strategies around customer requirements. The attitude of Indian companies needs to move drastically from the trading mentality to the customer service mentality. It must move from the culture of turning the face towards the boss, to turning the face towards the customer. Metaphorically speaking, when the face is to the customer, the employee can focus on customer needs and try to meet them. Such a change in focus clarifies where the energies need to be directed. In fact, how to win the customer's mind-share and keep it is the vexing question for all Indian companies today.

A dynamic interchange and interaction with the customer is required to enable understanding the mind of the customer, get feedback about the customer needs, etc. Their ability to provide value to the customer will define their competitiveness. In the absence of such a strategy, the organization may slip into degeneration mode. Figure 1.1 brings out that companies should strategize their actions by building sensitivity and awareness, not only regarding the present need of the customers but also their future need profile.

FIGURE 1.1: Customer Orientation

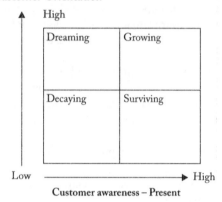

Source: Authors' own.

As Figure 1.1 brings out, high sensitivity about the present customer needs would ensure survival but it will not bring growth. Similarly, high sensitivity about future needs of customers devoid of awareness regarding present needs would be a mere utopian exercise and would create dreamers. Thus, organizations need to integrate both on the present and the future customer needs to grow and effectively compete. A deep grasp is required of what touches and moves the Indian customer. The strategies of MNCs like HLL provide an insight of how this can be done. Systematic data gathering and demographic profiling help to gain understanding of this phenomenon. A customer audit and research wing reporting to the CEO would be a useful mechanism to give the needed thrust.

The phenomenon of shortening product cycles and higher customer expectations necessitates greater customer involvement in product development—for example, GE India, as part of the six sigma initiative introduced in-depth focus group discussion with customers to find out their requirements. Likewise suppliers' views must also be heard through some forum, the idea being to make both partners in the activity contribute to product development. Listening to the voice of the customers and suppliers will provide invaluable feedback to the company.

The technology-based route to customer care is emerging as a promising one. In one of the dramatic examples, at the extreme end of the definition of customer care, is the innovation by Dell in selling custom-built computers. Dell has built a direct internet-based interactive model where the customer places orders for computers stating various configuration details. This has altogether done away with the middlemen involved in sales and service. Further, technical support is provided online and repeat buyers can save time by linking up to specialized web pages made to meet their requirements. In the Indian context, Mahindra & Mahindra allows you to build your own jeep from the vast choice of components, colors and consumables, via the company website. At Godrej and GE, virtual call centers have been setup to assist customers. Philips India has initiated a feedback mechanism in which customers have been asked to give the company their idea of a good TV. Banks like ICICI have revolutionized banking through mobile banking.

Despite the growth of technology-driven customer care initiatives, relationship marketing will however continue to be important. There is everything to be gained by companies where CEOs and top people also meet customers regularly to know the "moments of truth" in the words of Jan Carlson. This has been a common practice among multinationals. CEOs of Indian companies like Wipro and Hero Honda also follow the practice of personally meeting customers.

Some of the structural arrangements mentioned above help companies institutionalize the customer-centered approach.

Another big area crying for attention is the attitude to the internal customer. Indian organizations have to overcome the silo mode of functioning and encourage greater internal customerization that can be triggered inside the company by introducing cross-functional teams and task forces. Leading Indian companies like Maruti, and banks like ICICI have introduced cross-functional teams thereby tremendously increasing the inter-functional cooperation, learning, quality improvement focus, and internal customer service. Another intervention would be to bring a shift from cabin management to management-by-walking-around for increasing internal customerization. At Siemens-India, it was observed that introduction of the system of design group officers walking around on the shop floor, immensely helped in improving internal customerization. Companies can further increase internal customerization by introducing an Internal Customerization Audit to be done by the relevant client groups—both internal and external. The findings of such audits must be taken up and be discussed by the top management.

World class organizations like Motorola and GE pioneered the Six Sigma technique and achieved high levels of quality, cost, and delivery—the three factors which are vital for customer satisfaction. Leading companies globally introduced this technique and attained desired results.

Ultimately, at the heart of providing high quality customer service is the ability to streamline the internal processes. Six Sigma has helped GE deliver better quality, lower costs, and improved delivery.

The organizational structure should also be aligned to the customer centered mode. Most Indian companies (especially those in the public sector) have a functional and production-centered structure rather than a customer-centric structure. This tends to inhibit the customer orientation of these companies. The structure should empower the people at the field level so that they can respond to customer needs with speed, without having to refer to HQ and without having to bother too much about internal monitoring by HQ. It is high time Indian companies did monitoring online using a single format focusing on the basics which is enough to assess the health of the organization on key parameters.

Checklist 1.3: Customer at the Center

- Are people convinced that customer-centric, rather than production and product-centric strategies are essential to become a winning company?
- Does the company constantly ask the question: what business are we in and for whom?
- Has the company evolved mechanisms to continuously know the present and anticipate the emerging customer need profiles?
- Has the organization succeeded in bringing marketing to the workplace?
- Does the company involve the customers—present as well as future—in product development?
- Does the company organize customer meets and make regular customer visits where the CEO is also involved?
- Does the company have cross-functional teams?
- Does the company regularly conduct customer audits?
- Do we practice the style of management by walking around?
- Do people in the company believe that they are paid by the customer?

NURTURING INTELLECTUAL CAPITAL

Intellectual Capital (IC) is the reservoir of wisdom, built on the basis of the accumulated experiences and knowledge of the institution. Intellectual Capital is the software which gives the company its key competitive advantage. Without building such IC, the organization is only a shell, vulnerable to the slightest onslaughts from competitors. Nurturing and building IC is thus emerging as a big challenge for companies, as they prepare to vault to the next level of organizational evolution, moving from managing business processes to becoming knowledge-creating companies. Such evolution is imperative because increasingly the growth and effectiveness of companies is being closely linked to their ability to evolve and learn, so as to continually provide value. In this context the following factors become relevant:

(a) Attracting and retaining talent;
(b) Building systematic approaches to gather, share and retrieve knowledge; and
(c) Encouraging people to be creative and innovative.

(a) Attracting and Retaining Talent

With IC being available an increasing premium, organizations aiming for transformation will have to make special efforts to attract and retain people who can add value to the company. Companies can create special compensation schemes for the "Think Tank" groups and other key talents of the company. The members of such a group can be at any level and should be paid as per their ability to add value to the company operations. To attract such people, however, money is not the only factor. Equally important is the work culture—a culture where such people are treated as resources; where people are free to show their creativity and also where they are given enough elbow-room and personal space for experimentation. In this context it is particularly relevant to mention the experiments of Mr Damodaran when he worked as Chairman of UTI, IDBI, and subsequently SEBI.

(b) Building Systems to Gather Share and Retrieve Knowledge

To support the creation of a collective company pool of intellectual capital, companies must provide basic IT architecture to enable:

- gathering and maintaining databases regarding customer demographics, tastes, products, competitors, suppliers, and markets; and
- gathering and maintaining databases regarding the internal experiences, skills, and resources which others in the company can access when needed.

Operating and using IT requires a totally different mindset and habits in people. As such, an Indian organization undergoing renaissance must make efforts to grow such a culture, where IT infrastructure is used like a supporting and connecting nerve center of the company. As earlier attempts at using IT have shown, unless the habits and mindset for using IT are created, it becomes a wasted investment. Indian companies must invest more in IT and build systems which promote live sharing to convey experiences, knowledge and wisdom, and combine with a conducive culture. Today there are a large number of companies that have invested in IT. One has observed however that one of the slowest to change—despite investing in good IT infrastructure—are Indian banks; they need drastic measures to increase adaptation to usage of IT and internet.

(c) The Culture of Nurturing IC

(I) THE OUTSIDE-IN ROUTE
The hierarchical, seniority-centered styles of Indian companies must shift to a more open, idea-driven work culture. It is only in such a free culture that people would be able to create knowledge to effectively use it to make best decisions. Live knowledge about customers is available at the frontline of the company with executives who are in the field, and who interact daily with customers. The company needs to value these persons and their ideas and provide the needed support and also groom them. In Indian companies, the general experience has been that people at this level are stifled, their ideas are not valued and they are treated as dispensable.

The company must provide dignity to the people at this interface position, vest trust in them and "make us accountable, don't shackle us down by bureaucratic procedures"—as many Indian executives at the front line put it. Systems are needed to tap into this information—for example, keeping people networked so that experiences are shared and mutual learning takes place. Building brainstorming groups consisting of people involved across the chain from design to marketing are very helpful. Systems which facilitate information flow across functions and hierarchy would also be useful.

(II) THE TEACHING AND LEARNING ROUTE
Companies must also become teaching organizations as GE, Pepsi, Allied Signal, and others have shown. Companies must help their people understand the context, as well as, the language and numbers

of business. Company level perspectives, perception, and wisdom must be transferred and widely disseminated among the organizational members and a common mindset and perspective needs to be created. At L&T one of the first steps in the preparation for the transformation has been educating employees about the business environment. At Acer, managers learn from senior executives (including the CEO, Stan Shih) who share management philosophy and experiences with hundreds of trainees of the "Sea Dragon" program. As a learning and teaching organization, the company must use benchmarking (internal and external) to create the push factor to constantly improve their collective learning and implementation of the same.

Motorola Corporation exemplifies this philosophy, having invested in grooming and building people for the last three generations. Motorola has consciously built an intelligence group which helps management anticipate both competitive threats and market opportunities. The "intelligence group" has played a critical role in forming a number of key dances and joint ventures for the company. Motorola has also initiated the "Minority Report Approach"—this allows anyone with alternative or minority opinions to express them. New and fresh intelligence is gathered by using this mechanism and this is used as an aid to management decision-making.

(III) TOLERANCE OF MISTAKES

This is an important dimension to be built into the work culture for building IC. The spirit of tolerance for mistakes is revealed in companies like 3M and Johnson & Johnson. In 3M, the founder instilled the perspective that a management which becomes dictatorial makes bigger mistakes than the mistakes individuals make (provided they are essentially right). In Johnson & Johnson the perspective on mistakes has been that mistakes reflect that people are making decisions and taking risks, both considered to be key factors for company growth.

It is high time Indian companies acknowledged the importance of integration and networking with academic institutes of excellence for enhancing IC. Such a strategy is common practice in the Western countries. The above presentation clearly brings out that Indian companies will have to travel miles to nurture IC and generate wisdom for initiating corporate renaissance.

Checklist 1.4: Nurturing Intellectual Capital

- Does the company value an idea per se, or does it value an idea depending on who gives that idea?

- Does the company change its action modes based on latest knowledge?
- Does the company have appropriate systems to gather knowledge into a common pool?
- Does the company conduct knowledge audits?
- Is there institutional arrangement to set aside a part of the budget for promoting IC in the organization?
- Do we benchmark our company both in terms of processes and resources used for IC?
- Does the company have a well-defined approach to attract and retain explorers and innovative thinkers?
- Does the company allow organizational members to experiment and tolerate any unintentional mistakes and fallouts?
- Does the company have systems and organizational processes where people can continuously learn from each other?
- Is there a good system to recognize the contributions of idea people?
- Does company have a corporate board with representation of scholars working at the cutting edge of the discipline?

SOUL OF A STARTUP, HEART OF A COLOSSUS

The soul of a startup refers to the entrepreneurial spirit which pervades and drives the company to be flexible and seek new opportunities; heart of a colossus indicates the staying power of the company to last out the competition, to invest and to use wisdom and experience.

In the era of opportunity and competition, the quick footed and nimble have a better chance of winning as compared to the dinosaurs that get slowed down by sheer size. The quick and nimble footed are agile, flexible, and quick responding by virtue of their size. Startups are fueled by the entrepreneurial spirit, constantly seeking new business opportunities to capitalize upon. People in such companies thrive on the challenge of doing something new; they have a keen sense of ownership and desire to take advantage of business opportunities. Giant-sized companies on the other hand, are characterized by the twin perils of bureaucracy and hierarchy, which build inflexibility and rapidly threaten to convert companies into dinosaurs. Their strength lies in the wisdom, social, intellectual and process capital, deep pockets, and staying power, all of which are valuable for companies but seldom tapped adequately for budding competitive edge.

The challenge for the giants is to reinvent themselves in such a way as to infuse the startup spirit to revitalize their way of working. Giants thus have to mimic the form of startups so that the associated fervor and spirit that focuses on quality cost and closeness to the customer gets activated. The giants will dance or bumblebees will fly, only when the excitement, challenge, speed, innovation, sense of ownership, and drive charge up the company

Companies worldwide and to some extent in India are getting lean, having shed a lot of slack and fat. The major challenge for organizations is to get trim without becoming weak, as well as build the entrepreneurial spirit rather than becoming risk averse. Vibrant and entrepreneurial companies like 3M and Virgin have had the advantage of organic growth; 3M grew from the bottom up into 100s of Little organizations, with today over 50,000 products and a well-deserved reputation for innovation. Branson of Virgin creates a new business, involves himself with the ins and outs and then hands it over to a good MD (managing director) and FC (financial controller) who are also given a stake in the company. This approach has helped the company.

Winning companies will have to build the sense of ownership among their employees. Typically, in large organizations, this is a difficult task since size itself creates a sense of alienation. To build ownership, companies need to break up the operating structure of these behemoths into a smaller, more manageable size. This should be combined with total responsibility, authority, and accountability being provided to the units. Merely building profit centers is however not sufficient. The role of the corporate office and its control orientation is another aspect to be curbed, so that focus is less on controlling and more on facilitating. Entrepreneurial types of executives flourish when they have the freedom and authority, along with the accountability.

The work culture must be characterized by tolerance of mistakes in the pursuit of organizational goals. As ABB, 3M, GE, Airtel, ICICI, and others have shown, such a spirit is essential if people are to explore, experiment, try out, test out, and take risks.

In the whole process of building the entrepreneurial organization, the style of the top has to shift from imposing to facilitating, coaching, supporting, and guiding. For example, after Westinghouse was taken over by ABB, the erstwhile chief was astounded when the top team from corporate office made their first visit and simply asked them for their plans, and the support they needed. This attitude revealed trust, delegation, and a helping attitude on the part of management which immensely facilitated the turnaround.

The advantages of size—resources, knowledge pools, niche expertise—should be identified and shared across the units. This will bring the advantage of size (expertise, research, money) to the smaller units in the group. Unfortunately, most big corporations in India are slothful bureaucracies where work culture is rule bound, precedence focused, and activity driven, stifling individuality and creativity. To compete globally therefore, there is a need to infuse the Indian dinosaur-like corporations with the startup spirit which companies like Aditya Birla Group, L&T, and Airtel have shown.

Checklist 1.5: Soul of a Startup

- Is the entrepreneurial spirit nurtured in this company?
- Has the company identified an entrepreneurial corps and developed approaches to groom and nurture them?
- Does the company have the flexibility and quick responses to seek and capitalize business opportunities?
- Do people in this company have a sense of commitment and ownership to continued organizational growth and innovation?
- Is the sense of ownership built in the company?
- Does the company encourage creativity for its own sake or is it linked to furthering company goals?
- Is the company rule bound or results and solutions bound?
- Are there continuous efforts to make the organization leaner, responsive, and proactive?
- Does the company have passion for new ideas?
- Is there a culture which facilitates innovation and experimentation?
- Does the company have tolerance for mistakes?
- Does the company establish clear boundaries, spell out the direction in which innovative ideas are required, so that business is furthered and problem solving accelerated?
- Is the mindset of corporate office more that of a facilitator rather than as a controller?
- Towards this end what radical changes have been initiated in the company in terms of strategic reorientation, organizational restructuring, creating process focused organization and wealth maximization of stakeholders?

PREPARE TODAY FOR TOMORROW

This refers to the company mindset of not only capitalizing the opportunities today, but evolving strategies with tomorrow in mind. In an era of increasingly short product cycles (around six months in the case of IT organizations), companies have to constantly look ahead and prepare.

As Michael Dell, CEO, Dell Computers, puts it, "... in this business there are two kinds of people really, the quick and the dead." This dramatically sums up the speed at which one has to prepare for the future.

Great companies like Sears Distal, Wang Labs, British Leyland, and American Express were caught unaware because at the height of success they became complacent; they began living on present successes without looking at and preparing for the future demands and challenges. It is very evident therefore that today's competitive strength is temporal and companies will have to continuously find and build new strengths to compete for tomorrow.

Many Indian companies are today caught on the wrong foot and are in danger of obsolescence and death. They are still living in the past, unwilling and unable to accept the changing realities and reorient themselves accordingly. It is critical that company leadership must try to keep their finger on the pulse of the company, the business, the customer, and the market place all the time. Companies like Airtel, and ICICI are true Indian examples of companies which have prepared themselves for the future changing as frequently as required. More Indian CEOs have to demonstrate such an orientation, get out of day-to-day problem solving, look into the future and prepare for it. Companies like Wang Labs, makers of mini computers, lost out mainly because they could not fathom the change in the customer tastes which favored personal computers.

Coke recreates its brand by focusing on tastes of the new generation customer. The company looks into the future everyday, figuring out ways to make Coca-Cola more relevant for the present generation. These issues are then discussed and acted upon. It is evident that at Coke, the future is in focus and the company spends time and plans how to reach there. If tomorrow is not focused upon, the company is too busy living in the present and loses a grip of future scenario and requirements.

The computer industry has provided profound lessons regarding operating on the razor edge of competition. CEOs, like Grove of Intel, Bill Gates of Microsoft, anticipated the future and prepared their companies through a linear approach, e.g., faster chips produced by Intel. When it came to the new and discontinuous, for example, the burgeoning net-related opportunities, they found themselves unprepared relative to the competition and are scrambling to keep up.

Preparing for tomorrow happens in the context of what you are as a company today. Awareness of strengths and weaknesses through benchmarking approaches help the company to understand the extent of effort required to cope. Different companies handle this issue by focusing on different routes, depending upon their own competencies built over the years.

At Coke, there was a system of regular meetings of the EVP, John Hunter, with the country managers and their teams, where there were discussions and debates regarding strategies, for not only the next year but also the next three years. Issues relating to the consumer, the market the bottler system were focused upon and reviewed threadbare. Most importantly, the teams focused upon the goals three years down the road and action strategies to reach there.

Companies like Medtronic and 3M try to have a sharp focus on the future. Medtronic examines new technologies, even if they challenge their existing products. This approach ensures that they learn about it and prepare for it, rather than waiting for a competitor to get an edge over them by using the new technology. The company has built a system by which anyone can work on a new idea even if it is not directly related to one's own job profile. What is considered more important is the willingness of the person to work on the idea and examine its worth to the company. At 3M, technical people are in constant touch with customers, to understand the explicit and implicit needs so that technical people can help match technology to customer needs. These strategies of the company reveal the anticipatory orientation based on ground realities.

The above examples have clearly revealed winning companies build competitive edge by: Building clarity of where they want to go; Working on developing customer delight; Gathering feedback from within and outside the company through intense and regular meetings; Aligning all the processes towards levers of competitive edge; and Engaging in new search and inquiry.

Checklist 1.6: Preparing Today for Tomorrow

- Does the company live more in the past, present or future? Is the mode of operation proactive or reactive? What does the company need to do for tomorrow? How is the company preparing the people for the future? What are the challenges the company has to gear up for?
- Is the company building the business plan in the context of emerging opportunities?
- Are we adequately involving, sharing, and mobilizing people?
- Does the company have an institutional mechanism/an equivalent of alert antenna to continuously examine business plans in the light of emerging future?
- Has the company developed co-partnership with various stake-holders and used their ideas in evolving competing strategies?
- Is the company a path follower or a path maker?

CREATIVE DESTRUCTION

"Life begins from death," so goes the famous Indian saying. Creative destruction is an important route for the company to stay creative, youthful, lithe, and ever-renewing. Creative destruction is the act of deliberately decimating parts of the organization which are no longer relevant and adding value—parts of the organization in terms of structure, systems, styles, skills, processes, mindsets, and approaches. It also means giving up old habits and ways of doing business and substituting them with new, more appropriate approaches. The vision and goals of the company and the pace, at which it wants to move, are the only guiding light, which bring clarity to this exercise. Viewed in this way, the actions of the CEO of GE, Jack Welch, exiting from businesses where the company was neither number 1 nor number 2, makes perfect sense. At that time people were surprised at GE exiting businesses which were still profitable. The company deliberately killed or hived off businesses which were on the downswing (though profitable) in order to move ahead. Clear vision of the future helped Welch at GE, Barnevik at ABB, and Neil1 at Unipart realize the pace at which they had to renew themselves in order to safeguard the future of their companies.

It is evident that organizations with clear and focused vision, and direction have been able to embrace death, however painful. Without having the rocket-launch approach (discarding the used parts in flight), there is a drag on the speed at which the organization can move. Many organizations try to move ahead without a clear vision and suddenly find themselves unable to move forward. The lack of link up of vision and goal with the roadmap as well as reluctance to give up old habits are the basic source of the stagnation and decay.

In fact, the major challenge for building corporate renaissance is to prepare people to move out of the comfort zone of the known and familiar through educational and training programs as at Motorola and GE.

Success traps many organizations, lulling the best of companies into a false sense of security. There is a conviction, reinforced by their success that all their actions, strategies, and styles are right and need no change. In fact many companies fell into this trap; they became insensitive to the customer and to the new requirements. They continued with past approaches, relevant in the preceding situation, but out of sync with the changed business scenario.

Operating successfully in the fast-changing business scenario entails shedding the "I" feeling and the need for a continued alert observation and response to the competition. As Intel's Grove succinctly put it, "only the paranoid survive." It is the presence of such a mindset that helps keep the company balanced and ready with fresh moves before other companies catch up. Intel is a very apt example of a company which did not fall victim to the success syndrome, because it was not satisfied with its success and knew that today's success does not necessarily translate into success tomorrow.

The organization members have to be extensively educated regarding the need for creative destruction to build corporate renaissance. Many organizations built great plans for corporate renaissance, but failed miserably because the implementers were not involved and committed to the process. Clarifying vision and purpose, building awareness about the problems, getting people's views and preparing them to get rid of irrelevant modes, are all important steps in the process. Such practices have been used by successful Indian organizations like ICICI Bank, L&T, and Airtel.

Planned and deliberate strategies should be worked *out for* creative destruction, aimed at making the company youthful, aggressive, and excited about embracing value-adding activities. Induction of youthful people into the company will help provide the added dash and energy. While this is a necessary step, it is nevertheless insufficient. The process of creative destruction is facilitated through benchmarking, participative styles, and strategies which are designed to take advantage of the new opportunities.

Thus companies practicing creative destruction have been observed to build collective vision; move people from the comfort zones and into the zone of challenge; evolve clear mantras to communicate new messages; focus on building strategies to win in the game rather than being trapped in conducting a *post-mortem*; and view activities from the value-added lenses.

Checklist 1.7: Creative Destruction

- Where is the company going? Which path are we taking? Are all of us in the company clear about where we are heading? Is there a buy-in?
- What is the gap between the goal and our current position? What is the stage of the company in its life cycle?
- Are we consciously moving people from their zone of comfort?
- Is there a mechanism to keep the company perpetually youthful and its people in the learning mode?
- Does the company continuously examine and identify non-value-adding activities?
- Are there well-designed approaches to destroy non-value adding activities?

- Is there forward momentum generated in the company? Are people experiencing it?
- Does the company have a strategy to discard old products?
- Does the company have a strategy that a certain percentage of total turnover should come from new products?
- Is the company trapped by past glory and present success or is it focused on the future opportunities?
- Does the company continuously audit its systems and processes and destroy old and irrelevant ones?

TEAMWORK

One of the biggest shifts in mindsets which is needed in organizations today—especially in Indian organizations—is on the aspect of team working. Teamwork is the basic building block for channelizing collective energy and empowering people. Team working happens when people are comfortable about interacting, sharing, and moving together for organizational goal achievement. A basic assumption, which underlies organizations moving in the direction of team working, is that everyone, regardless of department, gender, geographical locations, has something valuable to contribute to the organization. Moreover, there is also a second underlying assumption—individuals may not have solutions for complex situations and problems; teams do.

The change in the working paradigm from centralized and individual to collective has to be triggered through leadership styles at the top. One of the earliest signals regarding the need for change in work culture has been at GE under Jack Welch. True to his style of intense company-wide communication, Welch gave slogans which signaled the change over in the work culture towards collaboration—"break down the walls (across departments) and build bridges." In this way, he initiated the move to expand the mental boundaries of executives to include the entire organization. Commenting on the work culture, one of the Crotonville Staff said, "Working across boundaries is a core value embedded here. We have moved away from the concept of silos. Wherever you are in our company you are looking at a GE leader, not a leader in a particular business." The shift in emphasis is also reflected in the selection process at GE. The interviews put a lot of emphasis on assessing the person's leadership style and his ability to build the team.

The next step is for the CEO and top management to demonstrate a consistent and systematic leadership style which encourages and facilitates group working. The top management must emphasize working together by demonstrating this to the entire company, creating the right climate, and atmosphere characterized by trust. Trust and liking are two important foundations for collaboration. The following factors must be taken care of to build such a climate:

- Create forums where people can bond together
- Redirect the normal competitive energies outward and towards killing the competition
- Reward collaboration
- Emphasize the higher goal
- Continuing education

(a) Forums for Bonding

In companies like South West Airlines, Wal-Mart, Virgin, leaders like Herb Kelleher, Sam Walton and Richard Branson provided personal touch, sharing of meals, celebrating the annual day. All these have contributed to building the informal culture in the respective companies.

(b) Directing Natural Competitive Instincts Outward

Companies like Intel have done this very effectively by giving slogans like "Crush Motorola" "Bag Ford". Such an approach powerfully redirects competitive energies constructively and helps achieve the organizational goals. Without such re-channelization, the energies can easily get directed with the company for negative ends, a phenomenon which has been observed in many large Indian organizations.

(c) Rewarding Collaboration

Evaluation and recognition are two techniques by which the company reinforces desirable pro team and collaborative behavior. At Xerox, intra-department teamwork and cross-functional teamwork are two critical attributes which have been identified, and all senior managers including the CEO are assessed on these parameters (among other parameters) every year. Collaboration and help are recognized at Xerox Corporation. The Eureka system networks 25,000 field representatives with laptops, which facilitates lateral communication—people are motivated to help each other through a system in which each time a colleague gives help, his name is flashed on the network. The team-based reward systems are also making a re-appearance, according to some researchers, in the form of profit sharing, gain sharing, team-based rewards, group incentives, etc. Companies must include a percentage of performance reward linked to group working to further encourage team working.

(d) Emphasizing the Higher Goal

This point has been powerfully emphasized in the Arthi-Smtiti. The sloka goes,

Tajait Ekam Kulam Syarthae
Gramam Syarthae Tajait Kulam . . .
Dharmarthae Prithvim Tajait

This roughly translates to mean—when people are clear about the higher goals they voluntarily sacrifice the lower goals: people are capable of sacrificing self-level goals for the village; those of the village for the (Janpada) district level goals; and likewise the goals of the Janpada for the nation, and above all, the national goals can be sacrificed for Dharma (for humanity).

The sense of collectivity can pervade the company, when the focus is shifted to a higher goal, linked to growth of the company. Efforts are needed to shift the focus of management as well workmen groups to build a sense of collectivity. Another powerful way of building collectivity is through greater information sharing and involvement of people in vision building.

(e) Continuing Education

Successful companies promote team work through the training route to educate people and provide them with interpersonal skills, and team working skills. Many times, inability at team working may also be an outcome of poor skills. Efforts must be made by companies to tackle this deficit by providing rigorous training and education.

In the Indian context, with the cultural predisposition towards hierarchy and tribalistic mentality, it is extremely important to emphasize team working, remind people, and bring them together. The spirit of the ancient Indian saying *Sanga Chhatwam, Sam Wadhatwam*—Let's live together, let's work together, let's enjoy together—should be inculcated.

Checklist 1.8: Team Working

- Does the company have an individual-based reward system or a group-based reward system?

- Does the company provide the opportunity for people to mingle informally?
- Does the company make efforts to develop a sense of community?
- Are there many cross-functional teams in the company?
- Does the company follow and provide rules and practices or enables people to work together?
- Are people trained to work together through programs like managing diversity and team building?
- Do people have a silo vision or helicopter perspective in the company?
- Is there cabin management or management by walking around?
- Do people freely walk into each others' cabins rather than communicating through memos, e-mails and phone calls?
- Is there a mechanism to remind people about the higher goal of the company?
- Do people have sufficient appreciation and understanding about the functioning of other departments?
- Have they got functional perspectives or general management perspective?
- Does the company continuously remind people about the power of collectivity, synergy-building through team-building programs?
- Does the company inculcate competencies and skills required for teamwork?

ETHICAL GOVERNANCE

It would be appropriate to begin by quoting the timeless philosophy from the Hindu scriptures—*Satya Mewa Jayate*—truth ultimately conquers. This underlies the basic tenet of winning and succeeding by using the right means—right as assessed by the extent to which it fosters rather than hurts, the interests of others in society. The Olympic Games symbolize the spirit of winning on prowess and ability rather than through unfair means. Otherwise outstanding athletes have been debarred from participating in the competitions, when they were found trying to win through unfair practices like taking drugs to boost performance. This principle of using ethical means holds good in organizations as well, from the standpoint of people working in them. Ethical behavior thus refers to the "ought" and the "ought not" in the context of the organization. Viewed from the social psychological perspective, an ethical mode of functioning reduces conflict within the organization and creates a healthy work atmosphere. At the psychological level, working for such an organization increases self-pride, individual commitment, and motivation.

Worldwide there is a move today to lay increasing emphasis on ethics in business. Over the last decade, various international movements have been gathering momentum under the aegis of the United Nations, the OECD, Organization of American States Action, Transparency International, the Caux Round Table, etc. With such developments taking place, it is evident that those companies nursing global ambitions will have to move towards ethical business conduct. The Caux Roundtable has adopted the principles of Kyosei (working and living for the common good—a conviction of Kaku, CEO-Canon) and human dignity in producing, "Principles of Business." This is the first international ethics statement for business. The aim is to set a world standard against which business behavior can be measured.

In this context, therefore, the statement by Nicolas Moore, Chairman—PWC, is very relevant and makes the case for putting ethical behavior at the core of the organization: "Ethics is not a luxury, but an important element that holds companies together. Ethical business improves stakeholder relationships, enhancing the company's public image, enabling it to attract and retain the best directors and employees and increasing consumer loyalty and shareholder returns. . . ." Unfortunately, few companies are able to see the link between ethics and company performance. Most organizations tend to see ethics in isolation from business, as something, which belongs to the moralistic, "do good" realm, not contributing to performance. As a consequence, many companies pay lip service to ethical practices and do not integrate it with the strategy. Simply put, ethical behavior in the context of the business organization refers to right actions and actions which do not harm the interests of the various stake-holders. Two aspects of the ethical organization functioning are now examined:

- Business Ethics—ethical treatment of customers, community, environment, shareholders
- Managerial Ethics—ethical practices within the organization

(a) Business Ethics

One of the earliest companies to establish business ethics and codes of conduct in the corporate sector has been Johnson & Johnson (credo published in 1943). In 1935, Gen. Johnson spoke about the corporation's responsibility to customers, employees, community, and stakeholders. Other companies known for practice of business ethics are Kao, GE, Texas Instruments, Motorola, and Canon. In the Indian context, the one name which stands out for its ethical code of conduct is the house of Tatas. Others like Aditya Birla Group, JSW, and Biocon have also built a name for themselves on their ethical orientation.

Worldwide a shift is taking place on the ethical posture of companies because of the public reaction against those companies which are perceived to be poor in discharging social responsibility to the community—e.g., the public boycott which took place in Europe, against policies of companies like Nestlé (decision to sell baby milk in the third world); and Shell (the decision to dispose the Brent Spar Oil Platform). Such protests affected the bottom line of these companies and they had to perforce reverse their decisions because of public pressure. In fact a number of researches have brought out that consumers' purchase decisions are linked to the ethical practices pursued by the company. This clearly reveals that companies cannot be successful for long by hurting the interests of people. After all, they are part of the larger social ecosystem and other parts of this system—the customer in this case—can hurt the company's interests. In fact, trends in the western countries reveal that whenever the consumer has a choice, he would prefer to buy products from a more ethical company.

Canon has been an example of a company which showed how the practice of the business ethic of "Kyosei"—Kaku's philosophy—benefits both the company and the community at large. Their Newport Virginia plant has successfully reduced solid waste by more than 90 percent. Production costs have come down and they are re-manufacturing copiers for resale, reducing the need for new resources. Another initiative is to collect copier cartridges from all over the world for recycling. They have completely eliminated use of CFCs and Trichloroethylene in an attempt to reduce environmental pollution.

Goizueta, the former CEO of Coca-Cola Corporation, made a strong statement about the imperative for organizations to be better corporate citizens. Alluding to the link between society and the company, he said: "We cannot for the long term exist as a healthy company in a sick society." Sensitivity to business ethics becomes even more important when companies work in a global context and have to respond to culture specific sensitivities on this dimension.

The recent implosion of Enron Corporation and the fall of Andersen consulting, the accounting firm which worked in collusion with Enron, has created a huge furor on the stock markets. The entire meltdown in the US, the fall of giants like Lehman Brothers has cast a pall of suspicion on the integrity of firms. Likewise has been the fall of Satyam Computers in India. The biggest losers have been the stakeholders (employees and investors).

(b) Managerial Ethics

History has thrown up ample examples where those fighting for a virtuous cause ultimately emerged as winners. The power of truth over non-truth has been affirmed by various scriptures and epics all over the world.

Few companies have realized the importance having clearly stated codes of conduct within the company. Business decisions and actions tend to have ethical and moral ramifications. Unless companies build clearly stated guidelines and make them the norms of performance, coordinated actions become difficult for the employees of the company, especially when they are operating in geographically dispersed locations.

A second crucial dimension is the way in which people are treated in the organization—if the company culture promotes dignity, respect for individuals, fairness, and integrity, then people respond with commitment and loyalty to the company. The typical concerns in the developed world have been around bribery, white-collar crimes, ecology, and environmental issues, as also focus on ethical treatment of customers, and the employees.

In the Indian context, companies need to spell out the work ethics regarding quality, performance standards, speed and cost standards—something which is perhaps not such an issue in the western context, where these are taken as a given. Such clarification is extremely important in the light of the Indian value system which predisposes people to give priority to affiliation rather than work values. Unfortunately, emphasis on such aspects, though essential is inadequate in Indian companies. It would be relevant to reflect on the consequences of unethical practices within the company. By using unethical means in dealing with various stakeholders, the inner core of the company gets weakened. People become manipulative, seek shortcuts, operate without integrity—they follow the styles of the organizational role models, who have legitimized such actions in the company. When the organization is weak at the core, its ability to learn, grow, value people, respond to customers, nurture talent, goes down. While those in the inner circle may feel motivated, by and large people would have lower levels of motivation and pride in the company. Once shortcuts, manipulation, cheating, and power mongering enter the bloodstream of the company, it becomes impossible to regulate and promote ethical behavior, and healthy work practices. Practices which are relevant for the company to stay fit are not cultivated and affects the ability to learn, and be responsive to the customer. Worse than this is the fact that the commitment of people would be more to the self and the boss and less to the institution.

Companies like Texas Instruments, General Electric, Hewlett-Packard, and Motorola have strongly stated beliefs and principles on how they deal with various stakeholders:

- At GE, in-house rules were drawn up in the 1980s with reference to ethical concerns, called "Integrity: The letter and spirit of our commitment." Texas Instruments' adopted a written ethics code more than 35 years ago and circulated the ethics booklet in 12 languages, listing out its core values—integrity, innovation, and commitments: integrity in action refers to supporting, respecting, valuing people, and being honest; innovation requires learning, creating, and acting boldly; commitment means taking responsibility and committing to win.
- At Motorola two key beliefs are emphasized which influence the way company deals with customers, shareholders, suppliers, competitors, communities, and employees:

  - Uncompromising integrity
  - Constant respect for people

Each of the company employees is expected to demonstrate these key beliefs in work.

- The Japanese company Kao has built strong ethical foundations based on Buddhist philosophy. Maruta, the CEO of Kao Corporation, believes that, at Kao, prosperity is an outcome of respect for the needs of the consumer. He further says,

  For our company to reach greater heights, we must recognize the equality of all people. We must create a shared code of conduct and encourage a sense of unity among the entire work force. . . I truly feel the result of respect and sharing is innovation.

- The HP management got together and put up a values statement in the year 1957 and this has shaped the strategies, and practices of the company. The enunciated values touch upon the employees, customers, as well as performance—trust and respect for individuals, high level of achievement, and contribution, conduct of business with uncompromising integrity, achieve common objectives through teamwork, encourage flexibility and innovation. In emphasizing integrity, the company has said,

We expect HP people to be open and honest in their dealings to earn the trust and loyalty of others. People at every level are expected to adhere to the highest standards of business ethics and must understand that anything less is unacceptable. It's a practical matter, ethical conduct cannot be assured by written HP policies and codes; it must be an integral part of the organization, a deeply ingrained tradition that is passed from one generation of employees to another.

These statements have framed the guidelines for the work culture of the company—the HP way—which is admired worldwide. Interestingly, at HP the values statement highlights profits as a value—"profit is not something that can be put off until tomorrow; it means that myriad jobs can be done correctly and efficiently. The day-to-day performance of each individual adds to, or subtracts from our profit. Profit is the responsibility of all."

- The pharma giant Merck strongly believes that innovation, values, and ethics are the key to achieve their long-term goal of bringing the best of medicine to the widest possible number of people. Merck has been able to have ethical business practices, as well as achieved high performance. According to the CEO, the company also cares about how it achieve these results. It expect it's leaders to set high standards for performance, treat others inside and outside the company with dignity and respect, and adhere to the highest standards of ethical behavior and integrity.

Some companies have spelt out the importance of both the means and the ends—whether in response to the customer, for example at Kao; or in terms of profit, for example at HP; or as commitment to take responsibility and win, for example at TI—as a part of the values and ethics. In this way, integration has been brought in terms of the objectives and the means. This has helped to make ethical decisions very pragmatic and doable.

Companies like GE, TI, Motorola, and HP have made ethical guidelines clear to their employees:

- GE has a network of toll free helplines for each business unit in the US. Employees can call up these hot lines anonymously to ask questions about the guidelines and report suspected violations.
- TI has a number of communications which help employees understand company expectations. TI News, a weekly electronic newsletter, has a column dealing with ethical dilemmas and solutions. A group of subject experts are also available for discussions to clarify employee

doubts on ethical dilemmas be they on safety or environment or on any other topic.

- At Merck, "principles and values have been ingrained deep into the blood stream of the company—and influence the selection of people for growth, modes of developing them, evaluating as well as compensating them," according to Ray Gilmartin, CEO.
- Motorola has a process called "Ethics Renewal." According to Bob Galvin, CEO-Motorola, "we have spent entire weekends taking the entire management team to do this with ethics, morals and culture...." The MERP workshops are held country-wise to clarify and set the ethics agenda. The company has an ethics committee that addresses ethical and legal issues in each country. The adherence to ethical business practices is so strong that for many years, the company did not enter into certain markets because they felt that the environment was not conducive to the company's ethical practices. At Motorola it is relevant to note that the Ethics Renewal Program is in the domain of HR rather than legal. This ensures a positive approach unlike the legalistic one where the vigilance departments operate as in various Indian public sectors, creating fear and constraining action, rather than helping managers' function effectively.

In all the above-cited companies, ethical practices have supported performance excellence because they have been linked to business strategy and therefore to performance. They have been practiced consistently, there are mechanisms for clarification as well as systems to support and implement. The consequences of practicing ethical conduct are evident in the above-cited companies: on the employee morale, on the image of the company, on the customer, and all these in turn contributing to the bottom line. As CEO, Merck put it:

> Aspiring to the highest standards of ethics and integrity motivates our people and gives them a sense of satisfaction about their jobs. It inspires confidence and trust inside and outside our organization, helping to create the positive relationships and productive environment that we need to do business in.

At Texas Instruments, Skooglund (Chief of HR) highlights the consequences of ethical practices: "Values and ethics absolutely play a role in an empowered workforce. This way we operate in an environment of trust rather than in one of command and control. We view our reputation as a result of 100s of decisions made day in and day out."

Examination of Indian companies in the background of the above cited examples shows that they have a long way to go. Although concerns are being raised, committees have been set up to examine issues of ethical governance; a lot needs to be done. Companies like L&T, Biocon, UTI, Airtel, and JSW are showing the way.

Excellence focus, human dignity, equity, justice, and fairness, sensitivity to stakeholders, corporate social responsibility, and good corporate citizenship are some of the important dimensions which Indian organizations must incorporate in the mode of transacting business. These are not mere moralistic exhortations; they are powerful business paradigms, since they contribute to achieving business excellence and competitive edge.

In addition, the companies must also evolve the code and norms of behavior at the individual level within the company. The one major area which needs re-emphasis is creation of a contribution focused mindset. This is important because in Indian society there is a mindset of entitlement in operation rather than one of contribution. Companies must raise the consciousness of people by emphasizing that contribution is their dharma; they must educate people regarding contribution as an important means to create higher meaning in life. "One is equal to his contribution" should be the ethical mantra of the organization. To promote contribution focus, companies must give continuous signals to be ingrained in the minds of people that, unless they contribute they stand to lose something.

BIBLIOGRAPHY

Barham, K. and C. Heimer (1998) "ABB—The Dancing Giant: Creating the Globally Connected Corporation," *Financial Times*. London: Pitman Publishing.

Bartlett, C. and M.F. Wolff (1999) "In the Organization of the Future, Competitive Advantage will be With Inspired Employees," *Research and Technology Management*, 42(4).

Beer, M. and N. Nohria (2000) "Cracking the Code of Change," *Harvard Business Review*, 78(3).

Collins, J.C. and J. Porras (1994) *Built to Last: Successful Habits of Visionary Companies*. Harper Business.

Farkas, C.M. and De P. Backer (1996) *Maximum Leadership: Five Strategies for Success From the World's Leading CEOs*. London: Perigee Books.

For information on GE, see Corporate codes of conduct, cited above; for information on TI, see Flynn G, op cit; for information on Motorola see Motorola web site; For information on Merck see Gilmartin, op. cit. For further information on H-P, see www.latinsynergy.org/hpway.htm

Ghoshal, S. and C. Bartlett (1997) *The Individualized Corporation: A Fundamentally New Approach to Management*. London: William Heinemann.

Gilmartin, R.V. (1999) "Leadership Roles in Changing Society: Perspectives for Today and Tomorrow," AMA, National Leadership Conference, March 21.

Hammer, M. (1996) "How the Process-Centred Organization is Changing our Work and Lives," *Management: Beyond Re-engineering*. New York: Harper Business.

Heller, R. (1989) *The Decision Makers*. London: Hodder and Stoughton.

Interview with Barnevik P., in Kets de Vries, MFR, and Florent—Treacy, E, *The New Global Leaders*, Jossey Bass, San Francisco, 1999.

Kets de Vries, M.F.R. and K. Balaz (1999) "Creating the Authentizotic Organization," *Administration and Society*, 31(2).

Kotter, J.P. (1997) *Matsushita Leadership: Lessons from the 20th Century's Most Remarkable Entrepreneur*. New York: The Free Press.

Rosen, R., P. Digh, M. Singer, and C. Phillips (2000) *Global Literacies—Lessons in Business Leadership and National Cultures*. New York: Simon and Schuster.

See "Corporate Codes of Conduct, ILO, Bureau for Workers activities," www.itcilo.it/english/actrav/telearn/global/ilo/code/mami.htm

See "Taking action on corporate social responsibility: Summary and research," www.2.conferenceboard.ca/ccbc/knowledge areas/csr/csrf.htm

Spiller, R. (1999) "Ethical Boards," *Management*, 46(2).

Tichy, N. and S. Sherman (1993) "How Jack Welch is Making GE the World's Most Competitive Company," *Control Your Destiny or Someone Else Will*. New York: Doubleday/Currency.

2

Strategic Positioning Choices for Indian Businesses: Beyond *Jugaad* into the Next Orbit

Arun Kumar Jain and Ajay Singal

CONCEPT OF STRATEGIC POSITIONING

Highly successful global companies learn and acquire competencies quickly relating to management of four simultaneously arising and inherently contradictory challenges. These challenges are globalization and localization; standardization and customization; market capitalization and social responsibility; technological convergences and social divergences.[1] The four challenges cover an entire axis of strategy, structure, and leadership. The priorities for these challenges have to be set by the board and communicated to internal and external audiences.

The 2010 list of top 500 global corporations by *Fortune* magazine has once again highlighted the fact that few Indian companies (eight this year) are there. In comparison there are 46 Chinese companies in the list. Taiwan and South Korea—much smaller Asian nations—have 10 and eight companies respectively in the list. In case of India, only three companies are privately owned viz. RIL, Tata Motors, and Tata Steel.

Indian firms, except those in the technology and pharmaceutical space, have had largely a domestic focus that has limited their strategic options of growth. Tata Motors and Tata Steel made large acquisitions across the globe to attain size. Reliance Industries, the biggest company by market cap, has now changed strategy and begun hunting for assets abroad. We are of the opinion that Indian managers especially the HR need a global perspective to form a view as to where their next orbit of growth lies. India is on a growth path and overall the Indian industry has done well. But there are two key questions:

---

[1] From Arun Kumar Jain (2010) "Indian Firms Need to Go Global," *Financial Chronicle*, July 12.

1. Can we ascertain the true nature of our firms overall competitiveness?
2. What do Indian companies lack that prevents (most of) them from competing and winning at global levels, despite economic reforms and liberalization policies of the last 20 years...?

This paper develops a robust framework to answer these two basic questions.

ABOUT STRATEGIC CONTROL MAP FRAMEWORK

The first question can be answered by using a tool called strategic control map (SCM). SCM is an important tool for understanding global competitiveness in terms of positioning and for deciphering choices available to identify growth opportunities.

SCM uses two parameters, viz. firm size and market performance. Firm size is measured by book equity value. Book equity is the invested capital that determines scale of operation and balance sheet strength. Market performance is what matters to the shareholders. It is measured by price-to-book ratio (PB ratio) and reflects the multiple that the market is willing to put on the shareholders equity. Multiplying PB ratio with book equity produces the firm's total market value or market capitalization. PB ratio is more sensitive to returns on equity. Therefore, growing earnings rapidly and achieving high ROE can increase market capitalization. Even though market capitalization keeps changing because of volatility in stock markets, yet it remains a significant indicator of current and future growth opportunities and expectations for a firm.

SCM classifies firms into four groups: vulnerable, complete control, partial control through performance, and partial control through size (Figure 2.1). Companies in the lower left quadrant have a small capital base, domestic focus and operate in mature businesses. They are most vulnerable to acquisition by global competitors looking for local assets to diversify. Those in the upper right quadrant generate high returns from a large capital base and are in complete control of their direction. Their distinct capabilities make them suitable for global play. On the basis of their market performance (high price to book multiples) they can make fresh acquisitions. Firms in the upper left quadrant enjoy high performance from small invested capital because of high proportion of intangibles and niche capabilities. These firms have partial control through performance

FIGURE 2.1: Strategic Control Map

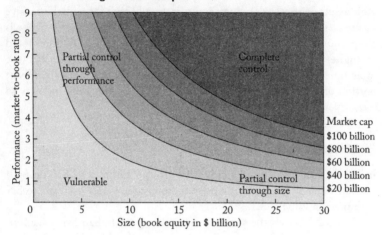

on their future courses of action like seeking newer products or markets. Companies in the lower right quadrant have a huge asset base, operate in capital intensive sectors, but have rather mediocre performance in stock markets. Such firms are difficult to be acquired, yet because of their size they can exercise partial control on the industry outcomes. For them, the challenge is to increase returns on their assets.

DATABASE AND SAMPLE

For the purpose of this paper we will restrict our analysis to firms forming a part of CNX100. This is a widely traded index representing 35 sectors of Indian economy and accounts for almost two-thirds of India's total market capitalization. Our sample consists of 82 firms from CNX100 (see Appendix 2.1 for list of firms). The subsidiaries of foreign firms were excluded from the sample as they were considered as part of global subsidiary networks of their parent companies. The data pertains to year ended 2008–09 for which financial reports are available.

We have used price to book ratio cutoff at 3.1 (median value of CNX100 index for financial year 2008–09) and book value cutoff at ₹100 bn (median value) to segregate above average performers. Mergers and acquisitions data pertains to period 2004–09 and has been collected from the ISI Emerging Market database, accessed online.

SCM on one hand measures tangible assets (horizontal axis) and intangible assets (vertical axis). Book equity is usually high for capital intensive businesses like infrastructure and capital goods. Market performance is the premium that markets place on a firm's book equity. This ratio should be higher for FMCG and other knowledge-driven industries because intangibles such as brands, goodwill, and patents contribute a significant portion of their market value. The capitalization varies from industry to industry and from firm to firm within an industry.

FINDINGS

In our data set firm capitalization varies from ₹15 bn to ₹2,810 bn with median value of ₹103 bn. The price to book ratio varies from 0.3 to 8.5 with median value at 3.1.

Figure 2.2 shows the strategic control map of Indian firms that are majority part of CNX100. Outliers data points (book equity greater than ₹200 bn or PB ratio greater than seven, 13 firms in total, refer to Appendix 2.1) are excluded. The Indian SC Map shows that firms are concentrated towards lower and left quadrant. There are few clear winners. Three isoquant curves (not to scale, used for explanation purposes only) at market capitalization of ₹50 bn, ₹200 bn, and ₹500 bn are also shown.

The SCM framework shows that there are no clear winners yet on the Indian horizon. Most firms are located in the lower-left quadrant (vulnerable portion) and are susceptible to acquisition by other firms, international or domestic. But some of those in vulnerable quadrant have made significant acquisitions abroad during period 2004–09.

FIGURE 2.2: Strategic Control Map of CNX100 Firms

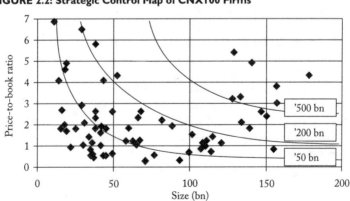

DISCUSSION

Table 2.1 shows the positioning of firms in a strategic control map (as in Figure 2.1). Firms like BHEL, HDFC, Infosys, ITC, L&T, ONGC, and TCS occupy a zone of complete control and hence are globally competitive. But HDFC and BHEL do not invest abroad and operate in fewer foreign markets. Further, 47 firms out of 82 are in the vulnerable zone, they have neither the equity base nor the market muscle to pursue opportunities in the foreign markets. These companies limit India's ability to go global. In banking, Bank of Baroda and Bank of India have size and are strong candidates for globalization provided they can improve returns on their assets. They have chosen path of organic growth and are improving upon their services to attract international business.

Eight financial institutions forming part of CNX100 (a widely traded index of large capital firms on National Stock Exchange: see Annexure 2.2) are concentrated domestically. Banks like Bank of Baroda and Bank of India despite having international orientation have not been able to attain the size anywhere close to their foreign-owned competitors.

To get a perspective we did try to find out the comparative size of some well-known global companies. We have global champions such as Intel, Microsoft, J&J, Apple, Siemens, BASF, Oracle, SAP, etc., which

TABLE 2.1: Competitive Position of Indian Firms on Strategic Control Map

Market performance (price-to-book ratio) 3.1	Adanient, Asian Paint, Bajaj-Auto, Cipla, Cromp Greav, Hero Honda, Lupin, Mundra Port, Sun Pharma	BHEL, HDFC, INFOSYSTCH, ITC, LT, ONGC, TCS
	A Birla Nuvo, ACC, Ambuja Cem, Andhra Bank, Ashok Ley, Axis Bank, Bank Baroda, Bank India, BEL, Bharat Forg, BIOCON, BPCL, Can Bk, CONCOR, Corp Bank, Dr Reddy, Federal Bnk, GAIL, Glenmark, GMR Infra, HCL Tech, HDFC Bank, HDIL, Hind Petro, IB Real Est, IDBI, IDFC, Idea, IFCI, Ind Hotel, IOB, JP Associat, JSW Steel, Kotak Bank, LIC Hsg Fin, McDowell-N, MRPL, Patni, Ranbaxy, Rel Capital, Sesa Goa, Suzlon, Tata Power, Tech M, TTML, Unitech, Zee	Axis Bank, Bank Baroda, Bank India, Bharti Artl, BPCL, Can Bk, DLF, GAIL, HDFC Bank, Hindalco, Hind Petro, ICICI Bank, Idea, Jindal Steel, M&M, NTPC, PNB, Power Grid, R Com, Reliance, Rel Infra, R Power, SAIL, SB In, STER, Tata Motors, Tata Steel, Wipro

0   ₹ 100 bn

Size (book equity)

continuously redefine global competition. These and other companies also ride on huge assets-base spread across the globe (Table 2.2).

TABLE 2.2: Hard Assets of Some Leading Global Companies

	Assets (bn dollars)
GE	800
P&G	134
Volkswagen	233
Nestlé	100
Sony	122
Pfizer	110

Box 2.1

Tata Steel follows its globalization strategy intensely—acquired NatSteel Asia, Singapore & Millennium Steel, Thailand in 2004–05 to capitalize on Asian opportunities, then Carborough Downs Coal Project in Australia to secure coal supply, and finally Corus in 2008 to produce value added products.

In terms of foreign assets, not a single Indian company figures in the top 500 companies of the world.

The question is: in the light of such huge companies with tangible and intangible assets and deep pockets, how do Indian companies compete?

The control map firms in the top right quadrant are fit to pursue globalization as they have the right kind of capitalization. But for this to happen, these firms ought to have specifically articulated global aspirations and benchmark their capabilities to global standards. Many companies in pharmaceuticals, auto components, and information technology have foreign focus and are able to compete successfully. These industries have developed product and service capabilities to serve international clients.

Tata Motors, Hindalco, and Tata Steel have made big ticket overseas acquisitions. Even smaller firms like Renuka Sugars, Astral Coke, Jubilant Organosys, Videocon Industries, Godrej Consumer Products, and UB group have made acquisitions of more than US $100 million. Our research shows that it is not that just large cap firms that can think of global ambitions, but firms in lower left quadrant are also global candidates provided they can decide on their distinctive competencies and remain focused. The Tata Steel – Corus deal in 2006 is a significant milestone reflecting maturity of Indian enterprises. It is an effort to improve competitiveness of Tata Steel in European markets through low-cost intermediate products from India and converting them into high-value, sophisticated finished products. Aspirations to be a global

---

Box 2.2

During 2005–08, Godrej Consumer Products bought three firms, one in the UK and two in South Africa. In 2010, it bought four, not including the buyout of Sara Lee Corp.'s stake in Godrej Sara Lee Ltd.

---

player, superior complementary com-binations, and greater hold over a geographic market are motivations such as these reflect a sense of supreme confidence to be globally competitive; a premise that is most essential to eventually become a multinational firm.

STRATEGIC CHOICES FOR VULNERABLE FIRMS[2]

The question is what should firms falling in the vulnerable portion do, although they may be champions in the "domestic" market?

In terms of strategic implications, the more efficient but smaller Indian firms are most vulnerable as acquisition targets by global champions. These "local" champions will provide cheaper and readymade access to huge Indian markets, and also be an excellent base for outsourcing and global manufacturing for the acquiring companies. Earlier, we had the classic case of Thums Up being sold out by the Chauhans to Coca-Cola and Godrej's soap-making assets bought out by alliance partner P&G. More recently, we had two cases where well-performing Indian companies were taken over by foreigners. The buyout of Delhi-based Indo Asian Fusegear by Legrand of France and Shanta Biotech by Sanofi are such examples, whereby, the foreign entrant gets ready access to the Indian market in the electric switchgear and pharma businesses. In a nutshell, they are liable to be acquired at a premium by foreign and domestic companies, or can simply wither away in the face of competition.

BEYOND *JUGAAD* TO WORLD-CLASS PATENTABLE INNOVATIONS

The asset-light businesses must shore up their R&D skills and come up with products that can be sold in global markets. This requires risk up front and specific skills to operate in global markets. Not to forget, speed is of essence—in the fight for survival between the tiger and deer, the one that can run faster will live to see another day.

---

[2] This section is based on, Arun Kumar Jain (2010) "Do We Lack the Killer Instinct?" *Financial Chronicle*, July 26.

Fortunately, we have great examples of success close to our home. First the Japanese firms showed us the way. Sony, Toshiba, Matsushita, Nippon Steel, Toyota, Honda, Canon, Fuji, Seiko, Epson, Hitachi, Fujitsu are just a few names in electronics, automobiles, precision instruments that struck the world. They could take on the much bigger and robust competitors on their home ground. Now, one can be in any part of the world and easily find hoardings and products from Samsung, LG, Acer, and Asus. Is not it surprising that some of the biggest consumer electronic and computer brands in the world are coming from small Asian countries? It is indeed a revelation that in a relatively short period of time these companies from small nations and without much comparative advantage have become bigger than the biggest companies in India. All of these are privately owned and are respected for cutting-edge technologies. Seldom do they bank upon domestic demand (which may simply not exist).

FOCUS, FOCUS, AND FOCUS[3]

Unless firms focus on scale, scope or competences, they will remain vulnerable. Globalization is just not about scale and scope, but also about managing backward and forward supply chain links. The local factors come into play when, for instance, jobs are to be protected. Standardization allows companies to put processes in place and go for economies of scale; customization challenges companies to provide individual customers their choices thereby making processes and learning vulnerable when customer loyalties are fickle. The notion of market capitalization is a tricky one. BP has lost substantial market value since the Gulf of Mexico crisis. Market capitalization economy imposes a strict discipline on companies to create wealth for the shareholders, while the social responsibility paradigm imposes a strict regimen for creating social wealth for the society for the company to gain acceptance in the marketplace. ADAG's Reliance Natural Resources in India has eroded shareholder value since a share-swap agreement with sister company Reliance Power was announced.

The four challenges mentioned at the beginning of this essay encompass the gamut of strategy, structure, and leadership inter-linkages. These also require a comprehensive understanding of local factors including government policy, expectations, local laws and customs, and social infrastructure. Suzlon found to its dismay that dealing with these areas in Germany and the US can lead to unintended consequences in its global forays.

---

[3] This Section is based on, Arun Kumar Jain (2010) "Indian Firms Need to Go Global," *Financial Chronicle*, July 12.

BLEND TECHNOLOGY WITH INNOVATION[4]

Here we must mention our penchant for *jugaad*s. India abounds in local-level *jugaad*s. These are functionally useful problem-solutions but usually physically dangerous and environmentally disastrous, and never patentable. For instance, we had a repair job done on our suitcase that made it almost new when all vendors said that this was beyond repair. It cost us a fraction of a price that a new one would have. But over-emphasis of this approach on adaptations can drift a company from a path of patentable innovations. Equally, catchy management jargons such as 'bottom-of-pyramid' can severely handicap a firm from properly slicing (segmenting) the market and designing products to the customer profile.

The real test of competitiveness is a firm's export competitiveness. A hi-technology innovation should lead to greater exports and reduced customer negotiation power. This is an area where we have failed collectively! For the last 60 years we have not been able to produce any "global" product or service that enhances our image as a technology or knowledge-based economy. In several emerging and sunrise industries such as bio-tech, nuclear, renewable energy, aeronautics, consumer electronics, and pharmaceuticals, our firms have not yet started on the innovation curve (barring exceptions). Where are our own hi-technology small and medium enterprises which form the backbone of German export competitiveness? South Korea and Taiwan are leading-edge countries in consumer electronics, while China has moved rapidly ahead in renewable energy, automobiles, and electronics hardware and software.

A good indicator of our global competitiveness is the number of patents filed and rejected within the country. We are far behind on this parameter compared to developed nations and even some other Asian countries. Digging deeper, we have no figures for number of patents granted for the money (dollars) invested in R&D which indices the efficiency of our investments. The other useful statistic could be the Return on Investment on Technology (ROIT). This important statistic can help develop a better commercial understanding of various research projects.

The main reasons for our collective inability to develop new hi-tech innovations can be summarized as:

(i)   Too much differentiation between process and product innovations. In the real commercial world these do not matter!

---

[4] This section is based on, Arun Kumar Jain (2010) "Blend Technology with Innovation," *Financial Chronicle*, August 24.

(ii) Low priority to engineering skills compared to managerial ones (in terms of monetary rewards and societal prestige)—leading to de-emphasis on systems-based problem-solving skills.

(iii) Poor or absent knowledge management in companies. The knowledge is much individual-based and once the person retires or leaves the firm, is stranded. An off-shoot of this mindset is the paucity of information in research journals and textbooks about innovations by Indian companies. Even today we depend on the Western world produced literature and case studies for our curriculum.

(iv) Poor or absent safeguarding structures and systems for the innovators. Often the research-minds are burdened with administrative duties, or worse, evaluated on normal bureaucratic parameters even in centers of excellence.

Overall poor results in hi-technology innovations are surprising and troubling at the same time. Pick up any issue of a major science or research-based journal, and one can find many Indians writing and contributing major pieces. In a recent issue of *Nature*, we counted at least nine Indians (single largest community) who were reporting state-of-the-art research commentary in major papers on subjects as diverse as physics, astronomy, chemistry, biology, and pharma-genetics. It also showed that our much-maligned universities are after-all not so bad for producing top talent.

IMPLICATIONS FOR STRATEGY AND HR MANAGERS

Firms will require globally competent managers who understand the four challenges highlighted earlier; can handle a multi-cultural workforce; liaison with regulatory bodies in different countries; and can mitigate business risks.

The issue before the Indian business leadership is not (lack of) strategies, or a level-playing field industry structure, or even government policy. It is purely a question of hunger and fire in the belly. Firms must define and articulate their aspirations in clear and simple terms. Our research points out that the aspirational and vision deficit in our firms is remarkable. We tend to get satisfied rather too quickly and by very few real achievements despite talent and potential. Sania Mirza is a classic example. Should our companies remain satisfied with being World No. 32? Or should they have Vishwanathan Anand and Saina Nehwal as role models?

This is the moot point. In 20 years since the economic reforms and liberalization process started, Indian companies have successfully managed the challenges of quality, cost, and output. But have they shown the necessary aggression and acumen to become global champions? In an ongoing research project, we found that few Indian companies have the leadership attributes and competences to manage large-ticket acquisitions or the internal vision to become truly global. This is a challenge for the HR managers of 21st century—how do we retain, and nurture talent that will take their firms into the next orbit.

APPENDIX 2.1: LIST OF FIRMS

Name	Abbreviation	Name	Abbreviation
ACC Ltd.	ACC	Corporation Bank	CORPBANK
Adani Enterprises Ltd.*	ADANIENT	Crompton Greaves Ltd.	CROMPGREAV
Aditya Birla Nuvo Ltd.	A BIRLA NUVO	DLF Ltd.*	DLF
Ambuja Cements Ltd.	AMBUJA CEM	Dr. Reddy's Laboratories Ltd.	DRREDDY
Andhra Bank	ANDHRA BANK	Federal Bank Ltd.	FEDERALBNK
Ashok Leyland Ltd.	ASHOK LEY	GAIL (India) Ltd.	GAIL
Asian Paints Ltd.	ASIAN PAINT	Glenmark Pharmaceuticals Ltd.	GLENMARK
Axis Bank Ltd.	AXIS BANK	GMR Infrastructure Ltd.	GMRINFRA
Bajaj Auto Ltd.	BAJAJ-AUTO	HCL Technologies Ltd.	HCLTECH
Bank of Baroda	BANK BARODA	HDFC Bank Ltd.	HDFCBANK
Bank of India	BANK INDIA	Hero Honda Motors Ltd.	HEROHONDA
Bharat Electronics Ltd.	BEL	Hindalco Industries Ltd.*	HINDALCO
Bharat Forge Ltd.	BHARAT FORG	Hindustan Petroleum Corporation Ltd.	HINDPETRO
Bharat Heavy Electricals Ltd.	BHEL	Housing Development and Infrastructure Ltd.	HDIL
Bharat Petroleum Corporation Ltd.	BPCL	Housing Development Finance Corporation Ltd.	HDFC
Bharti Airtel Ltd.*	BHARTI ARTL	ITC Ltd.	ITC
Biocon Ltd.	BIOCON	ICICI Bank Ltd.*	ICICIBANK
Canara Bank	CANBK	IDBI Bank Ltd.	IDBI
Cipla Ltd.	CIPLA	Idea Cellular Ltd.	IDEA
Container Corporation of India Ltd.	CONCOR	IFCI Ltd.	IFCI

Company	Symbol	Company	Symbol
Indian Overseas Bank	IOB	Reliance Communications Ltd.*	RCOM
Infosys Technologies Ltd.	INFOSYSTCH	Reliance Industries Ltd.*	RELIANCE
Infrastructure Development Finance Co. Ltd.	IDFC	Reliance Infrastructure Ltd.	RELINFRA
Jaiprakash Associates Ltd.	JPASSOCIAT	Reliance Power Ltd.	RPOWER
Jindal Steel & Power Ltd.*	JINDALSTEL	Sesa Goa Ltd.	SESAGOA
JSW Steel Ltd.	JSWSTEEL	State Bank of India*	SBIN
Kotak Mahindra Bank Ltd.	KOTAKBANK	Steel Authority of India Ltd.*	SAIL
Larsen & Toubro Ltd.	LT	Sterlite Industries (India) Ltd.	STER
LIC Housing Finance Ltd.	LICHSGFIN	Sun Pharmaceutical Industries Ltd.	SUNPHARMA
Lupin Ltd.	LUPIN	Suzlon Energy Ltd.	SUZLON
Mahindra & Mahindra Ltd.	M&M	Tata Consultancy Services Ltd.	TCS
Mangalore Refinery & Petrochemicals Ltd.	MRPL	Tata Motors Ltd.	TATAMOTORS
Mundra Port and Special Economic Zone Ltd.	MUNDRAPORT	Tata Power Co. Ltd.	TATAPOWER
NTPC Ltd.*	NTPC	Tata Steel Ltd.*	TATASTEEL
Oil & Natural Gas Corporation Ltd.*	ONGC	Tata Teleservices (Maharashtra) Ltd.	TTML
Patni Computer Systems Ltd.	PATNI	Tech Mahindra Ltd.	TECHM
Power Grid Corporation of India Ltd.	POWERGRID	Unitech Ltd.	UNITECH
Punjab National Bank	PNB	United Spirits Ltd.	MCDOWELL-N
Ranbaxy Laboratories Ltd.	RANBAXY	Wipro Ltd.	WIPRO
Reliance Capital Ltd.	RELCAPITAL	Zee Entertainment Enterprises Ltd	Zee
Indiabulls Real Estate Ltd.	IBREALEST		
Indian Hotels Co. Ltd.	INDHOTEL		

* Not considered in strategic control map, figure 2.

REFERENCES

Lowell L. Bryan (2007) "The New Metrics of Corporate Performance: Profit per Employee," *McKinsey Quarterly*.

Lowell L. Bryan, Timothy G. Lyons, and Rosenthal James (1998) "Corporate Strategy in Globalizing World: The Market Capitalization Imperative," *McKinsey Quarterly*.

Incandela Denise, Katheleen L. Mclaughlin, and Shi Christiana Smith (1999) "Building Cross Border Positions in Retailing," *McKinsey Quarterly*.

Ray, S. and S.R. Gubbi (2009) "International Acquisitions by Indian Firms: Implications for Research on Emerging Multinationals," *The Indian Journal of Industrial Relations*, 45(1): 11–26.

Thompson Art A., A.J.III Strickland, John Gamble John, and Arun Kumar Jain Kumar (2010) *Crafting and Executing Strategy: The Quest for Competitive Advantage Concepts and Cases*. Tata McGraw-Hill.

Web References

1. Bombay Stock Exchange, www.bseindia.com (last accessed July 1, 2010).
2. National Stock Exchange, www.nseindia.com (last accessed July 1, 2010).
3. http://www.nseindia.com/content/indices/ind_cnx_100.pdf
4. Company Annual Reports for FY 2008–09.
5. ISI Emerging Markets Database.

3

Finding the Future and Making It Happen

John Pisapia

Every few hundred years in western history there occurs a sharp trans-formation. We cross. . . a divide. Within a few short decades society rearranges itself, its world view; its basic values; its social and political structure; its arts; its key institutions. Fifty years later, there appears a new world. . . we are currently living through such a transformation. (Drucker, 1993: 1)

In my book, *The Strategic Leader: New Tactics for a Globalizing World* I present a puzzle posed as questions to leaders who want to find the future and to make it happen must solve it. What is going on here? Do we need to *jump the curve*? What needs to happen here? What is precious and what is expendable? How do we make it happen? How do we keep making it happen? These questions form the core elements of the strat-egic leadership system (SL System). When we answer these questions, as I do in this chapter, we are working in a strategic way to find the future and make it happen.

WHAT IS GOING ON HERE?

Leaders must identify the strategic forces in their environment that must be addressed. A natural place to start is to examine our worldview. World-view means the expectations and biases we bring to a situation before new data appears (Lakoff, 2002). To identify the strategic forces, we not only must understand our worldview but also the worldview of those people we are trying to influence if we wish to be successful in positioning our organizations. If we fail, our ideas will fall on deaf ears, and we will be out of sync with the direction the world is moving in. Our starting point is to understand how different worldviews give rise to alternative forms of leadership. My purpose in starting at this point is descriptive not pre-scriptive. Consequently, the focus is on what the dominant worldviews are; not what they should be.

The beginning point of this journey is an acceptance that there is a constant movement in society between stability and instability. A tool I introduced in *The Strategic Leader*—the power of the curve[1]—can be useful to explain this constant movement and the necessary transitions; how they come about, why leaders need to be agile and *jump the curve* when it is appropriate, and be artistic in executing innovations that are introduced as the initial curve plays out.

The curve I speak of is the sigmoid curve and the power comes when leaders are able to detect the beginnings of new curves that have the potential to replace the old sigmoid curve. A simple example of the power of the curve is that of the early automobile industry.

The transportation mode before 1907 was the—horse and wagon. By introducing a new product—the Model T automobile—Henry Ford jumped *the existing curve* based on horse and wagon transportation. Henry did not invent the automobile. The first ones were hand crafted and had a high price tag; they were unable to create a new curve. Henry surmised that a competitive product had to be cheap enough that many users could afford one and sturdy enough to withstand the wear and tear of potholes created by the rough terrain of unpaved roads. So the "Tin Lizzie", as the Model T was called, was bland and black; but it was affordable by the masses. In essence, Henry was able to create a new sigmoid curve by recalibrating his worldview and that of others. He reinforced this curve by introducing the assembly line technology to replace hand craftsmanship, to keep costs down, and enable his car to compete with and eventually outperform the horse and wagon. The curve Henry created remained in place for twenty years and the Ford Company captured the automobile market. He continued to make Model T's that withstood the wear and tear at an affordable price. To do this his cars came in one color—black and one body style—the Model T—to control costs.

As the century moved on, new strategic forces appeared. There were more paved roads, personal income increased, and American customers began to wonder why they could only own a car in one style and one color. Alfred Sloan, one of Henry's competitors with Chevrolet, was one of the first to understand these signals of change. He recalculated his worldview to match the emerging future and began to give consumers choices by offering several car models and colors at a comparable cost to the Model T. By 1925, the new curve was evident and Ford readjusted to meet his new competition; but it was too late to retain the dominance of the market

---

[1] Pisapia, 2009, pp. 2–4.

he had achieved when he first jumped the curve. To his credit, however, the Ford Company remained an important but not dominant player in the auto industry.

The account of the ebb and flow of the early automobile industry illustrates *the power of the curve*. If we fail to understand our worldview, we will fail to see the signals of change. If our worldview is not in sync with the direction the world is moving in, the signals cannot be seen and will fall on deaf ears. So what is the direction the world is moving in now?

The organizers of this enclave suggest that we are going through a transformation like Drucker described in 1993. They suggest that this transformation will realign power, financial markets, corporate strategy, process, and consumption patterns, business, competition, and collaboration. In this transition, capital will flow toward opportunity fast. Other observers also agree. The developed world is moving out of an investment driven economy into an innovation driven one fueled by competition (Porter, 2008a), innovation, and technology (Freeman et al., 2007) and the role of government to create conditions that support knowledge creation and diffusion, and resource fluidity necessary to move capital to strategic opportunities (Doz and Kosonen, 2008; Meyer et al., forthcoming). My observations indicate that four central strategic forces: technology, clash of ideologies, diversity, and competition are moving the world from stability to instability.

Technology and Innovation are In

More countries are moving from pig iron to silicon industries (Delos, 2010: 25). In developed and developing countries wireless communications, sensors, and social networks extend the reach of organizations. For instance, there are over 500 million cell phone users in China, 81 million in Indonesia, and 40 million in Nigeria (*CIA World Factbook*, 2009). Globally, the number of people doing knowledge work is increasing at a faster rate than those involved in production. Today the demand for cognitive skills is as important as technical skills. According to the recent *McKinsey* survey (Freeman et al., 2007), there are over 10 million social networking users worldwide which enable users to co-create content (i.e., Wikipedia, Facebook, and cloud computing). These web 2.0 tools enable individuals and organizations to access the best talent and skills from a wider pool, pay for these services as one does with a public utility, collaborate across organizational boundaries, and receive immediate data for analysis and experimentation to drive innovation.

Central Planning and Capital are Out; No Holds Barred State or Democratic Capitalism Fueled by Competition, Knowledge, and Innovations are In

This trend is being played out as a struggle between state and democratic capitalism. David Brooks (2010) the award winning *New York Times* syndicated columnist[2] characterizes this trend this way. On one side are the United States of America (USA), Japan, and Australia who believe that business creates wealth and governments regulate and enforce a level playing field. On the other side there are China, Saudi Arabia, Russia, and Iran who believe that government uses markets to "create wealth that finances the ruling party's survival." The two groups of countries invest differently. For example, India with a decentralized model focuses on low capital investment in IT, and high capital flow toward education. However, even in China with its traditional centralization, high capital investment in plants, steps are being taken to decentralize and introduce competition, and move from a planned economy to a market economy. Evidently this rivalry is an interdependent one unlike previous ideological clashes. Viewing these signals from a traditional worldview will prove to be inadequate to anticipate the shift from a bipolar world of the USA and the rest of the world to a multi-polar world where the USA, who still accounts for one-third of all the economic growth in the world over the last 15 years (Porter, 2008b) and leads the world in technology, patents, and higher education, will still be relevant but not the engine it has been historically. Looking at the world through a multi-polar lens, strategists must focus on combinations of forging a new path or fast following!

Diversity is In; Single Geopolitical Interests is Out

Another driving strategic force in the world is the explosion of diversity of consumers. Interestedly, this diversity is not so much ethnic (although it still exists) as much as it is in class structure, as the middle class in emerging countries of Russia, China, and Brazil explodes. Internally, the hiring of Millennials with their "backpacks and Kaki's" and the hiring of multinationals to work in and manage globalizing corporations require rethinking organizational processes, structure, and leadership styles. Diversity in these cases leads to fragmentation of the marketplace and reconfiguring organizations. Cherian Varghese (2010) suggests that organizations with these characteristics must possess three attributes: operate

---

[2] Brooks' ideas build off the work of Ian Bremmer the American Political Scientist and President of the Eurasia Group.

as networks, highly adaptable business model that can enter new markets quickly, diverse leadership teams, and multiple value systems co-existing in the same company.

Competition is In; Protectionism is Out

Competition, advocates assert, encourages the development of new products, services, and technologies leading to lower prices and better products. It works well when property rights and the rule of law are the underlying elements of the transactions. The fallacies in the logic of protectionism, restraint of trade, and barriers to trade are well accepted (Bhagwati, 2004). Relatively speaking, it is not by chance that none of the poorest economies in the world is free and none of the freest economies are poor (Kasper and Streit, 1998).

Competition is also evident in the education sector. For example, in China the preparation of school principals was assigned to one university. Each year 1,500 beginning principals are brought to China East Normal University in cohorts of 50 to study and live on campus for three months and become certified as a school principal. Now there are movements to introduce competition from other universities and private providers in the training of principals. Similarly, in the USA, K-12 public education's protected status is waning as more and more Charter Schools open. Traditional competition, however, is giving away to cooperative competition thus promoting mutual survival. Regardless if a nation or an organization is powerful or less powerful, value now comes from the interactions of interlocking players rather than one-on-one transactions. Management interlocks occur when two corporations share a board director or officer, a practice which may confer upon corporations benefits such as expertise, legitimacy, and cooptation of risk. Management interlocks have their problems but product interlocks can help ensure that a corporation has a steady and reliable stream of resources necessary for its business operations. Product interlocks occur when companies select partners for creation and distribution such as Apple's IPhone and AT&T, Shell Oil company's partnering with Qatar Petroleum, or the Chinese government, and the Disney Corporation joining forces to introduce Disney China. The global challenge and opportunity appears to be in finding local partners who can overcome local customs; but these product interlocks do not happen by chance.

The key for solving the first part of the leader puzzle is to ask, "How do these strategic forces impact my industry?" The second part of the puzzle is to determine what you need to do in order to address strategic forces in your environment. Do you need to *jump the curve*? How have others made this decision?

WHAT HAS TO HAPPEN HERE

Let us fast forward to the year 2006. After presenting my thoughts on strategic thinking at the NHRD conference in New Delhi, I hired a driver and set off to Agra to visit the Taj Mahal and returned by train.[3] The roadway was crowded with bicycles, auto rickshaws, small cars, tractors, motorcycles, and other forms of conveyance that could carry people from one place to another, even a wagon pulled by camels and another by water buffalos. The two wheelers particularly caught my eye. Men in helmets drove the bike with their spouse sitting side saddle on the back and without a helmet; often they were holding a baby. Sometimes a small boy or girl sat western style in front of their father.

After reflecting on my experience and observations, I came to the conclusion that this land is where chaos and opportunity is king. Ratan Tata, being the strategic thinker that he is, more than likely saw the same things I was seeing many times in his travels through the country and came to similar conclusions. Soon after taking control of the Tata Group he positioned Tata to globalize, be skill intensive, and be among the top three in an industry or exit. His main concern at the time was with mindset and attitudes. He saw the creation of a new mindset as his first job followed by allowing empowerment down the line, and encouraging sensitivity to customer needs. The changed mindset started with him.

Ratan made a move into passenger cars with the introduction of a station wagon and a sport utility vehicle. He said that passenger cars were chosen because India was a country of 700–800 million people but the incidence of ownership of the passenger car was extremely small. By 1999, Ratan noted that the country was consuming about a million cars and five million scooters and motorbikes annually. The population stood around a billion plus, with 18 million people added each year and 40 percent of the population under the age of 16. Ratan concluded that there had to be a growth potential in personal transport, not so much at the high end as at the lower end of the market.

---

[3] After becoming aware of Ratan Tata during my work in India I pieced together his story from sources such as Pete Engardio (August 2, 2007); Lala (2006); http://www.telegraph.co.uk/news/worldnews/1575181/Ultimate-economy-drive-the-andpound1,300-car.html http://www.accessmylibrary.com/coms2/summary_0286-33768505_ITM; http://www.indiacar.net/news/n73529.htm, and a series of interviews with Ratan Tata (http://www.tata.com) including those by Christabelle Noronha (January 2008) and (August 2008)

Based on his synthesis and interpretation of the opportunities afforded by the market in India and the strengths the Tata Group had displayed after its first foray into the passenger car market, Ratan invested US $400 million in the development of a four door hatchback that sold for just US $4,100. The car was officially named the Indica but informally it was known as "Ratan's folly." The Indica was positioned to compete with Suzuki as well as Ford, General Motors, Hyundai, and Daewoo. Ratan Tata staked his reputation on it and therefore gave the project much of his time; often spending weekends at the factory to help with the rollout. The Indica V2 became the third-biggest seller in India.

Ratan did not rest on his laurels for long. He had already seen the same potential customers on the motor bikes that I observed during my travels. He knew that India has approximately 65 million scooter owners and that only 58 million Indians, out of the country's 1.1 billion population earn more than US $4,400 a year. In 2003, he reframed the challenge to make the potential consumers at this low income segment of the market into car owners. He announced plans to build a car costing approximately US $2,500 dollars, with four doors so it could transport a family of five.

Dubbed the *People's Car* by the media, the car was meant to be within the reach of everyone who had ever dreamed of owning a car, not just the people who could afford one. When asked, Ratan explained:

Launching an automobile is a risky endeavor, as you point out. But we have been satisfied with the success of the Tata Indica and are undertaking the 1-lakh (US $2,500) car with an even stronger base of competence. We are confident that the investment will prove a wise one.

On January 10, 2008, at the New Delhi Auto Show, and with the immortal words "a promise is a promise," Ratan Tata unveiled the world's cheapest car—the US $2,500 Tata Nano. For Ratan, the event capped a 17 year quest to transform the Tata Group into a world brand.

The case of the People's Car provides a solid backdrop to answering the first two parts of the leadership puzzle: What is going on here? What has to happen here? Anticipating and finding the future and a willingness to *jump the curve* plays an important role in continuing success. Understanding the role of anticipating in strategic leadership, Ratan Tata scanned the environment and found opportunities in the form of a growing economy and population. He also found threats in the form of foreign corporations in the market place that had a significant head start in the design and engineering needed to manufacture cars. Knowing his penchant for strategic planning, I am sure Ratan used some formal analytic tools to collect, synthesize, and interpret the data he gathered such as the strategic thinking protocol that I advocate.

The key for solving the second part of the leader puzzle is ask, "How do we respond to the strategic forces impacting my industry?" Ratan Tata responded to his strategic forces by creating a car that the masses could afford. The third part of the puzzle is to determine how to address them. Do our leadership models need to change? Is there a model that shows promise in addressing 21st century strategic forces? Does our worldview of leadership models—western or eastern—need to change?

HOW CAN WE MAKE IT HAPPEN?

There are lessons to learn from these strategic forces. It is obvious that change is occurring at warp speed. We live in quicksilver environments; environments that are fluid, uncertain, complex, and sometimes ambiguous. In such environments the spoils go to the creative and not to the compliant; leaders who maximize their conceptual agility and their organization's adaptability, and flexibility; and organizations who focus on metrics, learning, self-management, and adaptability.

In such environments, leadership is critical. In quicksilver, it is impossible to predict long term changes and influences. Answers and direction emerge without prior planning while the search for absolute truth wanes. It is a period of time when leadership is needed the most and potentially has its greatest impact. This time demands that leaders work in a strategic way. This means that leaders need to understand the threats and opportunities presented, and develop actionable plans well before the end of a life cycle to prepare their organizations to move to the next S curve. Capra (1994) suggests that five universal elements underpinning the type of leadership are needed: *(a)* a shift from parts to whole, *(b)* a shift from structure to process, *(c)* a shift from objective to epistemic science, *(d)* a shift from building to networking, and *(e)* a shift from truth to approximate description.

The emerging context demands strategic leaders. Strategic Leadership (SL) is not a style, nor is it reserved for top echelon leaders. It is a way of thinking and way of working by managers and leaders throughout an organization. The central tenant of strategic leadership is that given the uncertainty and ambiguity presented by the context, leaders must work in a strategic way by cultivating themselves and then cultivating their organizations to change the atmosphere. Leaders work in a strategic way by bringing a philosophy, a system, and a way of thinking, and working that leads to sustained, not scattered success. At its core, working in a strategic way requires the ability to make and execute consequential decisions about ends, strategies, and tactics. It requires that managers and leaders are able to think strategically and execute change effectively with a profound appreciation for stability.

Philosophically, strategic leaders (SLers) know that that their ability to find the future and make it happen is dependent on people embracing solutions and acting upon them; not technical tools. The quality of their actions leads to quality actions by their followers.

- SLers create a shared reality and then a shared direction. They know that in every organization there is a *WE–THEY LINE*—the line where people above it say *WE DID IT* and people below it say *THEY DID IT*. SLers move this line lower in the organization to get more people above the *WE–THEY LINE* where vision and aspirations are shared.
- SLers take calculated risks; they are tenacious. They do not plan first. They create aspirations and actions; then they plan. They know that when opportunity comes—it is too late to prepare! SLers *RUN TO DAYLIGHT*—they stick to their principles and when opportunities come they pounce on them vigorously.
- SLers cultivate the conditions that support change. They operate as gardeners rather than mechanics. A goal is to manage at *the edge of chaos*. They learn to keep their balance by maneuvering and adjusting – adjust – adjust; not adjust, adjust, adjust and then try to move forward.
- SLers lead through generative processes and principles; not rules and procedures. They know that close scrutiny helps in the beginning, but constrains in the long term.
- SLers believe that performance is the result of a combination of effective intent and excellent execution. They prudently use non-gameable metrics to push their organizations to action. They recognize that you cannot manage what you cannot measure.

SLers work in a strategic way because they know that through self and organizational cultivation they can tilt the playing field in their direction and achieve sustained not random success. They honor the process by running the *SL System* which is formed around finding the answers to these strategic questions: What is going on here? What has to happen here? What is precious and what is expendable? How do we make it happen? How do we keep making it happen?

The key to solving the leader's puzzle is the ability to see the world as it is; not as you wish it to be. The Tata story, unlike Ford's, is an examples of a leader working in a strategic way. He looked, listened, learned, and then led. Strategic leaders are not simply great strategists. They are able to understand their context, get a team together, and agree on a target and how they are going to get there. Then they get there. They exemplify a new way of leading which I schematically characterize as Theory Z.

Theory Z is built on an integral post Western framework: cultivate yourself and then cultivate your organization. *Agility of the mind* and *artistry of actions* are the keystones which must be in place to think and act in a strategic way. A keystone is the architectural piece that locks other pieces into place. Thus the placement of keystones is extremely important structurally. I use the term figuratively to refer to the central supporting elements of Theory Z—*agility of the mind* and *artistry of actions*—without which the whole structure would collapse. The keystones are supported by two action competencies: the strategic thinking and strategic execution protocols.[4] Protocol as used here are a specified set of procedures to follow to develop intent and execute it. Schematically cultivating yourself and then your organization looks like Table 3.1.

TABLE 3.1: Theory Z Guides the Practice of Strategic Leadership

Self-Cultivation	*Organizational Cultivation*
Agility	*Strategic Thinking Protocol*
Strategic Mindset	Create a Shared Reality
New Science Principles	Generative Processes
Systems Thinking	Strategic Questions
Reflection	Strategic Conversations
Reframing	Create a Shared Direction
Artistry	*Strategic Execution Protocol*
Transforming	Concrete Clear Target
Managing	Track Performance
Bonding	Teach Organization's Point of View
Bridging	Make Learning a Priority
Bartering	Empower
	Hire for Cultural and Performance Fit
	Tie Rewards to Performance, Growth & Contribution

Source: Pisapia (2010).

Agility is the keystone of strategic thinking. It refers to the ability of leaders to use three strategic thinking skills: systems thinking, reframing, and reflection on ways that combines rational knowledge with intuition, and promotes individual and organizational self-discovery, and open

---

[4] The strategic thinking and strategic execution protocols are not discussed here due to space limitations (see Pisapia, 2009).

mindedness. There are several results from using these skills. First, the possession of strategic thinking skills result in a strategic mindset that guides thinking and is successful in interpreting environmental forces and identifying strategic initiatives. These skills also drive the strategic thinking protocol which results in a shared statement of strategic intent (an actionable plan) which is central to developing a high performing organization. It sets the direction. It describes the clear concrete target. It describes the values that the organization will hold itself up against. It identifies the initiatives that will move the organization along its path to high performance. And, it does all this on one front and back page. The statement of intent forms a psychological contract with followers and guides the organizational actions. It is meant to be a living guiding statement for the organization/team.

Artistry is the keystone of strategic execution. It refers to the ability of leaders to use five leader actions: managing, transforming, bonding, bridging, and bartering. Leaders use these actions to embed their strategy into the everyday work behaviors and practices of their organization to be successful. Artistry takes its cue from the fact that no amount of thinking will make change happen. The results of using these skills are many. First, the possession of artistic leader actions results in an ability to engage in a constant cycle of leading and managing; sometimes simultaneously. They also enable the leader to juggle the political realities required to sell their ideas to those who enact them while following the values identified as important by themselves, their colleagues, and the organization. Finally, they drive the strategic execution protocol which results in creating the conditions for high performance on measures agreed upon by the organization.

HOW DO WE KEEP MAKING IT HAPPEN?

So how do leaders load the dice in their favor? Consider how Carlos Ghosn, born in Brazil, schooled in Lebanon by Jesuit priests, with a degree in Engineering from France's prestigious Ecole Polytechnique works in a strategic way. In 1999, at the age of 46, he was sent to Japan to change the financial status of Nissan motors from US $50 million in debt to profitability in three years. Ghosn made it happen by using a "listen first, then think, and then speak" philosophy and a generative inclusive style.[5]

---

[5] I used the following sources to piece together Mr Ghosn's responses to the four questions; Fonda (2003: 78); Ghosn (2005); Greising (2002); Magee (2003); Taylor (2003); http://www.time.com/time/2001/influentials/ybghosn.html; http://www.businessweek.com/2001/01_02/b3714015.htm; and http://www.nissanusa.com/insideNissan/CorporateBiographies

What is going on here? Ghosn would say: establish with and within the company a very simple vision about the destination. He went to Nissan without any preconceived ideas—just a clean sheet of paper—and set about, with his top team, evaluating the company systematically to find the problems that were limiting performance. He personally interviewed over 300 employees at all levels and scoured financial and performance data. What Ghosn found was an unclear vision and vague goals. Ghosn fondly quotes a former teacher's words: "If you find things complicated, that means you haven't understood them. Simplicity is the basis of everything." This affection led him to capture Nissan's vision in a concrete and measurable number: 180. The number is short hand for Nissan's aspiration—add one million vehicle sales, achieve an eight percent operating margin, carry zero debt over three years. Ghosn would say diagnosis; interact with many people to make sure you have the right priorities and then share this diagnosis through a clear and concrete goal.

What has to happen here—What is precious—What is expendable or modifiable? Ghosn would say, the company for the most part determines its own faith. Develop a strategy, action plans, at every level of the company so everyone knows the contribution that is expected of them from the company. In Nissan's case, the point was not to change culture just for the sake of change. He wanted to change the culture for the sake of performance. In every step he took, he was very careful not to institute changes that were not based strictly on the advantages they give Nissan to improve company performance. By showing that every change made was for the sake of performance and benefit to the company, gradually these changes were approved and accepted.

How can we make it happen? Ghosn is convinced that the biggest mistake leaders make is not connecting with people. Leaders must feel the situation, understand the expectation of people, and respond to them in ways to improve overall performance. He believes people need to feel a strong personal and team commitment coming from the top. You have to listen deeply—not only to direct reports—into the organization. When you find something out of place act fast and empower as many people as possible to make decisions. Communicate not only what you are doing but the results also and then reward people. He believes that in the end, results cement everything. They give you credibility—make people feel safe and want to sign on for the journey.

How do we keep making it happen? Ghosn says that many times people make great speeches but frequently nothing happens. While words are important, they do not automatically translate into action. He believes that measurement pushes you into action. The only way you are going to make sure actions are going to follow talk is by measurement. He believes in straight talk focused on results from his managers and employees. But he also believes in having an appreciation for simplicity in setting up monitoring indicators and surveys; not just to see how our customers rate the quality of sales processes, but also to understand what is going wrong. He believes that measuring objectively the way individuals and teams have contributed to the performance of the company is more useful for motivation than subjective views.

SUMMARY

The world is changing at warp speed and demands new ways of leading. In such an environment, performance will result from a combination of effective intent and excellent execution. In this chapter, the SL System, in the form of a leader puzzle, was introduced to understand signals of change in environments, enable leaders to judge when to jump the curve, and then develop and execute actionable plans that lead to high performance. The solution of this puzzle was framed schematically through Theory Z which suggests that leaders in the 21st century work in a strategic way by becoming gardeners who cultivate the conditions that support change and performance not mechanics to drive it. To work in a strategic way, leaders must possess four competencies exemplified by Henry Ford, Alfred Sloane, Ratan Tata, and Carlos Ghosn, and many other 21st century leaders whose thought processes I investigated and actions I observed. These observations, codified under the concept of strategic leadership and guided by Theory Z, should enable leaders to find the future and make it happen.

REFERENCES

Ahlstrom, D. (2010) "Innovation and Growth: How Business Contributes to Society," *Academy of Management Perspectives*, 24(3): 10–23.

Bhagwati, J. (2004) *In Defense of Globalization*. UK: Oxford University Press.

Brooks, D. (2010) "The Larger Struggle." *The New York Times*. Op-Ed. Retrieved June 14, 2010 from http://www.nytimes.com/2010/06/15/opinion/15brooks.html

Capra, F. (1994) *From the Parts to the Whole: Systems Thinking in Ecology and Education*. Berkeley: Center for Ecoliteracy.

CIA World (2009) *Factbook*. Retrieved on June 31, 2010 from http://www.infoplease.com/ipa/A0933605.html#axzz0wDn7grwI

Delos, A. (2010) "How Can Organizations be Competitive But Dare to Care?" *Academy of Management Perspective*, 25–36.

Doz, Y. and M. Kosonen (2008) *Fast Strategy: How Strategic Agility will Help You Stay Ahead of the Game*. Philadelphia, PA: Wharton School Publishing.

Drucker, P. (1993) *Post-Capitalist Society*. New York: HarperCollins.

Engardio, P. (2007) "The Last Rajah," *Business Week*, August 2.

Fonda, D. (2003) "He Did So Well, Let's Give Him Two CEO Jobs: Carlos Ghosn Renault," *Time*.

Freeman, V., A. Woodwark, and E. Stephenson (2007) "Acting on Global Trends: A McKinsey Global Survey," *McKinsey Quarterly*. Retrieved from http://www.hbs.edu/centennial/businesssummit/market-capitalism/the-future-of-market-capitalism-panel.pdf (last accessed in March).

Ghosn, Carlos (2005) *Shift: Inside Nissan's Historic Revival*. NY: Doubleday.

———. (2007a) Nissan CEO, *Time*. http://www.time.com/time/2001/influentials/ybghosn.html.

———. (2007b) "Nissan Motors." *BusinessWeek*. Retrieved March 10, 2007, from http://www.businessweek.com/2001/01_02/b3714015.htm

Greising, D. (2002) "Nissan CEO Carlos Ghosn: Lets Team Drive Turnaround," *ChicagoTribune*, November 25.

Kasper, W. and M. Streit (1998) *Institutional Economics: Social Order and Public Policy*. Cheltenham, UK: Edward Elgar.

Lakoff, G. (2002) *Moral Politics: How Liberals and Conservatives Think*. Chicago: The University of Chicago Press.

Lala, R.M. (2006) *The Creation of Wealth: The Tatas from the 19th to the 21st Century*. New Delhi: The Eastern Book Corp.

Magee, D. (2003) *Turnaround: How Carlos Ghosn Rescued Nissan*. New York: HarperCollins.

Meyer, K., R. Mudambi, and R. Narula (forthcoming) "Multinational Enterprises and Local Contexts: The Opportunities and Challenges of Multiple Embeddedness," *Journal of Management Studies*.

Pisapia, J. (2009) *The Strategic Leader: New Tactics for a Globalizing World*. Charlotte, NC: Information Age Publishers.

———. (2010) "The Principles of Strategic Leadership," paper presented at the Chinese Executive Leadership Academy (CELAP), Pudong, Shanghai, China, May 20.

Porter, M. (2008a) *On Competition*. Boston: Harvard Business Review.

———. (2008b) "The Future of Market Capitalism. Working Knowledge." Boston: Harvard Business School. Retrieved from http://hbswk.hbs.edu/item/6195.html (last accessed in June 2010).

Taylor, A. (2003) "Nissan Shifts into Higher Gear: Carlos Ghosn Has Revved Up Profits at the Japanese Automaker. Now He Wants to Go Faster." *Fortune*, July 21.

Varghese, K.C. (2010) "Do Multinationals Really Understand Globalization?" *Bloomsburg Businessweek*. Retrieved from http://app.businessweek.com/UserComments/combo_review?action=all&style=wide&productId=108280&productCode=spec (last accessed on August 2).

4

Managing Performance:
Beyond Value-based Leadership

Shivganesh Bhargava

Performance of an organization, particularly the business organization, has been a serious field of research since many decades, for the students of management and behavioral sciences that led to a voluminous research outcome. Leadership emerged as relatively less disputed key factors of organizational success/growth/performance/effectiveness. In this paper, all these concepts are conceptualized within the framework of organizational performance. Leadership referred to that influential ability of the leader, which facilitates to get the best from the members towards achieving organizational objectives. Literature showed that factor such as age, education, socio-economic background, value framework, relationship with team, and level of self satisfaction of leaders plays an important role in enhancing leadership effectiveness without undermining the role of jobs, and the internal and external environment of an organization.

A study examining the relationship between leadership and organizational performance becomes necessary, when one looks at the secondary records of some surveys. One finds that around 71 percent global and 62 percent Indian companies declined their position in ranking in a decade from 1995 to 2005 (Fortune 500, 1995, 2005 and *Economic Times*, 1995, 2005). Further, a careful analysis of these ranking also reveal that decline (20 percent) and improvement (18 percent) of ranking of many companies over a decade was not very different in terms of percentage. So, sustainability of a business organization in this century of a competitive techno-market environment is a big challenge to the leaders, policy makers, and scholars.

Leadership accounts for a very significant percentage in explaining the organizational performance (20 to 45 percent by Day and Lord, 1988 and 14 percent by Joyce et al., 2003) and has got consistent evidence (Hogan and Kaiser, 2005; Javidan and House, 2002 [Global Leadership and Organizational Behavior Effectiveness {GLOBE} study of 62 countries], Stogdill, 1974) with a counter view as well that leadership is merely attribution (McElroy, 1982). Attempt has been made to see how leadership has scope to face the contemporary challenges of the organizations and look beyond the value-based leadership proposed by Bhargava (2003), keeping the existing framework of leadership models in background.

VALUE-BASED LEADERSHIP

Keeping the literature of leadership and values (Schwartz and Bilsky, 1987, 1990) in the background, Bhargava (2003) argued in favor of applying a value-based leadership for achieving organizational objectives and having sustainable performance. He analyzed the traits, behavior, situational, post-situational, and indigenous leadership theories and models and concluded that all broadly emphasize on maintenance of some core personal, professional, social, and environmental values on the part of a leader for having sustainable performance of the organization. Based on his consulting work, he was able to see a high correlation between value-based leadership and transformational leadership that was subsequently examined empirically (Kumar and Bhargava, 2003).

Trait theories (Stogdill, 1974) do emphasize on importance of traits on judging the effectiveness of a leader and even till date its importance is not diminished as the big five frameworks of personality (Judge and Bono, 2000), the five levels of leadership of Collins (2001) and charismatic leadership (Conger and Kanungo, 1998; Hunt and Conger, 1999) occupy tremendous respect. Led by an eminent scholars team, behavioral theories did classify leaders into categories like authoritarian, democratic, and *laissez-faire* (University of Iowa group) or setting goals and supporting subordinates to help them achieve goals (Ohio state university group) or employee centered and production centered (Michigan group). Here also classification is not value free. Popular situational theories (Fiedler, 1967; Hersey and Blanchard, 1969) do assume that a leader can vary his/ her leadership style to match the demand of situation. Others arguing for the path of goal theory of leadership (House, 1971), leader-participation model (Vroom and Yetton, 1973) and servant leadership (Greenleaf, 1977) also give importance to the values that a leader carries.

Even post-situational theories of leadership such as transformational leadership (Bass, 1985; Bass and Stogdill, 1990 and being centered or five levels of leadership (Fry and Kriger, 2009) are rooted around the values. Indigenous theories originated with the basic assumption that the values of the East are different from those of the West and most theories originated from the West and therefore, an indigenous leadership style may suit over the other (Khandwalla, 1995; Singh, 1982; Sinha, 1980, 1990). All the above theorists have predicted the effectiveness of their model at mostly all levels in the organization. These were also in the background to argue in favor of value based leadership as an effective model to lead organizations towards excellence in this competitive era. Values of the leader, as perceived by the stakeholders, have a significant impact on organizational performance. Look at Bill Gates of Microsoft, Jack Welch of GE and Robert Goizueta of Coca-Cola; it was an integration of their values that provided leadership in their companies to create wealth (performance) far ahead than other industry peers.

Herb et al. (2001) studied the impact of a new leadership based on organizational performance at 10 companies namely Proctor & Gamble, Gillette, Conagra, Unilever, Nestlé, Quaker Oats, Nabisco, Campbell Soup, Kellogg, and Allied Domecq in the consumer goods industry. It was found that in seven out of these 10 companies a change of leadership did not improve performance. This means that whenever a new leader comes, he or she comes along with his/her set of values that will have a significant impact in due course of time on the performance of people. Likewise, old leadership, even if a leader is not there, was grounded around a certain core set of values which will continue to have their role in influencing performance, as long as a new value set of the new leader do not occupy space in the mental framework of the stakeholders.

ORGANIZATION PERFORMANCE

As mentioned in the beginning organization performance in this paper incorporates all financial (tangible) and non-financial (non-tangible) aspects. It takes into consideration all concepts such as profit, efficiency, growth, performance, and effectiveness including measures like return on sales, return on equity, earning per share, market share, quality and sense of ownership. Recent evidence reaffirms the relationship between values and organization performance (Lancau et al., 2007). To examine relationships between the leadership and performance and substantiate the model of value-based leadership, we are following two studies performed by a team of my students. The first study is based on the analysis of secondary records while second study is more systematic, having base of primary as well as some secondary data base also. Studies did not directly focus on revisiting the value-based model but inferences are drawn from the main findings of both studies confirming merits of the model and revising it.

Study I: Leadership Success Stories (Marathe and Ramesh, 2008)

A study by two of my master of management students as a part of project of a course was carried out voluntarily using secondary data and public documents available on success stories of top 20 leaders of India representing five different sectors.

Profile analyses of these successful leaders show an average age of 58 years ranging from 41 to 85. Most of them were from the family-owned business (50 percent) while first generation entrepreneurs were (15 percent) and others (35 percent). They have done their post graduation and 75 percent have studied from universities like MIT, Harvard Business School, Yale, Stanford, Purdue, University of California, University of England, and Wales. Interestingly, 80 percent of these leaders were MBAs. Their professional experience was around 34 years including 20 years in non-family owned businesses. Normally, they spent around 10 years in one job. So, from profile analysis of successful business leaders, it can be concluded still they represent the upper middle class or middle class of India.

These leaders attributed their success in different public platforms and forums to the factors such as getting an opportunity to work in the right sector at the right time, liberalization as a turning point in their success, a low capital business in the Indian market and a strong leadership team. This finding shows that most of the factors are external to the individual leader, which does not fall in line with the traditional literature of attribution. This also reflects on the reality of the business environment of India and a deep understanding of business by the Indian leaders—a very healthy sign for India, Indian business, and the global market.

For their success, they gave credit to the family (parents and wife) for inspiration and guidance. Without undermining the importance of the father, for most of them, the mother was the main inspirational factor. Credit to wife (spouse) also reflects a healthy balance of business and family of leaders, which is extensively talked about these days as the "work-life balance." Analyses also revealed that mostly all emphasized on core professional values like integrity, commitment, and passion as well as sociocultural values such as humility and philanthropy, as the mantras of their sustained business growth and success in the business world. Importance of good higher academic studies, sticking to the job for a longer duration, ability to see market opportunities and strong leadership (belief on self and self confidence) were other factors that were attributed to play significant role in developing one as a successful leader of this decade. The findings of this study also provide direction to accept the framework of value-based leadership (Bhargava, 2003) and demand attention to have a deep sense of business understanding depending upon environment.

Study 2: Further Examination of Value-based Leadership (Agrawal, 2010)

As a part of doctoral work, Agrawal (2010) conducted a rare study on 322 top management team (TMT) members (prospective CEOs) and 53 chief executive officers (CEOs) representing 67 organizations from across seven industry sectors of India to examine the merit of the value-based leadership. Findings of this study confirmed the significant impact of leadership on organizational effectiveness of business organizations. He argued that time has come now to see beyond value based leadership as the value framework is also dependent on many factors and is dynamically changing. He advocated in favor of a strategic leadership framework as an alternative framework to manage performance in the business organizations. Some of his striking findings, grounded around the framework of value-based leadership, are summarized in the following paragraphs.

Leadership has significant impact on some non-tangible measures of organizational effectiveness such as job satisfaction, engagement, ownership, and organization citizenship behavior. A novel and striking finding of this study was that it did not find any mediating effect of the external environment while examining relationships between leadership and organizational effectiveness. This means that while the external environment, such as the issue of recession for example, may have adverse impact on tangible measures (profit) of organizational performance but not on the effectiveness measures such as job satisfaction, ownership, engagement, and OCB which can still sustain if processes of the organization are in order. This finding is in line with the framework of value-based leadership. A mediating effect of the monetary rewards on examining the relationship between the extent/breadth of participation and ownership of this study has implications to the policy makers firmly believing that strong monetary incentives will always improve performance. Creating a sense of ownership should not be undermined. This study reaffirmed the need for having empowered culture and healthy (quality) leader-follower relationship for organizational effectiveness.

In this study, CEOs as well as TMT members were asked to rank five organization values, in order of importance given to these values in their organization. In ranking of values, the CEOs followed an order of result orientation, customer orientation, integrity, passion for excellence, and innovation; while the TMT members ranked them in order of integrity, customer orientation, result orientation, passion for excellence and innovation.

This finding substantiates my thesis that role-responsibility is a powerful empowering facilitator while developing the future leaders of tomorrow. All TMT members know that it is only the integrity that will enable them to be placed on the top leadership position of the company and therefore, any kind of their exceptional performance should be grounded around/ by preserving the integrity for which one is known (perceived) for years (past services and contributions).

Very interestingly, the same person, when changed to the role of CEO, values the result orientation if he aspires to continue as the CEO of the company. Traditionally, the head of the family in the joint family system of India, will not enjoy the respect and command, if most members of the family are not taken care well (education, health, etc.) and there is no money or food to preserve the identity and status of the family. Equally notable is that to be labeled as the ideal son/daughter you have to maintain the integrity required to achieve that role/position. From the Indian epic of Mahabharat, Yudhisthir was more preferred as the successor of Hastinapur over Duryodhana by the public because one reflected on the maintenance of integrity while the other did not and this explains this thesis value based leadership framework as well.

Both the aspirants for the top position may have a similar profile but both cannot be made the CEO and only one can get the chance. Question is who will get it? It is the value framework of the chair that will give weight to something and one will be left out, while the other will be given the chance. This puts a question mark on the existing framework of value-based leadership (Bhargava, 2003) wherein the value framework alone is not adequate enough to explain the final decision (outcome) as many factors inside and outside the person and organization also play crucial role. This warrants incorporating factors outside the value framework also. Even in Agrawal's (2010) work he did not find a significant profile difference between the CEOs and the TMT members as they were, in general, from the same homogeneous talent pool.

Looking at the business opportunities in India today, one has to see a relationship between the background factors and leadership effectiveness differently and therefore, the way factors like age, education, experience, past achievements use to be treated as the predictors of performance may not have same power. In fact, quality of life, life expectancy, and the retirement age of Indians even in the government and public sectors have increased. In corporate houses senior executives are not retiring. Even those, who retire from one organization, get absorbed in other competitive organizations, at least in the top management positions. Therefore, the value based identity of an executive will have a long term impact on others. This however, should not be taken as a mathematical equation or a management mantra, as can be seen from the success stories of many CEOs.

Dhirubhai Ambani (Reliance) was not an MBA from a top business school but built up a large and successful organization while his children (Ambani brothers) are examples of highly qualified professionals reshaping big organizations in the next generation too. Kumar Mangalam Birla represents an affluent background while Narayan Moorthy (Infosys) may represent a relatively modest socio-economic background. From these examples one finds that there are no universal characteristics, which are necessarily correlated with effectiveness of a leader but they lead to organization performance (Certo et al., 2006).

BEYOND VALUE-BASED LEADERSHIP

The kinds of changes that have taken place during the last few years including the effect of the recession have impacted the relook on the original framework of my (Bhargava, 2003) value-based leadership model, wherein the main thesis was focusing on maintaining core professional values in spirit and action by the leader and will open the door of winning trust of people (all stakeholders) and lead towards organizational performance. Based on the findings related with the role of background and profile factors on the success of business leaders and the powerful impact of the internal and external environment on performance of business organizations, it has become the need of the time to revise the original framework of the value-based model in this paper, ground around the findings of my other work with the studies of my students. A revised framework is depicted in Figure 4.1 and is self explanatory. No explanation and elaboration has been done here, as the framework is only directional.

CONCLUSION

The works of Kouzes and Posner (2002) have also reported the important core characteristics, in the context of leadership challenges, in the order of honesty, forward-looking, competence, inspiring, intelligent, fair-minded, broad-minded, supportive, straightforward, dependable, cooperative, determined, imaginative, ambitious, courageous, caring, maturity, loyalty, self-controlled, and independent. These may help facing leadership challenges in this century.

A careful scrutiny of these characteristics clearly show that most of the non-personality and non-skill-based characteristics do reflect the importance of values in facing contemporary challenges of this century's

FIGURE 4.1: Framework of Value-based Leadership and Organizational Performance

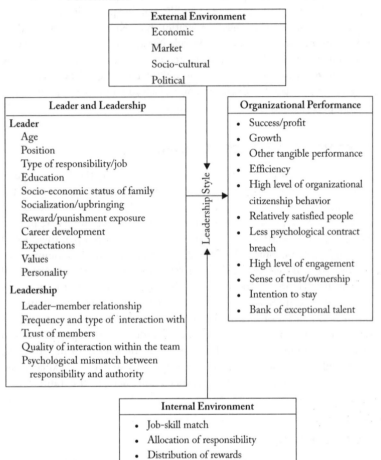

leaders and therefore, the importance of a value-based leadership becomes significant. One should not ignore that leadership is a complex social process and its effectiveness acts as a key of business performance. Therefore, one has to see it beyond the quality of a person. A value framework should be seen as a product of largely invisible inner feelings, thoughts, states, and intuitions of the person oriented towards achieving the visible processes of the organization led by the leader. Thus, focus on images, vision and values, which are central of social construction of organizational reality becomes more crucial for enhancing the performance of organizations through an effective leadership.

In this paper, the thesis has been extended to broaden the value framework from the self to also include input, management (process) and outcomes. In other words, stakeholders are fully aware about the kind of framework being applied by the company on behalf of the leader's value framework for identifying and selecting inputs (is there any scope to get entry with any kind of compromise), rewarding and punishing talented or average people and placing product in the market on excessive demand that was not cleared by all functionaries of the organization. This means that a value based leadership is not person-centric. It refers to the approach and process applied by the leader for taking people, product and performance together within the framework of the core values of leader and the organization, which should not be very different.

Changes in the external environment affect the financial performance of the organization but an organization can still sustain itself with its performance, if the process is appropriate. The leadership of the organization determines the long-run performance by developing new processes and nurturing existing processes across the system. It is not only the value framework of individual leaders but also the overall functioning of all aspects of the organization and stakeholders. Effectiveness of process is treated as more important than maintenance of core professional values and desirable/ideal characteristics of successful leader. A leader has to focus on core values after looking at the external and internal complexities of an organization and opting for the architecture of the organization that can integrate the cultural fabric of all stakeholders and continuously marching towards achieving organizational performance.

REFERENCES

Agrawal, A. (2010) "Examining Impact of Strategic Leadership on Effectiveness of Business Organizations." Unpublished doctoral dissertation. Bombay: Shailesh J Mehta School of Management, Indian Institute of Technology.

Bass, B.M. (1985) *Leadership and Performance Beyond Expectations*. New York: Free Press.

Bass, B.M. and R.M. Stogdill (1990) *Handbook of Leadership: Theory, Research and Managerial Applications* (Third Edition). New York: The Free Press.

Bhargava, S. (2003) *Transformational Leadership—Value-based Management for Indian Organizations*. New Delhi: Sage Publications.

Certo, S.T., R.H. Lester, C.M. Dalton, and D.R. Dalton (2006) "Top Management Teams, Strategy and Financial Performance: A Meta-Analytic Examination," *Journal of Management Studies*, 43(4): 813–839.

Collins, J. (2001) *Good to Great*. New York: HarperCollins Publishers Inc.

Collins, J.C. and J.I. Porras (1997) *Built to Last*. New York: HarperCollins.

Conger, J.A. and R.N. Kanungo (1998) *Charismatic Leadership: The Elusive Factor in Organizational Effectiveness*. London: Jossey-Bass Publishers.

Day, D.V. and R.G. Lord (1988) "Executive Leadership and Organizational Performance," *Journal of Management*, 14: 453–464.

Eisenhardt, K.M. and C.B. Schoonhoven (1990) "Organizational Growth: Linking Founding Team, Strategy, Environment, Growth Among U.S. Semiconductor Ventures, 1978–1988," *Administrative Science Quarterly*, 35(3): 504–529

Ensley, M.D. and A.W. Pearson (2005) "An Exploratory Comparison of the Behavioral Dynamics of Top Management Teams in Family and Non-family New Ventures: Cohesion, Conflict, Potency and Consensus," *Entrepreneurship Theory and Practice*, 29(3): 267–284.

ET 500 (1995) Economic Times Intelligence Group, March 1996, Mumbai.

———. (2005) Economic Times Intelligence Group, June 2005, Mumbai.

Fiedler, F.E. (1967) *A Theory of Leadership Effectiveness*. New York: McGraw-Hill Book Company.

Fields, D.L. (2002) *Taking the Measure of Work*. Thousand Oaks, California: Sage Publications.

Fortune 500 (1995, 2005). Download from http://money.cnn.com/magazines/fortune/fortune500/archive/fully1995

Fry, L. and M. Kriger (2009) "Towards a Theory of being Centered Leadership: Multiple Levels of Being as Context for Effective Leadership," *Human Relations*, 62(11): 1667–1696.

Greenleaf, R.K. (1977). *Servant Leadership*. Mahwah, NJ: Paulist Press.

Herb, E., K. Leslie and C. Price (2001) "Teamwork at the Top," *Mckinsey Quarterly*, 2: 32–43.

Hersey, P. and K.H. Blancherd (1969) *Management of Organizational Behavior: Utilizing Human Resources*. New Jersey: Eaglewood Cliffs.

Hogan, R. and R.B. Kaiser (2005) "What We Know about Leadership," *Review of General Psychology*, 9(2): 169–180.

House, R. (1971) "A Path-goal Theory of Leader Effectiveness," *Administrative Science Quarterly*, 16: 321–339.

Hunt, J.G. and J.A. Conger (1999) "From Where We Sit: An Assessment of Transformational Charismatic Leadership Research," *Leadership Quarterly*, 10(3): 335–343.

Javidan, M. and R.J. House (2002) "Leadership Cultures around the World: Findings from GLOBE. An Introduction to the Special Issue," *Journal of World Business*, Special issue(1): 1–2.

Joyce, T.A., N. Nohria and B. Roberson (2003) *What Really Works: The 4+2 Formula for Sustained Business Success?* New York: Harper Business.

Judge, T.A. and J.E. Bono (2000) "Five Factor Model of Personality Transformational Leadership," *Journal of Applied Psychology*, 85(5): 751–765.

Khandwalla, P.N. (1995) *Management Styles*. New Delhi: Tata McGraw-Hill.

Kouzes, J. and B. Posner (2002) *The Leadership Challenge*. San Francisco: Jossey-Bass.

Kumar, M.P. and S. Bhargava (2003) "An Emotionally Intelligent Leadership Style," in S. Bhargava (ed.), *Transformational Leadership*. New Delhi: Sage Publications.

Lancau, M.J., Amason Ward, N.G. Thomas, J.A. Sonnenfield, and B.R. Agle (2007) "Examining the Impact of Organizational Value Dissimilarity in the Top Management Team," *Journal of Managerial Issues*, 19(1): 11–34.

Marathe, C. and C. Ramesh (2008) *Leadership Success Stories*. Unpublished project report as a part of leadership and vision course of Professor S. Bhargava, Bombay: Shailesh J. Mehta School of Management, Indian Institute of Technology.

McElroy, J.C. (1982) "A Typology of Attribution Leadership Research," *Academy of Management Review*, 7(3): 413–417.

Schwartz, S.H., S. Roccas, and L. Sagiv (1990) "Universals in the Content and Structure of Values: Theoretical Advances and Empirical Tests in 20 Countries," *Advances in Experimental Social Psychology*, 25.

Schwartz, S.H. and W. Bilsky (1987) "Toward a Universal Psychological Structure of Human Values," *Journal of Personality and Social Psychology*, 53(3): 550–562.

Singh, P. (1982) "Leadership Styles: Changing Indian Scenario," *ASCI Journal of Management*, 11: 171–184.

Sinha, J.B.P. (1980) *The Nurturant Task Leader*. New Delhi: Concept.

———. (1990) *Work Culture in the Indian Context*. New Delhi. Sage Publications.

Stogdill, R.M. (1974) *Handbook of Leadership: A Survey of Theory and Research*. New York: Free Press.

Vroom, V.H. and P.W. Yetton (1973) *Leadership and Decision Making*. Pittsburgh: University of Pittsburgh Press.

5

Empowerment Practices and Corporate Effectiveness: Either be Democratic or Go Bust

Subir Verma

INTRODUCTION

Since the time the knowledge revolution has launched what Alvin Toffler (1991) called the gigantic third wave of economic, technical and social change, management scholars have studied radically new and continually shifting ways in which businesses have been forced to operate. Gibsons (1997) wrote that in this era of discontinuous change, market uncertainty and chaos, the winning firms will be those that stay ahead of the change curve, constantly redefining their industries, creating new markets, blazing new trails, reinventing the competitive rules and challenging the status quo. In the next orbit, the winning firms would be those who continuously invent the world rather than just respond to it. In our view, one way through which organizations can invent the world and vault their way to the trajectory of high performance in a sustainable way is by creating structures and processes that institutionalizes empowerment, thereby turning the organization democratic.

Indeed structures, processes, and practices which by definition, content and outcome belong to the realm of organizational democracy are getting back in. For, as Child and Mcgrath (2001) reported, successful organizations have responded to the challenges of interdependence, disembodiment, velocity, and power by jettisoning the traditional mechanism of command and control and by spawning new organizational forms such as "federalism," "network organizations," "virtual corporations," "post-entrepreneurial organizations," etc. In India, as Khandwalla (2002) reported, organizations have increasingly tended to become a strong information acquiring, information processing, quickly learning, and adapting organism to retain their viability. Pettigrew et al. (2003) in their survey on innovative forms of organizing in Europe, Japan, and the USA, discovered that organizations have used de-layering, operational and strategic decentralization, and IT to unite all parts of organization in the process of intense exchange of information and co-adaptive exploitation of cross business synergies. Whatever be the reasons, effective corporate response in terms of organizational processes for capability building for sustainable and continuous strategic advantage, organizational forms, governance structure and management practices have brought home the strategic importance of empowerment.

Traditionally empowerment has been viewed from two perspectives. In the first, it has been described as psychological empowerment denoting a motivational construct manifested in an employee's feeling of meaning, competence, self-determination, and impact on their job or work role (Conger and Kanungo, 1988; Spreitzer, 1995) The second view of empowerment is as a set of managerial practices that give employees increased decision making authority in execution of their primary work tasks. This relational construct involving decentralization and delegation which are directed towards giving employees more autonomy or control over their work is also described as "high involvement management" (Lawler, 1986) and includes initiatives such as job enrichment, self-management, teamwork, quality circles, and total quality management.

All these notions of empowerment miss the essential fact that organizations are also sites of power. Indeed, organizations provide the interaction context and the institutional milieu in and through which power operates to shape the capacities of people. So when this power is hierarchically organized and asymmetrically distributed in terms of resources, opportunity and capacity for the display of autonomy, they lead to structures of domination and even oppression. All in the name of empowerment. In so much as that, empowerment through structures and practices like decentralization, voice, delegation, open communication, involvement and participation in decision making and symbolized by terms like "un-management" and "self leadership" actually are dis-empowering and anti-democratic. For, since empowerment does not occur in a vacuum but within the relations of power, individuals experience domination, unless they have the ability to use and develop their essentially human capacities.

According to Boje and Rosile (2001), one way in which empowerment can be made to occur is to organize it around the concept of "co-power," a term which they have drawn from the works of Mary Follet and Stewart Clegg. This paper argues that, if the notion of empowerment means structures and practices that can bring about an increase in power defined in terms of individual capacity that grows in a democratic space contingent in a situation of co-relationship between the individual and the network of relations and systems that define the organization, then the construct of "freedom related practices" offers a philosophically and empirically robust basis for empowerment and its exercise. This is because such practices would be organizational in its sweep and impact. It will impact upon the design of the organization in all its pivots: structures, systems, processes, cultures and values, and the management styles.

Indeed the present study is directed towards establishing the hypotheses that corporate organizations that are more democratic or have structures, processes and practices which are perceived to be more freedom giving are more effective than those corporate organizations that have been configured on its denial or its limited promulgation.

CONSTRUCT OF FREEDOM: THE NEW FONT OF EMPOWERMENT

Ontologically, freedom is the state or the quality of being free. Transmuted into political principles, it is the quality that involves both freedom from arbitrary restraints as well as freedom to realize "self-mastery" (Berlin 1982: 118–31; Laski, 1948; Hayek, 1960: 135–37; Held, 1995: 147). While in political systems, such freedom is represented through bundle of rights, in corporate organizations these express themselves through management practices and organizational processes. Thus, in the context of corporate organizations, the notion of freedom would incorporate management practices and organizational processes, incorporating both the notions of "free from" (encroachments from others, expressed denial, fear or absence of capacity or anything that hinders) and "free to" (enabling conditions or presence of capacity) in the achievement of excellence and ones' fullest potential within the rubrics of shared collective good. These could be the result of discretionary practices that were initiated by an enlightened top management and later accepted by the lower level managers because of their positive effects. In other cases, they may be the result of concessions granted to the managers because of the pressures exerted on the top management, who in turn may have accepted the justification behind it. In still others, these practices could be those that have by tradition and convention implicitly governed the corporate organizations.

Literature Survey

In both management theories and in the organizational context, instances of the practices relating to various dimensions of freedom have been advocated and instituted. On the one hand, this has been a part of a wider project of worker revolution and industrial democracy (Kelly and Kelly, 1991; Thorsrud and Emery, 1969). On the other hand, since Mayo and his associates' Hawthorne experiment on the social factors such as group affiliations and supportive leadership, concerns with employee involvement measures originated to sub-serve the need for organizational effectiveness and efficiency. With the neo-human relations advocates (Herzberg, 1968; Argyris, 1992; McGregor, 1960; Likert, 1961) it led to an espousal of concepts such as job enrichment, task discretion and person-centered leadership and with the successes of the Japanese management practices and advocacy by scholars like Ouchi (1981), Peters and Waterman (1982), and Lawler (1986), the value of mutual responsibility between employer and employee for the pursuit of excellence along a range of performance parameters began to be celebrated. These translated into practices that provided for downward communication and upward communication and organization development interventions woven around the themes of total quality management, quality of work life and empowerment (Kelly and Kelly, 1991; Ferris and Wagner III, 1985; Wilkinson et al., 1997; Nadler and Lawler, 1983; Conger and Kanungo, 1988). But participation was not advocated anymore as a mechanism through which a worker's self-protection could be realized. Instead, it was touted for instrumental reasons founded on unitarist tradition, which required that the organizational concerns be associated with values internalized by employees themselves (Barley and Kunda, 1992; Beaumont, 1992; Hyman and Mason, 1995). Studies on participation in decision making (Cotton et al., 1988; Locke and Scheweiger, 1979; Miller and Monge, 1986; Wagner III, 1994) revealed its impact on increased morale and satisfaction and their frequent concomitants—reduced turnover, absenteeism and conflict, as well as, those on outcomes pertaining to productive efficiency such as higher production, better decision quality, better production quality, and reduced conflicts and cost.

Freedom Related Practices

Based upon the review of literature in social and political theory and the examination of management practices and organizational processes, the following categories of freedom related practices along with their constituent bundle of practices can be conceptualized to exist in corporate organizations.

- **Autonomy related freedom:** those freedom related practices are personal and associational in characteristic. The specific management practices relate to providing proper working conditions, health and professional benefits, avenues to express viewpoints and even differences, voice suggestions for work related improvements, dissent and associate with others. Overall, these freedoms are labeled as autonomy related freedom practices.

- **Justice related freedom:** practices that provides for "justice as fairness" (Hayek, 1960; Rawls, 1973) in the workplace. These practices relate to communication of rationale for decisions that affect its beneficiary/victim, procedural fairness, and appeal against injustice.
- **Participation related freedom:** practices that enable managerial employees to participate in decision-making on a host of issues ranging from those that affect the individual, such as the setting of the key result areas and targets, to those that pertain to the work group/unit, such as budgeting and capital expenditure, to the issues that are corporate wide in their import and operation.

A look at the practices of the autonomy, justice, and participation related freedom, as delineated above, shows that at a higher level of abstraction freedom is a unity. Indeed, the autonomy related practices represent the degree to which they bring about a release of restraint and provide access to avenues for self-expression to employees who are considered the members of the community. The practices related to participation in decision making seek to fashion the collective will of the organization so that the individual pursuit of excellence is balanced with the norms of organizational solidarity based upon the notions of collective and organizational good. Finally, the justice related practices provide the regulative framework of rules and regulations founded on the principles of non-discrimination, procedural fairness and a provision for appeal and review of unjust decisions. The different categories of freedom incorporate the diverse concerns of democracy with regard to creation of that milieu in which individuals who are free and equal members are provided opportunities to determine the fortunes of the organization.

Freedom Related Practices and Corporate Effectiveness

For the purpose of this research, we adopted the stakeholder perspective of corporate effectiveness. The essential premises of stakeholder theory is that corporations affect and are affected by many stakeholders (Freeman, 1984: 25) and that the interests of all (legitimate) stakeholders have intrinsic value such that no set of interests is assumed to dominate the others (Clarkson, 1995; Donaldson and Preston, 1995). Corporate effectiveness was thus defined: "...as the ability of an organization to achieve its objectives and meet the needs of its various stakeholders, not-ably employees, owners, customers etc." (Khandwalla, 1995: 159).

An organization that is high on the presence of freedom related practices would have substantive impact on its functioning and outcome.

One is the effect of freedom related practices on organizational innovativeness. Innovation at the basic minimum is the adoption of an idea or behavior—whether a product, device, system, process, policy, program, or service—that is new or is perceived to be new to the adapting organization (Damanpour, 1987; Zaltman et al., 1973). Organizational innovativeness in a firm will be high the more the organization is characterized by adaptability, problem solving skills, experimentation, and risk readiness (Damanpour, 1991; Leventhal, 1997; Garud et al., 1997; Senge, 1990; Van de Van and Polley, 1992). Freedom practices, in particular those that enhance information flow, widespread interaction, involvement and participation, would thus facilitate idea generation. Its effect would be equally significant at the idea implementation stage. Spender and Kessler's (1995) recent work on the effect of participation on organizational innovativeness suggests that user involvement is an important moderating variable vis-à-vis impact on management strategy.

Then the management practices that grant freedom to the employees would also lead to greater attainment of satisfaction and morale. The equity theory states that human behavior is motivated by the need to maintain fair relationships with others and to rectify unfair relationships by making them fair (Adams, 1963; Kanfer, 1990). Research on organization justice (Greenberg, 1987) has shown the importance of both the content (Adams, 1965; Homans, 1961; Walster et al., 1978) and the process (Blau, 1964; Summers and Hendrix, 1991) of distribution of outcomes for behavioral and attitudinal changes with regard to job satisfaction, performance, and commitment.

The work of Leventhal (1980), Konovsky and Cropanzano (1993), and Gilliland (1993) have identified practices and processes that prompt employees' fairness judgments. These are factors like people's ability to speak out, consistent treatment, accurate and bias free judgment, an opportunity for different positions to be aired, for decisions to be reversible and clear ethical standards. Tyler and Bies (1990) found that the criteria employees use to evaluate their interpersonal context include the decision maker's honesty and lack of bias, trust or sincerity of the motives of the decision maker, and treatment that shows respect and dignity. All these point to the importance of freedom related practices in affecting the fairness judgments, especially of the effect of participation in decision making. This has tremendous implications, in that organizational justice is likely to be positively related to staff trust, job satisfaction, identification with the organization, internalization of its values and ideologies, and with organizational citizenship behavior.

Finally, the followers of human relations school of management (Miller and Monge, 1986) have linked participation in decision making to employee's satisfaction. According to them, participation leads to greater attainment of higher order needs, such as self-expression, respect, independence, and equality that in turn are stated to increase morale and satisfaction.

Then are the effects of freedom related practices on the display of organizational citizenship behaviour. Studies have shown that organizational citizenship behaviour is the outcome of social exchange between the employees and the organization (Blau, 1964). This exchange is built upon the perception of fairness by the employees (Farh et al., 1990; Moorman, 1991; Organ and Konovsky, 1989), perceived organization support (Eisenberger et al., 1990; Moorman et al., 1998) and the quality of leader member exchange (Settoon et al., 1996). According to Dyne et al. (1994), it is not the social exchange that leads to the display of organizational citizenship. Instead it is the covenant that represents the responsibilities and values of citizenship in the organizational context. This covenant is characterized by open-ended commitment, trust and shared value between the individual and their community and is expressed in the mutual commitment of welfare. In any case, the freedom related practices would be instrumental in creating the conditions for the display of extra role behavior such as the organizational citizenship behavior, whistle blowing, principled organization dissent, and voice (Dyne et al., 1995; Near and Miceli, 1985; Graham, 1986). This is important, in that according to Katz (1964), organizational effectiveness depends upon the performance of both inrole (IRB) and extra role behavior (ERB) by the employees. It can thus be surmised that the organizations marked with a greater extent of freedom related practices will not only lead to the enhancement of effectiveness on traditional economic indicators, but also lead to the display of higher degree of corporate social responsibility, moral excellence, and corporate public image.

Another way in which freedom related practices could affect the individual and the organization is in terms of its effect on individual motivation towards effective performance. Employees' say in the decisions related to their job and working conditions (Karasek, 1979; Lawler, 1986); participation in goal setting and feedback to them about performance from the superior and the peers can enhance self efficacy which may motivate superior performance (Bandura, 1977; Conger and Kanungo, 1988; Erez and Arad, 1986; Earley and Kanfer, 1985; Gist and Mitchell, 1992; Locke et al., 1988; Miller and Monge, 1986).

In view of the above relationships between freedom related practices and the different dimensions of corporate effectiveness, the following is hypothesized:

H.1: *The greater the extent of freedom related practices in the corporate organizations, the greater is relative corporate effectiveness.*

METHODS

Questionnaire Development and Data Collection

The strategy adopted for this research moved through two phases. First, some corporate organizations were visited with a view to identifying their freedom related practices. Overall 67 interviews of duration between 45 and 90 minutes of managerial employees drawn from different levels of management across functions and locations were conducted. The case studies helped in the construction of the survey instrument.

The second stage involved the survey-based research. Its objective was to test the hypothesized model through an instrument developed from existing theories and the case studies that were conducted. The instrument to measure the constructs involved in the hypothesized relationship of freedom related practices were developed from three sources. First, the major categories of freedom related practices were derived from political philosophy. Second, they were supplemented/refined by the findings of the focused case studies on freedom related practices. Third, the measures of corporate effectiveness were adapted from the existing standardized instruments.

This survey yielded in all 1,043 responses from managers belonging to different levels and functions in 51 organizations out of which 962 responses from 50 organizations were found usable and accepted for the purpose of analysis. There were 642 missing cases. However, except for responses in four questions, in all the questions the percentage of valid response was above 98 percent.

Constructs and Measures

FREEDOM RELATED PRACTICES

The measures of freedom related practices involved 34 items suggested by political philosophy, and subsequently supplemented and refined through the case studies. The category of autonomy related freedom (17 items) consisted of practices related to *(a)* reasonable work conditions; *(b)* basic entitlements to health and career development; *(c)* expression of opinion; *(d)* formation, membership, and participation in the activities of staff association and professional associations; *(e)* conscientious dissent; and *(f)* voicing suggestions for improvement in the work procedures. The category of justice related freedom (11 items) consisted of practices related to *(i)* procedural fairness; *(ii)* communication of rationale for decisions to those affected; and *(iii)* to appeal if injustice were perceived. The participation related freedom practices included six items relating to the participation in decision making on *(a)* the modification of administrative systems by the relevant managers; *(b)* setting of the subordinate manager's key result areas, target and deadline for meeting them by the subordinate manager; *(c)* deciding inter-departmental issues by relevant managers; *(d)* the modification of HR practices; (e) setting the goals, objectives, and work plan of the work units; and (f) budgeting capital expenditure for the work unit.

These items were rated in terms of the 6 point Likert-type scales ranging from strong disagreement to strong agreement on the extent to which the respondent disagreed or agreed with the presence of the norm/practice in his/her organization.

CORPORATE EFFECTIVENESS

The effectiveness of the organization was measured through the 12-item scale developed by Khandwalla (2002). These items measure corporate performance on financial and non-financial parameters viz. profitability, growth, financial strength, operating efficiency, stability of performance, morale, adaptability, innovativeness, economic impact, public image, business ethics, and corporate social responsibility. The respondents were asked to rate them on a 6-point scale in terms of the extent of performance of their firm relative to the best performing organization in their sector/industry or in the line of activity.

DESCRIPTIVE STATISTICS, RELIABILITIES, AND CORRELATIONS

Table 5.1 discloses the descriptive statistics, reliabilities, and the intercorrelations amongst the composite freedom and its three individual dimensions: autonomy, justice, and participation. In order to facilitate our understanding of the phenomena of freedom related practices in corporate organizations, the descriptive statistics and the inter-correlations of the specific freedom related practices are disclosed in Table 5.2.

TABLE 5.1: Reliabilities and Descriptive Statistics of the Constructs

Variables	Mean	Range	Variability	1	2	3	4	5	6	7	8
1. Autonomy related freedom	65.6	49–80	10.2	[0.86]							
2. Justice related freedom	61.9	39–85	14.0	0.57***	[0.89]						
3. Participation related freedom	63.1	37–80	15.1	0.75***	0.85***	[0.87]					
4. Freedom (aggregate)	63.5	44–80	11.9	0.83***	0.91***	0.97***	[0.88]				
5. Corporate effectiveness (aggregate)	65.1	43–79	14.3	0.33**	0.21	0.30**	0.31**	[0.91]			
6. Ethical excellence				0.32**	0.15	0.2	0.24*	0.49***			
7. Innovative excellence				0.31**	0.55***	0.55***	0.53***	0.76***	0.25*	[0.83]	
8. Business excellence				0.15	-0.11	-0.01	0	0.86***	0.34**	0.40***	[0.85]

Notes: 1. Mean scores are in percentage; Variability = [std deviation/mean]*100.
2. Cronbach alphas of constructs and composite variables are in brackets on the diagonal.
3. *** significant at p <= 0.01 (2-tailed).
   ** significant at p <= 0.05 (2-tailed).
   * significant at p <= 0.1 (2-tailed).

TABLE 5.2: Descriptive Statistics and Inter-correlations of Freedom Related Practices

Freedom practices →	Mean	Range	Variability	1	2	3	4	5	6	7	8	9	10
Autonomy related freedom related practices													
1. Working conditions	74.6	52–88	10.4	1									
2. Basic entitlements	66.4	8–85	19.1	0.19	1								
3. Association	51.4	21–90	35.0	−0.09	0.31*	1							
4. Expression	62.4	42–80	14.0	0.46**	0.26	−0.11	1						
5. Conscientious dissent	61.3	38–92	18.5	0.31*	0.08	−0.01	0.81**	1					
6. Voice	77.2	58–95	10.7	0.42**	0.12	−0.04	0.80**	0.73**	1				
Justice related freedom practices													
7. Fairness	65.9	41–92	14.5	0.67**	−0.08	−0.28*	0.58**	0.57**	0.67**	1			
8. Information	60.6	27–83	19.0	0.50**	−0.05	−0.43**	0.78**	0.66**	0.73**	0.71**	1		
9. Appeal against injustice	59.3	39–80	15.4	0.27	0.35*	0.1	0.73**	0.76**	0.65**	0.50**	0.62**	1	
Participation related freedom practices													
10. Participation	63.1	37–80	15.1	0.63**	0.19	−0.02	0.85**	0.76**	0.84**	0.73**	0.79**	0.67**	1

Notes: 1. Mean scores are in percentage.
Variability = [std deviation/mean]*100.
2. **Correlations significant at p = 0.01 (2 -tailed).
* Correlations significant at p = 0.05 (2 -tailed).

Freedom Related Practices

The level of freedom, as disclosed in its aggregate dimensions in Table 5.1 and in terms of specific practices in Table 5.2, which is granted to employees in the organizations participating in the survey, was not very high. Quite remarkably there was not much difference amongst the scores on the three dimensions of freedom, which were all at about 60.

One way to identify the critical freedom practices is to assess the number of significant bonding of each practice with the other freedom practices in the organization. Thus, the most important freedoms as catalysts of other freedoms are the freedoms to express opinions, to voice suggestions, conscientious dissent, to participate in decision making, and to a fair process of work related decisions, communication of the rationale for decisions to those affected and avenues for grievance redressal to managers against any perceived injustice in treatment. The comparatively less critical freedoms are those that are directed to ensure physical safety, leisure, reasonable workload, health, and career growth of the employees. Finally, at the bottom is the freedom to associate with managerial employees. More importantly, there was a significant negative correlation between the propensity to associate and the extent of fair treatment and to be informed of decisions that affect the self. This on the face seems highly reasonable. The need to associate is likely to decrease, the more the employees are treated fairly and are kept posted of the rationale of the decisions that concern their interests and vice versa.

Overall, the scores on the freedom related practices reveal that organizations provide those freedoms to a far greater extent which enable the managers to contribute to the good of the larger entity and thus to actively perform their role as citizens of that organization. The analysis of inter-correlations establishes that in terms of their catalytic effect, these freedom practices were also more important than the others.

Corporate Effectiveness

Corporate effectiveness was measured through 12 dimensions. What stood out amongst the scores as displayed in Table 5.3 was the relatively large dispersion in the scores of almost all of the performance dimensions. The dimension on which the participating organizations reported the best performance was business ethics, and the worst was relative profitability of the firm. Overall, the firms have reported relatively low scores on their level of adaptability, innovativeness, social impact, and growth. On the other hand, the companies have reported relatively better performance

TABLE 5.3: Dimensions of Corporate Effectiveness: Descriptive Statistics and Correlation Matrix

Dimension of corporate effectiveness →

	Mean	Range	Variability	1	2	3	4	5	6	7	8	9	10	11	12
1. Profitability	59.5	23–92	29.2	1											
2. Growth	62.2	28–91	24.5	0.53**	1										
3. Staff morale	62.7	45–83	17.3	0.36**	0.44**	1									
4. Financial strength	71.5	32–97	23.6	0.83**	0.46**	0.33*	1								
5. Public image	73.3	42–94	16.9	0.44**	0.50**	0.53**	0.61**	1							
6. Adaptability	61.1	33–83	21.4	0.31*	0.65**	0.56**	0.35*	0.55**	1						
7. Stability	70.3	44–89	15.5	0.70**	0.59**	0.55**	0.73**	0.58**	0.54**	1					
8. Efficiency	62.4	40–83	19.2	0.77**	0.66**	0.66**	0.69**	0.53**	0.62**	0.77**	1				
9. Innovativeness	61.4	36–83	19.8	0.30*	0.56**	0.58**	0.26	0.49**	0.74**	0.51**	0.55**	1			
10. Economic impact	59.6	34–98	18.4	0.56**	0.57**	0.21	0.58**	0.33*	0.30*	0.56**	0.50**	0.31*	1		
11. Corporate social Responsibility	62.6	22–90	21.8	0.45**	0.30*	0.22	0.51**	0.32*	0.13	0.43**	0.39**	0.07	0.52**	1	
12. Business ethic	74.9	52–93	13	0.31*	0.25	0.19	0.42**	0.51**	0.35*	0.35*	0.30*	0.1	0.13	0.46**	1

Notes: 1. Mean is in percentage; Variability = [std deviation/mean]*100.
2. ** Correlations significant at p <= 0.01 (2-tailed).
   * Correlations significant at p <= 0.05 (2-tailed).

on the level of their financial strength, stability, and public image—which are all indices that reflect past performance.

DATA ANALYSIS AND HYPOTHESES TESTING

It was hypothesized that freedom related practices, in terms of the extent of its presence would lead to greater corporate effectiveness. While for the preliminary correlations, the 12 indicators of corporate effectiveness and composite corporate effectiveness were used, for subsequent regression analysis, the items were factor analyzed using the principal component method with varimax rotation. This unraveled that corporate effectiveness was a multi-dimensional construct. The first dimension consisting of items of adaptability, innovativeness, and morale of the staff was labeled the "innovative excellence" given that while adaptability was an essential ingredient of innovativeness, the very process of innovativeness in the organization usually brings about a tremendous upsurge of excitement and enthusiasm amongst the staff. The Cronbach alpha of the measure was 0.83. The indicators that loaded on the second factor (30 percent of total variance) were profitability, financial strength, and economic impact of the firm and the factor was thus labeled as the "business excellence" given that they indicated performance excellence on the usual indices of economic and financial returns. The Cronbach alpha reliabilities of the scale were 0.85. Only one indicator of effectiveness, business ethics followed by the firm, loaded the highest and significantly on the third component (14 percent of the total variance). This factor was therefore labeled as "ethical excellence." As for the other indicators viz. growth rate, operational efficiency, public image, performance stability, and corporate social responsibility, they cross loaded highly on at least two factors and therefore were dropped from the dimensions of corporate effectiveness. However, corporate effectiveness was also used as the composite outcome variable in view of the fact that the unrotated factor structure had yielded a first factor that explained about 52 percent of the total variance and that all the 12 indicators of corporate effectiveness had loaded significantly and highest on the first factor (approximately 0.5 and above).

RESULTS

Table 5.4 discloses the Pearson product moment correlation between aggregate freedom, the three dimensions of freedom viz. autonomy related, justice and participation related, the specific freedom practices and

Table 5.4: Correlation Matrix of Freedom Related Practices and Dimensions of Corporate Effectiveness

Freedom practices \ Effectiveness dimensions	Profitability	Growth	Morale	Financial strength	Public image	Adaptability	Stability	Efficiency	Innovativeness	Economic impact	Corporate social responsibility	Business ethics	Effectiveness (composite)
Specific freedom practices													
Working conditions	0.04	0.16	0.43***	0.06	0.21	0.34**	.28*	0.33**	0.23	-0.08	0.09	0.23	0.25
Basic entitlements	0.19	0.13	0.06	0.27	0.32**	0.00	0.10	0.11	-0.15	0.25	0.57***	0.42***	0.27
Association	0.09	0.05	-0.10	0.01	-0.07	-0.19	0.04	-0.06	-0.36**	0.25	0.33**	0.07	0.01
Speech & expression	-0.01	0.24	0.38***	-0.01	0.32**	0.54***	0.19	0.26*	0.47***	-0.04	0.06	0.22	0.28**
Conscientious dissent	-0.02	0.21	0.38***	0.02	0.31**	0.48***	0.23	0.16	0.51***	-0.02	-0.05	0.12	0.26
Voice	0.04	0.20	0.31**	0.08	0.20	0.43***	0.28**	0.29**	0.47***	0.04	0.12	0.14	0.29**
Fairness	-0.07	0.14	0.39***	0.02	0.30**	0.46***	0.31**	0.30**	0.50***	-0.02	-0.14	0.09	0.24
Information	-0.13	0.11	0.35**	-0.03	0.28**	0.52***	0.17	0.19	0.52***	-0.23	-0.20	0.12	0.18
Justice	-0.19	0.15	0.16	-0.11	0.23	0.41***	0.09	-0.03	0.31**	0.03	0.06	0.19	0.13
Freedom dimensions													
Participation related freedom	-0.01	0.26	0.42***	-0.01	0.24	0.52***	0.26	0.30**	0.49***	-0.00	0.08	0.20	0.30**
Civil freedom	0.12	0.24	0.31**	0.12	0.31**	0.32**	0.27	0.23	0.18	0.17	0.37***	0.32**	0.33**
Justice related freedom	-0.15	0.15	0.35**	-0.05	0.31**	0.54***	0.22	0.19	0.52***	-0.10	-0.12	0.15	0.21
Freedom aggregates													
Freedom	-0.03	0.24	0.41***	0.02	0.31**	0.52***	0.27	0.27	0.46***	0.01	0.10	0.24	0.31**
Appeal mechanism	0.05	0.10	0.06	0.02	0.01	0.09	0.11	0.04	-0.13	0.06	0.27	0.16	0.10

Notes: *** significant at 0.01 level (2-tailed).
** significant at 0.05 level (2-tailed).

the 12 dimensions of relative corporate effectiveness and the composite performance.

The results are remarkable. None of the freedom related practices were correlated significantly with any of the performance dimensions that were indicants of effectiveness in the financial domain—profitability, growth rate, financial strength, and economic impact of the firm. Indeed at the aggregate level, freedom was not associated at all with profitability, financial strength, economic impact and corporate social responsibility of the firm, and weakly associated with the growth rate of the firm, stability of performance, operational efficiency, and the pursuit of business ethics. However, the association of freedom related practices with staff morale, adaptability, innovativeness, public image of the firm, and with composite performance were both moderately strong and statistically significant.

As Table 5.1, earlier, had disclosed on the relationships between composite freedom variables and the three factor-analyzed dimensions of corporate effectiveness, none of the three dimensions of freedom viz. autonomy, justice related and participation, and the aggregate freedom were associated with the business excellence dimension of corporate effectiveness. On the other hand, the autonomy related freedom was the only dimension of freedom that was correlated with the ethical excellence of the firm. The relationship between the dimensions of freedom with innovative excellence was, however, positive and strong.

DISCUSSION

A perusal of the correlation, reveals that in terms of the frequency of significant relationships between the specific freedom and effectiveness dimension, the management practices related to *(i)* freedom of speech and expression in terms of differences in work procedure; *(ii)* voicing suggestions for its improvement; *(iii)* procedural fairness; *(iv)* information of rationale for decisions taken to those whom they affect; and *(v)* participation in decision making were more significant in terms of their catalytic effect, given the number of significant correlations they had with different dimensions of corporate effectiveness (net 5 to 6 correlations significant at 0.05 level).

This finding thus reiterates the importance of practices that empowers managers to contribute to organizational excellence. Indeed, practices that were premised on the principle that the managerial employees and organization have distinct, if not antithetical, interests as immanent in the freedoms of association and of entitlements to benefits, showed not only fewer relationships with performance dimensions but even low and negative relationships with dimensions that are possibly the conditions for future successes of the firm, such as adaptability and innovativeness. Not surprisingly, these practices had no association with a manager's morale and commitment. Nevertheless, the correlations showed that in the sample of participating organizations, the more the managers had the freedom to associate as a distinct entity and more their freedoms were secured against arbitrary and capricious violations by others, the more was the corporate social responsibility of the firms. This seems to be quite in conformance with the argument of the stakeholder approach to corporate social responsibility that the extent to which the distinct stakes of the employees are satisfied internally is positively associated with a greater display of corporate social responsibility by the firms.

Overall, the hypothesis that freedom related practices would lead to greater corporate effectiveness was supported. Amongst the three dimensions of corporate effectiveness, it was only for the innovative excellence that the hypothesized positive effect of freedom related practices was supported. Indeed, it seems that the grant of freedom related practices in the corporate organizations that participated in the survey may have been because of the realization and recognition by the top management that these were excellent management practices with a potentially positive effect on corporate effectiveness.

CONCLUSIONS

The most important theoretical significance of this study has been in terms of empirically demonstrating that democratic practices are significantly related with innovative excellence of the firm. Although these practices had no significant correlation with hard financial indicators of corporate effectiveness, one can also be comforted that the conditions for the hard indicators of financial performance of the firm gets established and strengthened in view of this relationship between democratic practices and firm's innovativeness.

In terms of individual empowerment related practices, the study identified the empowerment related practices that are significantly associated with corporate effectiveness. These were the freedom to *(a)* express opinion; *(b)* voice suggestions; *(c)* conscientious dissent; *(d)* participation in decision making; *(e)* fairness in terms of processes by which decisions are made; *(f)* information of the rationale for decisions on whom they affect; and *(g)* appeal against perceived injustice. All of them were found to be significantly related with the level of staff morale, adaptability, and innovativeness of the firm and, due to the freedom of participation in decision making and procedural fairness in the work related outcomes, with operational efficiency and public image of the firm. Indeed, the study has identified and established the significance and benefits of that set of management practices which obliges the corporate organizations to provide conditions and mechanisms through which the managers in these organizations can play the role of active citizens, as compared to those practices that are merely posited on the satisfaction of the needs of managers as a separate entity and passive recipients of the employee welfare measures.

In the end, it is necessary to reiterate the context that has driven this work—a context that is marked with hyper competition and hyper turbulence in which the only constant is change. These conditions require that an organization has to respond both systemically in terms of deployment of extensive uncertainty reduction, differentiation and integration mechanisms and strategically in terms of having fairly clear short and long term goals and its anchorage on the dimensions which could provide it with considerable competitive advantage.

Accordingly, such responses are tied to the presence of the freedom related practices within an organization. These practices would permit an enormous and unparallel amount of information acquisition, processing, learning, and adaptive capacity. Indeed, this study has at the minimum provided ample evidence that the presence of freedom related practices opens up the most inward looking, insular and staid bureaucratically managed state enterprises and leads them onto the path of innovative excellence. For more market challenged corporate organizations, the impact would be even more dynamic. The discharge of obligations attached to citizenship rights available to all, the control and coordination through multifunctional structures that at once facilitates broad, deep, and intense interaction amongst the citizens sufficiently informed and involved and the bearing of peer pressure through intensive vertical and lateral communication, personal commitment in decisions because they are the outcome of their voice and participation, and the sense of empowerment and commitment to super-ordinate values of self-development/emancipation in conjunction with that of the larger collectivity would lead to organizational excellence as a natural outcome. Indeed democracy pays.

REFERENCES

Adams, J.S. (1963) "Towards an Understanding of Inequity," *Journal of Abnormal and Social Psychology*, 67: 422–436.

Adams, J.S. (1965) "Inequity in Social Exchange," in L. Berkowitz (ed.), *Advances in Experimental Social Psychology*. New York: Academic Press.

Aldrich, H. (1979) *Organization and Environments*. Englewood Cliffs, NJ: Prentice-Hall.

Alvesson, M. (1993) *Cultural Perspectives on Organizations*. Cambridge: Cambridge University Press.

Argyris, C. (1992) "A Leadership Dilemma: Skilled Incompetence," in G. Salaman (ed.), *Human Resource Strategies*, pp. 82–94. London: Sage Publications.

Aycan, Z., R.N. Kanungo, and J.B.P. Sinha (1999) "Organizational Culture and Human Resource Management Practices," *Journal of Cross-Cultural Psychology*, 30(4): 501–526.

Bandura, A. (1977) "Self Efficacy: Towards a Unifying Theory of Behavioral Change," *Psychological Review*, 84: 191–215.

Barker, E. (1952) *Principles of Social and Political Theory*. Oxford: Oxford University Press.

Barry, B. (1989) *Theories of Justice*. London: Harvester, Wheatsheaf.

Barley, Stephen and Gideon Kunda (1992) "Design and Devotion: Surges of Rational and Normative Ideologies of Control in Managerial Discourse," *Administrative Science Quarterly*, 37(3): 363–399.

Beaumont, P.B. (1992) "Annual Review article 1991," *British Journal of Industrial Relations*, 30(1): 107–126.

Berlin, I. (1982) *Four Essays on Liberty*. London: Oxford University Press.

Bhalla, S.S. (1997) "Freedom and Economic Growth," in Axel Hadenius (ed.), *Democracy's Victory and Crisis*, pp. 195–241. Cambridge: Cambridge University Press.

Blau, P. (1964) *Exchange and Power in Social Life*. New York: Wiley.

———. (1970) "A Formal Theory of Differentiation in Organizations," *American Sociological Review*, 35: 201–218.

Boje, D.M. and G.A. Rosile (2001) "Where's the Power in Empowerment," *Journal of Applied Behavioral Science*, 37(1): 90–117.

Brooke, P.P., D.W. Russell, and J.W. Price (1988) "Discriminant Validation of Measures of Job Satisfaction, Job Involvement and Organizational Commitment," *Journal of Applied Psychology*, 73: 139–145.

Burns, T. and G. Stalker (1961) *The Management of Innovation*. London: Tavistock.

Bycio, P. and R.D. Hackett (1995) "Further Assessments of Bass's Conceptualization of Transactional and Transformational Leadership," *Journal Of Applied Psychology*, 80(4): 468–478.

Child, J. (1972) "Organization Structure and Strategies of Control: A Replication of the Aston Study," *Administrative Science Quarterly*, 17: 163–177.

———. (1977) "Organizational Design and Performance: Contingency Theory and Beyond," *Organization and Administrative Science*, 8: 169–183.

Child, J. and R.G. Mcgrath (2001) "Organizations Unfettered: Organizational form in an Information Intensive Economy," *Academy of Management Journal*, 44(6): 1135–1148.

Clarkson, M.B.E. (1995) "A Stakeholder Framework for Analyzing and Evaluating Corporate Social Performance," *Academy of Management Review*, 20: 92–117.

Conger, J.A. and R.N. Kanungo (1988) "The Empowerment Process: Integrating Theory and Practice," *Academy of Management Review*, 13 (3): 471–482.

Cotton, J., D. Vollrath, K.L. Froggatt, M.L. Lengnick-Hall, and K.R. Jennings (1988) "Employee Participation: Diverse Forms and Different Outcomes," *Academy of Management Review*, 13(1): 8–22.

Cyert, R.M. and J. March (1963) *A Behavioural Theory of Firm*. New York: Prentice-Hall.

Damanpour, F. (1987) "The Adoption of Technological, Administrative and Ancillary Innovations: Impact of Organizational Factors," *Journal of Management*, 13(4): 675–688.

———. (1991) "Organizational Innovation: A Meta Analysis of Effects of Determinants and Moderators," *Academy of Management Journal*, 34(3): 555–590.

Dess, G.G. and D.A. Beard (1984) "Dimensions of Organizational Task Environments," *Administrative Science Quarterly*, 29: 52–73.

Dewe, P., S. Dunn, and R. Richardson (1988) "Employee Share Option Schemes: Why Workers are Attracted to Them," *British Journal of Industrial Relations*, 26(1): 1–21.

Donaldson, L. (2001) *A Contingency Theory of Organizations*. Thousand Oaks, California: Sage Publications.

Donaldson, T. and L.E. Preston (1995) "The Stakeholder Theory of the Corporation: Concepts, Evidences and Implications," *Academy of Management Review*, 20: 65–91.

Dyne, L.V., L.L. Cummings, and J.M. Parks (1995) "Extra Role Behavior: In Pursuit of Construct and Definitional Clarity," in L.L. Cummings and B.W. Staw (eds), *Research in Organizational Behaviour*, pp. 215–285. Greenwich: Jai Press.

Dyne, L.V., J.W. Graham, and W. Dienesch (1994) "Organizational Citizenship Behavior: Construct Redefinition, Measurement and Validation," *Academy of Management Journal*, 37(4): 765–802.

Earley, P.C. and R. Kanfer (1985) "The Influence of Component Participation and Role Models on Goal Acceptance, Goal Satisfaction and Performance," *Organizational Behavior and Human Decision Process*, 36: 378–390.

Eisenberger, R., P. Fasolo, and V. Davis-LaMastro (1990) "Perceived Organizational Support and Employee Diligence, Commitment and Innovation," *Journal of Applied Psychology*, 75: 51–59.

Erez, M. and R. Arad (1986) "Participative Goal Setting: Social, Motivational and Cognitive Factors," *Journal of Applied Psychology*, 71: 591–597.

Farh, J., P. Podsakoff, and D. Organ (1990) "Accounting for Organizational Citizenship Behavior: Leadership Fairness and Task Scope Versus Satisfaction," *Journal of Management*, 16(1): 705–721.

Fayol, H. (1949) *General and Industrial Management*. London: Pitman.

Ferris, G.R. and J.A. Wagner III (1985) "Quality Circles in the United States: A Conceptual Re-evaluation," *Journal of Applied Behavioral Science*, 21: 155–167.

Freeman, R.E. (1984) *Strategic Management: A Stakeholder Approach*. Boston: Pitman.

Garud, R., P.R. Nayyar, and Z. Shapira (1997) "Technological Choices and the Inevitability of Errors," in R.Garud, P.R. Nayyar, and Z. Shapira (eds), *Technological Oversights and Foresights*, pp. 20–40. Cambridge: Cambridge University Press.

Gibsons, Rowan (1997) *Rethinking the Future*. London: Nicholas Brealey Publishing.

Gilliland, S.W. (1993) "The Perceived Fairness of Selection Systems: An Organizational Justice Perspective," *Academy of Management Review*, 18: 694–734.

Gist, M. and T. Mitchell (1992) "Self-efficacy: A Theoretical Analysis of Its Determinants and Malleability," *Academy of Management Review*, 17: 183–211.

Graen, G. (1976) "A Role Making Process within Complex Organizations," in M.D. Dunnette (ed.), *Handbook of Industrial/Organizational Psychology*, pp. 1201–1246. Chicago: Rand-McNally.

Graham, J.W. (1986) "Principled Organizational Dissent: A Theoretical Essay," in B.M. Staw and L.L. Cummings (eds), *Research in Organizational Behavior*, pp. 1–52. Greenwich, CT: Jai Press.

Greenberg, J. (1987) "A Taxonomy of Organizational Justice Theories," *Academy of Management Review*, 12 (1): 9–22.

Hage, J. and M. Aiken (1969) "Routine Technology, Social Structure and Organizational Goals," *Administrative Science Quarterly*, 14: 366–376.

Hall, R.H. (1963) "The Concept of Bureaucracy: An Empirical Assessment," *Administrative Science Quarterly*, 69: 32–40.

Hamel, G. and C.K. Prahalad (1996) "Competing in the New Economy," *Strategic Management Journal*, 17: 237–242.

Held, D. (1995) *Democracy and the Global Order: From the Modern State to Cosmopolitan Governance*. Cambridge: Polity Press.

Held, D. (1998) *Political Theory and the Modern State—Essays on State, Power and Democracy*. New Delhi: World View, Maya Polity Press.

Herzberg, F. (1968) *Work and the Nature of Man*. London: Staples Press.

Hill, S. and A. Wilkinson (1995) "In Search of TQM," *Employee Relations*, 17(3): 9–26.

Homans, G.C. (1961) *Social Behavior: Its Elementary Forms*. New York: Harcourt, Brace and World.

Hoogvelt, A.M.M. (1982) *The Third World in Global Development*. London: McMillan.

Hyman, J. and B. Mason (1995) *Managing Employee Involvement and Participation*. London: Sage Publications.

Jacobi, O., B. Keller, and M. Muller-Jentsch (1992) "Germany: Co-determining the Future," in A. Ferner and R. Hyman (eds), *Industrial Relations in the New Europe*, pp. 218–269. Oxford: Blackwell.

Jones, D.C. and T. Kato (1993) "The Scope, Nature and Effects of Employee Stock Ownership Plans in Japan," *Industrial and Labor Relations Review*, 46(2): 352–367.

Kanfer, R. 1990. "Motivation Theory and Industrial/Organizational Psychology," in M.D. Dunnette and L. Hough (eds), *Handbook of Industrial and Organizational Psychology 1*. Palo Alto, CA: Consulting psychologists press.

Katz, D. (1964) "The Motivational Basis of Organizational Behavior," *Behavioral Science*, 9: 131–146.

Katz, D. and R. Kahn (1966) *The Social Psychology of Organizations*. New York: Wiley.

Karasek, R.A. (1979) "Job Demands, Job Decision Latitude and Mental Strain: Implications for Job Redesign," Administrative Science Quarterly, 24: 285–308.

Kelly, C. and J. Kelly (1994) "Who Gets Involved in Collective Action? Social Psychological Determinants of Individual Participation in Trade Unions," *Human Relations*, 47: 63–88.

Kelly, J and C. Kelly (1991) "Them and Us: Social Psychology of the New Industrial Relations," *British Journal of Industrial Relations*, 29(1): 25–48.

Kerlinger, F.N. (1973) *Foundations of Behavioral Research*. New York: Holt, Rinehart and Winston Inc.

Khandwalla, P.N. (1977) *The Design of Organizations*. New York: Harcourt Brace Jovanovich, Inc.

Khandwalla, P.N. (1992) *Organization Design for Excellence*. New Delhi: Tata McGraw-Hill.

———. (1995) *Management Styles*. New Delhi: Tata McGraw-Hill.

———. (1999) *Revitalizing the State: A Menu of Options*. New Delhi: Sage Publications.

———. (2001) *Turnaround Excellence*. New Delhi: Response Books.

———. (2002) "Effective Organizational Response by Corporates to India's Liberalization and Globalization," *Asia Pacific Journal of Management*, 19: 423–448.

Klitgaard, R. and J. Fedderke (1995) "Social Integration and Disintegration: An Exploratory Analysis of Cross-country Data," *World Development*, 23(3): 357–369.

Konovsky, M.A. and R. Cropanzano (1991) "Perceived Fairness of Employee Drug Testing as a Predictor of Employee Attitudes and Job Performance," *Journal of Applied Psychology*, 76: 698–707.

Konovsky, M.A. and R. Cropanzano (1991) "Justice Consideration in Employee Drug Testing," in R. Cropanzano (ed.), *Justice in the Workplace*, pp. 171–192. Hillsdale, NJ: Lawrence Erlbaum Associates.

Laski, Harold (1948) *Grammar of Politics*. London: Allen & Unwin.

Lawler, E.E. (1992) *The Ultimate Advantage: Creating the High Involvement Organization*. San Francisco: Jossey-Bass.

———. (1986) *High Involvement Management*. London: Jossey-Bass.

Lawrence, P.R. and J. Lorsch (1967) *Organization and Environment*. Boston, MA: Harvard University Press.

Leventhal, D. (1997) "The Three Faces of Organizational Learning: Wisdom, Inertia and Discovery," in Raghu Garud, Praveen Nayyar, and Zur Shapira (eds), *Technological Oversights and Foresights*, pp. 167–180. Cambridge: Cambridge University Press.

Leventhal, G.S. (1980) "What Should be Done with Equity Theory?," in K.J. Gergen, M.S. Greenberg, and R.H. Willis (eds), *Social Exchange: Advances in Theory and Research*, pp. 27–55. New York: Plenum.

Liedtka, J.M. (1999) "Linking Competitive Advantage with Communities of Practice," *Journal of Management Enquiry*, 8(1): 5–16.

Likert, R. (1961) *New Patterns of Management*. New York: McGraw-Hill.

Locke, E.A. and D.M. Schweiger (1990) "Participation in Decision Making: One More Look," in L.L. Cummings and Barry Staw (eds), *Leadership, Participation and Group Behaviour*, pp. 137–212. Greenwich: Jai Press Inc.

Locke, E.A., G.P. Latham, and M. Erez (1988) "The Determinants of Goal Commitment," *Academy of Management Review*, 13(1): 23–39.

Locke, E.A. and D.M. Schweiger (1979) "Participation in Decision-making: One More Look," in B.M. Staw (ed.), *Research in Organizational Behavior*, pp. 265–340. Greenwich CT: Jai Press.

Marchington, M. (1990) "Unions on the Margin?" *Employee Relations*, 12(5): 1–24.

Marchington, M. and P. Parker (1990) *Changing Patterns of Employee Relations*. Hemel Hempstead: Harvester Wheatsheaf.

Marshall, T.H. (1973) *Class, Citizenship and Social Development*. Westport, Connecticut: Greenwood Press.

Mathieu, J.E. and J.L. Farr (1991) "Further Evidence for the Discriminant Validity of Measures of Organizational Commitment, Job Involvement and Job Satisfaction," *Journal of Applied Psychology*, 76(1): 127–133.

McGregor, D. (1960) *The Human Side of Enterprise*. New York: McGraw-Hill.

Miller, K. and P. Monge (1986) "Participation, Satisfaction and Productivity: A Meta-analytic Review," *Academy of Management Journal*, 29(4): 727–753.

Mintzberg, H. (1973) "Strategy Making in Three Modes," *California Management Review*, 16(2): 44–53.

Moch, M.K. and L.R. Pondy (1977) "The Structure of Chaos. Organized Anarchy as a Response to Ambiguity," *Administrative Science Quarterly*, 22: 351–362.

Moore Jr., B. (1973) *The Social Origins of Dictatorship and Democracy*. Boston: Beacon Press.

Moorman, R. (1991) "Relationship between Organizational Justice and Organizational Citizenship Behaviours: Do Fairness Perception Influence Employee Citizenship?" *Journal of Applied Psychology*, 76(6): 845–855.

Moorman, R., G. Blakey, and B. Niehoff (1998) "Does Perceived Organizational Support Mediate the Relationship between Procedural Justice and Organizational Citizenship Behavior?" *Academy of Management Journal*, 41(3): 352.

Mygind, N. and C.P. Rock (1993) "Financial Participation and the Democratization at Work," *Economic and Industrial Democracy*, 14: 163–183.

Nadler, D.A. and E.E. Lawler III (1982) "Quality of Work Life Programs, Coordination and Productivity," *Journal of Contemporary Business*, 11: 93–106.

Nadler, D.A. and E.E. Lawler (1983) "Quality of Worklife: Perspectives and Directions," *Organizational Dynamics*, 11(3): 20–30.

Near, J.P. and M. Miceli (1987) "Whistle Blowers in Organizations," in B.M. Staw and L.L. Cummings (eds), *Research in Organizational Behavior*. New Delhi: Jai Press.

Niehoff, B. and R. Moorman (1993) "Justice as a Mediator of the Relationship between Methods of Monitoring and Organizational Citizenship Behavior," *Academy of Management Journal*, 36(3): 534.

Nonaka, I. and H. Takeuchi (1995) *The Knowledge Creating Company: How Japanese Companies Create the Dynamics of Innovation*. New York: Oxford University Press.

Nozick, R. (1974) *Anarchy, State and Utopia*. Oxford: Basil Blackwell.

Nunally, J.C. (1978) *Psychometric Theory*. New York: McGraw-Hill Book Company.

Organ, D.W. (1990) "The Motivational Basis of Organizational Citizenship Behavior," in B.M. Staw and L.L. Cummings (eds), *Research in Organizational Behaviour*, pp. 43–72. Greenwich: Jai Press Inc.

Organ, D.W. and M. Konovsky (1989) "Cognitive vs. Affective Determinants of Organizational Citizenship Behaviour," *Journal of Applied Psychology*, 74(1): 157–164.

Ouchi, W. (1981) *Theory Z: How American Business Can Meet the Japanese Challenge*. Boston: Addison Wesley.

Pascale, R.T. and A. Athos (1981) *The Art of Japanese Management*. New York: Simon and Schuster.

Peters, T.J. and R.H. Waterman (1982) *In Search of Excellence*. New York: Harper and Row.

Pettigrew, A.M. and Massini (2003) "Innovative Forms of Organizing: Trends in Europe, Japan and the USA in the 1990s," in A.M Pettigrew et al. (eds), *Innovative forms of Organizing*, pp. 1–32. London: Sage Publications.

Pettigrew, A.M., Richard Whittington, Leif Melin, Carlos Sanchez-Runde, Frans Van Bosch, Winfred Ruigrok and Tsuyoshi Numagami (2003) *Innovative Forms of Organizing*. London: Sage Publications.

Przeworski, A. and F. Limongi (1997) "Democracy and Development," in Axel Hadenius (ed.), *Democracy's Victory and Crisis*, pp. 163–194. Cambridge: Cambridge University Press.

Pugh, D.S., D.J. Hickson, C.R. Hinings, and C. Turner (1968) "Dimensions of Organization Structure," *Administrative Science Quarterly*, 13: 65–105.

Rawls, J. (1973) *A Theory of Justice*. London: Oxford University Press.

Rothman, M., D.R. Briscoe, and R.C.D. Nacamulli (1993) *Industrial Relations around the World*. Berlin: Walter De Gruyter.

Schumpeter, J. (1934) *The Theory of Economic Development*. Cambridge, MA: Harvard University Press.

Senge, P.M. (1990) *The Fifth Discipline: The Art and Practice of Learning Organization*. New York: Doubleday.

Settoon, R.P., N. Bennett, and R.C. Liden (1996) "Social Exchange in Organizations: Perceived Organizational Support, Leader–Member Exchange and Employee Reciprocity," *Journal of Applied Psychology*, 81(3): 219–227.

Spender, J.C. and E.H. Kessler (1995) "Managing the Uncertainties of Innovation: Extending Thompson (1967)," *Human Relations*, 48(1): 35–56.

Spreitzer, G. (1995) "Psychological Empowerment in the Work Place: Dimensions, Measurement and Validation," *Academy of Management Journal*, 38: 1442–1456.

Strauss, G. (1990) "Workers Participation in Management: An International Perspective," in L.L. Cummings and B.M. Staw (eds), *Leadership, Participation and Group Behaviour*, pp. 213–306. Greenwich: Jai Press.

Suchman, M.C. (1995) "Managing Legitimacy: Strategic and Institutional Approaches," *Academy of Management Review*, 20(3): 571–610.

Summers, T. and W. Hendrix (1991) "Modeling Equity Perceptions: A Field Study," *Journal of Occupational Psychology*, 64: 145–157.

Tabachnik, B.G. and L.S. Fidell (1996) *Using Multivariate Statistics*. New York: HarperCollins College Publishers.

Thibaut, J. and L. Walker (1975) *Procedural Justice: A Psychological Analysis*. Hilsdale, NJ: Erlbaum.

Thiele, L.P. (1997) "Heidegger on Freedom: Political not Metaphysical," *American Political Science Review*, 88(2): 278–291.

Thorsrud, E. and F. Emery (1969) *Form and Content in Industrial Democracy: Some Experiences from Norway and Other European Countries*. London: Tavistook.

Toffler, Alvin (1991) *The Third Wave*. New York: Bantam Books.

Tyler, T.R. and R.J. Bies (1990) "Beyond Formal Procedures: The Interpersonal Context of Procedural Justice," in J. Caroll (ed.), *Applied Psychology and Organizational Settings*, pp. 77–98. Hillsdale, NJ: Erlbaum.

Van de Van, A.H. and D. Polley (1992) "Learning While Innovating," *Organization Science*, 3(1): 92–116.

Wagner III, J.A. (1994) "Participation's Effects on Performance and Satisfaction: A Reconsideration of Research Evidence," *Academy of Management Review*, 19(2): 312–330.

Wagner III, J.A., A. Buchko, and R.Z. Gooding (1988) "Aston Research on Organizational Structure: A Meta Analytic Examination of Generalizability." Paper presented at the annual meeting of the Academy of Management, Organization and Management Theory Division, Anheim, California, August.

Walster, E., G. Walster, and E. Berscheid (1978) *Equity Theory and Research*. Boston: Allyn, and Bacon.

Weber, M. (1947) "In the Theory of Social and Economic Organization," ed. T. Parsons. New York: Oxford University Press.

———. (1970) "In From Weber," ed. H.H. Gerth and C.W. Mills. London: Routledge.

———. (1978) *Economy and Society* (2nd ed). Berkeley, California: University of California Press.

Whittington, R. (2002) "Corporate Structure: From Policy to Practice," in A.M. Pettigrew, H. Thomas, and R. Whittington (eds), *The Handbook of Strategy and Management*, pp. 113–138. London: Sage Publications.

Wilkinson, A., G. Godfrey, and M. Marchington (1997) "Bouquets and Brickbats: TQM and Employee Involvement in Practice," *Organization Studies*, 18(5): 799–819.

Zaltman, G., R. Duncan, and J. Holbek (1973) *Innovation and Organizations*. New York: Wiley.

Zefanne, R.M. (1989) "Centralization or Formalization? Indifference Curves for Strategies of Control," *Organization Studies*, 10: 327–352.

6

Antecedents of Employee Performance and the Role of Job Satisfaction as a Mediator

Soumendu Biswas

INTRODUCTION

The increasing global spread of businesses and the growing prominence of multinational corporations (MNCs) in emerging economies have brought to fore the need to study management practices in different social and cultural contexts (Budhwar, 2003; Napier and Vu, 1998). In this connection, India is one such economy where global changes have had profound socio-economic influences (Biswas et al., 2006; Budhwar and Boyne, 2004). Not only have these changes affected the Indian socio-cultural milieu, but have also brought forth significant transformations in managerial policies and philosophies (Chauhan et al., 2005). Further, these changes have assumed contextual relevance, especially in the light of the resilience exhibited by the Indian economy in the period following the South East Asian financial crisis of 1997–98 (World Bank, 2001) which catapulted India into the league of the fastest evolving and most stable financial destinations for investors from the world over (Goldman Sachs, 2003).

In the context of the discussion about the flexibility and spirit displayed by India in the face of global changes, not all of which have been particularly encouraging, it is imperative to explore the cultural factors that have shaped the behavioral aspects of managerial effectiveness in Indian organizations (Biswas, 2006). This argument is corroborated by an earlier study by Zurcher (1968) wherein it was posited that in view of the growing worldwide commercial operations, it is necessary to study the behavioral facets of business within the contextual boundaries of socio-cultural events.

India is a country with a rich heritage of national culture. To a large extent, the socio-economic values and actions of Indians can be attributed to their long cultural history. Further, these cultural characteristics are deeply ingrained in the individual mindsets and markedly influence their cognitions and affect their personal, social, and professional environment (Rao and Abraham, 2003). At the same time, the indigenous culture of India has readily accepted alien customs and traditions while preserving its unique cultural norms and legacies (Biswas et al., 2006). This has put the Indian social order, as a classic example, on the map of the South East Asian cultural geography. With reference to the cross-vergent socio-cultural ethos therefore, India stands as a pioneer in establishing norms and reciprocities that govern managerial policies and procedures, especially in the light of the contemporary boundariless business environment (Ralston et al., 1997). In a cross-cultural framework, the preceding discussion indicates the elevated status of India in the global socio-cultural atlas. Inasmuch that Varma et al. (2005) have remarked that India's traditional cultural systems are acting as a fulcrum for the South East Asian business environment.

In this connection, it has been observed that during periods of environmental confusion and chaos, societies in emerging economies such as India follow a path of least-resistance that leads to stability. They accomplish this by falling on their prosperous cultural tradition that acts as a timely buffer. This implies that in order to maintain internal cohesion and familiarize themselves with the external transformations such societies focus on retaining certain behavioural models that are local and at the same time welcome some customs and mores that are foreign and novel. Given that organizations function within the domains of social norms and values, it becomes an issue that needs further examination in the context of such behavioural singularities. On the basis of this supposition, the objective of the current study was formulated wherein the interrelationship between four behavioral constructs were examined, namely the psychological climate, transformational leadership, job satisfaction, and employee performance. More specifically, the present study investigates the causal impact of the psychological climate and transformational leadership on employee performance through job satisfaction which acts as the mediator variable. The following section reviews literature related to the key variables.

THEORETICAL BACKGROUND

Prior to the introduction of the New Economic Policy (NEP) in 1991, the Indian business environment was apparent through the supremacy of firms in the manufacturing sector. These firms, whether public or private, were usually large organizations and were marked by mechanistic processes and bureaucratic practices (Biswas and Varma, 2007). In fact, firms belonging to the service sector such as, educational institutions, healthcare organizations, and media and communications were basically owned by the state. This was a direct consequence of Nehruvian welfare philosophy that emphasized pluralistic utilitarianism. The fall out of such a socio-political arrangement was the lack of emphasis on individual aspirations and expectations (Varma et al., 2005). Thus, till the privatization of the Indian economy in the early 1990s, Indian organizations were extremely bureaucratic and were characterized by one-way flow of decision making from the top to the bottom. Indeed, Hofstede (2001) observed that such managerial philosophies and practices are not uncommon in social cultures that are dominated by collectivism and high power distance norms.

However, with the liberalization of the Indian business environment managerial practices especially those related to cognitive and affective facets of individual employees at the workplace underwent major alterations. Furthermore, human resource (HR) practices in Indian firms have experienced a sea change, as contemporary HR policies and practices are designed in a manner that promotes individual involvement on-the-job and encourages extra-role behavior in addition to the in-role behavior of employees (Biswas, 2006; Budhwar and Khatri, 2001; Pattnaik and Biswas, 2005). As Biswas and Varma (2007: 666) observed that "HR practices in India are increasingly geared towards improving the way individual employees perceive their day-to-day working environment, or the way they perceive the *psychological climate* [italics added] in the workplace."

Thus, to understand the group of actions in relation to the administration of members of an organization, the appropriate literature recommends an investigation of those variables that are related to an individual's acuity *a propos* their immediate workplace atmosphere based on their everyday experiences (Schneider, 1975; Strutton et al., 1993). In this regard, it is worth noting that the relevant literature recommends the examination of the psychological climate as a primary antecedent of a variety of individual-level outcomes such as organizational commitment, job satisfaction, job involvement, and organizational citizenship behavior (James et al., 1990; Parker et al., 2003; Woodard et al., 1994). This article seeks to empirically inspect these theoretical suggestions in the context of the Indian management scenario.

Leadership refers to encouraging followers to track collective or at least joint objectives that symbolize the values and drive of both leaders and followers (Krishnan, 2003). Thus the concern for the need and requirements of the followers is at the core of leadership principles and practices. In this connection, Tichy and Devanna (1986) noted that the real need of followers was fulfilled by leaders who did not utilize their followership to attain their own ends, but who endeavored towards the realization of mutual development. Burns (1978) further notes that such leadership, which may be termed a moral leadership in itself, could not be a driver of need fulfillment of the followers unless it took the form of transformational leadership. According to Burns (1978: 20), transformational leadership "... occurs when one or more person engage with others in such a way that leaders and followers raise one another to higher levels of motivation and morality ...."

In continuation, literature reveals that transformational leadership is a significant correlate of the amount of effort exerted by followers, leader-member satisfaction, employee performance, and overall effectiveness of individuals and by extension, of the organization (Bass, 1998). According to Kirkpatrick and Locke (1996), the leader's vision and its implementation through job indications positively affect the subordinates' performance and attitudes. Thus, organizational policy makers should recognize that effective courses of action can be devised if one keeps in mind the role of transformational leaders, as predictors of such guidelines and practices.

According to Bass and Avolio (1994), transformational leadership contributes to organizations' attempts at improving operations by optimal utilization of its human resources. In order to do so, transformational leaders must chalk out appropriate designs related to HR practices and policies that are geared towards greater autonomy and augmented individual performance. In this connection, it was observed that transformational leadership led to follower-organization value congruence, which as a result, became a significant source of various positive outcomes in organizational and human resource management practices (Seltzer and Bass, 1990; Yammarino and Atwater, 1997).

Job satisfaction has been defined as "a pleasurable or positive emotional state resulting from the appraisal of one's job or job experience" (Locke, 1976: 1300). Wanous and Lawler (1972) identified several different operational definitions of job satisfaction examining different facets of job satisfaction and their combined effect in providing a general understanding of the job satisfaction construct. Job satisfaction has been found to be a multidimensional construct manifesting the emotional evaluations of individuals regarding their expectations and how well they have been met. Schnake (1983) conceptualized three dimensions of job satisfaction representing its intrinsic, extrinsic, and social aspects. In effect, Schnake's (1983) dimensions of job satisfaction cover cognitive and affective responses made by individuals in connection to their work environment.

Literature suggested that there are two forms of work performance: in-role and extra-role (Brief and Motowidlo, 1986; Williams and Anderson, 1991; Wolfe Morrison, 1994). In-role performance referred to an employee's action to fulfill the requirements of his/her job description (Williams and Anderson, 1991), whereas, extra-role performances were those that were outside the formal role requirements and are at the employee's discretion (George and Brief, 1992).

Studies suggested that participatory management practices such as open communication and participatory leadership style would be positively associated with higher levels of employee performance on both the counts, viz. in-role and extra-role performance. Indeed, such practices would enhance an employee's level of job satisfaction leading to better performance.

Based on the discussion earlier, the following propositions were formulated for the purpose of empirical testing:

P1: Psychological climate will have a significantly positive impact on job satisfaction of individual employees at work;

P2: Transformational leadership style will positively and significantly influence an individual employee's level of job satisfaction; and

P3: An employee with high level of job satisfaction will exhibit higher levels of performance.

DISCUSSION AND CONCLUSION

With reference to the opening paragraphs of the present study, one understands that the introduction of a new economic policy resulted in major changes in the economic behavior of the citizens therein. According to Cowling and Newman (1995), these types of socio-political upheavals lead to environmental transitions which in turn affect organizations and their members. Such changes in the business environment lead to quite a few adjustments at the individual as well as the organizational level. At the individual level, the primary factor that is affected would be individual perceptions about one's immediate environment (Martin et al., 2005). A perception about one's immediate work environment is what is known as psychological climate. Thus, changes in the business environment do have an impact on the psychological climate, which in turn affects many other individual behavior and outcomes.

The present study takes a cue from these past conclusions and notes that perceptions of organizational members become critical data for understanding and interpreting individual behavior and attitudes.

Such understanding shows that climate variables, individually interpreted, become pointers for an employee's level of job satisfaction (Drexler, 1977). Similarly, interaction between group members, supervisor–subordinate relationship, and an individual's own perception about his/her job description also play a role in the attitudinal outcome related to their job.

Work environment and its relatedness to work related attributes and behavior suggest that the work-place climate has a significant consequence on an employees' perception about the work context. In so far as the construct of climate is concerned, and extensive studies have confirmed (Katz and Kahn, 1978), that description of role clarity, supervisory support, and perhaps more importantly, an employee's perception about the various human resource policies and practices go to create a day-to-day environment of enjoyment and satisfaction. The above arguments are corroborated through the acceptance of the first proposition, that is, the psychological climate will have a significantly positive impact on job satisfaction of individual employees at work.

As the discussion earlier points out, individual and group level behavioral factors have significant impact on individual level outcomes. In this context, Bryman (1992) found that an important predictor of individual level outcomes, such as perceived extra effort at work, organizational citizenship behavior, and job satisfaction was transformational leadership. Similar to psychological climate, transformational leadership was also found to influence employee-related outcomes during periods of intense economic competition that required higher levels of creativity and innovativeness (Howell and Avolio, 1993; Keller, 1992; Niehoff et al., 1990). Thus, during these periods there are higher expectations about goal achievement. Due to the consequent role clarity provided by transformational leadership, it is expected that these enhanced goals shall be achieved and there is a general atmosphere of euphoric anticipation which leads to higher levels of job satisfaction.

Moreover, transformational leaders are those who enthuse and inspire their followers and base their relationship on mutual understanding and trust which involves fruitful non-verbal communication. Such leadership behavior inculcates a sense of self belief and confidence in the followers. This in turn, would make employees less lackadaisical and open to a more meaningful interpretation of their work related roles. This is the process by which transformational leadership affects individual job satisfaction levels.

The argument posited above supports the findings of the results wherein it was hypothesized that transformational leadership would significantly and positively influence an employee's level of job satisfaction, and where this proposition was found to be true, and thus accepted.

In this connection, positive levels of psychological climate and transformational leadership, leading to higher levels of individual employees' job satisfaction were hypothesized to lead to higher levels of employee performance. This implied that satisfied employees who are themselves enthused enough about their work roles will display higher levels of in-role and extra-role performance. As Voss et al. (2004) observe that augmented job satisfaction would result in higher levels of employee productivity in conjunction with employee group behavior. Indeed, in today's business environment, transformational leadership, by generating higher levels of job satisfaction ensures that employees are more motivated and that they perform even better.

In this context, what is posited to happen in a practical context is that an employee who is satisfied with his/her job, that is, in other words enjoys job satisfaction will definitely not wish to run down his/her status quo and would strategize to maintain the same (i.e., the current level of high job satisfaction) by displaying continuous improvement with regards to in-role as well as extra-role performance, the summation of which would reflect his/her overall job performance as an employee. The above argument presumes that job satisfaction improves employee performance within the ambit of day-to-day organizational life.

The above arguments provide justification for the acceptance of the third proposition that an employee with a high level of job satisfaction will exhibit higher levels of performance.

In the context of a liberalized and globalized business environment, there is a gradual shift of focus from the manufacturing sector to the service sector. Apart from this, there is also a notable decline in union-related activities. The fallout of this is a reduction in inter-departmental and/or inter-divisional rivalries and antagonism, and promotion of a culture where co-workers are looked upon as internal customers. This has led to a greater cordiality and harmony at the workplace which has in turn, improved individual employees' perceptions about his/her immediate work environment, making them more satisfied with his/her job. As a result, this has improved individual performance, the overall effect of which has been an enhancement of organizational effectiveness.

Furthermore, with increasing competition and superior levels of performance expectations, employees are now required to achieve higher targets than before. Thus, the element of challenge has increased in the present work context and meeting these challenges are intrinsically rewarding and satisfying at the individual level and it encourages employees to perform better. While the element of job satisfaction leading to better performance is clear from this argument, what is also revealed is that in such a climate of overall enhanced performance, there shall be a significant improvement in organizational effectiveness.

With regards to the limitations of the present study, it is believed that the predictor variables could have included organizational culture and its strength in shaping up the psychological climate. Future researchers in this area may examine relationships among the variables of the present study and look into the similarities and differences with respect to different industries, ownerships, and types of products and also include organizational climate, an organizational level construct along with psychological climate, an individual level construct as a predictor for the outcomes presented in the model of the present study.

REFERENCES

Alwin, D.F. and R.M. Hauser (1975) "The Decomposition of Effects in Path Analysis," *American Sociological Review*, 40: 37–47.

Arbuckle, J.L. and W. Wothke (1999) *Amos 4.0 User's Guide*. Chicago, IL: Smallwaters Corporation.

Arogyaswamy, B. and C.M. Byles (1987) "Organizational Culture: Internal and External Fits," *Journal of Management Studies*, 13(4): 647–659.

Baron, R.M. and D.A. Kenny (1986) "The Moderator-mediator Distinction in Social Psychological Research: Conceptual, Strategic, and Statistical Considerations," *Journal of Personality and Social Psychology*, 51(6): 173–182.

Bass, B.M. (1998) *Leadership and Performance beyond Expectations*. New York: Free Press.

Bass, B.M. and B.J. Avolio (1994) *Improving Organizational Effectiveness through Transformational Leadership*. Thousand Oaks, CA: Sage Publications.

Bateman, T.S. and D.W. Organ (1983) "Job Satisfaction and the Good Soldier: The Relationship between Affect and Employee Citizenship," *Academy of Management Journal*, 26: 587–595.

Baysinger, B.D. and W.H. Mobley (1983) "Employee Turnover: Individual and Organizational Analysis," in G.R. Ferris and K.M. Rowland (eds), *Research in Personnel and Human Resource Management*, pp. 269–319. Greenwich, CT: JAI Press.

Biswas, S. (2006) "Organizational Culture and Psychological Climate as Predictors of Employee Performance and Job Satisfaction." PhD Thesis, Indian Institute of Technology, Kharagpur.

Biswas, S. and A. Varma (2007) "Psychological Climate and Individual Performance in India: Test of a Mediated Model," *Employee Relations*, 29(6): 664–676.

Biswas, S., V.N. Giri, and K.B.L Srivastava (2006) "Examining the Role of HR Practices in Improving Individual Performance and Organizational Effectiveness," *Management and Labour Studies*, 31(2): 111–133.

Brief, A.P. and S.J. Motowidlo (1986) "Prosocial Organizational Behaviours," *Academy of Management Review*, 11: 710–725.

Bryman, A. (1992) *Charisma and Leadership in Organizations*. London: Sage Publications.

Budhwar, P.S. (2003) "Employment Relations in India," *Employee Relations*, 25(2): 132–148.

Budhwar, P.S. and G. Boyne (2004) "Human Resource Management in the Indian Public and Private Sectors: An Empirical Comparison," *International Journal of Human Resource Management*, 15(2): 346–370.

Budhwar, P.S. and N. Khatri (2001) "A Comparative Study of HR Practices in Britain and India," *International Journal of Human Resource Management*, 12(5): 800–826.

Burns, J.M. (1978) *Leadership*. New York: Harper and Row.

Business Week. (1986) Retrieved October 3, 2008 from http://www.businessweek.com

Chauhan, V.S., U. Dhar, and R.D. Pathak (2005) "Factorial Constitution of Managerial Effectiveness: Re-examining an Instrument in Indian Context," *Journal of Managerial Psychology*, 20(1/2): 164–177.

Cotton, J. and J. Tuttle (1986) "Employee Turnover: A Meta Analysis and Review with Implications for Research," *Academy of Management Review*, 11: 55–70.

Cowling, A. and K. Newman (1995) "Banking on People: TQM, Service, Quality, and Human Resources," *Personnel Review*, 24: 25–41.

Dean, J.W. and S.A. Snell (1991) Integrated Manufacturing and Job Design: Moderating Effects of Organizational Inertia," *Academy of Management Journal*, 34(4): 776–804.

Drexler, J.A. (1977) "Organizational Climate: Its Homogeneity within Organizations," *Journal of Applied Psychology*, 62: 38–42.

Drucker, P.F. (1990) *Managing the Non-profit Organization*. Harper & Row.

England, G.W. and R. Lee (1974) "The Relationship between Managerial Values and Managerial Success in the United States, Japan, India, and Australia," *Journal of Applied Psychology*, 59: 411–419.

Farh, J.L., P.M. Podsakoff, and D.W. Organ (1990) "Accounting for Organizational Citizenship Behavior: Leader Fairness and Task Scope Versus Satisfaction," *Journal of Management*, 16: 705–721.

Farrell, D. and C.E. Rusbult (1981) "Exchange Variables as Predictors of Job Satisfaction, Job Commitment and Turnover: The Impact of Rewards, Costs, Alternatives, and Investments," *Organizational Behavior and Human Performance*, 27: 78–95.

George, J.M. and A.P. Brief (1992) "Feeling Good-doing Good: A Conceptual Analysis of the Mood at Work-organizational Spontaneity Relationship," *Psychological Bulletin*, 112(2): 310–329.

Goldman Sachs Investment Bank (2003) *Dreaming with BRICs: The Path to 2050*. Retrieved from http://en.wikipedia.org/wiki/BRIC (last accessed on May 3, 2008).

Hair, J.F.H., R.E. Anderson, R.L. Tatham, and W.C. Black (1998) *Multivariate Data Analysis* (5th ed.). Engelwood Cliffs, NJ: Prentice-Hall.

Harrington, H.J. (1987) *Business Process Improvement: The Breakthrough Strategy for Total Quality, Productivity, and Competitiveness*. New York: McGraw-Hill

Hayes, H.R., H.C. Wheelright, and K.B. Clark (1988) *Dynamic Manufacturing. Creating the Learning Organization*. USA: Boek2 Antiquariaat.

Hofstede, G. (2001) *Culture's Consequences* (2nd Ed.). Thousand Oaks, NJ: Sage Publications.

Howell, J.M. and B.J. Avolio (1993) "Transformational Leadership, Transactional Leadership, Locus of Control, and Support for Innovation: Key Predictors of Consolidated-business-unit Performance," *Journal of Applied Psychology*, 78(6): 891–902.

James, L.R., L.A. James, and D.K. Ashe (1990) "The Meaning of Organizations: The Role of Cognition and Values," in Benjamin Schneider (ed.), *Organizational Culture and Climate*, pp. 40–84. San Francisco, CA: Jossey-Bass.

Katz, D. and R. Kahn (1978) *"The Social Psychology of Organizations* (2nd ed.). New York: John Wiley.

Keller, R.T. (1992) "Transformational Leadership and the Performance of Research and Development Project Groups," *Journal of Management*, 18(3): 489–501.

Kirkpatrick, S.A. and E.A. Locke (1996) "Direct and Indirect Effects of Three Core Charismatic Leadership Components on Performance and Attitudes," *Journal of Applied Psychology*, 81: 36–51.

Klein, R.B. (1998) *Principles and Practice of Structural Equation Modeling*. New York: Guilford.

Krishnan, V.R. (2003) "Power and Moral Leadership: Role of Self-other Agreement," *Leadership & Organizational Development*, 24(5/6): 345–351.

Locke, E.A. (1976) "The Nature and Causes of Job Satisfaction," in M.D. Dunnette (ed.), *Handbook of Industrial and Organizational Psychology*, pp. 1297–1349. Chicago: Rand McNally.

MacKinnon, D.P., G. Warsi, and J.H. Dwyer (1995) "A Simulation Study of Mediated Effect Measures," *Multivariate Behavioral Research*, 30(1): 41–62.

Martin, A.J., E.S. Jones, and V.J. Callan (2005) "The Role of Psychological Climate in Facilitating Employee Adjustment during Organizational Change," *European Journal of Work and Organizational Psychology*, 14(3): 263–289.

McEvoy, G.M. and W.F. Cascio (1985) "Strategies for Reducing Employee Turnover: A Meta-analysis," *Journal of Applied Psychology*, 70(2): 342–353.

Mobley, W.H. (1982) *Employee Turnover: Causes, Consequences and Control*. Reading, MA: Addison-Wesley.

Mobley, W.H., R.W. Griffeth, H.H. Hand, and B.M. Meglino (1979) "Review and Conceptual Analysis of the Employee Turnover Process," *Psychological Bulletin*, 86: 493–522.

Moorman, R.H. (1993) "The Influence of Cognitive and Affective Based Job Satisfaction on Relationship between Satisfaction and Organizational Citizenship Behavior," *Human Relations*, 46: 759–776.

Napier, N.K. and V.T. Vu (1998) "International Human Resource Management in Developing and Transitional Economy Countries: A Breed Apart?" *Human Resource Management Review*, 8(1): 39–77.

Niehoff, B.P., C.A. Enz, and R.A. Grover (1990) "The Impact of Top Management Actions on Employee Attitudes and Perceptions," *Group & Organization Studies*, 15(3): 337–352.

Organ, D.W. (1988) *Organizational Citizenship Behavior: The Good Soldier Syndrome*. Lexington, MA: Lexington Books.

———. (1994) "Personality and Organizational Citizenship Behavior," *Journal of Management*, 20: 465–478.

Organ, D.W. and K. Ryan (1995) "A Meta-analytic Review of Attitudinal and Dispositional Predictors of Organizational Citizenship Behavior," *Personnel Psychology*, 48: 775–802.

Organ, D.W. and M.A. Konovsky (1989) "Cognitive Versus Affective Determinants of Organizational Citizenship Behavior," *Journal of Applied Psychology*, 74: 157–164.

Parker, C.P., B.B Baltes, S.A. Young, J.W. Huff, R.A. Altmann, H.A. Lacost, and J.E. Roberts (2003) "Relationship between Psychological Climate Perceptions and Work Outcomes: A Meta-analytic Review," *Journal of Organizational Behavior*, 24: 389–416.

Pattnaik, S. and S. Biswas (2005) "The Mediating Role of Organizational Citizenship Behavior between Organizational Identification and its Consequences," Paper presented at the International Research Conference of the Academy of Human Resource Development (AHRD), February 24–27, 2005, Estes Park, CO.

Podsakoff, P., S. MacKenzie, J. Paine, and D. Bacharach (2000) "Organizational Citizenship Behaviors: A Critical Review of the Theoretical and Empirical Literature and Suggestions for Future Research.," *Journal of Management*, 26(3): 513–563.

Price, J.L. and C.W. Mueller (1981) *Professional Turnover: The Case of Nurses*. New York: Spectrum.

Ralston, D.A., D.H. Holt, R.H. Terpstra, and Y. Kai-Cheng (1997) "The Impact of National Culture and Economic Ideology on Managerial Work Values: A Study of the United States, Russia, Japan, and China," *Journal of International Business Studies*, 28(1): 177–207.

Rao, T.V. and E. Abraham (2003) "HRD Climate in Organizations" in T.V. Rao (ed.), *Readings in Human Resource Development*, pp. 36–45. New Delhi: Oxford and IBH Publishing Co. Pvt. Ltd.

Schnake, M.E. (1983) "An Empirical Assessment of the Effects of Affective Response in the Measurement of Organizational Climate," *Personnel Psychology*, 36(4): 791–807.

Schneider, B. (1975) "Organizational Climates: An Essay," *Personnel Psychology*, 28: 447–479.

Seltzer, J. and B.M. Bass (1990) "Transformational Leadership: Beyond Initiation and Consideration," *Journal of Management*, 16(4): 693–703.

Steers, R.M. and R.T. Mowday (1981) "Employee Turnover and Post-decision Accommodation Processes," in B.M. Staw and L.L. Cummins (eds), *Research in Organizational Behavior*, pp. 235–282. Greenwich, CN: JAI Press.

Strutton, D., L.E. Pelton, and J.R. Lumpkin (1993) "The Relationship between Psychological Climate and Salesperson-sales Manager Trust in Sales Organization," *Journal of Personal Selling and Sales Management*, 13(4): 1–14.

The Economist (1986) Retrieved from http://www.economist.com/printedition/ (last accessed on October 3, 2008).

Tichy, N.M. and M.A. Devanna (1986) *The Transformational Leader*. New York: John Wiley.

Varma, A., P. Budhwar, S. Biswas, and S.M. Toh (2005) "An Empirical Investigation of Host Country National Categorization of Expatriates in the United Kingdom," Paper presented at the European Academy of Management, May 2005, Munich, Germany.

Voss, M.D., S.B. Keller, A.E. Ellinger, and J. Ozment (2004) "Differentiating the Suppliers of Job Products to Union and Non-union Frontline Distribution Center Employees," *Transportation Journal*, 43(2): 37–58.

Wanous, J.P. and E.E. III Lawler (1972) "Measurement and Meaning of Job Satisfaction," *Journal of Applied Psychology*, 56: 95–105.

West, S.G. and R.A. Wicklund (1980) *A Primer of Social Psychological Theories*. Monterey, CA: Brooks/Cole.

Williams, L.J. and S.E. Anderson (1991) "Job Satisfaction and Organizational Commitment as Predictors of Organizational Citizenship and In-role Behaviors," *Journal of Management*, 17(3): 601–617.

Wolfe Morrison, E. (1994) "Role Definitions and Organizational Citizenship Behaviour: The Importance of the Employee's Perspective," *Academy of Management Journal*, 37: 1543–1567.

Woodard, G., N. Cassill, and D. Herr (1994) *The Relationship between Psychological Climate and Work Motivation in a Retail Environment*. New York, NY: Routledge.

World Bank (2001) *World Development Report*. New York: Oxford University Press.

Yammarino, F.J. and L.E. Atwater (1997) "Do Managers See Themselves as Others See Them? Implications of Self-other Rating Agreement for Human Resource Management," *Organizational Dynamics*, 25(4): 35–45.

Zurcher, L.A. (1968) "Particularism and Organizational Position: A Cross Cultural Analysis," *Journal of Applied Psychology*, 52(2): 139–144.

7

Managing Talent through Employee Engagement Strategies

Jyotsna Bhatnagar

INTRODUCTION

The India shining factor has lead to a spurt on India-based research and practitioner ideas. Cutting edge India-based research and case studies are on the rise, and increasing the responsibility to craft the Next Orbit strategies lies on the shoulders of Indian HR leaders and academicians. This essay investigates the emerging concepts and tries to present an integrated approach towards talent management and employee engagement. The section below delineates the conceptual flow of the essay.

Conceptual Schema

(a) Emergent context: Talent management, capability building, and employee engagement
(b) Academia and practitioner research bridge
(c) Emerging challenge: Innovation in talent management strategies
(d) Emerging model routing talent management and engagement strategies to the Next Orbit

EMERGENT CONTEXT

Indian organizations are not winning the war for talent, by competing on their talent and hiring "stars" from the external labor market. Instead, they leverage the talent by investing in the competencies of employees and building talent capabilities from within. The source of comparative advantage emerges from new and better ideas, superior execution and the process of *jugaad* that gets things done. These outcomes were traced to a holistic engagement with employees. Recent research found that 62 percent of the Indian firms tracked progress in overall talent management, compared to only 26 percent in the United States (Cappelli et al., 2010). Capability building in the context of intense growth, a cost arbitrage scenario with a constant vigil on the changing pulse of the business is a challenging and an onerous task, which many organizations, across the globe, struggle to sustain. We need talent management strategies that develop capabilities and competencies of internal talent, while all the time monitoring the cost factor.

In India, recently sectors like FMCG, consumer durables, and auto sectors were not planning to give another round of pay hikes. These sectors had given a pay hike, in 2007 (Puri, 2010). The IT sector in India has recently been witnessing a boom in compensation in order to retain and engage talent. There are mid-term reviews and hikes, and variable pay compensation practices to retain and engage talent (Puri, 2010). Diverse sectors reflect diverse results. Indian CEOs are not insensitive to labor cost issues, but they did not perceive the immediate or long-term competitiveness based on labor costs. Instead they perceived competitiveness and firm goals as moving up the value chain and doing so was based on innovation and superior execution. These outcomes were closely tied to superior talent, motivated employees, and an organization culture that encouraged synchronization of individual goals to organizational goals (Cappelli et al., 2010: 62–63). Much emphasis is on a leader who is the change strategist and architect who believes that emerging corporate battles in times to come will be won not on the might of technology but, on the power of human ideas and the innovation quotient. Innovation means offering new combinations and permutations, and not just offering incremental change. It means deconstructing one's own thought and self and offering an absolutely new product year after year. It also implies creating an environment where change is accepted instead of facing resistance. Instead of waiting for a competitor to destroy it for them, organizations create an environment where organizations cannibalize their own products, policies, and competencies (Singh et al., 2006). This kind of an innovative business strategy would have to be supported by synchronized capability building among the existing talent pool. Walia of Bharti, has reflected, on this need and how the global HR profile knows where to source quality and the right talent, build internal talent development, and leadership capability; and anchor it to innovative reward and recognition practices (National HRD Network Conference, 2007).

Capability building and employee engagement go hand in hand. The reflection of this relationship is on employee engagement quotient, which wavers as the context and the ground reality shifts. Recent research found that organizations that are serious about their talent engagement strategy spend 30 percent of their time on talent issues. This includes time spent on leadership pipeline development review strategies, networking with potential talent, and review of succession position candidates, at board and senior level meetings (Ulrich et al., 2008). Capability building is not on the priority list of many countries due to the recent economic trends. As is indicative from the research on US Organizations, capability building was ranked second last, with only 4 percent of American organizations reflecting it as a strategic value to their organizations. On the other hand, Indian organizations attributed it as the most important strategy, with 81 percent of the Indian organizations reported organizational capability building as an important purpose for employee learning (Cappelli et al., 2010: 75).

A global talent management strategy, aligned with business strategy has also been used by many organizations. Private banks like ICICI Bank and HSBC Bank have used talent pool identification, which comprises of middle and senior level managers. ICICI Bank uses a diversity based intervention which is integrated with the global talent management strategy. Diversity intervention targeted the shortage amongst the plenty syndrome at the bank and came into implementation in order to enhance the ICICI Bank's ability to attract, deploy, and retain a global talent pool (Bhuj, 2007).

On the other hand, HSBC's global talent pool identification followed a value proposition, where a customized talent development strategy was utilized. The first step was to identify the global talent pool, which comprised of senior general managers and world class specialists. The next step was to go beyond the senior managers and implement development programes for future leaders based on the level of experience and seniority. Capability ratings were reviewed based on a holistic panel of reviews, interviews, self and managers assessments', besides benchmarking the capability building framework against competitors and industry peers (Gakovich and Yardley, 2007).

In organizations such as HSBC, capability building was drawing on employee engagement, and was built upon employee value proposition. Corporate Leadership Council (2006) defines EVP as "a set of attributes that the labor market and the employees perceive as the value they gain through employment in an organization." At this organization the EVP was driven by four practices, which in turn drove employee engagement and retention. These were: reward and recognition; career development (training and succession planning); work environment (empowerment and communication) and work life balance.

Yet, the *Next Orbit* challenge for this organization was to manage the scope and breadth of talent management process which would lead to consistent high employee engagement. The challenge was to manage the talent identification and nomination process for all employees in 76 countries. It was important to refine the talent nomination process, improve talent assessment tools as well as establish talent nomination accountability. The challenge was to implement and adapt the best practices in talent identification leadership development, and customized retention programes to meet HSBC's global needs (Gakovich and Yardley, 2007: 205). HCL on the other hand, introduced *trust pay* to ensure stretch goals implementation for critical assignments and clients. It used empowerment as an important vehicle for engagement and integrated it with transparent feedback on performance at all levels. The CEO's office became a redundant concept and it implemented a bottoms-up approach of employee first and customer second. This is hailed as the next management practice (Nayar, 2010).

A recent annual Work Trends Report 2010, which sampled 29,000 employees across the world, on employee engagement found India to be ranking number one (71 percent) in engagement as opposed to Japan (38 percent) which was the lowest. The countries survey included India, the US, the UK, Australia, Brazil, Canada, China, Denmark, Finland, France, Germany, India, Italy, Japan, Mexico, the Netherlands, Russia, Spain, Sweden, Switzerland, and some nations in the Gulf Co-op Council. This report analyzed the importance of leadership and managerial effective-ness to employee engagement and organizational success. "The findings show that companies with highest level of employee engagement and best leadership will recover from the economic downturn faster and emerge stronger" (Wiley, 2010a). According to the latest research from the Kenexa Research Institute (KRI), an organizations' senior leadership team has a significant impact on the engagement levels, which have been linked to total earning per share and total shareholder return. In fact, employee engagement is a means to an end. The end is better business returns. This is true, in tougher times, where employee engagement draws upon inspiring and motivating leadership, which stands to support its employees (Wiley, 2010b). This is supported by the work of Ulrich et al. (2008) who state that: "Talent managers are like magnets. They get the most out of their managers, and are inspiring in their presence and lead to employee engagement."

In an economic downturn, and in a scenario of fearfulness and blamegames—where employees are anxious and worried about the future—the onus for effective employee engagement lies on the powerful, understanding, empathic shoulders of the leader. With the context of recession, upgrading talent in these times of recession to increase employee engagement was found by the research of Guthridge et al. (2008) who reported that, organizations can improve the engagement of key talent by redesigning jobs. Organizations can maintain their employer of choice brand attraction, by using cost cutting efforts as an opportunity to redesign existing jobs, by increasing the span of control. Case in point is of Cisco which did that during the last recession in 2001. Yet, an argument may be made that these findings on talent management and engagement are from the practitioner driven lens. We look towards academia to provide grounded answers bridging theory and practice, and providing robust research based linkage for talent management and employee engagement strategies.

ACADEMIA AND PRACTITIONER RESEARCH BRIDGE

Bridging the gap between the practitioner and academic world for retaining talent through robust employee engagement strategies is the *Next Orbit* research agenda, which few research studies have started addressing. More recently, academic scholars (Macey and Schneider, 2008; Bhatnagar, 2007, 2009; Rich et al., 2010) have tried to address this need.

Rich et al. (2010: 617) have investigated the linkage between employee engagement and task performance in the Western context, theorizing upon Khan's (1990) seminal work on engagement. They conceptualized engagement as the investment of an individual's complete self into a role, providing a more comprehensive explanation of relationships with performance than do well-known concepts that reflect narrower aspects of the individual's self. The theorizing of engagement is physical, cognitive, and emotional engagement with effects on task performance. Employee engagement emerged as a mediator between value congruence; perceived organization support and core self-evaluation as antecedents and organizational citizenship behavior and task performance as consequences.

In an Indian context, research (Bhatnagar, 2007, 2009) found employee engagement as a tool for employee retention and for effective talent management strategies. This was found in the ITES sector and challenged the findings of the Gallup research. Further, it revealed the emergence of the concept of "employee engagement" which at times is confused with an employee's organizational commitment as an outcome variable and confusion persists in its definition (Saks, 2006; Bhatnagar, 2007).

Researchers (Halbesleben and Wheeler, 2008; Macey and Schneider, 2008: 3) state in their work that, engagement will make a stronger contribution to literature as a unique and distinct construct (Bhatnagar and Biswas, 2010). More recently, Biswas and Bhatnagar (2010) found in an Indian sample, that employee engagement emerged as a discriminant construct to organizational commitment and its antecedents were found in perceived organizational support and a person–organization fit. Employee engagement was theorized as job and organization engagement and emerged as a mediator between perceived organizational support and person–organization fit, as antecedents and organizational commitment, and job satisfaction as consequences.

A recent study (Aggarwal et al., 2010) has explored the linkage between employee engagement and innovation. The implications of work engagement on an employees' innovative work behavior and turnover intention were investigated on a sample of 979 managerial employees working in six service organizations from India. Results suggested there was a linkage between leader member exchanges which was positively related to work engagement. Engagement has effects on innovative work behavior and turnover intentions in the expected direction. Hausknecht et al., (2009) developed a content model of employee retention grounded in theory and past research, and tested it with a sample of 24,829 employees who were asked to comment on why they have stayed with their employer. This research developed and tested predictions grounded in ease or desirability of movement (March and Simon, 1958) and psychological contract (Robinson et al., 1994) rationales to explain why high and low performers and those at different job levels are more or less likely to emphasize particular reasons for why they choose to stay. The emerging framework, nested in the Western context, revealed that job satisfaction, extrinsic rewards, constituent attachments, organizational commitment, work life balance (described as flexible arrangements) and organizational prestige (associated with emerging as an employer of choice [Branham, 2005]) were the most frequently mentioned reasons for staying.

High performers and non-hourly workers were more likely to cite advancement opportunities and organizational prestige as reasons for staying, whereas, low performers and hourly employees were more likely to cite extrinsic rewards. This study highlights the need to differentiate and customize HR practices that have a distinct goal of retention of highly valued talent (Hausknecht et al., 2009: 269). Managing and developing talent is the high priority area in *The India Way* (Cappelli et al., 2010), and this throws up challenges for innovating existing talent management strategies.

EMERGING CHALLENGE: INNOVATION IN TALENT MANAGEMENT STRATEGIES

In order to maintain and sustain employee engagement and retention, there is a need for innovative talent management strategies and high performing work systems, organizational cultures which nurture innovation and strategic leadership that institutionalizes and encourages such a mindset.

Job Characteristics: Reward and Recognition and the Changing Psychological Contract Based on Talent Management Strategies

Referring to the research study cited above and the earlier work of Saks (2006), Bhatnagar (2009) recently investigated the linkage between the following factors and their integration into innovative and customized talent management strategy. There is a need to build challenging assignments for high performing talent, balance and customize it to a need–fitment based on the reward and recognition strategy which would address the changing psychological contract of the talented employees. A case in point is of Sasken technologies which customized the reward and recognition basket, from which employees choose as per their demographic profile and emerging needs. This customization would lead to enhanced and sustained engagement levels, and retention of critical and valued talent.

Diversity and Inclusiveness based Talent Management Strategies

Ollapally and Bhatnagar (2009) state that, some of the reasons that cause organizations to embark on diversity management include shortage of skill or talent (Devine, 2007), globalization, a high turnover (Robinson and Dechant, 1997) and the management style of the CEO (White, 2000). Buttner et al. (2008) demonstrated that when employees perceived a breach in the psychological contract pertaining to promises made, with respect to diversity, they showed lower commitment and higher intentions to leave. The above study also showed the effect of the interaction of procedural justice and the implementation of diversity practices, indicated by organizations on the commitment of employees. Diversity practices as part of the definition of high performing work systems was associated positively with employee productivity and innovation, and negatively with turnover (Amstrong et al., 2008). Coca-Cola India is known for inducting women based sales representatives in their work force. Pepsico, ICICI Bank, IBM, and Microsoft are some of the well-known examples of diversity based talent pool, and emerging diverse competencies, which address the unique needs of the diverse customer base (Ollapally and Bhatnagar, 2009).

Employer Branding and Employer of Choice-targeted Talent Management Strategies

Recently while working on employer branding and employer of choice strategies, Srivastava and Bhatnagar (2010), reported the consequences of the anticipated permanent shortage of a competent workforce, which brought forth a need for a strong talent acquisition strategy. This is possible, after finding out what differentiates the organization from the competitors and then market the unique employment proposition it can offer (Ewing et al., 2002; Keefe, 2007). Employer branding (Ambler and Barrow, 1996) is one such relevant HR strategy in the context of employment, especially in a knowledge based and service economy where competent employees are often in short supply. Where traditional recruitment strategies are short-term, reactive and subject to job openings, employment branding is a long-term strategy designed to maintain a steady flow of skills in the organization. A tight labor market gives highly competent employees many choices (Srivastava and Bhatnagar, 2008), especially in professional, information/knowledge based, technical, and service driven organizations (Ewing et al., 2002). Prospective employees are as particular about choosing the right organization as about choosing the right job (Rynes and Cable, 2003). Hence, organizations are increasingly trying to assess and enhance their attractiveness to prospective applicants (Highhouse et al., 1999), by using employer branding strategies. This has critical consequences for organizations into heavy recruitment (Rynes, 1991) as it leads to the most pressing problem of talent acquisition: of attracting people with the right skill set and competencies, who also fit the need and the culture of the organization (Bhatnagar and Srivastava, 2008). The power of the employer brand has been rightly summed up by Fernon (2008: 50) as

> its ability to deliver organizational success by attracting and retaining the right people, providing an environment in which employees live the brand, improving organizational performance in key business areas of recruitment, retention, engagement and the bottom line and differentiating employers from each other, creating competitive advantage. (Srivastava and Bhatnagar, 2010)

Work Life Balance Integration into Talent Management Strategies

Shankar and Bhatnagar (2010), note that in contemporary times, employees want it all. It is not restricted to one domain of work or life but rather a rich synthesis of the two. "Generations X and Y are keeping the pressure on companies to devise flexible, innovative options that give high-performing employees more choice and control in managing the competing demands of work and family" (Klun 2008). Research in this domain emerged at a time when the number of women entering the labor market grew and resulted in a focus on working mothers and dual earner families. It was found that those with high job involvement tended to have higher work interference with family (Byron, 2005). In Fortune's 100 best companies to work for, each company was ranked on the basis of what it did towards "Work-Life Balance" of its employees. Three aspects within work life were surveyed: job sharing, compressed work week, and telecommuting. The 10 best organizations, which Fortune (2009) quoted, are the ones, where employees feel "encouraged to balance their work and personal life." Future Leave is one work life balance practice that provides employees with the flexibility to address various generational work-life issues and enables Accenture to retain the high performers. Many employers continue to strive to create better work-life Balance in order to:

- Increase employee commitment and engagement
- Improve retention
- Improve mental health and productivity (Gallinsky, 2005; Shankar and Bhatnagar, 2010).

Leskiw and Singh (2007: 454) report "Arrow Electronics in the USA encourages seasoned employees to take a ten-week sabbatical after every seven years of service. This allows other employees to temporarily fill the role and develop their leadership skills."

EMERGING MODEL ROUTING TALENT MANAGEMENT AND ENGAGEMENT STRATEGIES TO THE NEXT ORBIT

The above conceptualization of innovative talent management and engagement practices leads us to the model of research for the Next Orbit. Refer to Figure 7.1 for a depiction of this holistic TM Model based on innovative and customized talent management, engagement, and retention strategies.

FIGURE 7.1: Holistic Talent Management Strategies, Outcomes, and Firm Performance Indicators, Moderated by Changing Psychological Contract

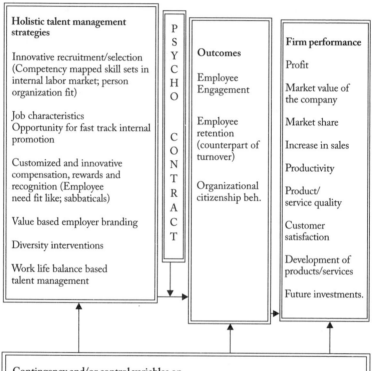

Source: Some part of this model is adapted from Bhatnagar (2009).

CONCLUSION AND IMPLICATIONS

HR leaders and managers need to develop holistic talent management strategies which would lead to employee engagement and retention and will give a "return on talent" (Chowdhury, 2010). There is a need to develop an innovative mindset which will always take into account cost and talent arbitrage (Prahalad and Krishnan, 2008). A need to develop a holistic mindset with integrated talent management strategy which is customized to the unique need fitment criterion of a pivotal talent pool is required to be replicated across all industry sectors. As is evident, a few aggressive industry sectors like IT/ITES, telecomm, banking, pharmaceuticals, and the automobile industry, knowledge and service based firms have these interventions in place. Other sectors like manufacturing, media, dairy, etc., need to develop and replicate these futuristic interventions. When we will witness this kind of replication we will be able to move the talent management practices to the Next Orbit. This is a tall order, but can be fulfilled if HR leadership in India takes charge of the business and talent manage-ment synchronization, in order to yield higher return on investment and an attractive employee value proposition. The focus should be on a industry ready talent pool, rather than compensation driven, capability building race, as reiterated by Bhuj (2007).

REFERENCES

Aggarwal, U., S. Dutta, S. Bhargava, and S. Blake-Beard (2010) "Linking Work Engagement and LMX to Innovative Work Behaviour and Turnover Intentions." Paper presented at Academy of Management Conference, Montreal, August 6–10, 2010.

Ambler, T. and S. Barrow (1996) "The Employer Brand," *Journal of Brand Management*, 4(3): 185–206.

Amstrong, C., P.C. Flood, J.P. Guthrie, W. Liu, S. MacCurtain, and T. Mkamwa (2008) "Should High Performance Work Systems Include Diversity Management Practices?" Paper presented at the Academy of Management Conference.

Bakker, A.B., E. Demerouti, and W.B. Schaufeli (2005) "The Crossover of Burnout and Work Engagement among Working Couples," *Human Relations*, 58: 661–689.

Bhatnagar, J. (2007) "Talent Management Strategy of Employee Engagement of Indian ITES employees: Key to Retention," *Employee Relations*, 29(6): 640–663.

——— (2009) "Exploring Psychological Contract and Employee Engagement in India," in P.S. Budhwar and Jyotsna Bhatnagar (eds), *The Changing Face of People Management in India.* London: Routledge, Taylor and Francis.

Bhatnagar, J. and P. Srivastava (2008) "Strategy for Staffing: Employer Branding and Person-organization Fit," *Indian Journal of Industrial Relations*, 44: 35–48.

Bhatnagar, J. and S. Biswas (2010). "The Mediator Analysis of Psychological Contract: Relationship with Employee Engagement and Organizational Commitment." Paper presented at 11th International Human Resource Management Conference June 9–12, 2010, Aston Business School, Birmingham, UK (*Forthcoming Thunderbird Internal Review*).

Bhuj , M.P. (2007) "ICICI Bank: Diversity in a Global Environment," NHRDN conference presentation, Kolkata.

Biswas, S. and J. Bhatnagar (2010) "P-O Fit and Perceived Organizational Support as Antecedents of Organizational Commitment and Job Satisfaction Mediated by Employee Engagement: Exploring a Latent Variable Model in an Indian Context." *Under review article.*

Branham, L. (2005) "Planning to become an Employer of Choice," *Journal of Organizational Excellence*, 24: 57–68.

Buttner, E.H., K.B. Lowe, and L.B. Harris (2008) "An Assessment of the Effect of Diversity Promise Fulfilment on Minority Professionals Outcomes." Paper presented at the Academy of Management Conference.

Byron, K. (2005) "A Meta-analytic Review of Work–family Conflict and Its Antecedents", *Journal of Vocational Behaviour*, 67: 169–198.

Cappelli, P., H. Singh, J. Singh, and M. Useem (2010) *The India Way*. Boston, Massachusetts: Harvard Business School Press.

Corporate Leadership Council (2006) "The 2006 Employment Value Proposition (EVP) Survey". Unpublished participant report. Corporate Executive Board.

Chowdhury, S. (2010) *The Talent Era*. New Delhi: Pearson.

Devine, F., T. Baum, N. Hearns, and A. Devine (2007) "Cultural Diversity in Hospitality Work: The Northern Ireland Experience," *International Journal of Human Resource Management*, 18(2): 333–349.

Ewing, M.T., L.F. Pitt, N.M. de Bussy, and P. Berthon (2002) "Employment Branding in the Knowledge Economy," *International Journal of Advertising*, 21(1): 3–22.

Fernon, D. (2008) "Maximizing the Power of the Employer Brand," *Admap*, 43: 49–53.

Fortune (2009) http://money.cnn.com/magazine/fortune/bestcompanies/2009/benefits/work_life.html

Gakovich, A. and K. Yardley (2007) "Global Talent Management at HSBC," *Organization Development Journal*, 25(2): 201–205.

Gallinsky, E. (2005) The Changing Workforce in the United States: Making Work "Work" in Today's Economy. "International Research on Work and Family: From Policy to Practice," Inaugural Conference of the International Center of Work and Family, IESE Business School, Barcelona.

Guthridge, M., J.R. McPherson, and W.J. Wolf (2008) "Upgrading Talent: A Downturn Can Give Smart Companies a Chance to Upgrade Their Talent," *The McKinsey Quarterly*, December.

Halbesleben, J.R.B. and A.R. Wheeler (2008) "The Relative Roles of Engagement and Embeddedness in Predicting Job Performance and Intention to Leave," *Work & Stress*, 22: 242–256.

Highhouse, S., M. Zickar, T. Thorsteinson, S. Stierwalt, and J. Slaughter (1999) "Assessing Company Employment Image: An Example in the Fast Food Industry," *Personnel Psychology*, 52: 151–169.

Kahn, W.A. (1990) "Psychological Conditions of Personal Engagement and Disengagement at Work, *Academy of Management Journal*, 33: 692–724.

Keefe, T.J. (2007) "Know Thyself: Developing a Strong Employer Brand," *American Water Works Association Journal*, 99(8): 20–21.

Klun, S. (2008) "Work-Life Balance is a Cross-Generational Concern—And a Key to Retaining High Performers at Accenture," *Global Business and Organizational Excellence*, 27(6): 14–20.

Leskiw, Sheri-Lynne and Parbudyal Singh (2007) "Leadership Development: Learning from Best Practices," *Leadership and Organization Development Journal*, 28(5): 444–464.

Macey, W.H. and B. Schneider (2008) "Engaged in Engagement: We are delighted We Did It," *Industrial and Organizational Psychology*, 1: 76–83.

March, J.G. and H.E. Simon (1958) *Organizations*. New York: Wiley.

Nayar, V. (2010) *Employees First, Customers Second: Turning Conventional Management Upside Down*. Boston, USA: Harvard Business School Press.

Ollapally, A. and J. Bhatnagar (2009) "Holistic Approach to Diversity Management: HR Implications," *Indian Journal of Industrial Relations*, 44(3): 454.

Prahalad, C.K. and M.S. Krishnan (2008) *The New Age of Innovation: Driving Co-created Value Through Global Networks.* USA: McGraw-Hill.

Puri, M. (2010) *Retaining Talent: IT Companies Line Up Hikes, Economic Times,* http://economictimes.indiatimes.com/news/news-by-industry/jobs/Retaining-talent-Its-the-season-of-hikes/articleshow/6633212.cms (last accessed on September 27, 2010).

Rich, B.L., J.A. Lepine, and E.R. Crawford (2010) "Job Engagement: Antecedents and Effects on Job Performance," *Academy of Management Journal,* 53(3): 617–635.

Robinson, G. and K. Dechant (1997) "Building a Business Case for Diversity," *Academy of Management Executive,* 11(3): 21–31.

Robinson, S.L., M.S. Kraatz, and D.M. Rousseau (1994) "Changing Obligations and the Psychological Contract: A Longitudinal Study," *Academy of Management Journal,* 37: 137–152.

Rynes, S.L. (1991) "Recruitment, Job Choice, and Post-hire Consequences: A Call for New Research Directions," in M.D. Dunnette and L.M. Hough (eds), *Handbook of Industrial and Organizational Psychology,* pp. 399–444. Palo Alto: Consulting Psychologist Press.

Rynes, S.L. and D. Cable (2003) "Recruitment Research in the Twenty-first Century," in W.C. Bouman, D.R. Ilgen, and R.J. Klimoski (eds), *Handbook of Psychology: Industrial and Organizational Psychology,* pp. 55–76. Hobroken, NJ: Wiley.

Saks, A.M. (2006) "Antecedents and Consequences of Employee Engagement," *Journal of Managerial Psychology,* 21: 600–619.

Schaufeli, W.B. and A.B. Bakker (2004) "Job Demands, Job Resources, and Their Relationship with Burnout and Engagement: A Multi-sample Study," *Journal of Organizational Behavior,* 25: 293–315.

Shankar, T. and J. Bhatnagar (2010) "Work Life Balance, Employee Engagement, Emotional Consonance/Dissonance and Turnover Intention," *The Indian Journal of Industrial Relations,* 46(1).

Singh, P., A. Bhandarker, and J. Bhatnagar (2006) "Future of Work: Mastering Change," in P. Singh, J. Bhatnagar, and A. Bhandarker (eds), *A Future of Work.* New Delhi: Excel Books.

Srivastava, P. and J. Bhatnagar (2008) "Talent Acquisition Due Diligence Leading to High Employee Engagement: Case of Motorola India MDB," *Industrial and Commercial Training,* 40(5): 253–260.

Srivastava, P. and J. Bhatnagar (2010) "Employer Brand for Talent Acquisition: An Exploration towards Its Measurement," *Vision,* May.

Ulrich, D., N. Smallwood, and K. Sweetman (2008) Rule 3: Engage Today's Talent: Cardinal Rule for Effective Leadership, in *The Leadership Code : Five Rules to Lead by.* Boston, USA: Harvard Business School Press.

Wefald, A.J. and R.G. Downey (2009) "Job Engagement in Organizations: Incubator Fad, Fashion, or Folderol?" *Journal of Organizational Behavior,* 30: 141–145.

White, M.B. (2000) "Are We There Yet?" *Diversity Factor,* 8(4): 2–6.

Wiley, J.W. (2010a) cited in "Indian cos rank highest in employee engagement: Study." *Economic Times,* September 25, 2010. http://economictimes.indiatimes.com/Corporate-Trends/articleshow/6614097.cms (accessed on September 27, 2010).

——— (2010b) "The Impact of Effective Leadership on Employee Engagement," *Employment Relations Today,* 37(2): 47–52.

8

Bharat Petroleum: Building Capabilities through Competency Modeling

S. Mohan

ROLE BASED COMPETENCIES

In the early 1970s, industrial psychologists and human resource managers were seeking ways to better predict job performance. There was significant evidence to show that personality testing was very poor at predicting job performance (about 10 percent success rate was achievable). At the same time, a number of studies showed that traditional academic aptitude, knowledge tests, school grades, and credentials did not predict job performance.

In the year 1973, Dr David C. McClelland, Professor of Psychology at Harvard University, wrote a seminal paper: "Testing for Competence Rather than Intelligence" (McClelland, 1973), which created a stir in the field of industrial psychology. According to his research and findings, traditional academic aptitude and knowledge content tests seldom predicted on-the-job performance. They were however good predictors of scholastic achievement. He went on to argue that the real predictors of outstanding on-the-job performance were a set of underlying personal characteristics or "competencies." Since then, Dr McClelland's findings have been cross-culturally validated by 30 years of global competency research.

Competencies are any measurable characteristics of a person that differentiates level of performance in a given job, role, organization or culture. According to Dr McClelland, competencies were best described in the form of an iceberg, with an individual's knowledge and skills representing the tip of the iceberg and long enduring personal characteristics (like Self-Confidence, Initiative, Empathy, Achievement Orientation, etc.) representing what lay hidden below the surface, the vast, submerged bulk of the iceberg. With the "shelf-life" of knowledge and skills becoming shorter and shorter in today's ever-changing world, the long-enduring characteristics are the ones which have a more substantive impact on how an individual performs on the job. Refer to Figure 8.1 for more details.

FIGURE 8.1: What are Competencies?

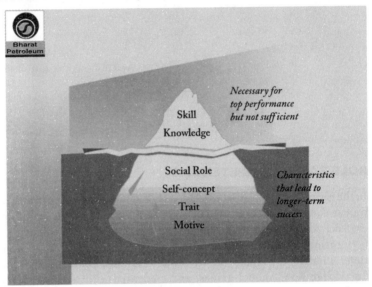

Competency-based performance management processes are becoming more prevalent in many organizations, but they are particularly appropriate for organizations where there are:

- Uncertain environments
- Qualitative/process service jobs
- Self-managed teams
- Developmental jobs
- Changing organizations

COMPETENCY BASED APPROACH IN BPCL

Changes in the market place, or major changes within the organization, often lead to revisiting the business strategy. The 1990s saw rapid changes in economic policies of the Government, paving the way to opening up of the market and the infusion of a greater degree of competition.

The oil and gas sector had been under the Administered Pricing Mechanism (APM) of the Government for around 25 years and the movement towards open market competition called for a critical review of the existing strategies and an urgent need to reorient them to meet the emerging challenge of market determined pricing and competition.

One of the first products to move out of the Administered Pricing Mechanism was "Lubricants." The private players in the market had made a major dent in the market share of the public sector oil companies and the price deregulation therefore was a welcome opportunity to try and regain the market share. It was very soon realized that the freedom to fix prices is an important and necessary requirement to compete but by no means a sufficient condition to be successful. Re-organizing within, to become agile and respond quickly to the ever-changing needs of the customer, was an important step to meet the challenge. While the other products were still under the APM, in the early 1990s, the senior management of the corporation, in consultation with the major stakeholder, the Government of India, decided to initiate the change process to cope with a totally free market competitive situation.

The process of identifying and implementing the changes that were required has been a long and an exciting exercise and it would perhaps need a separate paper to describe how we in BPCL did it.

However some of the key elements of the change process, which have had a positive impact in implementation are quickly summarized as they have been crucial for introducing the Competency Based Performance Management System.

- First, it was recognized that the change that had to come about did not depend on technology or change in statutes or practices of other industry members but was squarely dependent on the change in the mindset of the people within the organization.
- Second, the identification of what needs to change and thereafter also implementing it, it was realized, had to be done by people from within the organization, with expert help where required. In other words, we had to make the changes happen.
- Third, while several proven techniques such as Kaizen, TQM, and many others in their own right have been successful, what would work for BPCL would have to be uniquely identified by us.

Armed with this understanding, the internal processes to meet customer requirements were very critically examined and the end-to-end process from procurement to delivery of the customers' needs was realigned for greater effectiveness. This needed the organization structure to be modified to enable this to happen smoothly. Six Strategic Business Units (SBUs) thus came into existence for Retail, LPG, Aviation, Lubricants, Industrial, and Commercial, which were customer facing, along with one asset based SBU: Refinery.

In the year 2000 we had completed two years in the new structure of SBU's and we had done very well in terms of both top and bottomline growth in each of these Business Units. In shifting from a function-based organization to a process-based organization, it became evident that the competencies which had served us in the past were not the ones which would hold us in good stead in the context of the emerging customer focused initiatives. In the process of restructuring, 140 territories had been formed across the five markets facing SBUs. All the territories had performed well, but about some of them, did better than the rest.

It is at this point in time that we started exploring what we needed to do to sustain this advantage. Amongst other things, competency modeling was identified by us as one of the enabling initiatives to sustain the positive changes which we had brought about.

It is in this context that a study was undertaken to understand the competencies exhibited by outstanding performers in the new structure and develop it into a model to serve as a guide for the aspiring leaders of the future.

ENLISTING PEOPLE

BPCL's transformation into the new SBU structure was supported by the formation of "Lateral Linking Mechanisms." One of the important requirements of the new structure was that the staff working in different business units or entities should decide on matters having enterprise-wide implications, taking a corporate view as against the perspective of the individual units. These objectives were meant to be achieved through the medium of business/governing councils. At the top there were two governing councils viz., Apex Council and Executive Council, to decide on the broad strategy matters. Each SBU and support service teams have their councils to operationalize the strategies at their own level. Separate councils have also been formed in functions like HR, Brand, and Finance, where the members comprise Business Unit Heads and Heads of major support services. These cross-functional councils help to take major decisions in important areas wearing the corporate hat, so that there is a consistency in approach, commitment to execution, as well as, a greater buy-in of the proposal.

The HR team, which conceived of coming up with the Competency Model created the buy-in, by discussing the proposal in the HR Council. It was decided here that robust competency models should be developed for critical positions in the company.

With this mandate we identified the best consultants in the field who could help us develop these models. Concurrently, key personnel were also identified in each of the business/entities who would be able to provide a perspective of the business in the market context and the focus that is expected of the critical jobs.

A working group of interested staff was also identified, as to who would work with the consultants to ensure transfer of learning so that in the future competency modeling could be done in-house.

A SNAPSHOT OFF THE PROCESS ADOPTED

To begin with, competency modeling is of one of the most critical jobs in the corporation, viz., a Territory Manager is taken up. A Territory Manager manages a fairly self-contained unit and is focused on a particular customer group.

The process of competency modeling was initiated by holding a strategy clarification and a culture survey workshop with the Apex, Business and major Entity Heads. Subsequently, meetings were held with representatives and Business Heads of each SBU to identify their strategies, challenges, and what type of role they foresaw their Territory Managers performing.

The next key step was to identify a sample of outstanding Territory Managers from each of the SBUs who could be interviewed using a technique called Behavioural Event Interview (BEI). In addition to these, a set of average performers in these roles were identified to provide a base reference. The trained consultants conducted these interviews. Each of these interviews were recorded with the permission of the interviewee and later transcribed. These transcripts were sent to expert coders' to identify the competencies demonstrated by these interviewees.

Finally, all the data was pooled in and analyzed in a "Concept Formation" workshop which was attended by the working group from BPCL, facilitated by the consultants. The findings, thereafter, were put together to develop the Straw Competency Model for Territory Managers.

Subsequent validation workshops were held with CMD, Directors, and Business Unit Heads and based on their feedback, the final model was developed. A "Competency Development Guide Book" was prepared consisting of the 15 competencies placed in three clusters. Each competency has been explained using live behaviour examples and tips to develop each competency.

The findings were communicated to the entire community of around 140 Territory Managers and their endorsement to the findings were sought. Also invited to attend this meeting of the 140 Territory Managers were their bosses, viz., the Regional Managers, and the HR representatives from the Business Units.

A peer level evaluation was done, to validate the findings of the competency model and to develop a profile of each Territory Manager in addition to evaluation by the Line Manager. All the Territory Managers were requested to fill out a self-evaluation questionnaire and nominate three peers who could be approached to provide input on their behavior. Feedback was also taken from their bosses, the Regional Managers. Consolidated data generated from these was now available was a database to begin a developmental exercise in respect of each of the Territory Managers.

COMPETENCIES IDENTIFIED

Competency Model illustrates the point that outstanding Territory Managers in BPCL always look for opportunities to do things differently, be it in thought or action. There is always this urge to "go against the tide," to break away from normal and take novel and positive steps to bring success to the SBU and the larger organization.

The research done in BPCL shows that an outstanding TM demonstrates an array of behaviors consistently over a period of time and across tasks in comparison to others similarly placed. These behaviors have underlying themes, which seem to cluster into three areas: Personal Mastery, Breakthrough Performance, and Passion for Customer. The competencies within each cluster are shown in Table 8.1.

There are tipping points ranging from 1 (lowest) to 5 (highest) identified for each competency and indicated as Level 1 (L1), Level 2 (L2), ..., Level 5 (L5) which distinguishes the outstanding performer from the average. He however does not need to have all the competencies above the tipping point to be outstanding. Several combinations of the competencies with

TABLE 8.1: Territory Manager Competency Clusters

Sr. no.	Personal mastery	Sr. no.	Breakthrough performance	Sr. no.	Passion for customer
1.	Self-confidence	7.	Driving results	11.	Focusing on customers
2.	Taking charge	8.	Thinking analytically	12.	Initiative
3.	Tuning into self	9.	Thinking conceptually	13.	Information seeking
4.	Integrity	10.	Influencing others	14.	Understanding others
5.	Coaching			15.	Networking
6.	Team effectiveness and collaboration				

TABLE 8.2: Different Ways to be Outstanding

Sr. no.	Different ways to be outstanding		
1.	Breakthrough Performance Driving Results (L4)	Must have	☑
2.	Thinking Analytically (L3) Influencing Others (L3)	Either	☑ ☐
3.	Passion for Customer Focusing on Customers (L3)	Must have	☑
4.	Initiative (L1) Information Seeking (L3)	Either	☑ ☐
5.	Personal Mastery Self-confidence (L4) Taking Charge (L5)	Either	☑ ☐

a few from each of the cluster are sufficient to lead to being outstanding as depicted in Table 8.2.

A brief description of each of the competencies is as follows:

Self-confidence

It is a belief in one's own capability to accomplish a task and select an effective approach to a task or problem. This includes confidence in one's own ability as expressed in increasingly challenging circumstances and confidence in one's decisions or opinions.

Taking Charge

Implies the intent to hold people accountable to clear standards and agreed performance targets. It means using one's position or one's personality appropriately and effectively with the long-term good of the organization in mind. It includes a theme of "telling people what to do."

Tuning into Self

It means the ability to understand ones own emotions, recognize their impact on one's performance, and the surrounding environment having a "gut" sense. The "environment" refers to the people that the Territory Manager comes into contact within the course of work. This knowledge is used to inspire and motivate others as well as one to strive to achieve to make good of an unpleasant situation.

Integrity

Acting in a way that is consistent with what one says is important; that is one's behavior is consistent with one's values (values may come from business, society, or personal moral code).

Coaching

Coaching involves a genuine intent to foster the long-term learning or development of others. Its focus is on the developmental intent and effect rather than on a formal role of training.

Team Effectiveness and Collaboration

It implies the intention to work cooperatively with others, to be a part of the team as well as to lead it, as opposed to working separately using explicit "control and command" structures. The "team" here refers to the Territory Team at the field level.

Driving Results

It means having a concern for working well or for surpassing a standard of excellence. The standard may be one's own past performance (striving for improvement); an objective measure (results orientation); outperforming others (competitiveness); challenging goals set or even what anyone has ever done (innovation).

Thinking Analytically

Thinking analytically means understanding a situation, issue, problem, etc., by breaking it into smaller pieces or tracing the implications of a situation in a step-by-step way. Thinking analytically includes organizing the part of a problem, situation, etc., in a systematic way, making systematic comparisons of different features or aspects, setting priorities on a rational basis, and identifying time sequences, causal relationships or if–then relationships.

Thinking Conceptually

It is an ability to identify patterns or connections between situations that are not obviously related and to identify key or underlying issues in complex situations. It includes using creative, conceptual or inductive reasoning.

Influencing Others

Implies an intention to persuade, convince, influence, or impress others (individuals or groups) in order to get them to go along with or to support the speaker's agenda. The "key" is: understanding others, since influencing others is based on the desire to have a specific impact or effect on others where the person has his/her own agenda, a specific type of impression to make or a course of action that he/she wants the others to adopt.

Focus on Customers

This means focusing one's efforts on discovering and meeting the customer or client's needs. The "customer" in the BPCL context refers to final customers, distributors, dealers, internal "customers" or "clients."

Initiative

Initiative means the identification of a problem, obstacle or opportunity and taking action in light of this identification to address current or future problems or opportunities. Initiative should be seen in the context of proactively doing things and not simply thinking of future actions. The time frame of this scale moves from addressing current situations to acting on future opportunities or problems.

Information Seeking

This means getting driven by an underlying curiosity and desires to know more about things, people or issues. It may include pressing for exact information; resolution of discrepancies by asking a series of questions or a less focused environmental scanning for potential opportunities or miscellaneous information that may be of future use.

Understanding Others

It is the ability to hear accurately and understand unspoken or partly expressed thoughts, feelings, and concern of others. This understanding of others may at times result in a certain degree of respect for others point of view.

Networking

The ability to understand and learn the power relationships in one's own organization and in other organizations, this includes the ability to identify who the real decision-makers are as well as the individuals who can influence them. It also involves building and nurturing relationships with networks of people who may be able to assist in reaching business goals.

TRANSFERENCE OF LEARNING

Subsequently, the working group with hand holding from the consultants has created competency models for Location Heads, frontline staff in Sales, Operations, and Engineering. The consultants have also developed competency models for leadership positions such as Business Unit/Entity Heads and Regional Managers. We have also developed generic competencies for roles not covered by any of the aforesaid specific models.

The process of transference of knowledge from the consultant to the company has been effective, and we now have a dedicated band of staff members fully capable of developing Competency Models for any new positions that emerge.

WHERE DO WE GO FROM HERE?

The Competency Model is an important element in the HR lexicon. Success of competency based approach will be evident only when necessary changes are made in other HR processes. Three areas, which warranted change, were:

- monitoring of the competencies by bringing about corresponding changes in the Performance Management System;
- changes needed in the Performance Management System, incorporating the critical competencies, have already been done;
- reorientation of Training and Development to cater to competencies now identified.

Based on the competency models that have been developed, staff are being profiled by our trained internal people. Developmental plans for each one of them are also being chalked out. The corporate Learning Center is drawing up its calendar taking cognizance of the emerging competency based training needs.

WHAT ARE THE TAKEAWAYS FROM OUR EXPERIENCE?

- Competency by itself, while very important, cannot be a stand-alone initiative. It would have to be a part of a larger strategy aimed at moving towards a better fit between job and individual, and a performance focus. Competency models produce a great competitive advantage when they are part of the delivery of the business strategy. A company which wants to increase its market share by getting more from its current employees and hiring the best in the outside market will gain a great deal in bottomline savings from an accurately defined model of superior performance. This review of strategic direction and its effects on the business area concerned is a prerequisite to competency modeling.

- Any initiative needs a buy-in, and this calls for a commitment to a consultative process, and putting every forum available to achieve this participation. This again, as would be realized, cannot be independently transplanted into an organization, but has to be a part of the culture of the organization.
- Third, the involvement of the top and senior management is a must for the initiative to take root in the organization.
- And finally, as stated in the beginning of this paper, there has to be a sound business case for the initiative, and one which unequivocally has to be established right in the beginning.

REFERENCES

Hartle, Franklin (1997) *Transforming the Performance Management Process*. London: Kogan Page.

Hay/McBer (1997) *People and Competencies: The Route to Competitive Advantage*. London: Kogan Page.

McClelland, David (1973) "Testing for Competency Rather than Intelligence," *American Psychologist*, 28(1): 1–14.

Spencer, Lyle M. and Signe Spencer (1993) *Competence at Work: Models for Superior Performance*. New York: Wiley.

9

Architectural Innovation and SAIL's Strategic Response

Shubhabrata Basu

INTRODUCTION

The present work draws its inspiration from the seminal work on Architectural Innovation by Henderson and Clark (1990). While revisiting that work we felt that contextuality may have overtly influenced the concept development. To elaborate, the semi-conductor photolithographic alignment equipment industry was characterized by small players. This meant that the players were not characterized by adequate resources to sustain successive rounds of creative destruction (Schumpeter, 1950). Thus financial resource constraints, leading to inadequate R&D manpower, more than organizational inertia, may have forced firms to conform to dominant design (Utterback and Abernathy, 1975).

Second, the industry chosen, operated under a dynamic environment with four waves of architectural innovations hitting it in about two decades. These observations have serious implications. It raises questions about the dominance of dominant design and the sustainability and competitive advantages likely to be derived from architectural innovations. Put differently, if the entire reconfiguration exercise provides neither sustainability nor competitive advantages, then *probably*, as a concept, it is strategically not appealing.

Finally, we have reservations on the extendibility of the concept of architectural knowledge into the domain of large incumbent firms. We feel, the assumption, that large incumbent firms cannot respond by Architectural Innovation (or find it difficult to do so), is a strong one. In our opinion, the empirical evidences showing the path dependence of large firms are more of an advantage than not. Path dependence lends focus both holistically as well as at the component level. Both literature and practice provide evidences of large incumbent firms choosing and implementing radical (Chandy and Tellis, 1998) as well as incremental innovations. In all fairness, the beauty of the concept lies in its abstraction to the systems and processes impeding the recognition of Architectural Innovation.

Having said so, we face the following questions. If incumbent firms can occupy the two extremities of the innovation continuum, will the position of Architectural Innovation remain vacant? Leaving apart incremental-ism, incumbent firms decisive enough to cannibalize their own successful products, do exhibit radical innovation (Chandy and Tellis, 1998). Then by deduction, firms not enamored by their historical success can and should also exhibit traits of Architectural Innovation without much difficulty.

Of greater significance are the questions—what factor(s) determine the preference, of different types of innovation in general and Architectural Innovation in particular, by incumbents, if at all? Thus our agenda is to investigate, whether large incumbent firms facing changes in technol-ogy and or in competitive conditions (i.e., an environmental shift) can respond through Architectural Innovations. We restrict and differentiate our investigation to process innovations in its architectural sense. We draw legitimacy from the assertion of Henderson and Clark (1990) on its extendability to process domains.

The context of our search is the Indian State Owned Enterprise (SOE), the sample being Steel Authority of India Limited (SAIL). The industry is a relatively matured and stable one as opposed to the photolithographic industry. The firm is the biggest steel producer in the Indian steel market. And finally the firm, being an SOE, should have more than its fair share of system and process inertias impeding a quick response.

We have adopted the case method as it affords thick description (Geertz, 1973; Yin, 1994). SAIL had faced changes in competitive con-ditions and consequently, environmental shifts following the economic liberalization of India in 1991.

The remainder of the paper is arranged in the following order. In the next section, we define innovation and undertake an extensive literature review to classify the different types of innovations and their character-istics and implication. This we do to ensure legitimacy and consistency to what we set out to achieve. We also put forth a set of propositions to validate our research agenda. In the following section we present our case and the evidences it furnishes. Finally, we present a framework abstracted from empirics along with and conclusion.

GENERALIZING INNOVATION CHARACTERISTICS

The literature on defining innovation is too divergent to speak the least. Myriad numbers of author have attempted to define the same beginning with Schumpeter (1934). Using a chronology, others who have attempted the same include, Rowe and Boise (1974), Rogers (1983), Dewar and

Dutton (1986), Urabe (1988), Utterback (1994), Amabile et al. (1996), Afuah (1998), Fischer (2001), Garcia and Calantone (2002), McDermott and O'Connor (2002), Luecke and Katz (2003), Pedersen and Dalum (2004), Davila et al. (2006), and Mckeown (2008). The list is certainly not exhaustive and leaves out stalwarts like Nelson and Winter (1977), Christensen (1997), Fagerberg (2004), and von Hippel (2005).

However, there are points of convergence in all these definitions namely, some concepts of *novelty*, some prospects of *commercialization* and an intension to *implement* it. Thus, an idea or a concept which exists without any commercial implications (in product or services) does not constitute innovation. For the purpose of this paper however, we intend to adopt the definition as proposed by Afuah (1998) that captures innovation from three dimensions: *technological, market* and *administrative or organizational.* To him innovation is new knowledge captured or incorporated in products, processes, and services.

To substantiate, technological innovation, per se, constitutes of knowledge of the whole as well as the parts of the deliverables. In other words, it is the knowledge that goes to the components, the linkages amongst the components as well as the processes and techniques that go into their making into a product, service or a process. Thus, technological innovation can be decomposed in terms of its two subsets, namely product or service innovation and process innovation. Product or service innovation deals with introduction of new products or services. Process innovation concerns introduction of new elements into the line of operation like input materials, task specifications, work and information flow mechanisms and equipments used (Afuah, 1998). In a sense, process innovation precedes product innovation although introduction of one is not necessarily contingent upon the other in broader sense. The outcome of both is aimed at satiating the need of some existing or new market.

Market innovation can be broadly segregated into two—that happening within the firm boundary and outside in the environment. Market innovations within the firm boundary are captured in the products, their applications and distribution channels to deliver the same. In the environment, the market innovation embodies appropriate knowledge about customer expectations, preferences, needs, and wants (Afuah, 1998). The central tenet is the knowledge on demand and acceptability of the new deliverables through improving their components and mix. The Frascati Manual (2004) specifies that market innovation concerns marketing of new products and covers activities in connection with the launching of a new product. These activities may include market tests, adaptation of the product for different markets and launch advertising, but exclude the building of distribution networks for market innovations.

Administrative innovation deals with innovations in the firm structure and administrative process and relates to strategy, structure, systems (including process), and people.

The generic classification of innovation as proposed by Afuah (1998) is adopted and presented in Table 9.1.

TABLE 9.1: A Summary of Innovation Classification

Technological	Market	Administrative
Process	Products (inside)	Strategy
Product	Applications (inside)	Structure
Service	Distribution channels (inside)	Systems
	Market testing, product adaptation, launch advertising (midway)	Internal process
	Customer expectations and preferences (outside)	People
	Customer needs and wants (outside)	

Afuah's chief contribution lies in establishing the linkages between innovations at the technological as well as those at the market level, conditioned by the changes at the administrative level of the firm. It may be noted that a number of authors have combined technology and market perspectives in their development of theoretical models of innovation. Four influential models, by Abernathy and Clark (1985), Henderson and Clark (1990), Tushman et al. (1997), and Chandy and Tellis (1998) are briefly used to explain the different types of innovations that have evolved based on the technology-market paradigm.

The Abernathy and Clark (1985) model focuses on the interactions of the firm's technological knowledge and capabilities with that of its market acceptability. In fact, it is an optimistic model for the firm. It stresses that firm's market related knowledge can come to its rescue even when it faces technological obsolescence at the product/service level. From the market–technology interaction, they have derived four types of innovations namely, Regular Innovations, Niche Innovations, Revolutionary Innovation and Architectural Innovations

The second model proposed by Henderson and Clark (1990) sharpens the focus and attempt to answer, why firms may face technological obsolescence in the first place. They focus on the component part of the technology and come to the conclusion that besides technology, market linkages and component level linkages also affect innovations. The changes in the component level linkage affect the architecture of the product which they termed as architectural innovation. The combination of component and architectural knowledge produces four types of innovation namely Incremental, Radical, Modular, and Architectural.

The third model by Tushman et al. (1997) is a successor to Abernathy and Clark's model (1985) that differentiates itself by suggesting opportunism in place of optimism. Thus Tushman's model suggests firms to wake up or evolve to the possibility of newer markets by changing their technological capabilities. They too have suggested four types of innovation namely Architectural, Incremental, Major Product or Service Innovations, and Major Process Innovations. The authors also came up with a fifth type of innovation which strengthens the evolution process and which they term as Generational Innovation that caters to changing market and technology.

The fourth model by Chandy and Tellis (1998) is in line with Henderson and Clark (1990) to the extent that both investigate the causes of success or failure in the face of a particular type of innovation. For Chandy and Tellis, the question was why some incumbents are more successful in bringing radical innovations than other. In the process of looking into the internal systems of the firm, they too have come to four types of innovation namely, Incremental, Market breakthrough, Technological breakthrough and Radical Innovation. The four models are collated and represented in Table 9.2 and are adopted from Popadiuk and Choo (2006) that is marked by its parsimony in presentation.

It is evident that the classifications of innovation are done in terms of both product and process besides market and technology. However, there is a predominance of product level innovation than process. Also, apparently, process level innovations leading to new market entries have remained under explored. Another emergent aspect is the apparent existence of a continuum with incremental and radical innovation occupying the poles. The foundations of the continuum are the technology and market impact factors.

STRATEGIC IMPORTANCE OF ARCHITECTURAL INNOVATION

Of the various types of innovation stated above, architectural innovation perhaps holds more promise than the others. Some of the reasons being familiarity with the concepts captured in the components, markets that they cater to and not to forget the investments involved. Firm's research resources involved in architectural innovation, intuitively should be less than that involved in radical innovation. Besides, the outcome of architectural innovation opens the market for new entrants (Henderson and Clark, 1990). It is thus pertinent to revisit the concept of architectural innovation to make it our point of departure.

TABLE 9.2: Evolving Models of Innovation

(1) Abernathy and Clark Model (1985)

Market knowledge	*Technical capabilities*	
	Preserved	*Destroyed*
Preserved	Regular Innovation	Revolutionary Innovation
Destroyed	Niche Innovation	Architectural Innovation

(2) Henderson and Clark Model (1990)

Component knowledge	*Architectural knowledge*	
	Enhanced	*Destroyed*
Enhanced	Incremental Innovation	Architectural Innovation
Destroyed	Modular Innovation	Radical Innovation

(3) Tushman et al. Model (1997)

Market	*Technology (R&D)*	
	Incremental	*Radical*
New	Architectural Innovation	Major Product, Service Innovation
Existing	Incremental—Product Process, Service	Major Process Innovation

(4) Chandy and Tellis Model (1998)

Newness of Technology	*Customer need fulfillment per dollar*	
	Low	*High*
Low	Incremental Innovation	Market Breakthrough
High	Technological Breakthrough	Radical Innovation

Abernathy and Clark (1985) conceptualized architectural innovation as new technology that departs from the established systems of production and in turn opens up new linkages to the markets and users. Innovation of this sort defines the basic configuration of products and processes and establishes the technical and marketing agendas that would guide subsequent developments. Abernathy and Clark extract three themes from the architectural pattern of innovation namely, breaking the grip of the prior industries on the technological structure of the new industry. Second, such innovations are durable and finally, the role of science is not overarching, rather other peripheral processes contribute to the development of this type of innovation. Architectural innovation destroys existing markets and technical capabilities.

Henderson and Clark (1990) refined architectural innovation and embedded it in the components that go into the making of the product. To them, the architectural aspect lies in the arrangement of the components and the linkages that exist due to the existing configuration. Architectural innovation happens when there is a reconfiguration of the existing components leading to a new product. The existing product architectural knowledge is rendered obsolete and new stream of knowledge emerges from the reconfiguration. Another winner in the process is the enhanced knowledge about the components themselves, specifically that which is an outcome of the reconfiguration process.

Tushman et al. (1997) described architectural innovation as one where the technological contribution is incremental while market contribution is substantial and novel.

In developing the concept of architectural innovation, the authors have convergence on certain parameters Enabling (E) or Inhibiting (I) the process. They are enumerated as follows:

Enablers

1. Focus on the importance of the parts rather than the whole.
2. Transformation of technological concepts into commercial utility by capturing them within the components and arranging the same into the commercial deliverables.
3. The limited conceptual novelty extended at the component level in architectural innovation.
4. The willingness, on the part of some, to experiment with component configurations and in the process discovering newer linkages.
5. The new linkages established due to component reconfiguration leads to newer market opportunities.

6. The rearrangement of the parts affecting the whole broadens the horizon of the concept's potentials and enhances component knowledge.
7. The relative difficulty in identifying an architectural innovation (using the same components) by incumbents due to their path dependence and information filters.

Inhibitors

1. Incumbents using the older configuration (the dominant design) are surprised by the new entrants who render the market knowledge of the incumbents obsolete.
2. The optimal arrangement of the components agreed upon by the incumbents constituting the dominant design. The emergence of the dominant design through iterative stages (Utterback and Abernathy, 1975; Clark, 1985).
3. Firm's reluctance to tamper with the arrangement of components (product architecture).
4. Firm's efforts to optimize at the component level in an effort—either to reduce cost or add incremental values—to prevent commoditization of products. This is the basic characteristic of incremental innovation.
5. The level of comfort settling down within the organizational structures and processes once the dominant design has emerged and incremental innovation has started.

The central tenet of architectural innovation is that of reconfiguration and integration, of coordination and combination, a sentiment that has found reflection in dynamic capabilities framework (Teece et al., 1997). Thus Henderson and Clark (1990) provided an answer as to why some firms, un-encumbered by existing routines, could affect minor systems level changes that have profound industry level impacts. Moreover, the concept of architectural innovation, though operationalized at the product level is extendable to process as well. In a sense, architectural innovation anticipated the advent of the concept of disruptive innovation of Christensen (1997).

Point of Departure and Propositions

Architectural innovation conveys the feeling of an easy ticket for new entrants. It probably assumes that the key concept(s) embedded in the components is an open source—to be seen and deciphered at will by the uninitiated new entrants. Alternatively, the entry barriers for the new entrants are low. Component and architectural knowledge are also assumed to be homogenized along the length and breadth of the incumbent's structure. This probably is an overstatement. While rationalization of ideas and optimization of firm resources do happen within the firm, yet resource heterogeneity (Barney, 1991) is also an established fact. Whereas Henderson (1993) found that incumbents faced with industry wide disruption failed to respond, counter views also exist. Chandy and Tellis (2000), for example, found that large incumbent firms are equally adept to radical innovations provided they are willing to cannibalize their successful products. In short, the game of creative destruction of Schumpeter, sustains the incumbent.

We propose to further this argument and say that, if incumbent firms are successful in radical innovations, then there should also exist, cases for architectural innovations. Firms that are successful in radical innovations are characterized by a willingness to learn, unlearn, and relearn. This conspicuously is a function of decision trade-off. One may argue that the very channels, filters and strategies that impede the possibility of alternative architectures, are actually optimization tools meant to maximize returns from the dominant design. One may even argue that resource rich incumbents faced with architectural innovations might have actually responded through radical innovation that did not fructify.

In view of the above, we propose the following:

Proposition 1: Large incumbent firms faced with environmental discontinuity resort to Architectural Innovation as one of the preferred strategic responses.

Proposition 2: The choice of innovation type depends, interalia, on the Executive Response and the available Organizational Slacks.

Proposition 3: The Executive response is a function and in turn affects of the Organizational Slacks within the firm.

We investigate the validity of these propositions in light of the evidences from SAIL.

THE CASE ON SAIL

SAIL is a state owned enterprise of the Central Government of India (GOI), with the President of India holding over 86 percent of the share on behalf of the nation. It came up to mitigate market failure and bridge the technological gap for a newly independent nation. The firm consists of four integrated steel plants besides three specialized steel plants and a few subsidiaries that produce steel using the traditional blast furnace route. Process diagrams of three integrated steel plants are provided in Appendix 9.1. The integrated steel plants came up in the late 1950s and early 1960s. They were considered priority technological projects under a socialist regime and were built with foreign collaboration using Blast Furnace (BF) and Basic Oxygen Furnace (BOF) route.

Subsequently, its technological priorities declined and became sources of employment generation rather than mitigating market failures. The resultant excess manpower ate away funds meant for modernization and for over 30 years no major modernization activities took place. Of the four integrated plants, only one remained profitable which some how kept the corporate balance sheet from sinking to red. However, following the balance of payment crisis and the subsequent conditional bail out by the International Monetary Fund, the Government liberalized the economy and de-licensed the steel sector. This change in the environment had two pronged effects. On the one hand, it allowed the entrance of private players (Indians) and on the other hand it stopped the subsidy provided to the SOEs.

The first action gave rise to two types of new entrants. In came the large private integrated players who would use the Direct Reduction (DR) and Corex Technology as opposed to the BF-BOF route. The second type of entrants was the sub million ton mini steel plants that used the induction furnace route to produce steel. Close to the heel of the new entrants came the worst ever global recession in steel industry augmented by cheap imports from CIS countries flooding the domestic market. To top it all, the only other incumbent in the sector, a private corporate house decided to enter the value added segment by commissioning an ultra modern and cost efficient cold rolling mill (CRM). When completed, this incumbent with its newly commissioned CRM would be the lowest cost steel producer, globally.

The second act meant that the Government was forced to end the operating subsidies for the SOEs including the SAIL. With only one plant making profit and others in red, the overall corporate financial performance took a serious hit. Modernization plans in the mid-1990s added high interest debt to the capital structure. The firm sank of red between 1998 and 2003. SAIL encumbered with obsolete technology and consequently high cost of production and low financial slacks was threatened with exclusion from the industry.

The Nature of Technological Change of the New Entrants

Let us stop a while and take a stock of the technological changes introduced by the competitors. The dominant process design that emerged in the steel industry post World War II was the BF-BOF route. Here lumps of iron ore, calcite flux and coking coal were charged inside the blast furnace and molten iron was taken out either as pig iron and sold or was charged into the BOF (LD Converter). The products from LD converter were the Steel Ingots which were successively reduced in cross section to blooms, billets or rolled into plates. Each item is termed semi finished as well as sellable steel which is sold to secondary rollers. The secondary re-rollers, mostly private entrepreneurs, rolled them in their merchant mills for final products like bars, rods, structural sections or cold rolled coils. Thus, SAIL hardly produced the final value added products.

In India, this arrangement supported an entire ecosystem of steel manufacturers and helped mitigate market failure (because steel making is a capital intensive sector). However, heating was required at every step and there were finishing losses with metals wasted in shaping and finishing. Also, availability of good quality cooking coal is a bottleneck; India through blessed with rich iron ore deposits, lacks cooking coal.

With liberalization, alternative approaches to steel making were brought in by Indian Corporate bodies like DR and Corex Process. In a direct reduction process, iron ore was reduced in rotary kilns to sponge iron with higher iron content of around 93 percent. It is also free from the usage of coke and the sponge iron could be directly fed to BOF. The alternative Corex Process substitutes the usage of coke for coal and thus saves on input costs. The smaller players reduce metal scraps through induction furnace route and directly feed the same to merchant mills via an intermediate section. Besides, they being private enterprises were not into employment generation. Thus, the private players entered with three distinct advantages, a radically new *energy saving technology*, an *optimized manpower*, and *input options* all leading to lower cost of production.

And finally, the long standing incumbent competitor in the industry through a 5-phase modernization ending in June 2000, has emerged as the lowest cost steel producer in world delivering value added end products like cold rolled coils and corrosion resistant bars.

Innovative Response of SAIL

SAIL's response to these changes in competitive conditions was moderated by several issues. Primarily, it is a state owned enterprise with multiplicity of goal objectives. Second, its strategic decisions involving financial investments and work force rationalization had to be vetted by the concerned ministry. The process of evaluating critical proposals like modernization involved inordinate bureaucratic delays. Third, it had started reporting losses from 1998 and, even prior to that, its financial performance was unenviable with only one plant reporting profit. Its reserves and surpluses were grossly inadequate to fund its modernization plans and had to look up to the Government to obtain loans. Fourth, its resource slack was fully scrambled. While it had operational slack out of apparent inefficiencies, financial and customer relation slacks (Voss et al., 2008) were grossly inadequate. However, slacks from human resources were adequate. Its managers historically came from the premier engineering and management institutes. Besides, it has a dedicated management training institute which is supplemented through training programes in the premier management schools of the country. Finally, SAIL was fully path dependent on the existing BF-BOF production process and changing the same was deemed impossible, even to stand scrutiny. Yet, SAIL affected a complete turnaround excellence and had been a dream run ever since. Even, if we *control for the general buoyancy in the steel prices* at the international market, there are clear evidences that it took actions that are thought through and innovative in nature.

PROCESS RECONFIGURATION

The Blast Furnace

As the firm was path dependent on the BF-BOF route, hence any operational improvement must include improvements in the performance including efficiency in these routes. The blast furnace is constrained by volume limitations that determined its rated capacity and indeed the plant capacity. Hence, a production improvement (exhausting efficiency slack) could only happen if the raw material mix is reconfigured. That meant, the volume increase of hot metal has to come at the cost of some other inputs like coke or flux. SAIL did not seek another blast furnace (that would be operating using the same process inefficiencies) or a Direct Reduction Kiln. Instead, it went on to install sintering plants at the back end of all the four Integrated Steel Plants. Sinters being already reduced have higher iron content than hematite ore. This also meant that Coke can be substituted for coal or even coal tar. And finally, quantity of hot metal increased at the expense of discarded gangue.

Subsequently, SAIL have made in house modifications in its blast furnace design so that they are configured to use even LNG (liquefied natural gas) having a higher calorific value. The net result of these process changes have been:

- Increased output of hot metals per charging cycle with reduced slag output.
- Substitution of Coke (imported from Australia) with ordinary coal, coal tar, or even LNG.
- Increased durability of refractory linings of the Blast Furnace.
- Feeding back the Blast Furnace flue gas to facilitate sintering process.
- Reduced overall input cost per ton of hot metal.

The Continuous Casters

Previously, the hot metal fed from the BF was further purified using the LD converters or BOF which was then cast into Ingot moulds for further shaping. Now, the same is predominantly fed into the Continuous Caster (CC) which churns out different sections thus reducing the need of reheating. Though some dedicated ingots are still used for specialized mills like wheels and axles, yet the thrust clearly lies with the CC line. The output of the CC line can also be directly fed to the merchant mills for producing value added products.

The Value Adding Units

Previously, SAIL used to sell semi finished steels, thereby allowing the down stream makers to appropriate rent. The introduction of CC allowed them to directly feed the specialized mills producing value added end products. Thus, products like CRNO and CRCA coils and Corrosion resistant deformed bars and structural sections have given the firm access to the end users directly. Consequently, SAIL itself has entered newer markets which previously were beyond its reach. The process diagram of three Integrated Steel Plants (obtained from Company Website) is presented below along with their modifications (in colored and italics) in Figures 9.1, 9.2, and 9.3.

ADMINISTRATIVE RESPONSES—THE CHIEF EXECUTIVE

SAIL had traditionally promoted insiders into the position of the Corporate Chairman and Managing Director. This practice ensured that the chief executive knew precisely the shortcomings that afflict the firm. Consequently, the top management has taken several decisions that proved vital for the firm's success. Some of these measures are enumerated in the Figures 9.1, 9.2, and 9.3.

FIGURE 9.1: Process Flow Diagram of Bhilai Steel Plant, Chhattisgarh

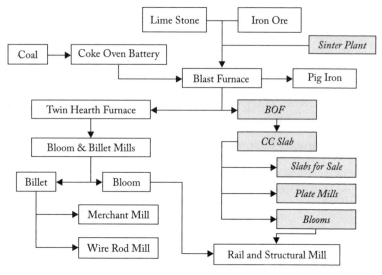

FIGURE 9.2: Process Flow Diagram of Durgapur Steel Plant, West Bengal

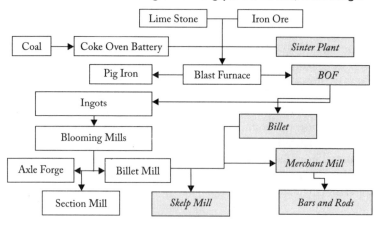

Work Force Rationalization

The executive decision to utilize a crisis scenario and a liberalized economy to reverse historic maladies deserves special considerations. SAIL, through three rounds of Voluntary Retirement Schemes have dispensed off with a third of its work force thus substantially reducing its fixed costs. It is

FIGURE 9.3: Process Flow Diagram of Rourkela Steel Plant, Orissa

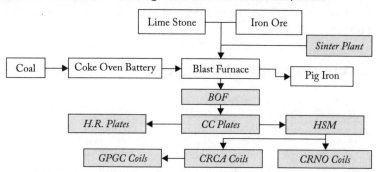

interesting to note that the current work force is a mix of some elderly employees but predominantly younger employees with an average of 10 years of experience (as on 2004). These newer employees are free from indoctrinated minds

Optimizing Organizational Slack

The firm restructured its capital structure by borrowing low interest yielding loans to ease out high interest yielding debts. It also was involved in cost cutting activities and optimizing on dividend pay outs to increase its reserves and surpluses. It also stressed on higher sales realization and improvements in its product mixes and enlarging the composition of value added products.

It laid stress in reorienting its marketing teams to focus and manage the Key Accounts that yields highest sales. To build up its financial muscles, it had even shown preferences to export at the cost of serving the domestic market—a clean shift in focus and recognition of quality outputs.

Goal Reorientation

The firm's goals and objectives are redefined in terms of efficiency and effectiveness parameters as a *quality steel producer*, with focus on *productivity, profitability,* and *customer satisfaction.* To effect this change, the top management has instituted a group of in house technologists to identify and improve productivity yields and eliminate inefficiencies. This exercise has lead the units of the firm to produce beyond their nominal rated capacities.

A frame of reference showing the environmental discontinuities, the executive response, the enablers and outcomes of those responses is provided in Appendix 9.1.

DISCUSSION AND ABSTRACTION

A Case for Process Innovation

The writings of Henderson and Clark (1990) have focused on the architectural configuration at the product level. However, as already stated the concept is extendable to the process level as well. We assert that SAIL responded strategically to environmental shift by effecting architectural innovation at the process level. The same is contingent upon the in situ resource slack of the firm and the executive responses. A proposed framework, supporting our propositions, is presented in Figure 9.4.

FIGURE 9.4: Proposed Frame Work

The Process Architectural Innovation

The Central tenets of Architectural innovation are characterized by reconfiguration and integration along with coordination and combination. The novelty of knowledge captured in the parts (components) is relatively small. The whole that emerges as a result of the reconfiguration exercise of the parts is capable of opening up newer markets. Accordingly, our empirical evidence shows:

Reconfiguration Exercise: The introduction of sintering plant and the continuous caster reconfigured, through minor relocation and restructuring of, the traditional BF-BOF-Ingots-Blooms-Billet layout and is a short cut that scores high on energy and overall cost savings.

Integration and Coordination Exercise: The same processes are seamlessly integrated both at the process level as well as worker knowledge level due to no amount of radical novelty in production process knowledge. Consequently the learning curve effect was seamlessly achieved.

Combination Exercise: While sinter and specially the CC units have been fully integrated, the older lines specific to dedicated processes still functions in conjunction with the newer ones. There had been no reported instance of worker dissatisfaction on account of transfer from one set of processes to another which strengthens the integration issues.

Component Novelty: The sinter plants as well as the Continuous Casters are relatively dated technologies that do not pose any challenge to the technical hand. However, when properly configured, it leads to quantum improvements in the production capacity and cost savings.

New Market Entry: With the CC in place, different sections can be directly made and fed to their respective mills for finished products. This leads to a decrease in semi finished steel production, reheating time and an increase in value added products. Consequently the firm can enter new markets hitherto reserved for the downstream manufacturers at competitive pricing.

THE ANTECEDENTS TO THE PROCESS ARCHITECTURAL INNOVATION

The Executive Directions

The choice of the aforesaid process innovations was contingent up on the executive directions. Stopping the entire production process and setting up a new process, for once, was simply not possible. What ever changes were needed to be done had to be effected without "*colding*" the blast furnace (within the existing process).

The executive directions commenced by setting the house in order. Its decision to cut the unproductive resources including manpower deserves special mention. Its direction to have productivity gains beyond nominal rated capacity, calls for, sufficiently challenging the routine oriented technical hands. The Executive Directions to enter new market including export market, at competitive pricing, lead to process changes and subsequent variable cost reductions.

The Executive Direction to set up in house expertise committee lead to newer process innovations, that enabled input substitution (Coke to LNG). And all these changes took place using the existing organizational slack of the firm.

The Resource Slacks

To fully appreciate the linkages between slack and executive directions, let us turn to the slack position of the firm. The firm had operational and human resource slack but less of financial and customer relations slack.

The immediate productivity increase was done by eliminating the operational inefficiencies and employee overheads. Again the decision to retain some of the older assets like ingot production line was specific to meeting the demands of the Indian Railways. SAIL produced wheel and axle from the ingots and supply the same to their dedicated customers

The firm's financial slack was insufficient to suo moto undertake modernization. Hence external debt capital was required and obtained from GOI which however was too tight.

Borrowing from external capital market, till the time of modernization, was not allowed. The debt which it took was high interest bearing and subsequently (with GOI relaxing capital market borrowing) took further softer loans to prepay the high interest loans. This reduced the fixed overhead even further and reinforced the financial slack.

The executive direction to utilize the HR knowledge slack is evident in setting up sinter plants that reduced the slag and increased the hot metal yield. Consequently, the firm continuously out performed the nominal rated capacity. Also, the rationalized human resources being free from indoctrination were quick to adapt to the process changes. Process changes invariably calls for routine changes (leading to developing new routines) which happens after much muddling through. The executive decision to go ahead with process changes was contingent upon the adaptability of the HR slacks. Slack in this context implies knowledge slack—the difference between the potential capacities of assimilation to actual assimilated knowledge.

Thus firms present or in situ resource slacks influenced executive directions and also shaped the choice of Architectural Innovation at the Process level.

CONCLUSION

The empirical evidence furnished above shows that the ability of firms to affect certain kinds of innovation is contingent upon certain internal factors within the firm. Firms seem to choose the type of innovation they need based upon their strategic perspectives that includes executive directions and resource slacks. Our evidences also suggest that Architectural Innovation can be one of the desired strategic responses of firms faced with changes in competitive conditions. The reason for the same is perhaps the desire of the firm to optimize on its resource position including slack resources and decision trade-offs. This finding also suggests that firms with superior financial capacity *may* follow a different trajectory of innovation but the success of the same depends on the performance by the critical resources, namely the human components both at the worker, as well as, at the managerial level. Put differently, slack positions constraints executive decisions on the emergence of different types of innovations. This in a sense validates why small firms in some typical industries were unable to respond properly to changes initiated by Architectural Innovations. Henderson's assertion that organizational channels and filters are a hindrance to understanding architectural innovation does not find support as the same is subsumed by a superior variable, i.e., the executive direction and its willingness to act, contingent upon the firm's slack position.

Finally, architectural innovation can also happen at the process level; but the concept needs an extension in terms of addition of minor components. This extension however is not sacrilegious as a closer look into the schematics of contact and proximity aligner would reveal—evidently gap setting mechanisms were introduced. These components though technologically insignificant, yet prove quite important in the overall design and perspective. These minor changes happen at the configuration level and strengthen the overall deliverables by enabling cost effective new linkages and new market entries which are the hallmarks of architectural innovation.

APPENDIX 9.1: SAIL's Strategic Response—the Enabling Factors and the Outcome

Response triggers	Executive responses	Enabling and emergent slacks	Outcomes
Environmental discontinuities in • Regulatory policies • Competition • Technology	1. Realignment of existing facilities 2. Relocation of existing and new units in existing layouts 3. Restructuring of production process	Available flexibility in Design and Layout—Operational Slack leading to Process Reconfiguration	Availability of In-Situ Slacks in Layout and Excess HR enabled the Executive to Optimize and Reconfigure the Processes—which is an innovation of the Architectural Type.
	Financial Restructuring: 1. Cost Cutting Activities—interalia through VRS 2. Optimizing between Dividend Payout and Retained Earnings 3. Loan Restructuring	Creation of Financial Slack for future exploitation—this reconfigured the capital Structure of the firm	Architectural Innovation in turn results in creation of other enabling slacks in finance and Customer Relationship which Enhanced SAIL's ability to respond to environmental discontinuities
	Rationalization through three rounds of VRS and retention of 1. Elder Employees with experience and Employees with less than 10 years of work exposure	Optimal Balance between experience and effort—Optimizing Human Resource Slack leading to flexibility in deployment and quick movement along the learning curve	
	Shift in Marketing Focus 1. Stress on Higher Sales Realization 2. Export preference to earn foreign exchanges 3. Stress on Key Account Management	Enhancing existing Customer Relationship and ability to leverage that relationship leads to Customer Relationship Slack	

REFERENCES

Abernathy, W. and J.M. Utterback (1978) "Patterns of Industrial Innovation," *Technology Review*, 14(1): 40–47.

Abernathy, W. and K.B. Clark (1985) "Mapping the Winds of Creative Destruction," *Research Policy*, 14: 3–22.

Afuah, A. (1998) *Innovation Management: Strategies, Implementation, and Profits*. New York: Oxford University Press.

Amabile, T.M., R. Conti, H. Coon, J. Lazenby, and M. Herron (1996) "Assessing the Work Environment for Creativity," *Academy of Management Journal*, 39(5): 1154–1184.

Barney, J. (1991) "Firm Resources and Sustained Competitive Advantage," *Journal of Management*, 17(1): 99–120.

Chandy, R. and G. Tellis (1998) "Organizing for Radical Product Innovation: The Overlooked Role of Willingness to Cannibalize," *Journal of Marketing Research*, 34(4): 474–487.

———. (2000) "The Incumbent's Curse? Incumbency, Size and Radical Product Innovation," *Journal of Marketing*, 64(July): 1–17.

Christensen, C.M. (1997) *The Innovator's Dilemma*. Boston, MA: Harvard Business School Press.

Davila, T., M.J. Epstein, and R. Shelton (2006) *Making Innovation Work: How to Manage It, Measure It, and Profit from It*. Upper Saddle River: Wharton School Publishing.

Dewar, R. and J.E. Dutton (1986) "The Adoption of Radical and Incremental Innovations: An Empirical Analysis," *Management Science*, 32(11): 1422–1433.

Fagerberg, J. (2004) "Innovation: A Guide to the Literature," in Jan Fagerberg, David C. Mowery, and Richard R. Nelson (eds), *The Oxford Handbook of Innovations*, pp. 1–26. Oxford University Press.

Fischer, M.M. (2001) "Innovation, Knowledge Creation and Systems of Innovation," *Annals of Regional Science*, 35: 199–216.

Frascati Manual (2004) A summary of the Frascati manual. Main definitions and conventions for the measurement of research and experimental development (R&D) OCDE/GD(94)84. (Retrieved August 2004, from World Wide Web: http://www. oecd.org/document/6/0,2340,en_2649_34451_33828550_1_1_1_1,00.html)

Garcia, R. and R. Calantone (2002) "A Critical Look at Technological Innovation Typology and Innovativeness Terminology: A Literature Review," *Journal of Product Innovation Management*, 19(2): 110–132.

Geertz, C. (1973) *The Interpretation of Cultures*. New York: Basic.

Henderson, R.M. (1993) "Underinvestment and Incompetence as Responses to Radical Innovation: Evidence from the Photolithographic Alignment Equipment Industry," *RAND Journal of Economics*, 24(2): 248–270.

Henderson, R. M. and K.B. Clark (1990) "Architectural Innovation: The Reconfiguration of Existing Product Technologies and the Failure of Established Firms," *Administrative Science Quarterly*, 35(1): 9–22.

Luecke, R. and R. Katz (2003) *Managing Creativity and Innovation*. Boston, MA: Harvard Business School Press.

McDermott, C.M. and G.C. O'Connor (2002) "Managing Radical Innovation: An Overview of Emergent Strategy Issues," *Journal of Product Innovation Management*, 19(6): 424–438.

Mckeown, M. (2008) *The Truth About Innovation*. Pearson: Financial Times.

Nelson, R. and S. Winter (1977) "In Search of a Useful Theory of Innovation," *Research Policy*, 6(1): 36–76.

Pedersen, C.R. and B. Dalum (2004) "Incremental versus radical change—the case of the digital north Denmark program." International Schumpeter Society Conference, Italy. DRUID/IKE Group, Department of Business Studies, Aalborg University. Retrieved August 2004, from World Wide Web: http://www.schumpeter2004.uni- bocconi. it/papers.php?tric=Pedersen&cric=author&Invia=SEARCH&Invia=SEARCH

Popadiuk, S. and C.W. Choo (2006) "Innovation and Knowledge Creation: How are These Concepts Related?" *International Journal of Information Management*, 26: 302–312.

Rogers, E.M. (1983) *Diffusion of Innovations*. New York: The Free Press.

Rowe, L.A. and W.B. Boise (1974) "Organizational Innovation: Current Research and Evolving Concepts," *Public Administration Review*, 34(3): 284–293.

Schumpeter, J.A. (1934) *The Theory of Economic Development*. Cambridge, MA: Harvard University Press.

———— (1950) *Capitalism, Socialism and Democracy* (3rd Ed.). New York: Harper.

Teece, D. J., G. Pisano, and A. Shuen (1997) "Dynamic Capabilities and Strategic Management," *Strategic Management Journal*, 18: 509–533.

Tushman, M.L. and P. Anderson (2004) *Managing Strategic Innovation and Change: A Collection of Readings* (2nd Ed). New York: Oxford University Press.

Tushman, M.L., P.C. Anderson, and C. O'Reilly (1997) "Technological Cycles, Innovation Streams, and Ambidextrous Organizations: Organizational Renewal Through Innovation Streams and Strategic Change," in M.L. Tushman and P. Anderson (eds), *Managing Strategic Innovation and Change: A Collection of Readings*. New York: Oxford University Press.

Urabe, K. (1988) "Innovation and the Japanese Management System," in K. Urabe, J. Child, and T. Kagono (eds), *Innovation and Management International Comparisons*. Berlin: Walter de Gruyter.

Utterback, J.M. (1994) *Mastering the Dynamics of Innovation: How Companies Can Seize Opportunities in the Face of Technological Change*. Boston, MA: Harvard Business School Press.

Utterback, J.M. and W.J. Abernathy (1975) "A Dynamic Model of Process and Product Innovation," *Omega, The International Journal of Management Science*, 3(6): 639–656.

von Hippel, E. (2005) *Democratizing Innovation*. MIT Press.

Yin, R.K. (1994) *Case Study Research: Design and Methods*. Thousand Oaks, London: Sage Publications.

10

CEO Leadership, Organizational Culture, and Employee Affect Responses at the Workplace

*Asha Bhandarker, Ashita Goswami,
and Kshipra Rustogi*

Northouse (1997) has identified several elements as central to the phenomena of leadership. Leadership is a social influencing process in getting things done through people. Leaders are able to realize their vision with the help of their teams and have to motivate, and inspire them in producing first-rate performance. Thus, leadership involves goal attainment, and teams try to achieve the desired results. It is required because someone has to set the direction and point the way. There is no doubt leadership attributes have an impact on various aspects of organization, e.g., organizational effectiveness, work culture, work environment, and on employees' satisfaction and motivation.

ORGANIZATIONAL CULTURE

It encompasses the values and norms shared by members of a social unit. These values and norms indicate accepted ways of relating to others (Schein, 1990). Schein's (1990) definition is probably the most widely accepted and used definition. He defines organizational culture as: *(a)* a pattern of basic assumptions, *(b)* invented, discovered, or developed by a given group, *(c)* as it learns to cope with its problems of external adaptation and internal integration, *(d)* that has worked well enough to be considered valid and, therefore, *(e)* is to be taught to new members as the *(f)* the correct way to perceive, think, and feel in relation to those problems.

LEADERSHIP AFFECTS ORGANIZATIONAL CULTURE

Schein (1985) considers that one is likely to see a constant interplay between culture and leadership. Leaders create the mechanisms for cultural embedding and reinforcement. Cultural norms arise and change because of what leaders tend to focus their attention on, their reactions to crises, their role modeling, and their recruitment strategies. Schein (1992) observes that organizational culture and leadership are intertwined. He illustrates this inter-connection by looking at the relationship between leadership and culture in the context of the organizational life cycle. Thus, during the process of organizational formation, the founder of a company creates an organization which reflects their values and beliefs. In this sense, the founder creates and shapes the cultural traits of their organization. However, as the organization develops and time passes, the created culture of the organization exerts an influence on the leader and shapes the actions and style of the leader.

Bass (1985) demonstrates the relationship between leadership and culture by examining the impact of different styles of leadership on culture. He argues that transactional leaders tend to operate within the confines and limits of the existing culture, while transformational leaders frequently work towards changing the organizational culture in line with their vision. In the Indian context, Singh and Bhandarkar (1989) extensively studied the role of transformational leadership in building the organizational culture. They found a positive association between the two.

Although Organizational Culture has been one of the most studied concepts in the areas of organization behavior (Denison, 1996; Giberson et al., 2009; Schein, 1985, 1992, 1990), there is a dearth of literature studying the mediating role of organizational culture. The present study attempts to bridge this gap.

HYPOTHESES

CEOs with Excellence Seeker Leadership style raise the bar of performance and continuously move the organization to the next orbit (Singh and Bhandarker, Forthcoming). They are restless, impatient with the status quo and continuously endeavor to move things from best to next. This style of leadership will be significantly positively related to Affective Organizational Commitment of the subordinates across senior and middle levels in the organization. Since a result-focused leader recognizes and encourages high performance, followers are likely to develop a high emotional commitment to the organization and feel a sense of pride in its achievements, continuously looking at raising the bar through new ways of doing things. A study by Bjorn et al. (2009) has shown that affective commitment is related to innovative behavior. Employee commitment to change is important as they play a crucial role in the actual implementation of change. An excellence centric culture emphasizes focus on improvement to build competitiveness. As a result, there is a speedy response to both internal and external demands and openness to new ideas, thereby nurturing innovation and entrepreneurship. Such an organization is result-focused and recognizes performance (Singh and Bhandarker, Forthcoming). Therefore, Excellence Seeker Leadership style will be positively related to Excellence Centric Culture. Research has also shown a positive correlation between rewarding organizational culture and affective commitment (Meyer et al., 2010; Behery, 2009). Therefore, the following hypothesis is formulated.

Hypothesis 1a

Excellence centric cultures mediate the relationship between the Excellence Seeker leadership style and Affective Organizational Commitment of followers.

Leaders with Excellence Seeker Leadership style also have ambitious plans for the organization and a global focus, always looking at pursuing excelling in everything. Consequently, they are demanding, performance-centric, and result-focused (Singh and Bhandarker, Forthcoming). This style will also be related to positive affectivity of subordinates, which reflects generalized well bring, competence, and effective interpersonal engagement (Watson et al., 1988). An excellence centric culture also emphasizes on continuous focus on improvement to build competitiveness and is result-focused, and recognizes performance. Therefore, as stated earlier, the Excellence Seeker Leadership style will be positively related to the Excellence Centric Culture. Hence, the following hypothesis is formulated.

Hypothesis 1b

An excellence centric culture mediates the relationship between the Excellence Seeker leadership style and the Positive Affectivity of followers.

Leaders with a Visionary Strategist Leadership style are both visionary and business strategists. They have the great capability to convert their vision into action, thus, enabling a smooth execution. In this process, they bring creative thinking and there is an entrepreneurial orientation to wealth creation (Singh and Bhandarker, Forthcoming). This leadership will be positively related to Affective Commitment. As this style involves creating and communicating the big vision to employees and continuously reinventing business strategies towards this vision, it will lead to an emotional commitment of employees towards the goals of the organization, aligning them with their personal goals. This style of leadership will also be positively related to positive affectivity. A study by Rubin et al. (2005) has shown that Positive Affectivity was positively related to transformational leadership which involves articulating a vision of the future, setting high expectations etc. This style is similar to the Visionary Strategist one, as they both involve a creative envisioning of the future. An experimenting centric culture is built on values of growth, advancement, and learning. It is an open and risk-taking culture that encourages experimenting with new ideas and approaches, as well as, celebrates the achievements of innovation and novelty. A Visionary Strategist leadership style will be positively related to an Experimenting centric culture since they both involve creative thinking and entrepreneurial approach. As previously stated positive correlation between organizational culture and affective commitment has been found in studies (Meyer et al., 2010; Behery, 2009). A study by Lok and Crawford (2004) found that there is a positive relationship between innovative cultures and organizational commitment. Therefore, the following hypotheses are formulated.

Hypothesis 2a

Experimenting centric culture mediates the relationship between the Visionary Strategist leadership style and the Affective Organizational Commitment of followers.

Hypothesis 2b

Experimenting centric culture mediates the relationship between the Visionary Strategist Leadership style and the Positive Affectivity of followers.

METHOD

Participants

Survey questionnaires were distributed to a total of 425 top and senior executives of five high performing organizations in India, namely Aditya Birla Group, Jindal Steel Works, ICICI Bank, Larsen & Toubro, and Biocon India. Approximately 83 percent of the executives returned the filled questionnaires. This survey was part of a larger study on leadership and organizational building of CEOs in seven successful Indian organizations. The average age of the respondents was around 49.7 years varying from 25 to 74 years; 91 percent respondents were male and 75 percent had post graduate degrees.

Measures

LEADERSHIP INVENTORY

Leadership was measured using the Leadership Inventory by Singh et al. (2010) This inventory was initially developed through focused group discussions conducted upon 175 executives with at least five years of work experience, in various post experience MBA programs conducted at a northern university in India. Based on content analysis of this data (using the grounded theory approach), a pool of 65 items were developed. Each leadership attribute was measured on a 5-point scale ranging from 1 (Least Visible) to 5 (Most Visible). The 65 items were then reduced to 35 based on factor analysis (α = .94). The inventory has six factors: Excellence Seeker (α = .68), Visionary Strategist (α = .78), Enabler (α = .95), Role Model (α = .65), and Direction Setter (α = .75). For the present study only two factors were used: Excellence Seeker and Visionary Strategist (Appendix 10A).

ORGANIZATIONAL CULTURE INVENTOR

Culture was measured by the Work Culture Inventory by Singh et al. (2010). This inventory was initially developed based on an extensive survey of the research literature. The initial pool of 62 items was subsequently administered on a sample of 333 executives. Each item of work place characteristics was also rated on a 5-point likert type scale ranging from 1 (Very Low Extent) to 5 (Very High Extent). It was rated on the basis of the extent to which that particular characteristic is visible according to them, in their organization. Based on content analysis of this data (using the grounded theory approach) 62 items were then reduced to 33 based on factor analysis (α = .94). The inventory has five factors: Goal and Role Clarity (α = .72), Boundary-less Communication (α = .73), Experimenting (α = .80), Excellence Centric (α = .90), and Stakeholder focus (α = .90). For the present study only two factors were used: Excellence Seeker and Visionary Strategist (Appendix 10B).

POSITIVE AFFECTIVITY

Positive affectivity was measured by the Positive Affectivity and Negative affectivity scale by Watson et al. (1988). It had ten items (α = .61). The measures were completed by subordinates who had frequent interactions with the CEOs. It was a 7-point scale ranging from 1 (strongly disagree) to 7 (strongly agree). The participants were required to indicate their general feeling state at work.

AFFECTIVE ORGANIZATIONAL COMMITMENT

This was measured using the affective organizational commitment scale developed by Allen and Meyer (1990). It was completed by subordinates who had frequent interactions with the CEOs. It had ten items (α = .73). It was a 6-point scale ranging from 1 (strongly disagree) to 6 (strongly agree).

Procedure

The data was collected online. Each respondent had filled four instruments: one was about their respective CEO's behavior based on his/her interaction with him, second was regarding the perception of the organizational culture, and the remaining two regarding their affective-level responses to the organization. The sample of participants was selected based on the frequency of opportunity to interact with the CEOs. Level wise they were all from the top and senior levels. The questionnaires were sent to each organization in the year 2008–09 via email.

RESULTS

All our hypotheses regarding the mediating role of organizational culture on the relationship between leadership styles and the criterion variables (i.e., affective organizational commitment and positive affectivity) were tested using the traditional Baron and Kenny (1986) approach. The following regression framework was used *(a)* regression of hypothesized mediator (organizational culture, i.e., excellence centric and experimenting) on the predictor (leadership styles, i.e., excellence seeker and visionary strategist) *(b)* regression of the criterion (affective organizational commitment and positive affectivity) on the hypothesized mediator (organizational culture), and *(c)* regression of the criterion (affective organizational commitment and positive affectivity) on the predictor (leadership styles). Mediating effect of organizational culture was assumed if *(i)* significant links were found between leadership styles and the criterion variables and *(ii)* the relationship between leadership styles and the criterion variables was reduced when the mediator, i.e., organizational culture was introduced into the analysis.

MEDIATING EFFECT OF THE EXCELLENCE CENTRIC CULTURE BETWEEN EXCELLENCE SEEKER LEADERSHIP STYLE AND AFFECTIVE ORGANIZATIONAL COMMITMENT

The correlation analysis (see Table 10.1) revealed that the Excellence Seeker Leadership Style was positively related to affective organizational commitment ($r = .31$, $p < 0.01$) and to excellence centric organizational culture ($r = .50$, $p < 0.01$). An Excellence Centric Organizational Culture was also significantly and positively related to affective organizational commitment ($r = .43$, $p < 0.01$). Multiple regression (Table 10.2) analysis demonstrated that the excellence seeker leadership style was a significant predictor of affective organizational commitment ($\beta = .31$, $p < .001$). When the excellence centric culture was entered into the model in the second step, the excellent seeker continued to remain significant, although the slope decreased ($\beta = .12$, $p = .028$). An excellence centric organizational culture showed significant contribution to affective organizational commitment

TABLE 10.1: Descriptive Statistics and Correlations among Leadership Styles, Organizational Cultures, Affective Commitment, and Positive Affectivity

	M	SD	1	2	3	4	5
1. Positive Affect	42.77	5.67	–				
2. Affective Commitment	52.02	5.85	.48	–			
3. Excellence Seeker	23.43	1.92	.19	.31	–		
4. Visionary Strategist	23.18	2.42	.2	.33	.56	–	
5. Experimenting	19.11	5.99	.19	.23	.17	.25	–
6. Excellence Centric	36.20	5.50	.40	.43	.50	.56	.37

Note: All correlations were significant, $p < 0.01$, $N = 361$.

TABLE 10.2: Hierarchical Regressions: Mediating Effect of Excellence Centric Culture on the Relationship between Excellence Seeker and Affective Commitment

	b	β	t	p	R^2
Step 1					.095*
Excellence Seeker	.94	.31	6.13	.000	
Step 2					.295*
Excellence Seeker	.37	.12	2.21	.028	
Excellence Centric	.40	.37	6.85	.000	

Note: Affective commitment is the dependent variable. $N = 361$. $\Delta R^2 = .200$ for step 2, $p = .000$.
*$p < .001$.

(β = .37, p < .001, ΔR^2= .200). Thus, it appears that an excellence centric organizational culture acts as a partial mediator, indicating that perceived excellence seeker leadership style showed a significant direct effect on organizational affective commitment of subordinates, controlling for the effect of perceived excellence centric culture.

MEDIATING EFFECT OF EXCELLENCE CENTRIC CULTURE BETWEEN EXCELLENCE SEEKER LEADERSHIP STYLE AND POSITIVE AFFECTIVITY

The correlation analysis (Table 10.1) revealed that the excellence seeker leadership style was significantly and positively related to positive affectivity (r = .19, p < 0.01) and to excellence centric organizational culture (r = .50, p < 0.01). Excellence centric organizational culture was also significantly and positively related to positive affectivity(r = .40, p < 0.01). Multiple regression analysis (Table 10.3) demonstrated that excellence seeker leadership style was a significant predictor of positive affectivity (β = .19, p < .001). When the excellence centric culture was entered in the model in the second step, the excellence seeker leadership style became insignificant (β = –.01, p = .877). Excellence centric organizational culture has a significant contribution to affective organizational commitment (β = .41, p < .001, ΔR^2 = .162). Thus, it appears that excellence centric organizational culture acts as a mediator indicating that the effect of perceived excellence seeker leadership style on positive affectivity of subordinates was fully explained by perceived excellence centric culture. This finding was supported in Hypothesis 1(b).

MEDIATING EFFECT OF EXPERIMENTING CENTRIC CULTURE BETWEEN VISIONARY STRATEGIST LEADERSHIP STYLE AND AFFECTIVE ORGANIZATIONAL COMMITMENT

The correlation analysis (Table 10.1) revealed that visionary strategist leadership style was significantly and positively related to affective organizational commitment (r = .33, p < 0.01) and to experimenting centric organizational culture (r = .17, p < 0.01). Experimenting centric organizational culture was also significantly and positively related to affective organizational commitment (r = .23, p < 0.01). Multiple regression (Table 10.4) analysis demonstrated that the visionary strategist leadership style was a significant predictor of affective organizational commitment (β = .33, p < .001). When experimenting centric culture into the model in the second step, visionary

TABLE 10.3: Hierarchical Regression: Mediating Effect of Excellence Centric Culture on the Relationship between Excellence Seeker and Positive Affectivity

	b	β	t	p	R^2
Step 1					.071*
Excellence Seeker	.57	.19	3.76	.000	
Step 2					.162*
Excellence Seeker	−.03	−.01	−.16	.877	
Excellence Centric	.42	.41	7.27	.000	

Note: Positive Affectivity is the dependent variable. N = 361. ΔR^2 = .162 for step 2, p = .000.
*p < .001.

TABLE 10.4: Hierarchical Regressions: Mediating Effect of Experimenting Centric Culture on the Relationship between Visionary Strategist and Affective Commitment

	b	β	t	p	R^2
Step 1					.111*
Visionary Strategist	.80	.33	6.68	.000	
Step 2					.135*
Visionary Strategist	.71	.29	5.78	.000	
Experimenting	.16	.16	3.16	.002	

Note: Affective commitment is the dependent variable. N = 361. ΔR^2 = .135 for step 2, p = .000.
*p < .001.

strategist leadership style remained to be significant, although the slope decreased (β = .29, p = .000). Experimenting centric organizational culture showed a significant contribution to affective organizational commitment (β = .16, p = .002, ΔR^2 = .135). Thus, it appears that experimenting centric organizational culture acts as a partial mediator indicating that the perceived visionary strategist leadership style showed a significant direct effect on organizational affective commitment of subordinates, controlling for the effect of perceived Experimenting centric culture. This finding did not support Hypothesis 2(a).

MEDIATING EFFECT OF EXPERIMENTING CENTRIC CULTURE BETWEEN VISIONARY STRATEGIST LEADERSHIP STYLE AND POSITIVE AFFECTIVITY

The correlation analysis (Table 10.1) revealed that the visionary strategist leadership style was positively related to positive affectivity (r = .27, p < 0.01) and to experimenting centric organizational culture (r = .17, p < 0.01).

Experimenting centric organizational culture was also significantly and positively related to positive affectivity ($r = .19$, $p < 0.01$). Multiple regression analysis (Table 10.5) demonstrated that the visionary strategist leadership style was a significant predictor of positive affectivity ($\beta = .27$, $p < .001$). When the experimenting centric culture was entered into the model in the second step, experimenting centric leadership style remained to be significant, although the slope decreased ($\beta = .23$, $p = .000$). Experimenting centric organizational culture showed a significant contribution to affective organizational commitment ($\beta = .14$, $p = .009$, $\Delta R^2 = .088$). Thus it appears that experimenting centric organizational culture acts as a partial mediator indicating that perceived visionary strategist leadership style showed a significant direct effect on positive affectivity, controlling for the effect of perceived Experimenting centric culture. This finding did not support Hypothesis 2(b).

TABLE 10.5: Hierarchical Regressions: Mediating Effect of Experimenting Centric Culture on the Relationship between Visionary Strategist and Positive Affectivity

	b	β	t	p	R^2
Step 1					.038*
Visionary Strategist	.62	.27	5.22	.000	
Step 2					.088*
Visionary Strategist	.54	.23	4.46	.000	
Experimenting	.13	.14	2.63	.009	

Note: Positive Affectivity is the dependent variable. $N = 361$. $\Delta R^2 = .088$ for step 2, $p = .000$. *$p < .001$.

DISCUSSION

The current study was conducted to test the mediational role of two kinds of Organizational culture, i.e., Excellence Centric and Experimenting. To test mediation, two kinds of relationships were hypothesized. First, subset of the hypothesized relationship was "Excellence centric culture mediates the relationship between the Excellence Seeker leadership style and Affective organizational commitment." Here the excellence centric culture was found to be a partial mediator, which meant after controlling the effects of culture, the excellence seeker leadership style of CEOs showed a significant direct effect on the organizational affective commitment of subordinates. One of the reasons could be that the study has been done on an Indian sample, where the superior-subordinate relation is of paramount importance. As a result, the emotional connectivity is relatively more with the leader than the culture. Brewer and Cheh (2007) have argued that East Asians, who are typically relational collectivists, are more likely to feel committed to specific individuals in organizations and not necessarily the institution they belong to. The second part of the first hypothesis stated that the Excellence centric culture mediates the relationship between the Excellence Seeker leadership style and Positive Affectivity. This was supported. This meant the effect of perceived excellence seeker leadership style of CEOs on positive affectivity of subordinates was fully explained by perceived excellence centric culture. Such a culture is characterized by a speedy response to both external as well as internal demands, openness to new ideas, and recognition of high performance. Thus, it results in a healthy work environment where employees' suggestions and opinions are valued, and they are driven towards continuous personal as well as organizational development. Consequently, such a culture creates enthusiasm, trust, and a drive amongst employees, which are positive affective states.

The first part of the second hypothesis stated "experimenting centric culture mediates the relationship between the visionary strategist leadership style and affective organizational commitment." Here experimenting centric organizational culture was found to be a partial mediator indicating that the perceived visionary strategist leadership style showed a significant direct effect on organizational affective commitment of subordinates. This has brought out the significant and direct role of CEO leadership in inculcating affective commitment of followers. In the Indian context, followers look up to the leader as a "father-figure" (Singh and Bhandarker, 1989, 1997). They have the desire to be mentored and guided by their leader's vision. Thus, the leader becomes one of the primary authority figures whose guidance motivates and gives direction. In the absence of such a mentor, the followers become alienated and emotionally disconnected to the organization as well. The second part of second hypothesis stated "experimenting centric culture mediates the relationship between the Visionary Strategist leadership style and organizational positive affectivity." It was found that the experimenting centric organizational culture acts as a partial mediator indicating that the perceived visionary strategist leadership style showed a significant direct effect on positive affectivity, controlling for the effect of perceived experimenting centric culture. Since a visionary strategic leader has strong inspirational and intellectual power over his followers, his compelling vision arouses positive emotions of interest, pride, and determination amongst them. Some researches have found similar effects of transformational leadership on positive affective states of employees, such that transformational leaders use their strong emotional influences of energy and enthusiasm to arouse emotions in employees that encourage them to achieve organizational vision (Cherulnik et al., 2001; George and Brief, 1992). Therefore, culture as a partial moderator in the second hypothesis shows that CEO leadership has a significant direct effect on both affective commitment and positive affectivity of followers.

BROADER IMPLICATIONS, LIMITATIONS, AND FUTURE RECOMMENDATIONS

From the result section it can be observed that leadership style had a significant direct effect on affective organizational commitment and positive affectivity. These leadership styles are: excellence seeker and visionary strategist. Training programs must focus on building these two types of leadership competencies to enhance positive affective states and commitment in followers. Both Positive Affectivity and Affective Commitment lead to a number of desirable outcomes such as low turnover (Blau et al., 2009; Carmeli and Freund, 2009; Chapman et al., 2009; David and Kopelman, 2009; Pedero, 2009). As positive affectivity denotes a generalized sense of well-being and competence, and effective interpersonal engagement (Watson et al., 1988), employees with high positive affectivity will contribute meaningfully to the organization and will have less interpersonal conflicts with their co-workers. Also incorporating these two leadership competencies to the existing selection procedures may be helpful. Additionally, the effect of perceived excellence seeker leadership style on positive affectivity of subordinates was fully explained by the perceived excellence centric culture, emphasizing the role of building such a performance-driven culture.

A limitation of this study is that the data has been collected from five high performing successful organizations in India. Including organizations with different levels of performance, particularly failing organizations, might provide meaningful insights on the phenomenon under study. Since the study has been on Indian organizations the generalizability of the results is restricted. However, building on culture-specific results pertaining to CEO leadership and culture, cross-cultural comparison can be done through future research.

APPENDICES

Appendix 10A: Leadership

Visionary Strategist
1. Is a strategic thinker.
2. Is innovative and creative.
3. Is entrepreneurial.
4. Is a visionary.
5. Business Strategist (growth, mergers, and acquisitions)

(Continued)

(Appendix 10A Continued)

Excellence Seeker

1. Is demanding and performance-centric.
2. Is result focused.
3. Has ambitious plans for the organization.
4. Pursues excellence in everything.
5. Has a global mind-set.
6. Business Strategist (growth, mergers, and acquisitions)

Note: This is a 5-point scale ranging from 1 (Least Visible) to 5 (Most Visible).

Appendix 10B: Culture

Experimenting Centric Culture

1. Openness and transparency
2. Culture of celebration of achievements and successes
3. Empowerment and Delegation
4. Tolerance of Differences
5. Support for Risk Taking
6. Excellence Centric Culture

Nurturing Innovation

1. Speed of response to external demands and challenges
2. Focus on continuous improvement
3. Speed of response to internal demands
4. Result Orientation
5. Performance Excellence
6. Openness to new ideas
7. Entrepreneurial
8. Focus on building on competitiveness

Note: This is a 5-point likert type scale ranging from 1 (Very Low Extent) to 5 (Very High Extent).

REFERENCES

Allen, N.J. and J.P. Meyer (1990) "The Measurement and Antecedents of Affective, Continuance and Normative Commitment to the Organization," *Journal of Occupational and Organizational Psychology,* 63: 1–8.

Baron, R.M. and D.A. Kenny (1986) "The Moderator and Mediator Variable Distinction in Social Psychological Research: Conceptual, Strategic and Statistical Considerations," *Journal of Personality and Social Psychology,* 51: 1173–1182.

Bass, B.M. (1985) *Leadership and Performance Beyond Expectations.* New York: Free Press.

Behery, M.H. (2009) "Person-Organization Job Fitting and Affective Commitment to the Organization," *Cross Cultural Management: An International Journal,* 16(2): 179–196.

Bjorn, M., S. Ralf, and S. Karlheinz (2009) "Affective Commitment to Change and Innovation Implementation Behavior: The Role of Charismatic Leadership and Employees' Trust in Top Management," *Journal of Change Management,* 9(4): 399–417.

Blau, G., R.S. Pred, T. Daymont, H. Arthur, K. Karen, J. Portwood, S.A. Edelson, K. Crowne, and D.S. Tatum (2009) "Explaining Relationships to Three Types of Occupation

Perceptions-Forced to Stay in Occupation, Voluntary Occupational Withdrawal Intent and Involuntary Occupational Withdrawal," *Journal of Applied Health*, 38(1): 31–38.

Brewer, M. and Y.R. Chen (2007) "When (Who) are Collectives in Collectivism? Toward Conceptual Clarification of Individualism and Collectivism," *Psychological Review*, 114: 133–151.

Carmeli, A. and A. Freund (2009) "Linking Perceived External Prestige and Intentions to Leave the Organization: Mediating Role of Job Satisfaction and Affective Commitment," *Journal of Social Service Research*, 35: 236–250.

Chapman, S.A., B. Gary, R. Pred, and V. Lindler (2009) "Testing for Correlates of Intent to Leave One's Job Versus Intent to Leave One's Occupation Among Cancer Registrars," *Journal of Applied Health*, 38(1): 24–30.

Cherulnik, P.D., K.A. Donley, T.S.R. Wiewel, and S.R. Miller (2001) "Charisma is Contagious, the Effect of Leader's Charisma on Observer's Affect," *Journal of Applied Social Psychology*, 31: 2149–2159.

David, J.P. and R.E. Kopelman (2009) "Comparative Work-family Practice Availability and Employees' Attitudes," *Psychologist-Manager Journal*, 12(2): 79–96.

Denison, D.R. (1996) "What is the Difference between Organizational Culture and Climate? A Native's Point of View on Decade of Paradigm Wars," *Academy of Management Review*, 21(3): 619–654.

George, J.M. and A.P. Brief (1992) "Feeling Good—Doing Good: A Conceptual Analysis of the Mood at Work—Organizational Spontaneity Relationship," *Psychological Bulletin*, 112: 310–329.

Giberson, T.R, C.J. Resick, M.W. Dickson, J.K. Mitchelson, K.R. Randall, and M.A. Clark (2009) "Leadership and Organizational Culture: Linking CEO Characteristics to Cultural Values," *Journal of Business and Psychology*, 24(2): 123–137.

Lok, P. and J. Crawford (2004) "The Effect of Organizational Culture and Leadership Style on Job Satisfaction and Organizational Commitment," *The Journal of Management Development*, 23(4): 321–338.

Meyer J.P. and N.J. Allen (1997) *Commitment in the Workplace*. Thousand Oaks, CA: Sage Publications.

Northouse, P.G. (1997) *Leadership: Theory and Practice*. Thousand Oaks, CA: Sage Publications.

Pedero, N. (2009) "Readiness for Change: Contributions for Employees Level of Individual Change and Turnover Intentions," *Journal of Change Management*, 9(2): 215–231.

Rubin, R.S., D.C. Munz, and W.H. Bommer (2005) "Leading from Within: The Effect of Emotion Recognition and Personality on Transformational Leadership Behavior," *Academy of Management Journal*, 48(5): 845–858.

Schein, E.H. (1985) *Organizational Culture and Leadership: A Dynamic View*. San Francisco: Jossey-Bass.

———. (1990) "Organizational Culture," *American Psychologist*, 45: 109–119.

———. (1992) *Organizational Culture and Leadership*. San Francisco, CA: Jossey-Bass.

Singh, P. and A. Bhandarker (1989) *Corporate Success and Transformational Leadership*. New Delhi: Wiley Eastern.

———. (1997) "Mantras to Lead," *Vision*, July–December: 1–10.

———. (Forthcoming) *In Search of Change Maestros*. New Delhi: Sage Publications.

Singh, P., A. Bhandarker, and A.K. Jain (2010) "In Search of a Leader: Followers' Quest," in P. Singh and S. Verma (eds), *Organizing and Managing in the Era of Globalization*. New Delhi: Sage Publications.

Watson, D., L.A. Clark, and A. Tellegen (1988) "Development and Validation of Brief Measures of Positive and Negative Affect: The PANAS scales," *Journal of Personality and Social Psychology*, 54: 1063–1070.

11

Managerial Work Values in Public Sector Banks in India: An Exploratory Study

Deepa Mazumdar

INTRODUCTION

The emerging manpower crisis in public sector banks is becoming an issue of great concern. The shortage of personnel in specialized areas such as treasury businesses, risk management, IT infrastructure management, etc., is already been felt. Arun (2009) stated that only a fifth of the 700 Public Sector Banks (PSB) employees are managing these areas of banking. Further, mass retirement of officers who joined in the 1970–80 will leave a vacuum of experience and wisdom; these positions are most likely to be filled by the young generation differing from the older generation at least by three decades in age, experience, industry knowledge, work values, and culture. The intent of this study is to explore the existing work values of PSBs, and to observe if they are appropriate to the present market demand.

Work value is an extension of personal value, i.e., employees have an expectation that their organization will facilitate the satisfaction of their values at work. These work values will differ in degree and level for each employee and at different times. The effect of changing values created by the market culture is being felt more and more in management practices and in its philosophy. Management philosophy has become more people-centric and management practices have developed strategies to enhance human capital that will facilitate the organization to generate quality business. The aim of this study is to explore the relevance of the existing work values of the Indian PSBs.

THE PRESENT SCENARIO OF PUBLIC SECTOR BANKS

The PSBs are still maintaining the traditional management philosophy and practices of mechanistic and functional culture, possibly because it continues to remain under the protection of the regulator and the government (Shirreff, 2005). This process has both its advantages and disadvantages. The advantages are the protection of interests of depositors and stability of the financial sector, which also contributes to the disadvantages of cost of regulation, holding back innovation and change; as a result, bankers have been discouraged from incorporating a high achievement-oriented approach. In this state of protection, banks have little inclination to compete with other institutions offering similar services. The article "Open Wider" in the *Economist* (2005) makes three assessments of the Reserve Bank of India; its concern with "systemic risk" has not encouraged a competitive behavior in banks; "fear of failure" is more dominant than an "approach to succeed" and when the banks default or fail, the central bank plays the role of the saviour mostly by merger and acquisition. The existing style of management with its traditional systems and procedures is hindering the PSBs to confront the upcoming challenges of mass retirement, which will create a large vacuum in domain knowledge and experience at every management level. This group of future retirees belonged to a generation that believe in organizational loyalty, with a mental makeup of relationship management, and acceptance of hierarchy and status quo. The traditional managerial practices have been more towards valuing compliance, caring for subordinates, showing affections, taking personal interests in the well-being of the employees, and commitment to their growth. Moreover, emphasis was put on organizational stability than on organizational goal of maximizing profit. Compared to other countries, Indian managers gave higher importance to organizational stability, emphasizing on status, hierarchy, and security, employee welfare than profit maximization, change and innovation (England, 1978; Sinha, 1991).

Organizations generally operate on an incremental level of innovation with their own magnitude of degree of freedom. The bottom level being the *material level* with minimum degree of freedom, traditional and with a high bonding with the past, the *financial level* with moderate degree of freedom, moving to and fro between tradition and the present market culture, and finally the *conceptual level* with a high degree of freedom is totally broken from the past and focused on future development of the organization (Malik, 2003). Very few PSBs have managed to attain the financial level, whereas, many remain attached to the material level. How will these banks cope with the forthcoming change of old timers leaving and a new generation entering their threshold?

The bank operations will soon be taken over by generations X and Y, who are visibly more divergent compared to the old guards. The globalization has introduced a market culture, which is creating tension with the relationship management of the traditional managerial values and practices (Sinha and Sinha, 1990; England, 1978; Chatterjee and Pearson, 2000). The new emerging generation of managers is influenced by the market culture, which is technology driven, and focuses on consumerism, foreign investment, media, trade union, and a changing infrastructure (Kao et al., 1995). From the cultural context, transition from the bureaucratic to a mission culture, from the organization context, the shift from a closed to an open system is already happening, and from the individual context a shift towards development and challenges (Pearson and Chatterjee, 1999).

WORK VALUES

Systems and procedures shape the culture and climate of an organization, which in turn contribute to influencing, forming and establishing employees' work values like achievement, power, and affiliation. Research indicates that people with a high need for achievement prefer to work in private sectors and those with low need for achievement prefers to work for the public sector. Satisfaction of achievement of goals is more difficult to meet in the public sector than in the private sector (McClelland, 1953; Stahl, 1986; Cohen et al., 2004). This could be due to a strong hierarchical order, where decisions are made only at the top echelon and communication mostly flows downward. Based on this premise, this study is intended to find the work values of the Indian PSBs.

Work values are relatively stable goals that people aim to satisfy through work (Sverko and Super, 1995); they are seen as reflections of basic values at work context (Ros et al., 1999). Personal values are standards that guide behavior at work contexts and define how we work and how we relate to our work environment. They differ in the context that organizational values are narrowed down to accommodate the diverse values of the employees. The general practice in private organizations is that, those who find the fit, stay back, while others either quit or are asked to quit. Work values make more impact than tenure, education and salary. Values evolve and continue to develop just as an individual grows and develops. Values determine work behavior and attitude related to job satisfaction, performance, turnover, commitment to goals; other similar values can predict the effect on coordination, satisfaction and commitment (Judge and Bretz, 1992; Frieze et al., 2006; James and James, 1989; Ravlin and Megliano, 1987 ; Megliano et al., 1989).

Work values have been found to be closely related to the Psychological Contract existing between the organization and the employees. A psychological contract is an implicit understanding of the organization's and employees' expectations of satisfying each others goals (Rousseau, 1995; Shore and Tetrick, 1994). Generally, work values evolve from an early work life to development and finally to maturity (Wellin, 2007) and are also subject to change, as a result of the employees' experience (De Vos et al., 2005) during the course of the individuals career. Generally, people in their early years of work life will express an aspiration of career advancement and/or to earn a higher salary. If these needs are not met within 10 years, there is a possibility of value change to a lower order need (Alderfer and Schnieder, 1973). The work value adopted for this study is based on McClelland's three learned motives, i.e., achievement, affiliation, and power.

McClelland's 3 Work Values

Achievement is related to performance, and measured in terms of outperforming others, internal standard of excellence, unique or innovative accomplishment, and long range planning/career involvement.

Affiliation is measured in terms of establishing close and friendly relationships, concern about separation and disruption of relationships, and seeing group activities as social.

Power is composed of *personalized and socialized* power, related to being perceived as strong, effective, and influential. Personalized power is used for personal enrichment and controlling others. Socialized power is used for a larger good, such as the organization or society in general. Power is measured by taking forceful action that affects people, giving unsolicited support or advice, controlling or regulating people's lives, influencing, persuading or making a point, impressing individuals and the world at large, acting in ways that generate strong positive or negative emotions in others, and having a concern for reputation or position.

McClelland (1961) stated that a high need for achievement predisposes an individual to seek out an entrepreneurial position in order to attain more achievement satisfaction than could be derived from a managerial position, concluding that there is a positive relationship between achievement, satisfaction, economic growth, and development. McClelland has also found that need achievement (n-Ach) is a learned behavior, and indicated that an increase in entrepreneurial behavior of small businessmen in India occurred after they received n-Ach training (McClelland and Winter, 1969). Moderate level of n-Ach may be found where the connection between individual effort and goal accomplishment is quite weak. McClelland did not limit n-Ach only to entrepreneurs, and research done using this criterion has not been certain in identifying n-Ach differences between entrepreneurs and managers nor between entrepreneurs and the general population. Perhaps this is a condition resulting from variation in samples, construct validity issues, and measurement problems (Johnson, 1990). McClelland and Burnham (1976) posited that n-Ach has two separate bases, i.e., *hope of success* and *fear of failure*, and both result in achievement of satisfaction. Hope of success is linked with positive reinforcement, whereas, fear of failure is connected with negative reinforcement, which may not result in high level of achievement satisfaction.

Need for power (n-Pow) is dichotomized in two parts, i.e., *social or institutional power and personal power* (McClelland, 1970). Social power is positive in nature—influencing others to reach larger goals, which is considered to be more important than achievement for effective managers and leaders. Personal power is negative power that is involved in controlling and directing others, attaining prestige, and status through position for the sake of demonstrating personal dominance and superiority.

Need for affiliation (n-aff) has received the least attention; it has two bases, i.e., *hope of inclusion* and *fear of exclusion or rejection* (DeCharms, 1957). Excessive n-Aff prevents managers from dealing objectively with subordinates (McClelland and Burnham, 1976), and may create role conflicts as a manager (McClelland and Winter, 1969) and not associated with effective managerial leadership (McClelland and Boyatzis, 1982). Research has shown that senior executives were found to be the lowest scoring group in n-Aff compared to high scoring groups, such as blue collars workers, ministers, (religious) and non-supervisory nurses. Senior executives were also found to have the highest scores in power, which was significantly correlated to managerial performance appraisal scores.

Within each organization there are sub-units and groups that share the common organizational culture, but they differ from each other in their department culture on the basis of the differences in their functions (e.g., HRD vs. treasury), their leaders', and members' values and their professional, and educational level. This value system gets transmitted from higher levels to the bottom of the organization's structure, where individuals acquire through the process of socialization. Congruence of values between the employee and supervisor have an effect on job satisfaction, organizational commitment, and production; for shorter-tenured employees, commitment level for high and low congruence with supervisors showed similar results, and among the longer tenured employees, commitment level was substantially lower with those with low congruence with their supervisor (Megliano et al., 1989). Individuals belonging to the same group share the same values that differentiate them from other groups and create a group-level culture. For example, employees of an HRD unit are selected into the unit because of their interpersonal style and human relation expertise. Their leader also typically facilitates the display of these personal characteristics because they are crucial for developing human capital. Thus, all members of this unit develop a similar core value, which differentiates them from other organizational units (Bhagat et al., 2005).

Managers, being in a structured environment tend to focus less on risk-taking compared to entrepreneurs, who most often function as the decision makers in a more unstructured environment (Gasse, 1982). Achievement, rather than being the universal solvent, was being defined more narrowly; McClelland later thought that it would have been better to have named it "Efficiency" instead. The person who is high in n-Ach is preoccupied with completing a series of tangible tasks that produce rewards (Lemann, 1994).

The private sector banks, contrary to the public sector banks, have got themselves initiated in this new culture form, the formers' work culture is more entrepreneurial and technology oriented, and accept attrition as a "neo-age" reality. Recruitment and selection is mostly on contract basis, with an emphasis on performance. Effectiveness of certain managerial behavior is dependent on the organizational culture that endorses that behavior, which explains the link between managerial practices and behavior (Selmer, 1996). Greenwald (2008) identified two kinds of lifestyles, the *belonger* and the *experiential*. Belongers focus on home, family, and job and the experientialists focus on invention, product development, and tasks requiring creativity and risks.

The banking industry, like the insurance industry, tends to be more socially conservative (Greenwald, 2008); the symptoms are seen in the resistance to get into horizontal expansion or vertical integration, tendency to remain region specific and risk aversion. Technological development is slow compared to most other industries and the preference of recruiting the belonger to ensure stability is still apparent. Now, with the increasing number of knowledge workers in the market, the number of experiential's is increasing and belonger's is decreasing, the evidence is found in the high attrition rate of IT employees recruited by banks.

METHOD

Subjects

The sample consisted of 500 bank officers/managers from scale I to scale VII employed in 11 PSBs of both big and small size. Table 11.1 depicts

TABLE 11.1: Sample Distribution

Level	Scale 1	68	Junior management	68
	Scale 2	72	Middle management	161
	Scale 3	89		
	Scale 4	80	Senior management	154
	Scale 5	74		
	Scale 6	65	Top management	117
	Scale 7	52		
Age			<31	56
			31–40	100
			41–50	177
			51–60	167
Branches/Location			Head office	104
			Metro	132
			Urban	123
			Semi-urban & rural	141

the sample distribution of different scales, age groups, and branches/location.

Measures and Procedures

Personal Value Questionnaire (1991) based on the research of McClelland's three variables of social motive that contains 30 items was given to the respondents. The questionnaire contains 36 items, of which 30 items assess the three work values (10 each), and six items fillers, with a 6-point Likert scale, ranging from 0 (not important) to 5 (extremely important). The work values have been derived from McClelland's classification of achievement, affiliation, and power. McClelland considered only achievement to be a positive value for economic progress and individual development (Lemann, 1994). The reliability of the questionnaire is Cronbach's alpha coefficient .90.

Data Analyses

An analysis of data has been computed in following stages.

- Descriptive statistics to find the mean and standard deviation of each category of the sample (see Table 11.2).
- Factor analysis to obtain the latent dimensions generating from the 30 items, applying correlation matrix, Kaiser's criteria, and quartimax

TABLE 11.2: Mean and Standard Deviation Scores

Groups	n-Ach Mean	σ	n-Aff Mean	σ	n-Pow Mean	σ
Total Sample	3.74	.59	3.38	.58	2.95	.77
Jr. mgmt	3.73	.64	3.31	.65	2.82	.90
Mdl. mgmt	3.64	.61	3.42	.58	2.91	.77
Sr. mgmt	3.84	.52	3.34	.55	3.00	.73
Top mgmt	3.99	.53	3.31	.63	3.22	.60
< 41 yrs	3.82	.60	3.35	.57	3.04	.76
41–50 yrs	3.73	.59	3.41	.61	2.88	.81
51–60 yrs	3.71	.58	3.35	.56	3.02	.71
H.O.	3.84	.55	3.24	.59	3.09	.72
Metro Br.	3.76	.61	3.41	.56	2.97	.74
Urban Br.	3.70	.60	3.33	.62	2.93	.77
Semi-U & Rural Br.	3.62	.60	3.48	.51	3.03	.72

rotation was carried out to minimize the number of factors that explain each variable, which helps us to identify which items belong to which dimension. This was also used to optimize the factors (see Appendix 11.1).

- Finally, Analysis of Variance (ANOVA) of these dimensions as dependent variables was carried out to explore any group differences, using management levels, scales, age, and branch locations as predictors.

RESULTS

The overall picture we derive from Table 11.2, is that the top management's mean score of achievement indicates to be an important work value. The difference in mean score is small between groups spreading longitudinal (hierarchy and age) and latitudinal (branch/location) limits. The individual items that have mean scores above 4, i.e., *very important* are, "close, friendly, cooperative relations with others at work" (n-aff; mean 4.20, σ .88) and "maintaining high standards for the quality of my work" (n-ach; mean 4.17, σ .83), and the item with the lowest mean score, i.e., of "some importance" is "taking forceful action" (n-pow; mean 2.00, σ 1.33).

Factor Analysis

The 30 items measuring the three values were reduced to eight dimensions (see Appendix 11.1) based on the principle component analysis with quartimax rotation, correlation coefficient, and loading of ± .45 and above has been taken into account for the interpretation of factors. The Kaiser criteria retained eight orthogonal factors which account for 58.4 percent of the total variance.

Items relating to power values correlate significantly with items measuring affiliation and achievement values, whereas, items relating to affiliation value have low correlation with items relating to achievement value. The affiliation item "to be able to spend a great deal of time in contact with other people" does not have a significant loading (< .45), but it is significantly correlated to the power item "opportunities to be known" (r^2 = .45), and this item has not been considered for any interpretation due to a low loading (Guertin and Bailey, 1970). Henceforth the eight factors will be referred as values representing the work values of this sample.

The value *leisure* is not directly linked to work, *relationship* and *social* represent the employees' expectation from the organization, *leadership* (comprising of 8 power related values), *achievement, self-actualization,* and *advancement* represent what the employees desire to proffer to the organization. See Table 11.3 for more details.

Analysis of Variance—ANOVA

SCALES
Achievement (F = 4.558[**]),[1] relationship (F = 9.815[**]), and social (F = 2.172[*]) appeared to be significant. The *Achievement* value of scale VI (DGM) is significantly higher than that of scale II (manager), and scale III (senior manager); *relationship* values at work is less for scale V (AGM) compared to scales I (probationary officers), II (manager), II (senior manager), and IV (chief manager); scale VI's (DGM) *relationship* value is significantly less than scale III (senior manager). Social value did not bring out any significant group difference.

MANAGEMENT LEVEL
Achievement (F = 9.098[**]), self-actualization (F = 2.657[*]), relationship (F = 14.887[**]), social (F = 2.889[*]), and advancement (F = 3.047[*]) appeared to be significant. The top management's *achievement* value is significantly higher than that of junior and middle managements; senior management's achievement level is also higher than the middle management. Concerning *relationship*, middle management values it more that senior and top managements. *Social* value is preferred more by senior management than

---

[1] [**] = < .01, [*] = < .05.

TABLE 11.3: Work Values Related to Indian Bankers

Work value	Motives	Loading
Leadership	30. The opportunity to exercise control over an organization or group.	.70
	24. Opportunities to become widely known	.70
	29. Being well like by people.	.68
	20. To be in leadership position in which others work for me and look to me for direction.	.63
	14. A position with prestige	.60
	23. Opportunities to influence the decisions that are made in any group I am part of.	.58
	12. Opportunities to influence others.	.54
	13. Doing things that have strong effect on others.	.52
	7. Important positions and projects that can give me recognition.	.51
	25. The opportunities to be part of a team.	.45
Achievement	4. Opportunities to take on more difficult and challenging goals and responsibilities.	.72
	5. Continuously new, exciting and challenging goals and projects.	.69
	11. Opportunities to create new things.	.65
	17. Taking forceful actions.	.46
Self-actualization	28. Personally producing work of high quality.	.73
	18. Personally doing things better than they have been done before	.66
	22. Maintaining high standards for the quality of my work	.60
	26. Projects that challenge me to the limits of my ability	.45
Relationship	16. To be able to work with people who are also my close friends.	.70
	10. Not being separated from the people I really care about.	.68
	19. Maintaining close relationship with the people I really care about.	.64
Leisure	27. Having plenty of free time to spend with my friends	.74
	8. Having plenty of time to spend with my family	.71
Efficiency	9. Feedback on how well I am doing or progressing towards my objectives	.69
	15. Concrete way to be able to measure my own performance	.63
	3. Possessions that are impressive to others	.45
Social	1. Close, friendly, cooperative relations with others at work.	.77
	5. The freedom and opportunity to talk and socialize with others at work	.61
Advancement	7. Important positions and projects that can give me recognition	.58
	2. Continual opportunities for personal growth and development	.56

top management. Self-actualization and advancement did not demonstrate any significant group difference.

AGE
Self-actualization (F = 2.907*), relationship (F = 3.724*), leisure (F = 2.722*), and advancement (F = 4.977**) appeared to be significant. The difference is observed in relationship and advancement values. The age group between 41–50 years prefers *relationship* at work more than the age group below 30 years. Groups below 30 years and between 31 to 40 years prefer *advancement* at work more than group between 41–50 years. Self-actualization and leisure did not show any significant group difference.

BRANCH/LOCATION
Self-actualization (F = 3.755*), relationship (F = 3.736*), and advancement (F = 9.583**) appeared to be significant. Officials posted at the head office values *self-actualization* more than the officials posted in the metro and rural sectors, and officials posted in metros valued it higher than those posted in the rural sector. Officials posted in the rural areas valued *relationship* more than those posted at the head office. As for *advancement* at work, those at the head office valued it significantly more than those posted in the urban and rural sectors.

DISCUSSION

In this study, we observed that the achievement value is high among the younger employees at the entry level and those who have already attained a certain amount of success in their career; whereas, the middle management level shows a preference for non-work values. The achievement work value is absent in the middle management, employees aged between 41–50 years, and there are those who are physically distanced (urban and rural) from the head office. Earlier, it was noted that individuals belonging to the same group share the same values that differentiate them from other groups and create a group-level culture. The mean results indicate that among the respondents, none of the work values appear to be either "very important" or "extremely important." Only the top management scores the maximum in achievement at a "just important" level. Power appears to be least valued due to a possible cultural reason. Hoftede's study has demonstrated that achievement is highly correlated with individualism, and Indians are collective by nature and hence affiliation's need and belief in power distance are high, i.e., respect for hierarchy (Hofstede and Hofstede, 2005).

Work values like achievement, advancement, and social relationships, and in one instant self-actualization emerges as determining factors of group difference. The degree of preference for achievement is closely linked to career success. The middle management value relationships at the work place, probably because the "socio-emotional" goals are dominating the "official" goals (Greenwald, 2008). The difference is clearly visible between the scales. Scales V and VI score higher in values related to achievement than scales II and III, whose preference is related to relationship oriented values.

Concerning the difference between the age groups, those aged below 30 and between 31–40 years, show a very high preference for advancement and those above 40 years tends to value relationship. Nair's study (2004) found that *(i)* junior managers of private sector organizations, showed a high concern for values such as entrepreneurship (composed of independence), achievement and creativity, and little concern for job security, and *(ii)* young managers aged between 28–44 years valued money, quick promotion, relationship with co-workers, leisure and free time, whereas the older managers, aged above 45 years, valued pride in craftsmanship, hard work, organizational commitment, and service to others.

The difference between officials of different branch/locations shows that those in the head office and metros have a preference for self-actualization and advancement compared to those in the semi-urban and rural sectors. Those who are placed farthest (rural) from the centre of decision making (head office), show a significant preference for relationship at work as compared to those in the head office, and at other extremes of advancement are those who are posted at the head office and metro; this indicates that those close to the central network enjoy better "energizing relationships" than those at the periphery (rural) who are farthest from the network of communication (Johnson-Gamer et al., 2007), especially of the implicit or the informal kind.

Considering the factor *leisure* does not consist of any variable directly related to work and performance, it can be concluded that the group/s who value attachment and relationships to be more the "disengaged" workers for whom work is not as Guest and Conway (Wellin, 2007: 32) stated "is a central life interest and seek no emotional tie to their employer." In this case, these groups are middle management (90.5 percent), scales II (27.2 percent) and III (63.3 percent) who are above 40 years. In Scale III, 97.9 percent are over 40 years.

The results indicate that the need for achievement and advancement appears to be high among the top management, young officers aged below 41 years, and those having proximity to the head office. The challenge lies in how to motivate the middle management to develop a work value high on achievement. PSBs have employees, especially in the middle management, who are in their second half of working life, experiencing the "ceiling effect." The three high achievement categories, viz; top management, age below 41 years and proximity to the head office—can be the reason to initiate the change required in the redesigning of the HR systems and procedures.

PSBs need to increase their support to employees and improve on their technology, update their developmental process, or else it will become difficult to compete with foreign and private banks which are already providing better facilities and incentives. Improved quality of work life and business practices can have a very positive effect on profitability and competitiveness. HR can employ the existing senior management to motivate and encourage the young officers below 41 years, who are in readiness to achieve. This will install an achievement and entrepreneurial culture in banks. Second, approach to training and development should be that of investment. ROI should be measurable in terms of performance and linked to employees' balance scorecard. Third, HR should also have an audit of human capital. The balance sheet of human capital can be in ratio of the bank's cost of maintaining the employee to the employee's capability and potential. If the asset is higher than the liability, focus should be on talent retention and management, leadership, multi-tasking performance, e-learning, and e-training. In case the liability is higher than the asset, then the bank can work on to bring a balance between cost and capability through a job-person fit or further training or replace him. Finally, the above can be facilitated if banks invest on an effective HRIS.

This study was aimed to present the existing work values in PSBs and it depicts how "active inertia" has set into the Indian banking industry. Strategic patterns, processes, relationships, and values that have enabled the organizations to succeed can become a failed formula when business conditions change (Sull, 2000). The process that necessitates achievement does not follow the demands of a mechanistic culture of compliance, conformity or acquiescence.

CONCLUSION

Effective organizations aim to create new work values, and enable the individuals' to develop a psychological contract with the organization. Considering the age of Indian banks and their need to last in the competitive market, there is a need to bring a change in the employees' attitude to work to bring about a shift from extrinsic motivation to intrinsic motivation, from bureaucracy to adhocracy. Management has moved from the benevolent paternalistic relationship between employer and employee to a relationship of adults; personal accomplishment has scored over promotion as an indicator of growth, needless to mention that attrition is healthy and a reality. The new knowledge worker defines his own identity instead of waiting to be carved out by the organization (Wellin, 2007). Some of these transformations can be brought in through a process of culture change. A well conceived and a well-managed organization culture can mean the difference between success and failure in today's demanding environment. Morgan's typology of business relationship of the focal organization emphasizes that the internal relationship of the organization is a "necessary precondition for effective, external, agile relationship which is generally overlooked and assumed." The focus is on the market economy where individuals are in effect asked to pursue selfish interests, because the market mechanism will exactly measure the contribution of each person to the common good, each person can be compensated exactly for personal contributions. The emphasis made here is that reward is proportional to the quality and not quantity of work.

Changing the culture of any organization is a lengthy and complex process. The change process itself is influenced by the culture in place. If the ongoing culture is strong, i.e., when shared beliefs, values and norms consistently drive behavior, then the change process becomes more difficult. Such is the current situation in the banks. Ouchi (1981: 84–85) expresses the logic of the social mechanism of bureaucracy "do not do what you want, do what we tell you because we pay you for it," he adds further that "this bureaucratic mechanism alone produces alienation, anomie and a lowered sense of autonomy." Today, the drawbacks of reduced autonomy due to absence of trust, more control and less innovation, and slow procedural changes have become impediments to competitive advantage.

Banks can introduce an open system that encourages teamwork, communication, and autonomy leading to high inner commitment. The system will be based on the idea that people would want to contribute; operations and decision-making will be guided by the vision and mission of the organization with the view that contribution is being made to the society rather than for self-gain, moreover, access to resources need to be equal for everyone irrespective of hierarchy and perceiving failure as learning from mistakes rather than personal inadequacy. To facilitate this, leaders need to apply the required expertise to bring forth the transformation. Leadership has become a critical dimension for the successful continuity of any organization that intends to remain as leaders in the competitive market. For future growth managers have to go beyond managing to focus on leading and inspiring proactive techniques. According to Haslam (2001: 234–35) shifting from extrinsic to intrinsic motivations, transforms the superior's power into social influence, and subordinates detachment into organizational commitment.

A 6-step process can be reflected upon.

1. Step 1: Vision Statement needs to communicate the route to the goal. A good vision statement is able to respond to *what, why, how, where,* and *when* of the goals.
2. Step 2: Assessment of inequitable power, individual goals, and nature of support needed to achieve the goal.
3. Step 3: Setting Challenges: Share organizational goals; develop the individuals to transit from extrinsic goals to more intrinsic goals through coaching, delegating, and mentoring. During this process constant monitoring by the supervisor is important.
4. Step 4: Performance evaluation will indicate the progress to the desired goal.
5. Step 5: Feedback and reward will be a strong indicator of support and recognition.
6. Step 6: Setting further goals.

Providing the appropriate tools to empower executives can facilitate their contribution in improving the PSBs' bottom line. With measures and assessments, banks can deliver additional value, savings, and increased productivity to the business, and also articulate to the board the crucial role of culture change in business success.

Appendix 11.1: Rotated Component Matrix

	Leadership	Achievement	Actualization	Relationship	Non-work	Efficiency	Social	Advancement
aff_1	.04	.11	.09	-.02	.07	-.04	**.77**	-.03
ach_2	.25	.34	.11	.02	.07	.14	.15	**.56**
pow_3	.39	.01	-.31	.06	.21	**.45**	.17	.01
ach_4	.12	**.72**	.16	.08	-.13	-.02	.14	.17
aff_5	.07	.32	.07	.06	.16	.04	**.61**	.12
ach_6	.10	**.69**	.08	.09	-.01	.16	.16	.21
pow_7	**.51**	.24	-.06	.07	.03	.03	.01	**.58**
aff_8	-.01	.03	.07	.24	**.71**	.17	.14	.29
ach_9	.26	.23	.15	-.03	.09	**.69**	.03	.07
aff_10	.13	-.01	.06	**.68**	.31	.10	.02	.18
ach_11	.16	**.65**	.04	.06	.02	.35	.04	-.14
pow_12	**.54**	.41	.04	-.04	.35	.08	-.05	-.06
pow_13	**.52**	.39	.18	-.24	.14	-.11	-.01	-.05
pow_14	**.60**	.13	-.02	.02	-.01	.30	-.19	.36
ach_15	.24	.28	.20	.11	.03	**.63**	-.10	.11
aff_16	.20	.17	.01	**.70**	.03	.08	.04	-.27
pow_17	.24	**.46**	.23	-.17	.35	-.17	-.32	.11
ach_18	.19	.13	**.64**	.10	.05	.10	-.03	.04
aff_19	.32	.12	.30	**.64**	.01	-.10	-.01	.14
pow_20	**.63**	-.08	.15	.06	-.11	.18	.14	.05

aff_21	.40	.36	-.07	.20	.18	-.14	.13	-.34
ach_22	.22	.29	**.60**	.09	-.04	.05	.18	.00
pow_23	**.58**	.07	.24	.05	-.05	-.10	.01	.06
pow_24	**.70**	.20	-.03	.07	.04	.18	-.08	-.09
aff_25	**.45**	.32	.23	.12	-.08	.21	.26	-.27
ach_26	.26	.32	**.45**	.08	.01	.24	.07	-.09
aff_27	.19	-.02	.15	.10	**.74**	.03	.11	-.17
ach_28	.29	.01	**.73**	-.01	.23	.01	.05	.02
aff_29	**.68**	-.16	.18	.23	.13	-.06	.17	-.05
pow_30	**.70**	.02	.03	.04	-.01	.03	-.09	.15

BIBLIOGRAPHY

Alderfer, C.P. and B. Schnieder (1973) "Three Studies of Need Satisfaction in Organization," *Administrative Science Quarterly*, 18: 489–505.

Arun S. (2009) "Report on HR Practices in Public Sector Banks by March," *Business Line*, Tuesday, December 1.

Bhagat, R.S., N.R. Buchan, M. Erez, C.B. Gibson, and K. Leung (2005) "Culture and International Business: Recent Advances and Their Implications for Future Research," *Journal of International Business Studies*, 36(4): 357–378.

Chatterjee, S.R. and C.A.L. Pearson (2000) "Indian Managers in trasion Orientation, Work Goals, Values and Ethics," *Management International Review*, 40(1): 81–95.

Cohen, A., Y. Zalmanovitch, and H. Davidesko (2004) "The Role of Public Sector Image and Personal Characteristics in Determining tendency to Work in Public Sector," in Vigoda-Gadot and Cohen (eds), *Citizenship and Management in Public Administration-Integrating behavioral Theories and Managerial Thinking*, pp. 235–260. Northampton, USA: Edward Elgar.

DeCharms, R. (1957) "Affiliation Motivation and Productivity in Small Groups," *Journal of Abnormal and Social Psychology*, 55(2): 222–226.

De Vos, A., D. Buyens, and R. Schalk (2005) "Making Sense of a New Employment Relationship: Psychological Contract-related Information Seeking and the Role of Work Values and Locus of Control," *International Journal of Selection and Assessment*, 13(1): 41–52.

England, G.W. (1978) "Managers and Their Value System: A Five-country Comparison Study," *Columbia Journal of World Business*, 13: 35–44.

Frieze, I.H., J.E. Olson, A.J. Murrell, and M.S. Selvan (2006) "Work Values and Their Effect on Work Behavior and Work Outcomes in Female and Male Managers," *Sex Roles: A Journal of Research*. Online Access.

Gasse, Y. (1982) "Elaborations on the Psychology of the Entrepreneur," in K.D. Sexton and K. Vesper (eds), *Encyclopaedias of Entrepreneurship*, pp. 57–71. Englewood Cliffs, NJ: Prentice-Hall.

Greenwald, H.P. (2008). *Organizations: Management without Control*. Thousand Oaks: Sage Publications.

Guertin, W.H. and J.P. Bailey Jr. (1970) *Introduction to Modern Factor Analysis*. Ann Arbor, Michigan: Edwards Brothers Inc.

Haslam, S.A. (2001) *Psychology in Organization: The Social Identity Approach*. London: Sage Publications.

Hofstede, G. and G.J. Hofstede (2005) *Culture and Organization: Software of the Mind*, New York: McGraw-Hill.

James, L.A. and L.R. James (1989) "Integrating Work Environment Perceptions: Explorations into the Measurement of Meanings," *Journal of Applied Psychology*, 74: 739–751.

Johnson, B. (1990) "Toward a Multidimensional Model of Entrepreneurship: The Case of Achievement Motivation and the Entrepreneur," *Entrepreneurship Theory and Practice* 14(3): 39–54.

Johnson-Gamer, M.E., S. Panse, and R.L. Cross (2007) "Managing Change through Networks and Values," *California Management Review*, 49(3): 85–109.

Judge, T.A. and R.D. Bretz Jr. (1992) "Effect of Work Values on Job Choice Decisions," *Journal of Applied Psychology*, 88(3): 261–271.

Kao, H.S.R., D. Sinha, and S.H. Ng (1995) *Effective Organization and Social Values*. London: Sage Publications.

Lemann, N. (1994) "Is There a Science of Success?" *The Atlantic Monthly*, 273(2): 82.

Malik, Pravir (2003) "Business of Transformation through the Creation of a Complex Adaptive System," *Journal of Human Value*, 9(2): 153–161.

McClelland, D.C. (1953) *The Achievement Motivation*. New York: Appleton-century-Crofts.

———. (1961) *The Achieving Society*. Princeton, NJ: Van Nostrand.

———. (1970) "The Two Faces of Power," *Journal of International Affairs*, 24: 29–47.

———. (1991) *The Personal Value Questionnaire*. Boston: McBer & Company.

McClelland, D.C. and D.G. Winter (1969) *Motivating Economic Achievement*. New York: Free Press.

McClelland, D.C. and D.H. Burnham (1976) "Power is the Great Motivator," *Harvard Business Review*, 54(2): 100–110.

McClelland, D.C. and R.E. Boyatzis (1982) "Leadership Motive Pattern and Long-term Success in Management," *Journal of Applied Psychology*, 67: 737–743.

Megliano, B., E.C. Ravli, and C.L. Adkins (1989) "A Work Value Approach to Corporate Culture: A Field Test of the Value Congruence Process and its Relationship to Individual Outcomes," *Journal of Applied Psychology*, 74(3): 424–432.

Morgan, R. (2004) "Business Relationship and Technology," *Journal of General Management*, 29(4): 77–92.

Nair, S.K. (2004) "Managerial Work Values in Indian Private Sector," *Productivity*, 45(2): 245–251.

Oliver, N. (1990) "Work Rewards, Work Values and Organizational Commitment in an Employee-owned Firm: Evidence from the U.K.," *Human Relation*, 43(6): 513–526.

Ouchi, W. (1981) *Theory Z*. Reading, MA: Addisson-Wesley.

Pearson, C.A.L. and S.R. Chatterjee (1999) "Managerial Work Goals and Organizational Reform: An Empirical Study of Senior Indian Managers," *Asia Pacific Journal of Economics and Business*, 3(1): 1–16.

Ravlin, E.C. and B.M. Megliano (1987) "Effect of Values on Perception and Decision Making: A Study of Alternative Work Value Measures," *Journal of Applied Psychology*, 72(4): 666–673.

Ros, M., S.H. Schwartz, and S. Surkiss (1999) "Basic Individual Values, Work Values and the Meaning of Work," *Applied Psychology, An International Review*, 48(1): 49–71.

Rousseau, D.M. (1995) *Psychological Contracts in Organizations: Understanding Written and Unwritten Agreements*. Thousand Oaks, CA: Sage Publications.

Schwartz, S. (1999) "A Theory of Cultural Values and Some Implications at Work," *Applied Psychology, An International Review*, 48(1): 23–47.

Selmer, J. (1996) "What Expatriate Managers Know about the Work Values of Their Subordinates: Swedish Executives in Thailand," *Management International Review*, 36(3): 231–243.

Shirreff, D. (2005) Interviewed in *The Economists*, May 19.

Shore, L.M. and L.E. Tetrick (1994) "The Psychological Contract as an Explanatory Framework in the Employment Relationship," in C.L. Cooper and D.M. Rousseau (eds), *Trends in Organizational Behavior*, pp. 91–109. New York: John Wiley and Sons.

Sinha, D. (1991) "Values and Work Behavior," *Abhigyan*, Spring: 1–4.

Sinha, J.B.P. and D. Sinha (1990) "Role of Social Values in Indian Organization," *International Journal of Psychology*, 25: 705–714.

Stahl, M.J. (1986) *Managerial and Technical Motivation: Assessing Needs for Achievement, Power, Affiliation*. New York: Praeger.

Sull, Donald N. (2000) "Why Good Companies Go Bad," *Harvard Business Review on Culture and Change*, 83–106.

Sverko, B. and D.E. Super (1995) "The Findings of the Work Important Study," in D.E. Super and B. Sverko (eds), *Life Roles, Values and Careers*, pp. 349–353. San Francisco, CA: Jossey-Bass.

The Economist (2005) "Open Wider: International Banking," SURVEY, May 19.

Wellin, M. (2007) *Managing the Psychological Contract: Using Personal Deal to Increase Business Performance.* Gower Publishing Limited.

Yukl, G.A. (1981) *Leadership in Organizations.* New Jersey: Prentice-Hall Inc.

12

Emergence of the Born Global Entrepreneur: An Indian Case Study

Sumati Varma

INTRODUCTION

The rise of MNEs from emerging economies as important players in the global economy has been a distinctive development of the present century. The emergence of these firms from unique institutional and resource environments (Hoskisson et al., 2000; Khanna and Palepu, 2000) has been fraught with challenges (Lall, 1983; Wells, 1983; Khanna and Palepu, 2000) as many of them have emerged as latecomers (Mathews, 2002) from economies with underdeveloped institutions and market intermediaries, overcoming resource disadvantages such as financial capital, advanced technologies, and managerial capabilities (Guillen, 2000). The period 2000–07 witnessed an unprecedented boom in outbound M&A activity from India, Pradhan (2007); Nayyar (2008), led by firms in the IT and pharmaceutical sectors (Varma, 2009). Twelve percent of these cross-border M&As were done by firms which were less than five years old at the time of acquisition, hence the use of the nomenclature Born Global Acquirers (BGAs) to describe them.

Innovations in manufacturing, information, and communication technology and increasing liberalization in the global economy have enabled the birth of a new class of start ups that view the global market as their natural home. A multitude of small and medium sized firms have increasingly developed important sources of competitive advantage by organizing foreign operations at the time of founding or shortly afterwards, including not only exports but also more complex forms of internationalization such as joint ventures, wholly-owned subsidiaries or franchising networks. Variously described as "global start-ups," "born globals," or "international new ventures" (Rennie, 1993; Oviatt and McDougall, 1994, 1995; Bloodgood et al., 1996; Kohn, 1997; Madsen and Servais, 1997; Knight and Cavusgil, 2004; Rialp et al., 2005), these bring to the fore complex forms of entrepreneurship involving high levels of uncertainty leading to their inclusion in international entrepreneurship literature (McDougall and Oviatt, 2000; Oviatt and McDougall, 1994).

Born globals are exemplar highly entrepreneurial small firms that challenge the belief that the strategic options of small firms are constrained by resource poverty. Considerable research has already been undertaken and is ongoing (Rialp et al., 2005). In general, the born global literature assigns a prominent role to the founder manager, including his prior experience (Knight, 2001; Madsen and Servais, 1997), visible in a recent attempt by some to build a unified conceptualization of the accelerated internationalization of born global firms (Weerawardena et al., 2007), who have conjectured that born global owner managers, with a global mindset and an international entrepreneurial orientation, build and nurture a set of dynamic capabilities leading to early and rapid entry of markets. This paper examines the role of the entrepreneur as an initiating force in the accelerated internationalization of five Born Global firms from the Indian IT sector which made an international acquisition within five years of coming into existence.

The primary purpose of this paper is to initiate the process of applying insights from entrepreneurship research to explain the emergence of born global firms and their consequences for economic development. Most studies undertaken on the phenomenon of the born global firm have been in the context of industrial economies with a focus on manufacturing and process innovations using export as the mode of internationalization. There is no study on the phenomenon in the Indian context—this paper seeks to fill that gap and initiate discussion. In doing so it shifts the focus from the process and timing of internationalization to the discovery, evaluation, and exploitation of international entrepreneurial opportunities and the consequent emergence of the Born Global Acquirer. It thus contributes to the existing literature firstly by adding to existing knowledge on born global firms in an international entrepreneurship framework; secondly, it is the first such effort in the context of India which is an important emerging market; it therefore contributes to a better understanding of internationalization in this area, and thirdly, it profiles a specific kind of born global firm—the BGA.

The rest of the paper is organized as follows: Section II outlines the theoretical underpinnings of international entrepreneurship; section III specifies the research methodology; section IV develops the theoretical model; section V contains the analysis and discussion and section VI concludes.

INTERNATIONAL ENTREPRENEURSHIP

Entrepreneurship studies can be traced back to the work of Richard Cantillon (circa 1730) and Jean Baptiste Say (1816). Cantillion saw entrepreneurs as bearers of uncertainty, while Say (1816) saw the entrepreneur as the agent who united all means of production in order to make profits. These ideas about what entrepreneurs did were rediscovered in the 20th century. Thus, Frank Knight (1921) emphasized the entrepreneur's role in coping with the uncertainty of market dynamics, arguing that entrepreneurs were also required to perform fundamental managerial functions such as direction and control. Harvey Leibenstein in the 1960s and 1970s saw the entrepreneur as the agent, which resolved market deficiencies through input completing activities (Athreya, 2010).

A somewhat different twist to the advantages of entrepreneurship was given by Joseph Schumpeter (1934) who saw the entrepreneur as a heroic innovator who implements change within markets through the carrying out of "new combinations" of various kinds. From the Schumpeterian perspective, the entrepreneur disrupts the circular flow of the market by introducing actions that entail novel combinations of existing resources. These actions are "disequilibrating" in the sense that they disrupt established means-end relations and generate new sources of uncertainty (Smith and Di Gregorio, 2002). This has also been referred to as the strong premise for entrepreneurial action (Venkataraman, 1997) or Schumpeterian opportunities (Shane, 2003). From the Schumpeterian perspective, entrepreneurial action contributes to economic development by increasing the potential value in an economic system, also referred to as adaptive efficiency (Moran and Ghoshal, 1999; North, 1990; Schumpeter, 1934).

The perspective of the Austrian economists such as Israel Kirzner emphasizes the role of the entrepreneur in moving markets back towards equilibrium by recognizing market opportunities and acting upon them. From this perspective, markets are imperfect due to the dispersion and divergence in knowledge, and opinions across time and space. Utilizing a market cue such as the price mechanism, entrepreneurs correct ignorance by engaging in arbitrage of tangible goods as well as information. These "equilibrating" actions move the market toward equilibrium (Smith and Di Gregorio, 2002). The Austrian perspective has been referred to as the weak premise for entrepreneurial action (Venkataraman, 1997), or Kirznerian opportunities (Shane, 2003).

Entrepreneurial action contributes to economic development by enhancing the allocative efficiency of the system, since actions that exploit the dispersion of knowledge and other resources end up reducing that dispersion. The greater the dispersion of knowledge (e.g., across national borders), the greater will be the opportunities to engage in entrepreneurial action to profit while reducing the dispersion of knowledge.

International entrepreneurship as a newly emerging research arena began with an interest in new ventures (Oviatt and McDougall, 2005), whose existence, evolution and performance were explained using a broad range of theoretical frameworks (Rialp et al., 2005) with somewhat inadequate attention to the international entrepreneurship perspective (Di Gregorio et al., 2008). It has also focused on comparisons of entrepreneurial behavior in multiple countries and cultures as well as organizational behavior that extends across national borders and is entrepreneurial. The link between international new ventures and entrepreneurship has been acknowledged (Oviatt and McDougall, 1994), and recent research has addressed this link more explicitly (Autio, 2005; Oviatt and McDougall, 2005; Zahra, 2005; Zahra and George, 2002; Acs et al., 2003; Dimitratos and Jones, 2005).

Three major perspectives of international entrepreneurship have emerged in the literature.

The strategic management perspective of international entrepreneurship emphasizes brokering, resource leveraging or stretching, value creation, and opportunity seeking through a combination of innovative, proactive, and risk-seeking behavior (Covin and Slevin, 1989; Miller, 1983). It also implies that all international activities are entrepreneurial because they can only occur through brokering, leveraging, and risk-taking practices. Proponents of this perspective define international entrepreneurship as a combination of innovative, proactive, and risk-taking behavior that crosses national borders and is intended to create value in organizations (McDougall and Oviatt, 2000).

A second perspective views international entrepreneurship as a nexus of individuals and opportunities. Proponents of this perspective opine that international entrepreneurship entails the discovery, evaluation, and exploitation of opportunities to introduce new goods and services, ways of organizing, markets, processes, and raw materials through organizing efforts that previously had not existed (Shane and Venkataraman, 2000). Opportunities are situations in which people believe they can use new means-ends frameworks to yield novel resource combinations for generating profit (Shane, 2000). Individuals typically discover opportunities based on their prior knowledge which comes to bear on how they perceive external stimuli. These authors build on the works of Schumpeter and Austrian economics, for which entrepreneurial activity drives the market process and economic development by moving markets away from or toward equilibrium, while creating and resolving differences in knowledge and resources across time and space. Following Schumpeter (1934), entrepreneurs create value that contributes to economic development by engaging in novel combinations of resources. In line with Austrian economics, the knowledge gained through the discovery of entrepreneurial opportunities by individuals makes markets more efficient. To them, entrepreneurship is viewed as focusing on opportunities that may be bought and sold, or they may form the foundation of new organizations. The emergence of international new ventures is explained by the geographic dispersion of the key elements in the entrepreneurial process: individuals, the experience and other resources that individuals control, and opportunities for new international combinations of resources and/or markets. The core of this view is the nexus of individuals and opportunities (Gregorio et al., 2008). In the words of Shane (2003: 21) "This framework examines the characteristics of opportunities; the individuals who discover and exploit them; the process of resource acquisition and organizing; and the strategies used to exploit and protect the profits from those efforts."

A third perspective views entrepreneurship as a process of enactment and discovery. Proponents of this perspective do not agree that opportunities are "objective phenomena" that do not require subjective creation among people who are influenced by their social milieu (Baker et al., 2005). They argue that opportunities may be enacted (Weick, 1995) as well as discovered. That is, people act and then interpret what their actions have created, and sometimes those creations are economic opportunities. Based on this, they define international entrepreneurship as the discovery, enactment, evaluation, and exploitation of opportunities across national borders to create future goods and services (Oviatt and McDougall, 2005).

The aforementioned perspectives provide a base to conceptualize international entrepreneurship as a capability. It may be defined as a firm-level ability to leverage resources via a combination of innovative, proactive, and risk-seeking activities to discover, enact, evaluate, and exploit business opportunities across borders. This capability allows the firm to leverage firm resources, discover, and exploit opportunities in the international market in order to achieve superior business performance (Zhang et al., 2009).

This capability view is particularly helpful for born global firms because most born global firms are small firms with scarce financial, human, and tangible resources. Thus, developing organizational capabilities, such as international entrepreneurial capability, to leverage firm resources for achieving superior performance in international market is essentially important to them.

RESEARCH METHODOLOGY

Research Context

Recent years have witnessed the rise of MNEs from various emerging economies including China and India (Zhang et al., 2009), Varma (2009, 2010) including those termed born globals. Emerging economies refer to "low-income, rapid growth countries using economic liberalization as their primary engine of growth" (Hoskisson et al., 2000). One of the defining features of emerging economies in the last couple of decades has been the policy of economic liberalization favored by their governments (Hoskisson et al., 2000; Wright et al., 2005). Economic liberalization is a unique and powerful environmental contingency faced by firms in developing economies, which significantly changes the business environment by increasing competition, changing regulations, and creating new business opportunities. The forces of economic liberalization acting on firms from emerging economies are therefore equivalent to significant "institutional transitions" introducing fundamental and comprehensive changes to "the formal and informal rules of the game that affect organizations as players" (Peng, 2003) and encourage entrepreneurial behavior. There is, however, scant literature, which explicitly examines entrepreneurship within the context of the emerging economy firm's attempts to internationalize. This paper seeks to fill that gap and initiate discussion in that regard.

Method and Sample

Since the study focuses on an initial exploratory analysis, it has chosen the case study method as the research strategy. The case study method is suitable for model and grounded theory development along with a focus on complex processes that take a long time to unfold (Yin, 1991). As there is practically no theory on the phenomenon of born globals in India, the paper chose to ground model development on actual case data complemented with a deep review of received theories on internationalization (Eisenhardt, 1989).

Following Eisenhardt (1991), Miles and Huberman (1991) the paper focused on case studies of Indian IT firms that had made an international acquisition within five years of coming into existence. The sampling frame was defined following Miles and Huberman (1994) setting-event-actor-process parameter setting. Accordingly, we focused on Indian IT born global acquirers (setting), on the early and rapid internationalization process (event), on the top management team of these firms (actors) and the process of making an overseas acquisition early in the organization's life (process). Consistent with Eisenhardt's recommendation for a theoretical sampling strategy, we introduced variance along important theoretical dimensions by including both hardware and software firms, with varying areas of specialization and firms with both public and private listing in the sample. Consistent with established sample selection criteria in born global research, all firms were less than five years old at the time of international venturing and derived significant competitive advantage from the use of resources and sale of outputs in multiple countries from inception.

Data Sources

The data for this study is based on the M&A activity of the Indian IT industry during January 2001 to March 2007. It uses secondary reported firm-level data from studies by consulting firms such as UBS, Accenture and MAPE, as well as "Prowess," the Centre for Monitoring Indian Economy (CMIE) database. The study also examines published firm-specific information and media coverage (including their websites) to assemble a final data base. Data is based on the statements made by the top management of the firms in addition to reports in popular and business media (print and internet sources) to undertake a content analysis of the motives behind these cross-border M&A activities.

Firms included in the study are those that have undertaken a merger or an acquisition between 2001 and 2007, and are incorporated in India. The study excludes acquisition activity by firms that are subsidiaries of foreign firms and have been used as a vehicle of acquisition.

While primary data through a survey or questionnaire may be the ideal method for a study such as this, problems of low response, subjective bias, and a lack of research culture in the emerging economy scenario preclude their use. The use of data from "Prowess" has been increasingly vouched for by researchers such as Khanna and Palepu (2000b), Khanna and Rivkin (2005), and Chacar and Vissa (2005).

SAMPLE SELECTION

Between 2000 and 2007 there were over 521 overseas acquisitions from India out of which 133 (25.5 percent) were from the IT sector carried out by 47 firms. Fifty-six percent of the acquisitions in the sample had a market-seeking motive, followed by product and efficiency seeking acquisitions. The study also found that 12 percent of total acquisitions in the sample were undertaken by firms which were incorporated less than five years before they made their first global acquisitions (Varma, 2009).

We call these firms the Born Global Acquirers and select some of them for the final sample based on the criteria discussed below.

SPEED OF INTERNATIONALIZATION

The first criterion to differentiate BGFs from traditional internationalizes is the speed of internationalization. It can be described by two different time spans, namely:

> *(a)* The time span between founding and the first foreign market entry, and *(b)* the time span between the first and the following foreign market entries.

In previous studies, the time span between founding and the first foreign market entry is most commonly used to differentiate BGFs from traditional internationalizers. For example, Rennie (1993), Knight and Cavusgil (1996), and Kandasaami and Huang (2000) postulate a time span of two to three years from the time of founding. This definition is based on the consideration that it is hardly possible to speak of a global vision when the first internationalization step takes place after more than three years.

The time span between the first and the second foreign market entry is only mentioned by a few authors (Lindqvist, 1991; Autio et al., 2000; McNaughton, 2000; Stray et al., 2001). For example, Melin (1992) points out that, firms in technology-intensive industries show shorter time spans until their next internationalization step than firms in other industries. The study of Stray et al. (2001), however, reveals that technology-based firms show different speeds of internationalization. Generally, it is agreed that this time span should be shorter than between founding and first foreign market entry.

Since this paper is focused on a specific category of BGFs—viz., BCAs we designed an alternate criterion for classification:

(a) The first acquisition took place within five years of incorporation
(b) The firm had a subsequent foreign entry within the next three years

THE GEOGRAPHIC SCOPE OF INTERNATIONALIZATION

The geographic scope of internationalization of a BGF can be measured by the following criteria: *(a)* number of countries, *(b)* number of cultural clusters, and *(c)* number of geographical regions in which the firm is present. To call a firm global, Kandasaami (1998) demands that it should have activities in at least five countries. Other authors claim that a further distinction between cultural clusters (Hofstede, 2001) and geographical regions is necessary to clarify the physical and geographical distance of foreign markets from the home market. For example, Switzerland and South Africa fall into the same cultural cluster but represent two different geographical regions. Therefore, according to Lummaa (2002), speaking of BGFs requires at least activities in two cultural clusters and geographical regions. The corresponding criterion for this paper is that the firm must have a geographical presence in at least three countries.

FOREIGN SALES

Besides the number of foreign markets, the proportion of foreign sales compared to total sales of a firm presents a further criterion of BGFs. Kandasaami and Huang (2000) suggest a minimum ratio of 10 percent of foreign sales compared to total sales. Madsen et al. (2000) claim at least a ratio of 25 percent is necessary to speak of a BGF. The study by Lummaa (2002) revealed in three of four cases even a ratio of 90 percent. This paper considers a ratio of 10 percent of foreign sales to be sufficient.

The firms and their relevant features are briefly described below.

SAMPLE DESCRIPTION

IBS SOFTWARE SERVICES: IBS, was incorporated in 1997 in response to the global need for a software solutions company in the fast growing travel, tourism, and logistics industry. It began global operations in 1998, had a presence in three different geographies by 2001, and made its first overseas acquisition in 2002. Its founder V.K. Mathews, an aeronautical engineer from IIT Kanpur, has varied global experience in the travel industry. It has used a strategic mix of alliances and acquisitions to emerge as a leading international player in the travel space. Some of its notable alliances were with Oracle Corporations, Sun Microsystems and BEA Systems in 2001 and with Cendant Corporation USA in 2004 and important acquisitions were TopAir, Avient Technologies, Discovery Travel Systems, and VISaer Inc.

FOUR SOFT LIMITED: Four Soft Limited is the world's largest transportation and logistics software products company. Initially promoted, as a private limited company, by technocrat Palem Srikanth whose global experience includes both his education at Stanford and prior global work experience in supply chain management. The company owes its existence to the government's EOU/STP scheme and has moved up the technological capability ladder by obtaining various ISO and SEI-CMMI certifications. It has used a variety of modes of international entry and has a global presence in 10 countries.

MPHASIS: MphasiS Limited (then, MphasiS BFL Limited) was formed in June 2000 after the merger of the US-based IT consulting company MphasiS Corporation (founded in 1998) and the Indian IT services company BFL Software Limited (founded in 1993). The company was founded by Jerry Rao and Jeroen Tas, both former Citibank employees. Starting out as a BPO and application services outsourcer in the BFSI segment, it subsequently moved into telecom and health industries as well.

Its global character was evidenced by an Indian CEO, a Dutch president and more than a dozen subsidiaries in Europe, the US, and Asia. It enhanced its technological capability through both domestic and overseas acquisition cum alliances based strategy, making it among the top software exporters of the country within a couple of years of coming into existence. It was acquired by software services firm EDS in 2006, which in turn was acquired by HP in 2008.

MOSCHIP SEMICONDUCTORS: Founded in 1991, Moschip made its first acquisition in 2001. A firm with a geocentric orientation, its chips are designed in India, manufactured in Taiwan and sold through its offices in USA. The firm's CEO K. Ramchandra Reddy is an electronics engineer with a global vision acquired through both his education at Winconsin and work in Silicon Valley USA. A serial entrepreneur, Reddy has several start ups to his credit, besides having the credit for designing the world's first DSP chip. He also has extensive experience in sub contracting and manufacture of semi conductors. The firm has a global presence in all the continents.

VMOKSHA TECHNOLOGIES: Vmoksha Technologies is an IT services company headquartered in Bangalore, India as a private limited company. Since its inception in May 2001, Vmoksha has emerged as a key player in the global IT outsourcing space. Vmoksha currently has operations in the US, Europe, and the Asia Pacific region (development centers in Bangalore and Singapore). It is the first company in the world to directly go for CMMI Level 5 assessment without being assessed at intermediate levels and the 16th IT company in the world to achieve CMMI Level 5. It is the second company in the world to be assessed for all the four disciplines of CMMI—Software Engineering, System Engineering, Supplier Sourcing, and Integrated Process and Product Development. The company was included among SMEs from India poised to succeed on account of the strong offshoring model and included among the top 100 out-shorers of the world in terms of revenue.[1]

THEORETICAL MODEL DEVELOPMENT

The basic purpose of this paper is to examine the role of the entrepreneur as an initiating force in the appearance of the Born Global Acquirer profiled here. The theoretical foundations for hypothesis development are based on constructs from the Resource-based View (RBV) (Penrose, 1959; Barney, 1991) and Institutional Theory (Hoskisson et al., 2000; Scott, 1995).

Resource Based View

The Resource Based View (RBV) of the firm (Porter, 1959; Barney, 1991) emphasizes the role of heterogeneous capabilities as drivers of firm strategies. According to Barney (1991) the term "resource" covers "all assets, capabilities, organizational processes, firm attributes, information and knowledge controlled by a firm." Organizational capability is a system of organizational routines that create firm specific and hard to imitate advantages. A firm's organizational capability consists of *(i)* static capabilities to consistently outperform rivals at any given point in time and *(ii)* dynamic capabilities that enable a firm to improve its performance and outperform its rivals Penrose (1968), Nelson and Winter (1982), Teece (1992). Nelson and Winter (1982) explain that a firm's capability development depends upon access to technological and organizational knowledge and is conditioned by its past learning. These capabilities are heterogeneous, conditioned by local factors and difficult to imitate or replicate. The heterogeneity of firm capability and its stickiness are responsible for the diversity of firm strategy. Knight and Cavusgil (2004) argue that the ability of born global firms to succeed in foreign markets is largely a function of their internal capabilities (Wu et al., 2007). Evolutionary economics (Nelson and Winter, 1980) elaborate on the superior ability of firms to develop particular organizational capabilities. According to this view, the superior ability of certain firms to create new knowledge leads to the development of organizational capabilities (Wu et al., 2007). There is growing evidence that competitive advantage often depends on the firm's superior deployment of capabilities (Christensen and

---

[1] www.sharedexpertise.org

Overdorf, 2000; Day, 1994). From the RBV, this advantage may result from development of capabilities over an extended period of time that become embedded in a company and are difficult to trade. Alternatively, it may possess a capability that is idiosyncratic to the firm (Dierickx and Cool, 1989) or embedded in a firm's culture (Barney, 1991). Thus, based on the RBV, capabilities are often critical drivers of firm performance (Eisenhardt and Martin, 2000; Makadok, 2001; Teece et al., 1997).

Capability based resources are especially important for born globals, as they deal with diverse environments across numerous foreign markets (Luo, 2000). Possession of such capabilities helps firms to attenuate their liabilities of foreignness and newness (Oviatt and McDougall, 1994). The ability to consistently replicate the firm's capabilities across numerous and varied markets produces value for born globals by supporting, especially, international expansion (Knight and Cavusgil, 2004). Based on the afore-mentioned discussion, the RBV seems appropriate as the supporting theory to this study.

Institutional Theory

This theory (Hoskisson et al., 2000; Scott, 1995) has been a useful tool for understanding phenomena related to emerging economies. Institutions are conceptualized as "the rules of the game in a society" (North, 1990: 3; Scott, 1995) and institutional transitions are defined (Peng, 2003: 276) as the "fundamental and comprehensive changes introduced to the formal and informal rules of the game that affect organizations as players." One of the defining features of emerging economies is the policy of economic liberalization favored by their governments (Hoskisson et al., 2000; Wright et al., 2005). Economic liberalization is a unique and powerful environmental contingency faced by firms from these developing economies compared to firms from advanced nations, which have traditionally been more market-oriented. Firms in the countries undergoing economic liberalization face significantly different business environment characterized by increasing competition, changing regu-lations, increasingly demanding customers, emergence of new business opportunities, etc. (Ray, 2003). The forces of economic liberalization ac-ting on the firms from emerging economies are therefore equivalent to significant "institutional transitions" (Peng, 2003) leading to a variety of strategic responses. Economic liberalization measures such as deregulation and privatization in hitherto protected economies such as India has been the source of both opportunities and threats. This may translate into a defensive strategic positioning aimed at protecting their position in the domestic market (which precludes internationalization) or an assertive strategy aimed at leveraging new strategies through internationalization (Ray and Chitoor, 2007).

In this context, the paper posits that government induced policy changes and institutional forces can act as a catalyst towards accelerated internationalization through increased entrepreneurial behavior leading to the appearance of born global firms.

The conceptual framework developed provides the starting point for the development of two basic hypotheses outlined below:

H1. The appearance of a BGA depends on firm specific capabilities vested in the entrepreneur.

H2. Institutional and policy induced changes act as a catalyst for entrepreneurial behavior, causing the appearance of a BGA.

The RBV of the firm (Grant, 1996a; Penrose, 1959; Rumelt, 1984; Teece and Pisano, 1994; Wernerfelt, 1984) helps to explain, how in the context of an innovative culture, knowledge and resultant capabilities are developed and leveraged by enterprising firms. Differential endowment of resources is an important determinant of organizational capabilities and performance (Barney, 1991; Grant, 1996a; Teece and Pisano, 1994; Wernerfelt, 1984). Foundational resources are particularly important in turbulent business environments, as they become the basis for stable strategy formulation (Grant, 1996a; Prahalad and Hamel, 1990). Knowledge is the most important resource, and the integration of individuals' specialized knowledge is the essence of organizational capabilities (Conner and Prahalad, 1996; Dierieckx and Cool, 1989, Grant, 1996a; Leonard-Barton, 1992; Nelson and Winter, 1982; Solow, 1957). In international business, knowledge provides particular advantages that facilitate foreign market entry and operations (Kogut and Zander, 1993). The integration of specialist knowledge hinges on the nature and quality of the firm's organizational routines, which involve conversion of especially tacit knowledge (Polanyi, 1996) into business activities that create value for customers. Tacit knowledge is embedded in individuals and cannot be expressed explicitly or codified in written form (Nonanka, 1994). We argue that smaller international firms such as born global firms may manifest specific resources that are instrumental to the conception and implementation of activities in international markets. Although these businesses tend to lack substantial financial and human resources, they may leverage a collection of more fundamental intangible resources that facilitate their international success. Peng (2001a) argue that the RBV can allow businesses to identify specific knowledge and capability as valuable, unique, and hard-to-imitate resources that separate winners from losers in global competition (Dev et al., 2002), allowing smaller firms to differentiate themselves and succeed abroad. The most important knowledge resources are unique, inimitable and immobile and vest in the individual entrepreneur.

H1a. The appearance of the BGA depends on the firm's entrepreneurial resources.

Various studies have chronicled personal resources as important initiating forces of BGFs. The international experience of the founder or top management team especially, has a positive effect on the appearance of BGFs (Lindqvist, 1991; Reuber and Fischer, 1997; Harveston et al., 2000; Schmidt-Buchholz, 2001; Westhead et al., 2001; Gaba et al., 2002; Rhee and Cheng, 2002; Mahnke and Venzin, 2003; Johnson, 2004). The same applies to foreign language competence (Schmidt-Buchholz, 2001) and a distinct international vision or geocentric mentality (Lindqvist, 1991; McKinsey & Co., 1993; Oviatt and McDougall, 1994, 1995; Kandasaami, 1998; Harveston et al., 2000; Johnson, 2004) which could, among others, be shaped by family background (McAuley, 1999; Westhead et al., 2001). Entrepreneurial competencies acquired as a result of previous employment, technological expertise, and existing networking links create an awareness of internationalization opportunities in niche areas (Keeble, 1998). Also the age of the founder or founders has a positive effect, meaning that elder (and ceteris paribus more internationally experienced) founders or top managers tend to an earlier and geographically more distant market entry than younger ones. Finally, the risk-taking propensity of BGFs is higher than those of traditional internationalizers (Harveston et al., 2000: 96).

H1b. The higher the internationality (international experience, foreign language competence, family background) of the founder or top management team of a company, the higher the probability of the appearance of a BGA.

International networking capability refers to a firms' ability to obtain resources from the environment through alliance creation and social embeddedness, to use in its activities in foreign markets (Granovetter, 1985; Gulati, 1998). Networking is one of the major strategies pursued by entrepreneurial firms in order to gain access to resources and cope with environmental uncertainty and impediments in their operations (Alvarez and Barney, 2001; Steensma et al., 2000).

According to Coviello and Cox (2006), "network" is a metaphor used to represent a set of connected actors. These actors may be either organizations or individuals, and the relationships that tie them together may take many forms such as those between customers, suppliers, service providers, or government agencies. Further, Kelley et al. (2009) described "networks" as containing sets of relationships linking finite numbers of members. They view networks as avenues through which the diverse and situation-specific knowledge needs of an innovation project can be accessed across the organizational environment. Such networks contribute to the success of firms by helping to identify new market opportunities and contribute to building market knowledge (Chetty and Holm, 2000; Coviello and Munro, 1995). Based on previous literature, networks are referred to in this paper as those organizational ties with customers, suppliers, service providers, or government agencies.

Concerning social resources, previous studies point out nearly consistently that there is a very close connection between the integration of a company or founders in formal and informal networks and internationalization speed (Linqvist, 1991; Coviello and Munro, 1995; McAuley, 1999; Schmidt-Buchholz, 2001; Mahnke and Venzin, 2003; Johnson, 2004). One reason could be that companies or founders with well developed networks are stimulated to a higher degree by their (potential) customers, suppliers or partners to internationalize (horizontal and vertical bandwagon and follower effect) (Crick and Jones, 2000). Due to scarce resources in the beginning, companies are often dependent on resources of their network partners to expand internationally (Oviatt and McDougall, 1994). Besides, companies with a strong network integration can benefit from their experiences and gain relevant market knowledge, as well as, general knowledge about internationalization sooner than other companies (Reuber and Fischer, 1997). According to the Uppsala model, this has again a positive effect on internationalization speed and the degree of geographic expansion.

Moyi (2003) points to the growing interest in social relationships and its affect on the development of outcomes. Collier (1998) argues that social interaction generates three main externalities. These include knowledge about the behavior of other agents, knowledge about the non-behavior (such as prices and technologies), and the benefits of collective action. A firm's relationship capability affects enterprise performance directly since it generates information on technologies and markets (Zhou et al., 2007; Etemad and Lee, 2003).

H1c. Integration of the company and its founders in formal and informal networks increases the probability of the appearance of a BGA.

Access to financial resources, particularly loan capital and the possibility of additional partners are important initiating factors in the appearance of BGAs (Lindqvist, 1991; Schmidt-Buchholz, 2001; Gaba et al., 2002). It is contended that firms with access to financial resources coupled with a geocentric orientation are likely to make an early appearance on the global stage. In the emerging economy context this is linked to institutional changes which make access to capital easier and faster.

According to the institutional economics perspective, the most significant role of networks in emerging economies is that it substitutes for external markets (Caves, 1989; Khanna and Palepu, 1997). The lack of an adequate legal framework and a stable political structure in emerging economies has resulted in the underdevelopment of strategic factor markets (Barney, 1986), which leads to difficulties in creating the competitive advantages necessary for international expansion. Networks substitute for the undeveloped external markets for product development, financial capital, and entrepreneurial and management know-how in emerging economies (Khanna and Palepu, 1997). Institutional network ties refer to linkages with various domestic institutions such as government officials and agencies, banks and financial institutions, universities, and trade associations and provide critical advantages for firms in emerging economies. From the resource dependence perspective (Pfeffer and Salancik, 1978), institutional networks are the resources that firms depend on in order to be able to operate in a market.

In addition to getting permission from the government, links with domestic trade associations and professional bodies can provide intelligence on different markets and access to those markets for international operations. Also, owing to the lack of credit history and the liability of foreignness, it is difficult or costly for emerging-market firms to secure financial support in the host countries. On the other hand, the banking systems in most emerging economies are relational in nature, and banks are willing to provide long-term loans. Hence links with domestic financial institutions are another valuable tie that firms need to obtain for successful international venturing.

H2a. Access to financial resources as a result of institutional changes and liberalization increases the probability of appearance of Born Global Acquirers.

In addition to firm specific ownership advantages, firms in emerging economies have to undertake corporate entrepreneurial activities so that they can accumulate venturing capabilities, knowledge, and experience for successful international venturing.

Corporate entrepreneurship is defined as encompassing three types of process: innovation, venturing, and strategic renewal (Guth and Ginsberg, 1990; Zahra, 1996). Innovation refers to the firm's commitment to introducing new products, production processes, and organizational systems, and venturing refers to new business creation (Covin and Slevin, 1991; Lumpkin and Dess, 1996). Strategic renewal refers to the creation of new wealth through new combinations of resources (Guth and Ginsberg, 1990). It involves changing a firm's scope of business, competitive approach, or both (Stopford and Baden-Fuller, 1994), and building and acquiring new capabilities and creatively leveraging them to add shareholder value (Zahra, 1996). All three processes are relevant to the transformation of firms from emerging economies to become competitive players in the global market.

The adoption of corporate entrepreneurship represents a fundamental change in a firms' strategic behaviors in response to institutional changes (Spenner et al., 1998). For firms that have been embedded in the former planned economy for a long period of time, the presence of corporate entrepreneurship cannot be assumed. It is commonly believed in mature markets that a firm without the ability to have some levels of corporate entrepreneurship will fail. However, this is not necessarily the case in an emerging economy, where the role of the government and the operation of the economy are significantly different from those in mature economies. As the firm moves internationally, an entrepreneurial transformation of these firms is necessary for achieving efficiency, improving productivity, and creating wealth (Baumol, 1996).

H2b. Institutional changes lead to the emergence of corporate entrepreneurship facilitating the emergence of a Born Global Acquirer.

An organization has a certain mix of organizational learning capabilities (OLC) and may evolve to certain generic capabilities (Bhatnagar, 2006). OLC has been defined as formal and informal processes and structures in place for the acquisition, sharing, and utilizing of knowledge and skills in an organization (Dibella et al., 1996); as capabilities for self-reflecting and planning and environmental scanning to disseminate and share information to act and experiment (Shukla, 1995); and as dynamic capabilities that integrate/build/reconfigure competences to address rapidly changing environments (García-Morales et al., 2006). Based on these previous researches, we define international learning capability as a firm's ability to actively acquire, share, and utilize its advantage intelligence to plan and disseminate information in order to address rapidly changing environments on foreign market in this study.

Existing literature indicates that organizational learning forms a key dimension of organizational culture in the organization theory literature (Brown, 1998; Moorman, 1995). Bertels and Savage (1999) stress the significance of organizational learning in keeping up with market needs. The adaptive firm would foster learning norms that strengthen its ability to expand in foreign markets (Kitchell, 1995). Compared with traditional firms, born global firms may be characterized by their ability to overcome learning impediments that hamper the ability to adapt to and grow in new environments (Autio et al., 2000). Also, when the firm seeks to foster entrepreneurship as it expands worldwide, it has to maximize the knowledge flows and learning across its different countries (Zahra et al., 2000, 2001; Ireland et al., 2001). In the context of countries like India, the emergence of the National Innovation System plays a significant role in skill formation and organizational learning of firms prompting them to undertake overseas acquisitions.

H2c. The emergence of the Born Global Acquirer is facilitated by organisational learning which is the result of institutional and policy changes and the emergence of the National Innovation System.

ANALYSIS AND DISCUSSION

This paper has profiled the international entrepreneurial orientation as a driver of five Born Global Acquirers from the Indian IT industry. These firms came into existence with the geocentric orientation that helped them consider the global market as their natural home, driven by personal characteristics of their entrepreneur and facilitated by changes in the institutional environment. Keeping in mind the fact that the paper focuses on a specific type of "born global" firms viz., born global acquirers (BGAs) from India, the results and findings should be viewed in this light.

The findings of the study point towards a more rapid pace of internationalization than is usually reported in the classic stages theory literature as it profiles five young firms which have made global acquisitions within a few years of incorporation. The firms profiled here belong to the IT industry which is the most globalized and internationalized sectors of the Indian economy. The industry has rapidly moved up the value chain from body shoppers to customized product development (Parthasarthy, 2004; Bhatnagar, 2006), assisted by government policy which focused on investment in technical education leading to the development of a pool of English speaking trained manpower suitable for low cost programming and software development services.

The story of the IT industry's outward orientation began with the establishment of linkages through exports. Starting merely as providers of manpower, initially to be expatriated to firms elsewhere, time and cost arbitrage ensured that the IT industry were to become off-shore centres where efficiency mattered. And subsequently it grew vertically toward product development. The firms enriched in cash by providing manpower and in-sourcing found in customer acquisition the sustainability of revenues and profitability; while other players relied on the acquisition of products to move in the hierarchy of capability maturity.

In the current context, institutional policy change as a result of liberalization of the domestic economy facilitated aggressive venturing into global markets through the acquisition route. The 1980s witnessed the earliest cautious efforts to liberalize private investment and trade (Sridharan, 1996), leading to the enactment of policies aimed at ensuring India's inclusion in the global software boom. Using a "flood in flood out" feature which led to the growth of "thousands of small software companies in the country ... increasing export as well as local development" (Dataquest, 1987: 87) marked the beginning of networks of learning for the industry, which were later enhanced into personal networks of valuable reputations based on quality and productivity and got utilized for aggressive outward venturing.

The acquisition experience of these firms has been the result of innovation springing from internal R&D drawn from its own accumulated knowledge of the IT industry and domain experience gathered elsewhere. The linkages developed by entrepreneurs through prior experience in the IT industry and other domains enabled them to take the decision to acquire, facilitating leapfrogging and spring-boarding behavior to be able to leverage their resources for acquisition purposes in the global market.

All firms profiled in the study have been led by individuals with prior international experience of both the IT industry and also other domains, using opportunities in prior networks and the tacit knowledge vested in these leaders for rapid internationalization. This is consistent with Keeble et al. (1998) that competencies embodied in the founder/entrepreneur often relate to "a new and specialised technological niche which provides the opportunity for internationalization." These competencies are derived from previous employment, prior networks and technological expertise which makes them aware of new international opportunities that others remain unaware of.

As regulations relating to overseas investment were eased in the 1990s in the current phase of liberalization, it paved the way for all modes of international ventures (Nayyar, 2008). Simpler rules and easier access to money thus created a conducive environment in India for shopping overseas. Post liberalization, many Indian firms became more profitable as a result of an ever-booming economy and could access significantly more capital than in the past. A significant factor explaining acquisition activity therefore was the cash availability in the Indian market since many companies were under leveraged and did not have much debt. This enhanced their borrowing capacity which could be deployed for acquisitions.

Unlike most international M&A transactions that typically feature stock swaps in the financing arithmetic, Indian acquirers have for the most part paid cash for their targets, helped by a combination of internal resources and borrowings. Indian companies were also creating new international financial vehicles such as special purpose vehicles (SPVs) and setting up subsidiaries to route payments and take advantage of favorable tax regimes in countries like Mauritius. Private equity funds also emerged as a major source of money for Indian acquirers of overseas companies.

CONCLUSION

This paper has focused on the discovery, evaluation, and exploitation of international entrepreneurial opportunities of a specific kind of BGF— the Born Global Acquirer in the Indian context, as per a pioneering study. Born Globals are emerging in substantial numbers worldwide, and reflect an emergent paradigm, with the potential to become a leading species in the ecosystem of international business. In this sense, the born-global phenomenon is heartening because it implies the emergence of an international exchange system in which any firm, regardless of age, experience, and tangible resources, can be an active international business participant. Although large global corporations and the negative aspects of globalization often dominate reports in the popular press with respect to the emergent world order, the increasing role of born globals implies a more optimistic view. In relative terms, born globals might be seen to herald a more diverse international business system in which any firm can succeed internationally. Future research should aim at deepening our understanding of early adopters of internationalization, which represent a widespread, ongoing trend.

This study points towards international entrepreneurial capability as a key driver in the emergence of the Born Global Acquirer. It highlights the importance of networks and prior learning as the key to the emergence of the born global, assisted by institutional transitions. Despite their resource limitations these firms are rich in organizational learning capability, which is leveraged for their emergence on the global stage.

Being a pioneering study, the value of the present research lies in its exploration of hitherto uncharted territory. It has focused on international ventures with a deeper commitment than is normally considered in the literature on Born Globals since the Indian IT industry has mainly developed as an export oriented one and therefore merely exporting firms were thought unsuitable for the categorization considered here.

However, greater research effort is required to test the theoretical constructs developed here on a larger data base including "born global" firms from other industries and also in a cross-country comparative manner.

REFERENCES

Alahuhta, M. (1990) *Global Growth Strategies for High Technology Challenger*. Helsinki: ACTA Polytechnica Scandinavia.

Almor, T. (2000) "Born Global: The Case of Small and Medium Sized, Knowledge-intensive, Israeli Firms," in T. Almor and N. Hashai (eds), *FDI, International Trade and The Economics of Peacemaking*. Rishon LeZion, Israel: The College of Management, Academic Studies Division.

Aspelund, A. and O. Moen (2001) "A Generation Perspective on Small Firm Internationalization: From Traditional Exporters and Flexible Specialists to Born Globals," in C.N. Axinn and P. Matthyssens (eds), *Reassessing The Internationalisation of the Firm*, pp. 197–225. Amsterdam: JAI Press.

Autio, E., H.J. Lummaa, and P. Arenius (2002) "Emergent 'born globals'. Crafting early and rapid internationalization strategies in technology-based new firms." Paper submitted to the 22nd Annual International Conference of the Strategic Management Society, September 22–25, Paris, France.

Autio, E., H.J. Sapienza, and J.G. Almeida (2000) "Effects of Age at Entry, Knowledge Intensity, and Imitability on International Growth," *Academy of Management Journal*, 43(5): 909–924.

Barney, J. (1991) "Firm Resources and Sustained Competitive Advantage," *Journal of Management*, 17(1): 99–120.

Barkema, H., J.D. Bell, and J. Pennings (1996) "Foreign Entry, Cultural Barriers and Learning," *Strategic Management Journal*, 17: 151–166.

Bell, J.D. (1995) "The Internationalization of Small Computer Software Firms," *European Journal of Marketing*, 29(8): 60–75.

Bhatnagar, S. (2006) "India's Software Industry," in Vandana Chandra (ed.), *How Some Countries Got it Right*, pp. 95–124. Washington DC: World Bank

Bloodgood, J.M., H.J. Sapienza, and J.G. Almeida, J.G. (1996) "The Internationalization of New High-potential U.S. Ventures: Antecedents and Outcomes," *Entrepreneurship Theory and Practice*, 20(4): 61–67.

Bonacorsi, A. (1992) "On the Relationship Between Firm Size and Export Intensity," *Journal of International Business Studies*, 23(4): 605–625.

Busch, A. et al. (2004) Macht im Netz. Wirtschaftswoche, 30: 42–47.

Caves, R.E. (1971) "International Corporations: The Industrial Economics of Foreign Investment," *Economica*, 38(1).

———. (1996) *Multinational Enterprise and Economic Analysis* (2nd edition). Cambridge: Cambridge University Press.

Chacar, A. and B. Vissa (2005) "Are Emerging Economies Less Efficient? Performance Persistence and the Impact of Business Group Affiliation," *Strategic Management Journal* 26(10): 933–946.

Chandler, A.D. (1986) "The Evolution of Modern Global Competition," in M.E. Porter (ed.), *Competition in Global Industries*. Boston: Harvard Business School Press.

———. (1990) "The Enduring Logic of Industrial Success," *Harvard Business Review*, 68(2): 130–140.

Collis, D.J. and C.A. Montgomery (1998) *Corporate Strategy: A Resource-based Approach*. Boston: McGraw-Hill.

Coviello, N.E. and H.J. Munro (1995) "Growing the Entrepreneurial Firm," *European Journal of Marketing*, 29(7): 49–61.

Coviello, N.E. and A. McAuley (1999) "Internationalization and the Smaller Firm: A Review of Contemporary Empirical Research," *Management International Review*, 39(3): 223–256.

Crick, D. and M.V. Jones (2000) "Small High-technology Firms and International High Technology Markets," *Journal of International Marketing*, 8(2): 63–85.

Dataquest (1987) The new Software Policy: Dr Seshagiri Clarifies. January, 82–95.

DeChiara, A. and A. Minguzzi (2002) "Success Factors in SMEs' Internationalization Processes: An Italian Investigation," *Journal of Small Business Management*, 40(2): 144–153.

Eisenhardt K.M. (1989) "Building Theories from Case Studies Research," *Academy of Management Review*, 14(4): 532–550.

———. (1991) "Better Stories and Better Constructs. The Case for Rigor and Comparitive Logic," *Academy of Management Review*, 16(3): 620–627.

Freeman, J., G. Carroll, and M.T. Hannan (1983) "The Liability of Newness: Age Dependence in Organizational Death Rates," *American Sociological Review*, 48(5): 692–710.

Fujita, M. (1995) "Small and Medium-sized Transnational Corporations: Salient Features," *Small Business Economics*, 7: 251–271.

Gaba, V., Y. Pan, and G.R. Ungson (2002) "Timing of Entry in International Market: An Empirical Study of U.S. Fortune 500 firms in China," *Journal of International Business Studies*, 33(1): 39–55.

Gabrielsson, M. and V.H.M. Kirpalani (2004) "Born Globals: How to Reach New Business Space Rapidly," *International Business Review*, 13(5): 555–571.

Ganitsky, J. (1989) "Strategies for Innate and Adoptive Exporters: Lessons from Israel's Case," *International Marketing Review*, 6(5): 50–65.

Gankema, H. G.J., H.R. Snuit, and K.A. Van Dijken (1997) "The Internationalization Process of Small and Medium Sized Enterprises: An Evaluation of the Stage Theory," in R. Donckels and A. Miettinen (eds), *Entrepreneurship and SME Research: On its Way to the Next Millennium*, pp. 185–197. Aldershot: Ashgate Publishing Ltd.

Gomes-Casseres, B. (1997) "Alliance Strategies of Small Firms," *Small Business Economics*, 9(1): 33–44.

Hansen, N., K. Gillespie, and E. Genturck (1994) "SMEs and Export Involvement: Market Responsiveness, Technology and Alliances," *Journal of Global Marketing*, 7(4): 7–27.

Harveston, P.D., B.L. Kedia, and P.S. Davis (2000) "Internationalization of Born Global and Gradual Globalizing Firms: The Impact of the Manager," *Advances in Competitive Research*, 8(1): 92–99.

Hashai, N. and T. Almor (2004) "Gradually Internationalizing 'born global' Firms: An Oxymoron?" *International Business Review*, 13(4): 465–483.

Hedlund, G. and A. Kverneland (1985) "Are Strategies for Foreign Markets Changing? The Case of Swedish Investment in Japan," *International Studies of Management and Organization*, 15(2): 41–59.

Hofstede, G. (2001) *Culture's Consequences*. Thousand Oaks, London, New Delhi: Sage Publications.

Hoskisson, R., L. Eden, C.M. Lau, and M. Wright (2000) "Strategy in Emerging Economies," *Academy of Management Journal*, 43: 249–267.

Hurmerinta-Peltomäki, L. (2004) "Conceptual and Methodological Underpinnings in the Study of Rapid Internationalizers," in M.V. Jones and P. Dimitratos (eds), *Emerging Paradigms in International Entrepreneurship*. Cheltenham-Northampton: Edward Elgar Publications.

Hutzschenreuter, T., F. Guenther, and B. Oehring (2005) "Internationalization of Young, Fast-growing Companies: An Exploratory Study of the Organizational Design of the Headquarters-subsidiary Relationship," *Journal of Small Business and Entrepreneurship*, 18(1): 75–100.

Johanson, J. and J.E. Vahlne (1977) "The Internationalization Process of the Firm: A Model of Knowledge Development and Increasing Foreign Market Commitments," *Journal of International Business Studies*, 8(1): 23–32.

———. (1990) "The Mechanism of Internationalization," *International Marketing Review*, 7(4): 11–24.

Johanson, J. and Paul F. Wiedersheim (1975) "The Internationalization of the Firm—Four Swedish Cases," *Journal of Management Studies*, 7: 191–210.

Johnson, J.E. (2004) "Factors Influencing the Early Internationalization of High Technology Start-ups: US and UK Evidence," *Journal of International Entrepreneurship*, 2(1–2): 139–154.

Jolly, V.K., M. Alahutha, and J.P. Jeannet (1992) "Challenging the Incumbents: How High Technology Start-ups Compete Globally," *Journal of Strategic Change*, 1(1): 71–82.

Jones, M.V. (1999) "The Internationalization of Small High-technology Firms," *Journal of International Marketing*, 7(4): 15–41.

Jones, M.V. and N.E. Coviello (2005) "Internationalization: Conceptualizing An Entrepreneurial Process of Behaviour in Time," *Journal of International Business Studies*, 36(3): 284–303.

Kandasaami, S. (1998) "Internationalization of small- and medium-sized Born Global Firms: A Conceptual Model," Research paper, Graduate School of Management, Univer-sity of Western Australia.

Kandasaami, S. and X. Huang (2000) "International Marketing Strategy of SMEs: A Comparison of Born-global vs Non Born-global Firms in Australia," Paper presented at the ICSB Conference, Brisbane, June.

Keeble, D., C. Lawson, H. Lawton Smith, B. Moore, and F. Wilkinson (1998) "Internationalization Processes, Networking and Local Embeddedness in Technology Intensive Small Firms," *Small Business Economics*, 11: 327–342.

Khanna, T. and K. Palepu (2000) "The Future of Business Groups in Emerging Markets: Long run Evidence from Chile," *Academy of Management Journal*, 433: 268–285.

Khanna, T. and J. Rivkin (2001) "Estimating the Performance Effects of Business Groups in Emerging Markets," *Strategic Management Journal*, 22: 45–74.

Knight, G.A. and S.T. Cavusgil (1996) "The Born Global Firm: A Challenge to Traditional Internationalization Theory," in T.K. Madsen (ed.), *Advances in International Marketing*, pp. 11–26. Amsterdam: JAI Press.

———. (2004) "Innovation, Organizational Capabilities and the Born Global Firm," *Journal of International Business Studies*, 35(2): 124 –141.

Kuhn T.A. (1970) *The Structure of Scientific Revolution*. Chicago: University of Chicago Press.

Larimo, J. (2003) "Internationalization of SMEs: Two Case Studies of Finnish Born Global Firms," in A. Blomstermo and D.D. Sharma (eds), *Learning in the Internationalization Process of Firms*, pp. 258–280. Cheltenham-Northampton: Edwar Elgar Publishing.

Liesch, P.W. and G. Knight (1999) "Information Internalization and Hurdle Rates in Small and Medium Enterprise Internationalization," *Journal of International Business Studies*, 30(2): 383–395.

Lev, B. (2001) *Intangibles: Management, Measurement and Reporting*. Washington: Brookings Institution Press.

Lindqvist, M. (1991) "Infant Multinationals: The Internationalization of Young, Technology Based Swedish firms." Dissertation, Stockholm School of Economics, Institute of International Business.

Litvak, I. (1990) "Instant International: Strategic Reality for Small High-technology Firms in Canada," *Multinational Business*, 2(2): 1–12.

Lummaa, H.J. (2002) "Internationalization Behavior of Finnish Born Global Companies," Master Thesis, Helsinki University of Technology.

Luostarinen, R. (1979) *The Internationalization of The Firm*. Helsinki: Helsinki School of Economics.

Madsen, T.K., E. Rasmussen, and P. Servais (2000) "Differences and Similarities Between Born Globals and Other Types of Exporters," in A. Yaprak and H. Tütek (eds), *Globalization, the Multinational Firm, and Emerging Economies*, pp. 247–265. Amsterdam: JAI Press.

Madsen, T.K. and P. Servais (1997) "The Internationalization of Born Globals: An Evolutionary Process?" *International Business Review*, 6(6): 561–583.

Mahnke, V. and M. Venzin. (2003) "The Internationlization Process of Digital Information Good Providers," *Management International Review*, 1(Special Issue): 115–142.

McAuley, A. (1999) "Entrepreneurial Instant Exporters in the Scottish Arts and Crafts Sector," *Journal of International Marketing*, 7(4): 67–82.

McKinsey & Co. (1993) *Emerging Exporters: Australia's High Value-added Manufacturing Exporters*. Melbourne: Australian Manufacturing Council.

McNaughton, R.B. (2000) "Determinants of Time-span to Foreign Market Entry," *Journal of Euromarketing*, 9(2): 99–112.

McNaughton, R.B. and J.D. Bell. (1999) "Brokering Networks of Small Firms to Generate Social Capital for Growth and Internationalization," in A.M. Rugman, and R.W. Wright (eds), *Research in Global Strategic Management. International Entrepreneurship: Globalization of Emerging Businesses*. Stamford: JAI Press.

Melin, L. (1992) "Internationalization as a Strategic Process," *Strategic Management Journal*, 13(8, Special Issue): 99–118.

Miles, M.B. and A.M. Huberman (1994) *Qualitative Data Analysis: An Expanded Sourcebook*. Thousand Oaks, CA: Sage Publications.

Nayyar, D. (2008) "Internationalisation of Firms from India: Investment, Mergers and Acquisitions," in *Trade and Globalisation*. New Delhi: Oxford University Press.

Nelson, R. and S. Winter (1982) *An Evolutionary Theory of Economic Change*. Harvard University Press, Cambridge Massachusetts.

Nilsen, F.I. and P.W. Liesch (2000) "International Market Entry of Small Knowledge Based Firms: Towards a Synthesis of Economic and Behavioral Approaches." Paper presented at the Academy of International Business Annual Conference, Phoenix, Arizona.

North, D. (1990) *Institutions, Institutional Change and Economic Performance*. Cambridge: Cambridge University Press.

Ohmae, K. (1990) *The Borderless World*. New York: Harper Business.

Oviatt, B.M. and P.P. McDougall (1994) "Toward a Theory of International New Ventures," *Journal of International Business Studies*, 25(1): 45–64.

———. (1995) "Global Start-ups: Entrepreneurs on a World-wide Stage," *Academy of Management Executive*, 9(2): 30–43.

Parthasarthy, Balaji (2004) "India's Silicon Valley or Silicon Valley's India? Socially Embedding the Computer Software Industry in Bangalore," *International Journal of Urban and Regional Research*, 28(3): 664–685.

Peng, M.W. (2003) "Institutional Transitions and Strategic Choices," *Academy of. Management Review*, (28): 275–96.

Penrose, E. (1959) *The Theory of the Growth of the Firm*. Oxford: Oxford University Press.

Porter, M.E. (1991) "Towards a Dynamic Theory of Strategy," *Strategic Management Journal*, 12, Winter: 95–117.

Pradhan J.P. (2007) "Growth of Indian Multinationals in the World Economy: Implications for Development," *ISID WP No 2007/04*. Institute for Studies in Industrial Development, New Delhi.

——— (2007b) National Innovation System and the Emergence of Indian Information and Software Technology Multinationals, *ISID WP no 2007/09*, Institute for Studies in Industrial Development, New Delhi.

Preece, S.B., G. Miles, and M.C. Baetz (1999) "Explaining the International Intensity and Global Diversity of Early-stage Technology Based Firms," *Journal of Business Venturing*, 14(3): 259–281.

Rasmussen, E.S. and T.K. Madsen (2002) "The Born Global Concept," Paper presented at the 28th EIBA Conference, Athens, Greece.

Ray, and Chitoor (2007) "Internationalisation as a Strategic Response to Institutional Transition: Evidence from the Indian Pharmaceutical Industry," *WPS 608/2007*, IIM Kolkata.

Ray, S. (2003) "Strategic Adaptation of Firms During Economic Liberalization: Emerging Issues and a Research Agenda," *International Journal of Management*, 20(3): 271–281.

Rennie, M.W. (1993) "Global Competitiveness: Born Global," *The McKinsey Quarterly*, 3: 45–52.

Reuber, A.R. and E. Fischer (1997) "The Influence of the Management Team's International Experience on the Internationalization Behaviors of SMEs," *Journal of International Business Studies*, 28(4): 807–825.

Rhee, J.H. and J.L.C. Cheng (2002) "Foreign Market Uncertainty and Incremental International Expansion: The Moderating Effect of Firm, Industry, and Host Country Factors," *Management International Review*, 42(4): 419–439.

Rialp, A. and J. Rialp (2003) "Faster and More Successful Exporters: An Exploratory Study of Born Global Firms From the Resource-based View," Conference Paper, 7th Vaasa Conference on International Business, August 24–26.

Ruigrok, W. and H. Wagner (2003) "Internationalization and Performance: An Organizational Learning Perspective," *Management International Review*, 43(1): 63–83.

Rugman, A.M. and R.W. Wright (1999) *Research in Global Strategic Management. International Entrepreneurship: Globalization of Emerging Businesses*. Stamford: JAI Press.

Scott W.R (1995) *Institutions and Organisations*. Thousand Oaks, CA: Sage Publications.

Schmid, S. and A. Schmidt-Buchholz (2002). "Born Globals: What Drives Rapid and Early Internationalization of Small and Medium-sized Firms from the Software and Internet Industry?" in J. Larimo (ed.), *Current European Research in International Business*, pp. 44–63. Vaasa: University of Vaasa.

Schmidt-Buchholz, A. (2001) Born Globals: Die Schnelle Internationalisierung von High-tech Start-ups. Lohmar: Josef Eul Verlag.

Stray, S., S. Bridgewater, and G. Murray (2001) "The Internationalization Process of Small, Technology-based Firms: Market Selection, Mode Choice and Degree of Internationalization," *Journal of Global Marketing*, 25(1): 7–29.

Sridharan, E. (1996) *The Political Economy of Industrial Promotion: Indian Brazilian and Korean Electronics in a Comparative Perspective* 1969–1994. London: Praeger.

Storey, D.I. (1994) *Understanding the Small Business Sector*. London: Routledge.

Stuart, T.E., H. Hoang, and R.C. Hybels (1999) "Inter-organizational Endorsements and the Performance of Entrepreneurial Ventures," *Administrative Science Quarterly*, 44(2): 315–349.

Utterback, J. (1996) *Mastering the Dynamics of Innovation*. Cambridge: Harvard Business School Press.

Varma, Sumati (2009) "International Venturing by IT Firms: A Motive Analysis," *Journal of Emerging Knowledge On Emerging Markets*, 1(1). http://www.icainstitute.org/ojs/index.php/working_papers/article/view/24/11

———. (2010) "Born Global Acquirers from Indian IT—An Exploratory Case Study," *International Journal of Emerging Markets*.

Westhead, P., M. Wright, and D. Ucbasaran (2001) "The Internationalization of New and Small Firms: A Resource-based View," *Journal of Business Venturing*, 16(4): 333–358.

Wright, M., I. Filatotchev, R.E. Hoskisson, and M. Peng (2005) "Strategy Research in Emerging Economies: Challenging the Conventional Wisdom," *Journal of Management Studies*, 42(1): 1–33.

Yli-Renko, H., E. Autio, and V. Tomtit (2002) "Social Capital, Knowledge and the International Growth of Technology-based New Firms," *International Business Review*, 11: 279–304.

Zahra S.A. and G. George (2001) *International Entrepreneurship: The Current Status of the Field and Future Research Agenda*. Atlanta: Georgia State University.

13

Orchestrating Change: Shared Intentions is the Key Factor Enabling Change to Happen

Davide Sola, Marie Taillard,
and Giovanni Scarso Borioli

In an environment where some of our most respected household brand names can vanish overnight, firms undergo emergency mergers under duress, become the recipients of exorbitant government bailout packages, or have no choice but to reinvent themselves to survive—the notion of corporate change or transformation has taken on a whole new dimension. Transformation is no longer simply a matter of forward-thinking or opportunistic strategy, but rather the impact at the corporate level of a much broader system-wide metamorphosis of the global economy. Now, more than ever, it is incumbent upon researchers in organizational science to find answers to the question of how to successfully orchestrate the change process.

To provide some of these answers, we believe, requires a dual perspective—on the one hand, it is clearly important to look at the organization as a whole to understand the dynamics of organizational change; on the other hand, a thorough understanding of the psychological mechanisms that actually make change happen for one individual at a time is needed.

Corporate transformations are intricate organizational processes that require the concerted efforts often of large numbers of people with very different agendas and objectives. Experts estimate that 70 percent of change programs end in failure (Kotter, 2008), due to organization-wide parameters like firms' culture, communication, and corporate structure. However, when one examines corporate transformation from a "layman's" point of view, a simple conclusion is that change is really a matter of lots of people not just taking action, but doing so in a coordinated way so as to amount to a coherent whole.

In this chapter, we aim to show that current research on shared agency offers insight into organizational transformational processes, by highlighting two main points:

1. collective plans and individual action require individuals to form individual intentions to act,

2. individual intentions to act within a collective plan and towards a common goal must be coordinated or structured in some way in order for the project to be undertaken as a coherent whole.

We start our investigation by focusing on human agency in order to understand how and why collective action is undertaken. We then propose a change management blueprint that will help managers to successfully orchestrate change by fostering the conditions needed for individuals to take action in a coordinated fashion.

PLANS, INTENTIONS, AND PLANNED BEHAVIOR

Understanding the nature of human action has been an important pre-occupation for philosophers for millennia, and more recently a common thread of research among academics from diverse disciplines. In general, action is understood to be purposeful behavior, and is often contrasted to impulsive or unplanned behavior. Actions are the result of planning and are the deployment of means for the attainment of specific ends.

The nature and role of intentions are an important aspect of our investigations into human action. The late 20th century saw increased interest in the subject of intentions and intentionality on the part of philosophers as well as psychologists. Michael Bratman's (1987) *Planning Theory* bridges the gap between the two disciplines. He proposes that intentions are specific states of mind whose function of guiding, coordinating and organizing actions in future-directed and partial plans enables humans to achieve complex goals across time and interpersonally. According to Bratman, humans organize intentions into plans, which allow them to achieve complex goals even with limited cognitive resources. In this way, intentions are efficiency enablers, and can be seen as adaptive from an evolutionary point of view.

More recent work in neurophysiology and cognitive psychology offers further insight that complements Bratman's work. Reasoning is the main function of our conscious mind, the process that allows us to solve problems and make decisions in order to progress towards our goals. It happens by means of representational mental models. An inference leading to the solution of a problem is achieved by combining the existing models of the problem's premises with those other relevant models in our set of beliefs (knowledge) to generate new models of possible solutions (Johnson-Laird, 2008). For reasoning to take place, all such models must be kept active in our mind. The limitation of this process is our working memory, the capacity of the brain to keep active enough models and for

FIGURE 13.1: Individual Planned Agency

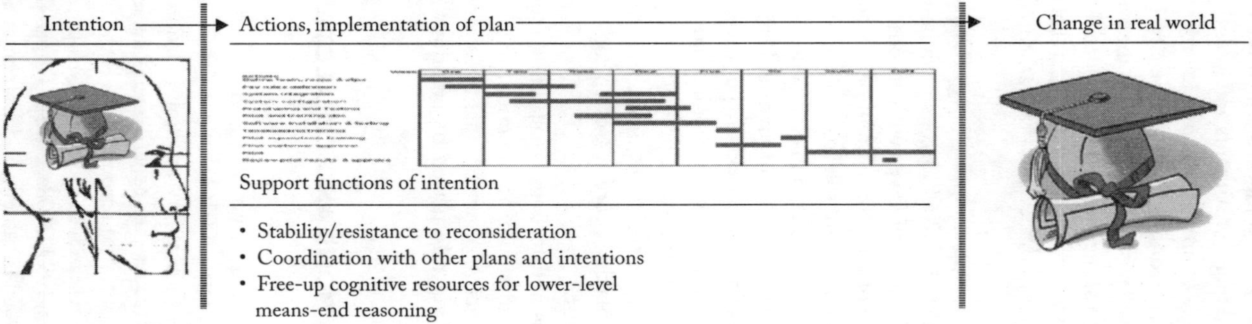

Intention → Actions, implementation of plan → Change in real world

Support functions of intention

- Stability/resistance to reconsideration
- Coordination with other plans and intentions
- Free-up cognitive resources for lower-level means-end reasoning

long enough to allow for decisions to be made and inferences finalized. Evolution allows us to overcome this difficulty by making us "planning" creatures. Plans, and their constituents and intentions, are a way to freeze all the previous stages of problem solving in order to save computational power and particularly working memory capacity. In other words, we first reason on higher-order possibilities related to the overall goal, we develop a high-order intention and commit to the associated course of action and then shift our cognitive attention to the next level of means-end reasoning, and so on until we get to the level of practical details that allows us to act (Bratman, 1987).

Recent developments in neurophysiology (Damasio, 1994) and psychology (e.g., Johnson-Laird, 2008) have shown how rational deliberation and reasoning are closely interwoven with unconscious and irrational processes, namely those of emotions. Emotions in fact are more and more viewed as playing an important role in cognition and behavior, as a bridge between the world of rationality and consciousness and that of biological regulation and innate mechanisms of survival (Damasio, 1994). According to Damasio's (1994) Somatic-Marker hypothesis, emotions and feelings play an active role in the process of reasoning and deciding in the personal and social domain by exercising a pre-selection of possible models of the future. Without such emotion-guided pre-deliberation our personal and social decision-making processes, often complex and time-sensitive, would be less efficient.

Clearly emotions and feelings constitute a fundamental step in the generation or consolidation of an intention, and we strongly believe that a full account of effective organizational transformation must take into account the important role played by emotions in intentionality and practical reasoning.

SHARED INTENTIONS AND COLLECTIVE PLANNED BEHAVIOR

Human beings are unique, according to biologists and psychologists (Tomasello and Racoczy, 2003; Warneken et al., 2006; Tomasello and Carpenter, 2007) in their ability to think individually while acting collectively in a way that takes each other's own plans and intentions, not just their observed behavior, into account. This is the field of shared agency, a very active area of research in biology, developmental psychology, and philosophy (Bratman, 1999, 2008a, 2008b; Tomasello and Racoczy, 2003; Warneken et al., 2006; Tomasello and Carpenter, 2007).

The sociality of human beings is key to their survival (Enfield and Levinson, 2006): we depend on each other to gain efficiency in accessing information and in performing required actions. Human action therefore might be conceived of on a continuum ranging from purely individual to more coordinated, to fully collaborative. While it is true that action at its physiological core is purely individual, it is also the case that some intentions are held uniquely and specifically by one single individual, while others happen to be shared with others. The ability to read other individuals' intentions is an important aspect of sociality and is the basis for many of our decisions as well as for human communication. As we will discuss below, emotions play an important role in facilitating intention reading. Depending on the intentions we perceive around us, we coordinate with others when our intentions are shared, change our course of action to allow or avoid collaboration, and, of course, persuade them to share intentions to suit our own needs.

Among the many important social functions of the human intention reading ability is its role in forming shared intentions, which we hypothesize to be mental models of future states requiring the corresponding intentions and actions of others. Intention reading lies at the very center of most of our sociality. Emotions and their physical manifestations provide (often unconsciously) specific hints or signals that facilitate and therefore play a central role in intention reading. We can speculate for instance that the notion of "responsiveness" introduced by Bratman (2002) as a condition for shared intentionality requires that we keep track of others' intentions as conditions evolve, and do so by interpreting visible signs of their emotions. In any case emotions seem to play an important role in the generation of shared intentions, at minimum as an instrument to constantly assess and check the status of intentions in the others, and possibly, as means to influence the deliberations towards the intended outcome by propagation of somatic markers.

When individuals act as a coherent entity, they are increasing the chance of reaching the desired shared outcome by agreeing, as a minimal condition, not to stand in each other's way. Beyond this minimal condition of non-interference, what constitutes shared intentions and distinguishes them from cases of coincidental joint action? Bratman (2008a) proposes a set of conditions, listed and developed below, that he argues are distinctive of shared intentionality in the absence of authority or explicit accountability that is characteristic of small informal groups.

(i) *"Intentions on the part of each in favor of the agents' joint activity."* This is a stronger requirement than an individual intention to contribute to a joint activity. The intention is for "our activity." If we share an intention that our family go for a walk, my own intention goes beyond intending to participate in a family walk.

(ii) *"Interlocking intentions."* Each agent's intention includes a reference to the role of each other agent's intention and vice-versa. Our shared intention to go for a family walk means that I intend that we take a family walk by way of you and other family members each intending that we take a family walk. Without your own intention to participate, there is no longer a shared intention for me to have.

(iii) *"Intentions in favor of 'meshing sub-plans'."* For us to have a shared intention means that we each have a commitment to having relevant sub-plans that are compatible with each other. We cannot share an intention to take a family walk if you only intend that we take a walk in the countryside and I only intend that we take a walk in the city. We must have a commitment to mutual compatibility of the relevant sub-plans to each other?

(iv) *"Disposition to help if needed."* Because of the interlocking feature, each agent must be sufficiently committed to each of the other agents' own intentions that they are disposed to help one another achieve their role in the joint action. I might help you finish your assignment so we can all take a family walk.

(v) *"Interdependence in the persistence of each person's relevant intentions."* Each agent is interdependent on the other's relevant intentions to persist over time. If we share an intention to have a family walk, we each depend on the others to stick to their intention.

(vi) *"Joint-action-tracking mutual responsiveness in the intentions and actions of each."* As the joint action unfolds, individuals need to be able to adapt means-end reasoning and further actions. Each of the individuals who share an intention tracks the joint action and is mutually responsive in their intentions and actions. If a family member needs to take a phone call as we walk out the door, we all respond by delaying our departure. The member on the phone knows to take it for granted that this is the case.

(vii) *"Common knowledge of conditions (i) to (vi) among the participants."* In a shared intention situation, individuals share the knowledge of the conditions just detailed.

In small informal groups with evenly distributed power, these conditions compensate for the lack of an authority figure or set of rules to dictate accountability. In doing so, the conditions ensure that shared intentions do indeed have all the characteristics necessary to qualify as

FIGURE 13.2: Planned Shared Agency

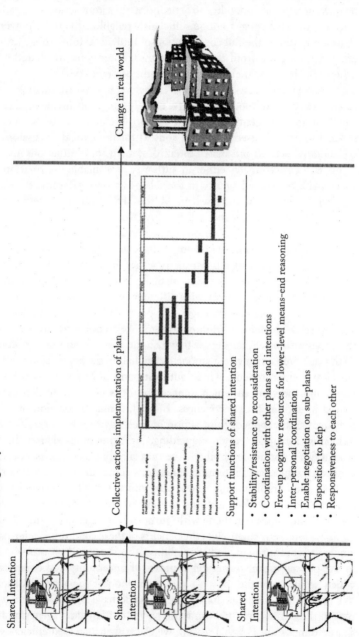

Shared Intention

Shared Intention

Shared Intention

Collective actions, implementation of plan

Change in real world

Support functions of shared intention

- Stability/resistance to reconsideration
- Coordination with other plans and intentions
- Free-up cognitive resources for lower-level means-end reasoning
- Inter-personal coordination
- Enable negotiation on sub-plans
- Disposition to help
- Responsiveness to each other

rational intentions for each individual: without these conditions, it would be unrealistic for an individual to actually intend a joint action as the commitment of others might not be sufficiently reliable. This is the power of shared intentions: the full commitment of individual intentions plus the efficiency resulting from the fact that these intentions are shared with others which makes them subject to conditions (i) to (vii).

The cooperative cases discussed so far belong to what Bratman (2008a) refers to as cases of modest sociality, namely situations involving a fairly small number of agents with equal authority (Bratman, 2008a). While modest sociality is used as a valid context for theoretical discussions of collaborative actions and shared intentions, many social situations involve some level of asymmetry either in authority or available information. Is there a role for shared agency in these larger groups? Recent strands of research in philosophy and law have addressed this issue and attempted to account for cases of non-modest sociality (Kutz, 2000; Shapiro, 2002).

We propose that organizations orchestrating change processes clearly do not meet the two criteria for modest sociality. They are too large and certainly do not present full symmetry either in terms of information or power. Indeed, change is usually instigated by only a few, while often requiring the actions of many with different agendas. In our opinion, the effectiveness of a change management program is directly correlated to the degree of "sharedness" of intentions to take on the necessary actions in the organization, i.e., the degree to which the shared intention conditions (i) through (vii) are prevalent among individuals in the organization. Firms are clearly environments where authority and information asymmetry reign, and therefore in which joint action does not have to depend on shared intentions for effectiveness. Instead, forms of coercion or other pressure can be applied. Joint action in such environments results from individual intentions, often coinciding, and sometimes shared. In the case of firms, the accountability issue that is resolved in modest sociality contexts by the shared intention conditions comes under external norms such as one's employment contract. In effect, by doing away with the need for the natural conditions for shared intentions under modest sociality and replacing them with authority or external norms, larger organizations deny themselves the benefits of these conditions in terms of efficiency, commitment, and adaptability. This is particularly problematic in the prevalent transformation contexts of uncertainty and complexity which would have the most to gain from modest sociality conditions. We believe however that shared intentions do have an important role to play in these cases, by combining the power of individual agency and its shared dimension. For this reason, we claim that increased efficiency in corporate transformations can be derived from fostering conditions of modest sociality. The means-end problem solving necessary to fully determine the detailed course of action to achieve a complex future oriented plan such as orchestrating corporate change is simply not possible in the initial instance, due to both humans' limited cognitive resources and limited information. Therefore, it is necessary that plans are constantly checked, revisited, and completed along the implementation process, and this requires participants to be actively involved in such creative process further and beyond the initial plan. Therefore, even when objectives and plans are shared, individuals will always generate different sub-plans along the way, hence conflicts will arise that authority structures won't always be able to deal with, as they are generated within the loose context of a common plan. This is where shared intentionality (hence conditions of modest sociality) can really boost the effectiveness of implementation, as it puts participants under rational pressure to negotiate and compromise on sub-plans, being responsive to each-other and prepared to help, since not only the objective is to achieve the intended goal(s) but it is to do it together with each other.

THE CHANGE MANAGEMENT BLUEPRINT

In order to successfully orchestrate the change process we propose a change blueprint that will foster conditions of modest sociality and prevail mutual commitment. Our findings result from our observation of several change programs (our examples will focus on two of these cases, an automotive firm and an international airline) and a thorough review of

FIGURE 13.3: The Change Management Blueprint

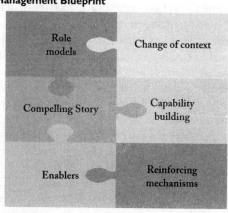

the most relevant scholarly papers. Together these two types of sources enable us to identify key elements of a change blueprint, and to challenge some current practices.

Setting the Scene

The first dimension of the proposed blueprint is about setting the scene so as to introduce and launch the transformation program. In particular, the team leading the change effort has to instill a need for change among all concerned. Much of the relevant literature recognizes that a prerequisite for change is a shared understanding that transformation is necessary and action is essential (Tushman and Romanelli, 1985; Burke and Litwin, 1992; Kotter, 1995; Roberto and Levesque, 2005). This step also allows change leaders to eliminate dysfunctional elements who fail to espouse the need for change and action (Schein, 1998). Many authors advocate the creation of a sense of crisis, real or simulated, to induce urgency (Galpin, 1996; Kotter, 1995), show current discrepancies (Armenakis and Harris, 2002) and illustrate that change is possible, appropriate, and desirable (Schein, 1998; Armenakis and Harris, 2002). Balancing disconfirmation of the current state and psychological safety in embracing the change (Schein, 1998) increases the awareness of indispensability of change and raises agreement and commitment toward change throughout the organization. A second widely recognized prerequisite is the articulation, discussion, and communication of a clear end-state. This involves drawing an easily understandable "picture" of what the organization should look like as a result of the change program (Galpin, 1996; Kotter, 1995; Schein, 1998). More specifically, this representation points to the direction to be taken (Burke and Litwin, 1992), a set of instructions (Beer and Nohria, 2000) both in terms of concrete scope and objectives (Roberto and Levesque, 2005), and mindset and behavior characteristics (Charan, 2006). Finally, many authors also agree on the need to clearly communicate the strategic initiatives associated with the change effort, as well as the more specific plans that derive from it. This serves to align individuals behind the required processes and values necessary to implement the intended change (Galpin, 1996; Roberto and Levesque, 2005). Together, these three prerequisites are designed to introduce the implementation of new processes and systems, and to contribute to creating an effective context for change (Beer and Nohria, 2000; Roberto and Levesque, 2005; Charan, 2006).

The change programs we observed exhibited these prerequisites to different degrees. While the decision to undergo change resulted mainly from either an internal assessment or an external strategic study, we were struck by the fact that the key information emanating from these reports was kept confidential by top management, leaving the rest of organization wondering about the true state of affairs. When the information was indeed disclosed across the company, it resulted in tremendous general anxiety. In the automotive case, the manufacturer was close to bankruptcy. The fourth CEO in three years had recently been appointed and was faced with a highly demoralized organization that saw little hope that anything could be done to save it. The crisis resulted simply from years of poor management, from a culture of hiding ongoing and from the absence of any common goal. The new CEO set the scene by developing a set of clear "from–to" guidelines which he called "how to see the light at the end of the tunnel." These included the major cultural issues that required change, and a clear vision of what to achieve. Guidelines called for the organization to move from technocracy to merit, from authority to leadership, from mediocrity to continuous search for excellence, from an inward perspective to competitive spirit, and from vague promises to reliability. Alongside these guidelines, a set of clear initiatives provided direction for how to make the journey "from–to" each guideline.

Launch and Spread of the Change Effort

Change leaders generally have two aims in communicating with their teams: to gain their commitment to change and to support them through the painful process of change. In other words, communicating for change is about persuasion, or gaining on-going commitment in a cooperative fashion (Taillard, 2005).

Bruner (1985) establishes that there are two different modes of communication, narrative, and rhetoric. A communicator can affect his audience's attitudes either by telling a story, or by presenting a well structured rhetorical argument. While rhetoric will get the point across, we suggest that when it comes to garnering commitment and offering support, narratives may in fact be more effective. Narratives, or storytelling, have been shown to be a fundamental universal form of communication which develops early in childhood (Cook-Gumperz, 1993). Green and Brock (2000) establish the persuasive force of narratives which they attribute to "transportation," a term which captures the sense of immersion experienced when one is "caught up" in a story. This notion ties into the dual-route theories of persuasion proposed by them. Narratives have a social dimension that makes them particularly prone to being repeated and in doing so, to evolving in a way that increases in relevance to the narrating community, at the same time as building culture. A compelling change story describes the actions that are required by the audience.

Stories vary as to how detailed they are, their use of metaphors and their logical structure. Good narratives rely on emotional or affective response to modify their audience's attitudes and intentions, or at least to suggest the possibility of a different course of action.

Storytelling plays a key role in change by fostering commitment and providing support. Several articles have documented specific instances of narrative use in management. Shaw et al. (1998) discuss how 3M achieved greater organizational buy-in by moving away from "bullet points" to narrative business plans. A recent case (Amernic et al., 2007) analyzing GE CEO Jack Welch's use of metaphors in the letters he wrote to his shareholders also suggests some interesting features of persuasive storytelling in a transformational leadership context.

The success of storytelling in change management depends on the strategic crafting of a narrative with the following features.

- Simple, but featuring examples, numerical objectives and concrete actions and suggesting clear objectives and the means to attain them (Fox and Amichai-Hamburger, 2001; Beer and Nohria, 2000; Kotter, 2008, Roberto and Levesque, 2005). Simple stories are easily shared, memorable, and repeatable, and should integrate elements of the change strategy.
- Flexible enough to allow enough room for individuals to model the story to their own situation, project themselves as protagonists and allow the narrative to evolve as it spreads across the organization (Kotter, 1995; Beer and Nohria, 2000).
- Able to "transport" individuals into the desired end-state through novelty and relevance and by creating commitment. Successful compelling stories should feature a novel element which serves to reinforce commitment and to provoke "discontinuity" with the status quo. Novelty often emerges when strategy is translated into layman's term.
- Able to create cohesion as a result of excitement and drama. Cohesion results from exciting, ambitious goals that can be easily recalled.
- Conducive to organizational culture through transmission and natural evolution. Compelling and memorable simple stories spread easily and adapt to and strengthen organizational culture along the way.

A demonstration of the power of a compelling story can be found in the case of an international airline which we observed as it underwent a major turnaround. The organization was experiencing the worse crisis since its inception in the early 1920s. Sales and yield were shrinking, and competition had never been so fierce, with new low cost carriers exploiting innovative ways of doing business. The result was dramatic; the company was losing €2 to 3 million a day with no sign of being able to reverse the trend. In a bold move, the major shareholder installed a new CEO, with substantial turnaround experience. A thorough analysis was commissioned to establish the root causes of the situation, and was used by management as the basis of a series of stories which created a sense of urgency for change and set out a picture of what could be achieved if the crisis was overcome. Sub-stories were built to provide direction to each division and department, beyond that of the overall organization, and added to the credibility and relevance for every single individual in the firm. These stories created a sense of fear-tinged excitement that provoked individuals to undertake many of the change initiatives that had been considered before, but never endorsed. As stated by a senior executive, "Many consultants had explained to me how to leverage elasticity for pricing, but not until a colleague told me he could get a 20 percent premium on standard fares if we could offer lounge access to our clients did I realize why it is so important."

Role Models

Role models are individuals at any level of the organization that embody the mindset and behaviors intended for the entire organization to follow (Kotter, 1995; Beer and Nohria, 2000). Such individuals have objectives that are aligned with those of the organization (Kotter, 1995; Schein, 1998). While they may not have a formal management role, these individuals' leadership capabilities and potential are recognized across the organization as they are often in positions of "public standing" (Duck, 1993; Kotter, 1995). Role models spread the compelling story and reinforce the vision by communicating and recalling the change message (Kilmann, 1995), and by choosing the right channels and register for target groups. Role models and their behavior are scrutinized throughout the organization as their actions send strong messages about what is really important. Their acts demonstrate that leadership can "walk the talk" and reinforces intentions towards the intended behaviors. There are no recipes for how to become or promote a role model as different contexts will require different types of role modeling. In the automotive case discussed earlier, the CEO summarize his role as follows, "My job as CEO is not to make decisions about the business but to set stretch objectives and help our managers work out how to reach them. I am the conduit for change, but it's the people in my organization who actually make change happen." This was both a compelling story (in an organization built on the Great Man theory, where all important decisions come out of the executive suite) and a true reflection of his behavior. In fact, he would always intervene last in meetings to say, "I understand what you are telling me and what you intend to do. You are now in charge, let me know how I can help." Offering such accountability had been previously unheard of in the organization.

Enablers

Enablers serve as transmission relays for the compelling story and often help build up a role model status (Duck, 1993; Kilman, 1995). The extant literature does not consistently distinguish enablers' roles from that of role models, and sometimes characterizes them generically as a critical mass of engaged and committed people (Duck, 1993; Chan and Mauborgne, 2003; Sirkin et al., 2005; Charan, 2006). We argue that enablers have the specific role of accelerating change by leveraging their network or their professional status (Schein, 1998). These individuals are important at every level of the organization.

Evidence of the importance of enablers is found in our airline case where the timing and speed of change were of the essence, but where there was no room for errors. The challenge was to quickly identify enablers and get them onboard. A team member came up with the idea of sending an e-mailed survey to all members of the sales department, asking them to list the people to whom they would turn with a given issue or to gather certain information, either general (e.g., company news, gossip, etc.), organizational (roles and responsibilities within the department, targets, etc.), or regarding distribution (e.g., tariff access, incentive structure, etc.). In a matter of several days, a dozen individuals were identified, and began working with the change team and the role models who acquainted them with the details of the transformation plan. These enablers were then able to reach out to all the sales staff to communicate and explain the compelling story, and to vouch for the authenticity of the company's intentions, as embodied by its role models.

Change of Context

Small physical changes in context such as signage, decoration, or new uniforms can help promote the message that change is taking hold. Such changes need to be relevant, meaningful, and easily visible. Surprisingly, little attention has been given in the extant literature to this effective feature, with the exception of a short mention (Roberto and Levesque, 2005). In a specific case, Schein (1988) suggests that technology can be used as a coercive tool to force employees to adapt and to embrace the change.

Evidence of the critical role of the change of context in speeding up the process of change, can be found in both of our cases. In the automotive firm, the physical state of the factory premises including waste on the floors, poor lighting, dirt, and unattractive employee facilities had been a striking indication of the need for change, and impacted morale and disgruntlement. One of the first initiatives of the change program was to address this issue with general refurbishment programs. Childcare facilities and retail outlets were opened next to the facilities to provide better work/family balance.

The airline we observed had suffered from years of lack of investment and poor facilities and equipment created considerable problems. The change team defined a number of quick wins for the sales department based on two simple criteria: effort required for implementation and impact on productivity and morale or motivation. The following measures were chosen: implementation of a new highly lucrative performance incentive system for the distribution network which greatly limited the number of partner travel agencies, a complete overhaul of the sales reporting process and the replacement of old laptops with newest models, resulting in greater efficiency, and providing sales representatives with an important status symbol.

Capability Development

Capability development programs are specifically designed and include formal training as well as on the job coaching. They are based on adult learning techniques, discovery, and experimentation (Kotter, 1995; Roberto and Levesque, 2005). They facilitate the learning of new behaviors and mindsets while contributing to the transmission of knowledge throughout the organizations, and helping change "stick" both at the individual and the organizational levels. A holistic approach to capability development focuses on both professional and personal development to maximize their impact (Schein, 1998; Beer and Nohria, 2000).

As a result of its history as a state monopoly, the airline's sales department exhibited poor sales skills, management competence, and little performance focus. The change team launched three types of initiatives: tailored training programs for all staff requiring development of technical competences, sales competences and managerial competences, coaching less experienced members and hiring new experienced staff members from related sectors to reinvigorate the department.

Reinforcing Mechanisms

Reinforcing mechanisms are systems that recognize the adoption of new attitudes and behaviors (Schein, 1998; Beer and Nohria, 2000). They reward individuals who have embraced change financially (Burke and Litwin, 1992) and in kind (Kotter, 1995), and penalize those who have not, thereby sending a strong signal throughout the organization (Kotter, 1995). These mechanisms must be clearly linked to the intended change and their symbolic meaning suitably leveraged (Kotter, 1995; Beer and Nohria, 2000).

Reinforcing mechanisms can take several forms. In the airline case, a series of mechanisms were developed with the aim of providing tangible and visible proof of the help and support available to those who embraced the requested change. The reinforcing mechanisms implemented were mainly as follows: an incentive and bonus system based on both departmental and individual performance, requiring that departmental targets be reached for any payout, a structured career plan (previously inexistent) based on clear merit criteria to allow each member to understand development opportunities and plan their own career within the department based on their own ambitions and the dismissal of non-performing staff members. This was the action that probably had the most impact from an emotional point of view. The company had always been a state company where dismissal was practically unheard of.

DISCUSSION

We began this chapter by suggesting a potential role for shared intention in facilitating organizational change which we can summarize in the following "central proposition":

"Certain conditions can be put in place to allow individuals in an organization to develop shared intentions towards change and allow them to undertake the actions necessary for change in a coordinated and effective manner."

This proposition puts specific demands on the cognitive state of individuals in the organization, and on the organization itself. It requires for an organization to be able to foster shared intentions in order to drive effective change.

Our discussion will now center on our central proposition by showing that the blueprint elements we have identified actually foster shared intentions, and as a result, can facilitate organizational change. We argue that the effectiveness of this blueprint is not a random matter, but rather that the reason that these features of change programs are as effective as they are in promoting change is that they constitute the basis for the development of shared intentions among individuals across the organization.

The first condition to shared intentionality is the generation of individual intentions, or plans, towards the same objective, in this case the intended end state of the organization, or at least several degrees of alignment along the transformation plan. It is worth reminding that an intention can only be generated through personal deliberation and cannot simply be imposed or passed on via authority routes. The three prerequisites for change: communicating a clear sense of crisis or rupture, that a clear end-state is communicated, and a "high-level" plan is put in place to show the way forward, address precisely such conditions. In fact, each individual will have pre-existing plans and intentions related to the pre-change state of things, and such plans and intentions will be, by their own nature, resilient and resistant to reconsideration. The first precondition aims at forcing such reconsideration and urging a new deliberation. The second and third pre-conditions then aim at guiding the inferential process towards the desired end state, smoothing the individual cognitive process by showing a desirable goal and a clear path to reach it. Relying on these pre-requisites will also ensure that each individual believes that he can personally contribute to change through his actions by formulating a plan in consultation with each individual projecting his contribution to the change effort. This will enable each individual to believe that his own actions will indeed contribute to the objective. As discussed in the first part, though, human cognition doesn't follow a linear rational path, but it's pre-shaped by non-rational elements such as emotions. The blueprint elements of storytelling, role modeling, enablers and change of context, all somehow affect such condition, in different stages of the formation of an intention, or a plan, as illustrated in the blueprint account presented few paragraphs before. Finally, we believe that the reinforcing mechanisms and capability building elements of the blue print play a fundamental role in reinforcing the individual intentions along time, when it is more likely that the belief that the change is attainable trembles due to unforeseen difficulties or simply the passing of time.

While the pre-requisites will foster individuals to act towards the same objective of following a shared plan, this will not be enough to ensure that such intentions and plans are shared. For the shared intentions condition to stand, individual intentions must be both compatible and interdependent. Needless to say that an organization in which individuals' intentions towards the end-state are not compatible with each other, or possibly in conflict with each other will not achieve much. The interdependence requirement is crucial: unless individuals in the organization can rely on each others' own intentions towards the same end-state, the change project is compromised. Trust and communication are clearly required for shared intentions to take hold. Finally, the condition on mutual awareness requires that individual intentions and their "sharedness" to be made explicit.

As introduced in the first half of the chapter, storytelling is instrumental to make the communication about the change prone to be repeated and evolving. In other words, participants will tend to tell each other the story, making gradually their own sense of it. The narrative element of the blueprint will then serve to signal individuals' shared intention to each other and can help foster the trust and compatibility necessary for interdependent intentions.

As per the role models and enablers elements of the blue print, we believe that they both cover a similar role, just with different degree of reach. In fact, because of their unique position in the network of the organization, they are more likely to stand naturally in a condition of modest sociality with more people, therefore, fostering "sharedness" of intentions and plans. They constitute a hub in the informal networks, which is a fundamental factor in bridging shared intentionality among a high number of people that often stand in no relationship among each other and therefore would not otherwise share intentions and plans.

Interdependence, compatibility and mutual awareness can all be greatly enhanced when external signs of change (i.e., physical contextual changes) are recognizable to all. Particularly relevant are those changes of context that bring more people in contact, such as shifting from traditional layout to open-space offices, as they enable physical interaction therefore allowing intention-reading and sharing. Also the last two elements of the blue print, capability building and reinforcing mechanisms, play an important role in the process of fostering modest sociality and shared intentionality, particularly when they are designed in a way that enhance informal networks as opposite to reinforce authority structures. Courses and development programs in general, in fact, can generate links and relationships among the participants, and can be important moments of sharing plans and intentions, especially when they are carefully selected.

We have argued that the features of the blueprint for effective change each address specific conditions of shared intentions, and therefore serve as powerful tools to promote shared intentions. The resulting structure is represented in Figure 13.1.

CONCLUSION

Our research brings us to three conclusions. Firstly, we have opened a new perspective on change by bringing in insights from research on shared agency, showing that certain conditions of shared intentionality are strongly conducive to efficient joint action. Secondly, we have shown the important role of emotions in intentionality. Evidence indicates that any transformation program that does not leave room for the development and communication of emotional content also misses out on the opportunity to enable shared intentionality to take hold. Thirdly, we proposed a change management blueprint that will foster the conditions needed for individuals to take action in a coordinated and effective manner. However, the model still needs to be tested in order to enable it to reach its full potential as the basis for a theory of change management.

REFERENCES

Amernic, J., R. Craig, and D. Tourish (2007) "The Transformational Leader as Pedagogue, Physician, Architect, Commander, and Saint: Five Root Metaphors in Jack Welch's Letters to Stockholders of General Electric," *Human Relations*, 60(12): 1839–1872.

Armenakis, A. and S.G. Harris (2002) "Crafting a Change Message to Create Transformational Readiness," *Journal of Organizational Change Management*, 15(2): 169–183.

Beer, M. and N. Nohria (2000) "Cracking the Code of Change," *Harvard Business Review*, 78(3): 133–141.

Bratman, M. (2002) "Shapiro on Legal Positivism and Jointly International Activity," *Legal Theory*, 8(4): 511–517.

———. (2008a) "Reflections on the Philosophy of Action," in J. Ahuilar and A.A. Buckareff (eds), *Philosophy of Action: 5 Questions*. Automatic Press/VIP.

———. (2008b) "Shared Agency," in C. Mantzavinos (ed.), *Philosophy of the Social Sciences: Philosophical Theory and Scientific Practice*. Cambridge University Press.

Bratman, M.E. (1987) *Intentions, Plans, and Practical Reason*. Cambridge, Mass.: Harvard University Press.

———. (1999) *Faces of Intention*. Cambridge Studies in Philosophy.

Bruner, J. (1985) *Actual Minds, Possible Worlds*. Harvard University Press.

Burke, W.W. and G.H. Litwin (1992) "A Casual Model of Organizational Performance and Change," *Journal of Management*, 18: 523–545.

Chan, K.W. and R. Mauborgne (2003) "Tipped for the Top: Tipping Point Leadership," *Harvard Business Review*, 81(4): 60–69.

Charan, R. (2006) "Home Depot's Blueprint for Culture Change," *Harvard Business Review*, April, 84(4): 61–70.

Cook-Gumperz, J. (1993) "The Relevant Text: Narrative, Storytelling and Children's Understanding of Genre: Response to Egan," *Linguistics and Education*, 5(2): 149–156.

Damasio, A. (1994) *Descartes' Error: Emotions, Reason and the Human Brain.* Penguin Books.

Duck, J.D. (1993) "Managing Change: The Art of Balancing," *Harvard Business Review,* 71(6): 109–118.

Enfield, N.J. and S.C. Levinson (2006) "Introduction: Human Sociality as a New Inter-disciplinary Field," in Enfield and Levinson (eds), *Roots of Human Sociality: Culture, Cognition and Interaction.* Oxford: Berg.

Fox, S. and Y. Amichai-Hamburger (2001) "The Power of Emotional Appeals in Promoting Organizational Change," *Academy of Management Executive,* 15(4): 84–94.

Galpin, T. (1996) *The Human Side of Change: A Practical Guide to Organization Redesign.* San Francisco: Jossey-Bass.

Green, M., and T. Brock (2000) "The Role of Transportation in The Persuasiveness of Public Narratives," *Journal of Personality & Social Psychology,* 79(5): 701–721.

Johnson-Laird, P.N. (2008) *How We Reason.* Oxford University Press.

Kilmann, R. (1995) "A Holistic Program and Critical Success Factors of Corporate Trans-formation," *European Management Journal,* 13(2): 175–186.

Kotter, J.P. (1995) "Leading Change: Why Transformation Efforts Fail," *Harvard Business Review,* 73(2): 59–67.

———. (2008) *A Sense of Urgency.* Boston, MA: Harvard Business School Press.

Kutz, C. (2000) *Complicity: Ethics and Law for a Collective Age.* Cambridge: Cambridge University Press.

Roberto, M.A. and L.C. Levesque (2005) "The Art of Making Change Initiatives Stick," *MIT Sloan Management Review,* 46(6): 53–60.

Schein, E.H. (1998) "Models and Tools for Stability and Change in Human System Reflections," *The SoL Journal,* 4(2).

Shapiro, S.J. (2002) "Law, Plans and Practical Reason," *Legal Theory,* 8: 387–441.

Shaw, G., R. Brown, and P. Bromiley (1998) "Strategic Stories: How 3m Is Rewriting Business Planning," *Harvard Business Review,* 76: 42–44.

Sirkin, H.L., P. Keenan, and A. Jackson, (2005) "The Hard Side of Change Manage-ment," *Harvard Business Review,* 83(10): 108–118.

Sugiyama, M.S. (2001) "Food, Foragers and Folklore: The Role of Narrative in Human Subsistence," *Evolution and Human Behavior,* 22: 221–240.

Taillard, M. (2005) "The Balancing Act of Persuasion: A Relevance-theoretic Perspective." Unpublished doctoral dissertation, University of London, London.

Tomasello, M. and H. Racoczy (2003) "What Makes Human Cognition Unique From Individual to Shared to Collective Intentions," *Mind and Language,* 18(2): 121–147.

Tomasello, M. and M. Carpenter (2007) "Shared Intentionality," *Developmental Science,* 10(1): 121–125.

Tushman, M.L. and E. Romanelli (1985) "Organizational Evolution: a Metamorphosis Model of Convergence and Reorientation," in L.L. Cummings and B.M. Straw (eds), *Research in Organizational Behavior,* pp. 171–222. Greenwich: JAI Press.

Warneken, F., F. Chen, and M. Tomasello (2006) "Cooperative Activities in Young Children and Chimpanzees," *Child Development,* 77(30): 640–666.

14

A New Terrain of Leadership Development: An Indian Perspective

Meena Surie Wilson and Ellen Van Velsor

When organizations want to increase the effectiveness of upcoming managers, they typically think of sending them through one or more programs or a certification process. Most often, the programs or courses are offered in collaboration with a business school or by the company itself. This is a sensible approach when managers need to learn the principles of accounting, logistics chain management, marketing, or any other technical or functional skill. But to develop leadership competence, a one-shot seminar, or a stand-alone program or course, seldom makes sense in isolation.

Our assertion is supported by findings from the *Lessons of Experience* (LOE) program of research, conducted, primarily by the Center for Creative Leadership (CCL) in the U.S. since the 1980s (Morrison et al. 1987; McCall et al., 1988; Van Velsor and McCauley, 2004; Douglas, 2006). Between 2006 and 2009, to advance knowledge about how leadership is learned by managers in Asia, the LOE methodology was used to conduct research studies in India, Singapore, and China (Wilson, 2008; Yip and Wilson, 2008; Zhang et al., 2009). Findings from the three studies were compared with the most recent and comparable U.S. based studies (Conway et al., 2006).

Each of these four 21st century studies confirms that the role of experience is crucial: effective leadership most frequently evolves from learning leadership lessons from on-the-job experiences. Other studies also confirm that leadership is learned from experiences rather than genetically determined at birth (Arvey et al., 2007; Bennis and Thomas, 2002: Hymowitz, 2002; McCall, 1998; McCall and Hollenbeck, 2002: Thomas and Cheese, 2005; Turner and Mavin, 2008).

The lessons of experience studies show that there are *key events* from which critical *leadership lessons* are learned. Key events are experiences that stimulate learning and change. Leadership lessons are shifts in attitudes, values, knowledge, skills, or behavior that help managers to become more effective as leaders. The 70-20-10 thumb rule was generated by this suite of studies. According to 70-20-10—which is considered a broad guideline for developing leadership talent—companies should provide a mix of 70 percent of challenging assignments, 20 percent of developmental relationships and 10 percent of coursework, and training to emerging leaders. The recent studies in Asia update these ratios to 65-30-5, but the message is the same. For companies that want to unlock leadership potential, and for individuals who want to become outstanding leaders, undergoing *challenging assignments* is central to learning to lead effectively. *Developmental relationships*, and to a lesser extent *coursework and training*, also contribute to leader development.

In theory, the usefulness of experiences as a source of leadership learning has been widely accepted. Just as musicians, cooks, and athletes become outstanding through hours and years of practice, leaders too become effective primarily from learning and practicing leadership on work assignments that stretch them beyond their current capabilities (Day, 2010). In practice, organizations barely use experiences to develop leadership talent intentionally and systematically.

In addition, in a majority of organizations, it is not development per se but an almost Darwinian selection process that commands the attention of top level leaders and human resource (HR) practitioners. Often, the assumption that underlies selection processes is that the fittest leaders are those who survive and thrive through the rough-and-tumble of demanding performance measures. Performance measures continue to be refined for example, by instituting leadership competency models, nine-box metrics, and sophisticated 360-degree feedback mechanisms (the results of which are sometimes more political than developmental). Scant attention is paid to developing leaders by purposefully and systematically giving them opportunities to run on many different tracks of experience.

In this paper, we briefly summarize the research methods and findings from the 21st century LOE studies. The findings are the basis of the theoretical but grounded 65-30-5 framework that represents the current reality of how leader development happens in organizations. The framework can be a useful starting point for any organization that wants to put into place a sensible leadership development strategy. Then, in order to generate in-depth insights about how 65-30-5 applies to developing leadership talent among Indian business managers, the LOE study in India is described. The paper concludes by raising questions about how to close the knowing-doing gap—between knowing what is important and being able to execute that—with regards to leadership talent development in Indian business organizations.

RESEARCH METHODS

The central question that has driven the LOE program of research over three decades is: how do executives learn, grow, and develop over the years? The primary research question—adapted from the critical incident methodology (Flanagan, 1954)—uses the following prompt:

> When you think about your career as a manager, certain events probably stand out in your mind, things that led to a lasting change in you as a manager. Please identify at least three key events in your career, things that made a difference in the way you manage now. What happened? What did you learn?

In the India, Singapore, and China studies, 60 to 90-minute face-to-face interviews were conducted with executives in the top four levels of the management hierarchy. In India, we conducted 71 interviews in eight organizations across all regions and four industry sectors. In Singapore, we conducted 36 interviews across 30 ministries and statutory boards. In China, we conducted 54 interviews in six organizations—four were state-owned and two were private sector. In the comparable U.S. and Europe-based study, an open-ended survey was used with program participants in the Center's *Leadership at the Peak* © program, which is offered exclusively to executives at the C-level and one level below. Since the program is run in the U.S. and occasionally in Davos, Switzerland, participants are primarily, but not exclusively, U.S. executives. An overview of this information is presented in Table 14.1.

Each study was conducted by a different team, with teams including at least two indigenous researchers. One researcher from each study then participated in a following study. This was to ensure an overall consistent

TABLE 14.1: Overview of 21st Century Lessons of Experience Studies

Country	Year completed	Number of senior leaders	Organizations
China	2009	54	Four state-owned and 2 private-sector companies
Singapore	2008	36	Twelve government ministries and 18 government agencies
India	2007	71	Eight global private-sector companies
United States	2005	354	Participants in CCL's *Leadership at the Peak* © program: 72% of the sample were US-based, 28% were based internationally
Total		515	

Source: Adapted from Yip and Wilson (2010) (used with permission).

coding and analysis methodology across the studies. However, each research team used an emic approach to develop its own set of event and lesson categories and allow cultural differences to emerge.

At the team level, events and lessons in interview transcripts or surveys were independently coded by three researchers. Discrepancies were resolved by majority. Codes were assigned if two of three coders agreed and the event and/or the lesson were dropped if two of three coders did not agree. Statistically, inter-coder agreement of the codes accepted for further analysis was at least 67 percent in all studies.

For the India study, a team of three researchers collected and analyzed the interviews. Then a different cross-cultural team—which included one of the researchers on the original India research team—compared the India, Singapore, China, and U.S. study findings. Besides comparing the pattern of learning and growth of Indian executives with that of executives from other countries, the analyses had another major objective: to uncover whether in the Indian business context, certain experiences are more likely to produce specific leadership lessons. If so, we believed that anybody with responsibility for leadership development in organizations would gain important knowledge: they would be able to link each essential work experience with the specific leadership lessons that it was most likely to produce. The results of the analyses follow.

RESEARCH FINDINGS

Across studies, the variety of experiences cited by senior executives is encompassed by five broad clusters of experience: challenging assignments; developmental relationships; coursework and training; adverse situations or hardships; and personal experiences (Conway et al., 2006; Wilson, 2008; Yip and Wilson, 2008; Zhang et al., 2009). Cross-study comparisons resulted in the following definitions of the five clusters.

- Challenging assignments—tasks, promotions or postings that stretch managers beyond their current capabilities.
- Developmental relationships—memorable people who transmit leadership learning and influence managerial behavior.
- Coursework and training—formal training and development experiences.
- Adverse situations—unexpected and consequential events that cannot be fully controlled by the organization and its leaders.
- Personal experiences—various events that create emotion-laden memories and influence the leader's principles.

Strikingly, the cross-study analysis reveals that the pattern of distribution of experiences across the five clusters is similar for these four countries (see Figure 14.1). Further, this distribution corresponds to that obtained from earlier studies using the LOE methodology (McCall et al., 1988; McCall and Hollenbeck, 2002).

To draw out the practical implications of the research for organizations, McCall and his colleagues set aside two event clusters: hardships (which has since been relabeled adverse situations) and personal experiences. Instead, they focused on the primary contribution of challenging assignments and the secondary contribution of developmental relationships to leader development, suggesting that the contribution of coursework and training was minimal. Their rationale was simply that organizations can not orchestrate hardships or arrange personal experiences, just in order to develop managers. As noted earlier, the popular 70-20-10 rule of thumb for designing leadership development initiatives in organizations is a by-product of the findings from the early LOE studies.

(Incidentally, researchers at CCL and practitioners have maintained their interest in the leadership lessons learned from hardships; and the current economic recession makes this topic even more relevant. We have also learned that Indian and Chinese managers report learning about leadership from early life/personal experiences to a greater extent than U.S. managers. However, in this paper, these two clusters of experience are excluded from consideration. This is because organizations can extract

FIGURE 14.1: A Cross-country Comparison of Five Clusters of Experience

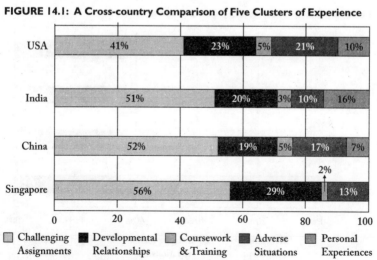

Source: Adapted from Yip and Wilson (2010) (used with permission).

leadership lessons from hardships and early life events reactively, but are not able to manage such experiences proactively.)

THE 65-30-5 FRAMEWORK

The current four-study analyses paint a similar picture (see Figure 14.2). Although the 21st century studies update 70-20-10 to 65-30-5, three clusters of experience—challenging assignments, developmental relationships, and coursework and training—continue to make the same relative contribution to leadership talent development. If this framework tends to be universal, there is a question that begs to be asked: how can the 65-30-5 framework get implemented in organizations? We use the findings and insights from the LOE-India research to probe this issue next: whether and how 65-30-5 can be applied by individuals and organizations in India.

BACKGROUND AND FINDINGS OF THE LESSONS OF EXPERIENCE-INDIA STUDY

The India study is based on stories told by 71 Indian business leaders from eight well-established homegrown global companies. These include Dr. Reddy's, ICICI Bank, JK Organization (Eastern Zone), ITC Ltd., Mahindra & Mahindra Ltd., Tata Chemicals, Tata Steel, and a public sector

FIGURE 14.2: A Cross-country Comparison of 65-30-5

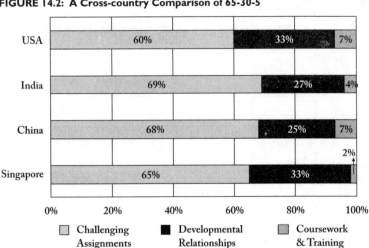

Source: Wilson (2010) (used with permission).

bank. All study participants had worked in organizations for a minimum of 15 years. Forty-five percent were 50 years or older; 55 percent were less than 50 years. Only three of the study participants were women. The organizational level of the 71 study participants is presented in Table 14.2.

The interviews yielded descriptions of 309 experiences from which 575 lessons were learned. Analyses resulted in the classification of these data into 26 event codes and 29 lesson codes. An overview of the initial analysis is depicted in Figure 14.3. In the follow-on analysis, the 26 event codes were conceptually grouped to yield 15 generic types of experiences. In alphabetical order, these are: *bosses and superiors; business crisis; coursework and training; dealing with labor/trade unions; early life and personal experiences; experience of ethical violations; first professional jobs; horizontal moves/transitions; increases in job scope; mistakes; negotiations; new initiatives; non-work role-models; turnarounds/fix-its; and cultural crossings.*

More to the point, a matrix was developed, linking every experience with all lessons learned. This was distilled into an "Opportunity Matrix" which includes experiences and lessons selected using two criteria: *(a)* cited

TABLE 14.2: Organizational Level of Study Participants

Organizational level	Number interviewed
President	9
Chief Executive Officer; Managing Director; Deputy Managing Director	10
Executive Vice President; Senior Vice President; Vice President	13
Chief Operating Officer; Chief Executive	9
Strategic Business Unit Head; Director	11
General Manager--including Senior, Deputy & Assistant General Manager	19
Total	71

Source: Wilson (2008) (used with permission).

FIGURE 14.3: Overview of Initial Analysis of *Lessons of Experience-India* Interviews

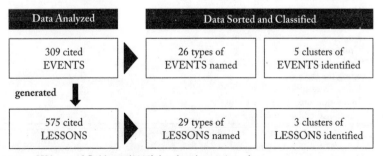

Source: Wilson and Sirbhaiya (2008) (used with permission).

the most frequently, relative to other experiences and lessons; and *(b)* cited by the highest percentage of interviewees. In other words, using our first criteria, we culled out experiences and lessons that were less frequently cited (experiences < 9 percent of total of 309 experiences; lessons learned < 8 percent of total of 525 lessons learned). Using our second criteria, we excluded experiences cited by less than 25 percent of interviewees and the lessons produced from those experiences. This distillation yielded a matrix of seven experiences and 11 leadership lessons.

For this paper, the "Opportunity Matrix" has been adapted to include coursework and training and the lesson most likely to be learned from formal coursework or training: *understanding individual differences.* The adapted version makes it possible to interpret the 65-30-5 framework (in the Indian business context) in a meaningful way. Presented as the *Current Terrain of Leadership Development in Indian Businesses,* Table 14.3 lists eight essential experiences and the 12 significant lessons learned from those experiences, as reported by the senior executives interviewed for the LOE-India study. The experiences are defined in Table 14.4.

TABLE 14.3: Current Terrain of Leadership Development in Indian Businesses: Significant Experiences and Leadership Lessons Learned

Lessons learned	Bosses and superiors	Creating change: turnarounds	Creating change: new initiatives	Horizontal moves & transitions	Cultural crossings	Increases in job scope	First professional job	Coursework and training
Leading Self								
Confidence	x	x	x					
Self-awareness		x	x					
Personal leadership insights	x						x	
Leading Others								
Managing and motivating subordinates	x					x		
Developing subordinates	x							
Navigating politics and gaining influence			x					
Engaging with multiple stakeholders				x				
Cross-cultural savvy					x			
Understanding individual differences								x
Leading the Business								
Effective execution	x	x						
Innovation and entrepreneurship			x					
Functional and technical expertise			x	x		x		

Source: Adapted from Wilson (2010) (used with permission).

Note: "x" signifies that an event-lesson link ≥ 4. That is, an "x" was assigned when a particular event produced the same lesson at least four times.

TABLE 14.4: Definitions of Types of Experiences

Type of experience	Definition
Boss or superior	Leader/s who is one or more levels above the manager and becomes a positive or negative role model, catalyst, or teacher.
Coursework & training	Formal training and development experiences that are sponsored by the organization or self-initiated.
Cultural crossing	Assignment involving cultural adjustment—based on learning about the views and practices of co-workers from different backgrounds—in order to achieve business goals.
First professional job	First exposure to the world of work and the demands of a professional career.
Horizontal move	Transition to another function, business unit, organization, or industry sector; may not involve a promotion but calls for acquiring new expertise; can be initiated by the organization or oneself.
Increased job scope	An increase in budget, number of people to manage, and access to resources; typically raises the manager's responsibilities and visibility and involves a promotion.
New initiative	Opportunity to develop or launch new products and services, adopt new technologies, craft a new policy or process, build a plant or unit from scratch, develop a new market, embark on a new line of business, or create a new business entity.
Turnaround	Fixing a failing or underperforming business operation; or implementing an organizational culture change.

Source: Adapted from Wilson (2008) (used with permission).

The 12 leadership lessons are further categorized as: *leading self, leading others*, or *leading the business*. Based on CCL's four decades of international experience with delivering programs and services to clients from a variety of industry sectors, we have learned that this categorization gives upcoming managers a sense of the scope of the leadership lessons that they need to learn. The three categories of leading self, leading others, and leading the business help them to focus their self-improvement efforts. Thus, leading self lessons are about improved ways of managing oneself—one's thoughts, emotions, actions, and attitudes. Examples are: *confidence* and *self-awareness*. Leading others lessons equip leaders to connect with people by improving their interpersonal and social skills. Examples are: *managing and motivating subordinates, navigating politics and gaining influence*, and *cross-cultural savvy*. Leading the business lessons make it possible to get work done in an organization and run a business. Examples are: *functional and technical expertise*, and *innovation and entrepreneurship*.

Reducing vast and intricate data into relevant and practical nuggets of knowledge is a complex undertaking; but it is a necessary first step for mapping the terrain of leadership development. We think that Table 14.3 (Current terrain of leadership development in Indian businesses) is a preliminary map that describes the reality of how leadership talent develops. This matrix-cum-map can guide senior leaders and HR professionals working in India, and managers themselves, about how development is currently occurring. For example, the matrix-cum-map permits the following observations.

- Relationships with bosses and superiors, and assignments characterized by creating change via a new initiative, seem to be the two experiences that produce the most leadership learning.
- Other experiences that produce several important leadership lessons are turnarounds, horizontal moves, and increases in job scope.
- Several experiences—such as cultural crossings, first professional jobs, and coursework and training—apparently teach more specific but equally important leadership lessons.

For those involved with developing leadership talent, these observations raise crucial questions related to: *(a)* the role of the boss; *(b)* the way in which different job assignments must be combined to provide a variety of leadership lessons; and *(c)* the part that coursework and training can play.

LIMITATIONS OF THE LESSONS OF EXPERIENCE-INDIA STUDY

Note that we recognize that managers' rich experiences at work, and what they learn from their experiences, cannot be represented in a table with 12 rows and eight columns even when the table is the result of rigorous analysis. For example, although our analysis shows that confidence is primarily learned from bosses and superiors, turnarounds, and new initiatives, confidence is also boosted by other experiences. Similarly, according to our analysis, college graduates start to form personal leadership insights based on impressions collected on their first professional job; obviously however, a first professional job yields new learning on many fronts (Wilson, 2010).

In addition, there are limitations to the LOE methodology. For example, in surging economies where companies are forging their way into a new future, perhaps it is not as helpful to look into the past experiences of current leaders. Also, since interviewees for the study were identified by the HR director—and not through a review process by the boss or peers or subordinates of the interviewee—we cannot be certain that we were interviewing the most effective leaders. Finally, although we elicited information about what the study participants were learning from their experiences, we did not gather data on whether and how they were applying what they learned. So there is little evidence concerning whether their learning was converted into practice.

Finally, the question of whether organizations should use the 65-30-5 framework to articulate a leadership strategy for individuals and for the organization itself remains to be addressed. In other words, although this framework is a starting point, can we be certain that the 65-30-5 menu of experiences (derived by analyzing interviews collected from four different studies) provides a nutritious diet for building leadership muscle? Or is this simply the diet on which today's leaders grew up?

Despite these limitations, simply by developing and presenting this matrix-cum-map, we have chosen to be pragmatic. Our pragmatism is echoed in this observation from futurist Alvin Toffler (1990): "As we advance into the terra incognita of tomorrow, it is better to have a general and incomplete map, subject to revision and correction, than to have no map at all."

In the next section, we delve more deeply into the issue of applying the findings to promote leadership development in business organizations. Our purpose is to simplify the complex phenomenon of leadership development without being simplistic.

INSIGHTS FROM THE LESSONS OF EXPERIENCE-INDIA STUDY

We start by emphasizing that our view of the current terrain (Table 14.3) captures only the most relevant findings of the LOE-India study. For example, the listed experiences encompass 215 of the total of 309 events gathered by the study; and the lessons produced—specifically by those experiences, encompass 394 of the total of 575 lessons learned. In other words, the matrix-cum-map of the current terrain zooms in on approximately 70 percent of all reported experiences and 69 percent of all leadership lessons learned.

To derive our insights, we delved deeper by noting the number and percent of citations of each of the eight experiences and 12 lessons. This is displayed in Table 14.5 in which every experience has been also classified as a challenging assignment (CA), developmental relationship (DR), or coursework and training (C&T). These data—a subset of all the experiences and lessons that were gathered—allow us to make the following observations in Table 14.5.

TABLE 14.5: Significant Experiences and Their Contribution to Leadership Learning: Events and Lessons Learned by Number and Percentage

Category	Experience	Event		Lessons Learned	
		Number	Percent [1]	Number	Percent [2]
DR	Boss or superior	53	25	91	23
CA	Turnaround	35	16	60	15
CA	New initiative	32	15	66	17
CA	Horizontal move	24	11	49	12
CA	Increased job scope	22	10	42	11
CA	Cultural crossing	20	9	31	8
CA	First professional job	19	9	37	9
C&T	Coursework & training	10	5	18	5
	Total	215	100	394	100

Source: Wilson (unpublished) (used with permission).
Notes: 1. Percent is computed as the number of events cited / 215.
     2. Percent is computed as the number of lessons learned
       (linked to a specific event) / 394.

- Challenging assignments: Six types of challenging assignments stand out as constituting 70 percent of experiences, and being a source of 72 percent of leadership lessons learned. These are: turnarounds, new initiatives, horizontal moves, cultural crossings, increases in job scope, and first professional jobs.
- Developmental relationships: At a remarkable 25 percent, or one in four of events, bosses, and superiors are the most frequently cited sources of leadership lessons, contributing to 23 percent of lessons learned. What this tells us is that bosses and superiors contribute more to leadership learning than any single challenging assignment.
- Coursework and training: Coursework and training seems to lack importance because this event comprises 5 percent of experiences cited and is a source of only 5 percent of lessons learned.

We need to explore what these insights mean for practitioners who want to take leader development to the next level. Can the findings be converted into practice? If so, how will this be achieved? Illustrative possibilities and issues follow.

- Companies for whom leader development is a high priority could identify their *experience tracks* or *tracks of experience* that upcoming leaders could tread. But what are the practical factors to consider for implementing experience-based tracks which future leaders can follow?

- Bosses and superiors are intermediaries who can not only identify challenging assignments for subordinates, but also support them in maximizing their learning from assignments. What are the barriers to making this happen?
- Coursework and training: in which participants bring their past experiences into the classroom and are helped to apply their classroom learning back at the workplace—is an important means of accelerating leaders' development. What changes in classroom content and exercises are needed to make this kind of integration more likely? What are the best integration strategies?

We believe that the 65-30-5 framework is an important guideline for forming a leadership development strategy for individuals and for the organization itself. This is especially possible in organizations committed to fostering a climate for learning, growth, and development among its managers. We conclude by exploring the factors that impinge upon translating this possibility into the reality of a new terrain for leadership development.

CONCLUDING REMARKS: CLOSING THE KNOWING-DOING GAP

While these studies make clear that learning from experience is a key element of leader development and a crucial piece of any good talent management strategy, we also know learning from experience is hard. The difficulties range from individual psychological factors to organizational culture and systems issues, to managers' orientations to their own roles as developers of others, as well as to characteristics of the learning process itself.

From the individual's perspective, learning usually signals risk and triggers anxiety. Every successful and experienced individual has a set of skills and behaviors that has worked for them for some time. These are likely to be closely aligned with preferences based on personality or early learning. We often refer to these preferences and habits as a person's "grain". To learn significant new lessons from one's experiences, a person has to be willing to go against their "grain" to some extent. The person has to take up new behaviors which will likely cause them to feel clumsy and unskilled and may not produce results with the same speed or efficiency to which others may have become accustomed. No one wants to be perceived as weak or incompetent and too often, expressing the need to learn is seen as an admission of inadequacy. Therefore, not only is it important that individuals have opportunities to understand their current areas of strength and weakness, but that they are also provided with support in the form of bosses who know how to (and have the patience to) support learning, and an organizational culture that supports and rewards the risks that learning entails.

The importance of bosses and cultures that support and encourage learning cannot be overemphasized, because otherwise inertia and past success can hold people back. Doing things the way one has always done them, using skills one has already attained, and continuing to see the world as one has always seen it, can be a source of comfort to a manager or employee busy with the daily tasks of work. People like to use their strengths to continue to be rewarded for what they have been rewarded for in the past. This approach also often seems like the most efficient use of valuable time. In most organizations, there is an active tension between producing immediate results (performance) and developing people (learning). Rather than give employees a developmental assignment where learning is accompanied by the possibility of failure, many organizations prefer to place high performers in key roles, doing what they already know how to do well. All of these factors can add up to inertia for the individual, and their inability to grow or change. This inertia can get worse the older people get, the more successful they have been, and the higher they have risen in the organization.

In addition to placing high performers in key roles, another common organizational practice that can get in the way of creating a learning culture is dependence on a competency based approach, rather than an experience based approach to performance assessment and improvement. Although competencies can seem to provide a convenient, one-size-fits-all elegance, that approach can also work to support some biases that managers often have about leadership and leader development (McCall, 2010). These biases include the belief that a person either is or is not a leader (in other words, that leadership is not developable), and the assumption that experiences are best used to test people (not develop them). Development through experience is inherently messy, a fact that is exacerbated by executives' inclination to think most often in the short term.

Through our research over the years, we have gained a better understanding of the learning process and the elements that are key drivers of leader development—elements that, most importantly, any organization can add to existing systems and processes to help managers learn and grow. These important elements are *assessment*, *challenge*, and *support*. When we look at any type of developmental experience, from training programs to job assignments, we find that they are most effective when all three elements are present. Regardless of whether assessment is formal (involving multi-rater instruments) or informal (providing a quick round of feedback on everyday issues), it creates the desire to close the gap between the *current self* and *ideal self* and provides clarity about needed change. Challenge forces people out of their comfort zones, motivates the desire for mastery of the new, and provides opportunity for experimentation, practice, and exposure to new perspectives. Challenge can be provided by new work, interaction with new individuals, or a skilled coach or mentor. Support gives people the confidence they need in their own ability to learn and grow and helps the individual to see that there is a positive value placed on change. Support is typically thought of as coming from people (a coach or mentor, a supportive boss), but it can also come from the organizational context—systems and culture that focus on and reward learning. Used together across a variety of experiences, organizations can develop a cadre of leaders who have not only learned a broad range of leadership skills, but who have also built their ability to learn from experience and to thereby effectively adapt to the ever changing challenges of the future.

REFERENCES

Arvey, R.D., Z. Zhang, R.F. Krueger, and B.J. Avolio. (2007) "Developmental and Genetic Determinants of Leadership Role Occupancy Among Females," *Journal of Applied Psychology*, 92(3): 693–706.

Bennis, W. and R. Thomas (2002) *Geeks and Geezers*. Boston: Harvard Business School Press.

Conway, R., E. Van Velsor, and C. Criswell (2006) "Learning from Experience: Critical Life Lessons of Senior Executives." Presentation at the annual conference of the Academy of Management, Atlanta, GA.

Day, D.V. (2010) "The Difficulties of Learning From Experience and the Need for Deliberate Practice," *Industrial and Organizational Psychology*, 3(1): 41–44.

Douglas, C. (2006) *Lessons of a Diverse Workforce*. Greensboro, NC: Center for Creative Leadership.

Flanagan, J.C. (1954) "The Critical Incident Technique," *Psychological Bulletin*, 5(4): 327–358.

Hymowitz, C. (2002) "Effective Leaders Say One Pivotal Experience Sealed Their Careers," *Wall Street Journal*, 240(41): B1.

McCall, M.W., Jr. (1998). *High Flyers: Developing the Next Generation of Leaders*. Boston: Harvard Business School Press.

———. (2010) "Recasting Leadership Development," *Industrial & Organizational Psychology*, 3(1): 3–19.

McCall, M.W., Jr. and G.P. Hollenbeck (2002) *Developing Global Executives: The Lessons of International Experience*. Boston: Harvard Business School Press.

McCall, M.W., Jr., M.M. Lombardo, and A.M. Morrison (1988) *The Lessons of Experience: How Successful Executives Develop On The Job*. Lexington, MA: Lexington Books.

Morrison, A., R. White, and E. Van Velsor (1987) *Breaking the Glass Ceiling: Can Women Make it to the Top of America's Biggest Corporations?* Reading, MA: Addison Wesley.

Thomas, R.J. and P. Cheese (2005) "Leadership: Experience is the Best Teacher," *Strategy & Leadership*, 33(3): 24–29.

Toffler, A. (1990) *Powershift: Knowledge, Wealth and Violence at the Edge of the 21st Century.* New York, NY: Bantam Books.

Turner, J. and S. Mavin (2008) "What Can We Learn From Senior Leader Narratives? The Strutting and Fretting of Becoming a Leader," *Leadership & Organization Development Journal*, 29(4): 376–391.

Van Velsor, E. and C. McCauley (2004) "Our View of Leadership Development," in C. McCauley and E. Van Velsor (eds), *Center for Creative Leadership Handbook of Leadership Development*, 2nd edition (pp. 1–25). San Francisco, CA: Jossey-Bass.

Wilson, M. (2008) *Developing Future Leaders for High-growth Indian Companies.* Technical report. Greensboro, NC: Center for Creative Leadership.

Wilson, M. and A. Sirbhaiya (2008) "Developing Future Leaders for High-growth Indian Companies: New Perspectives." Requested presentation at companies sponsoring the research in India.

Wilson, M.S. (2010) *Developing Tomorrow's Leaders Today: Insights From Corporate India.* Singapore: Wiley & Sons (Asia) Pte. Ltd.

———. (Unpublished) Computed from *Lessons of Experience-India* data.

———. (2010) "From Experiences to Leadership Lessons: Unpacking 70-20-10." Webinar Pesentation to the Council on Learning, Development and Organisational Performance and Leadership Development council. New York, The Conference Board.

Yip, J. and M. Wilson (2008) *Developing Public Service Leaders in Singapore.* Technical report. Greensboro, NC: Center for Creative Leadership.

———. (2010) "Learning from Experience," in E. Van Velsor, C.D. MCCauley, and M.N. Ruderman (eds), *Handbook of Leadership Development* (3rd edition), p. 65. San Francisco. Jossey-Bass.

Zhang, Y., A. Chandrasekar, and R. Wei. (2009) *Developing Future Leaders for Chinese Companies.* Technical report. Greenboro, NC: Center for Creative Leadership.

15

American Human Resource Management Techniques Fit Poorly in Latin America

Alfredo Behrens and James Wright

INTRODUCTION

Much of the discussion regarding the international expansion of American Human Resource Management techniques seems focused on measuring the extent of its prevalence and less on its fit to local cultures. Pudelko and Harzing (2007) have found evidence of an American Human Resource Management international dominance effect, even associating it to some benchmark of best practices. Tungli and Peiperl (2009) do not see much convergence yet in the managing of expatriates, but anticipate that some will occur. Still, host countries like Greece are different and practice less of the standard fare of multinationals like outsourcing (Galanaki and Papalexandris, 2007) though in Greece there may not be much difference in other practices (Myloni et al., 2004).

While these studies are illuminating, their focus on the prevalence of practices obscures their contribution to performance, which should be higher if the fit of the practices were adequate and made people happier and more engaged.

We have seen less quantitative work of this approach, despite evidence of different perceptions across cultures on the fairness of staff selection procedures (Steiner and Gilliland, 1996); or in reward preference (Chiang and Birtch, 2007) where culture does play a role despite the fact that all cultures except Finland showed a close relation to the U.K. one, and the respondents were engaged in the banking sector. The truth is that the closer to the ground research reaches, the closer it is to the cultural roots where the forces for divergence are larger, as seems to be the case in retail (Gamble, 2010) or as in differences in the role and extent of social networks in catering for the late adult, widowed or ill (Antonucci et al., 2001). Nonetheless, in some emerging markets there are a few, not many, but numerous, who have for generations dealt with commodities in international markets. Be the money, coffee or minerals, commodities have a known price and ready and large markets; those who deal in such markets are cosmopolitan, or have a global mindset, in modern parlance. Many of those circulate in the rarefied atmosphere of finance and tend to believe people can be managed in the same way everywhere. But come closer to the ground, like in agriculture, in industrial production lines or in retail, and the cultural differences become larger. It is to better manage these people, the millions, perhaps billions that this paper seeks to contribute to, set dangerously astride as it is, in arguable data and sources, while the intention remains honest.

INTERCHANGEABLE PARTS IS THE AMERICAN SYSTEM OF MANUFACTURE

As many technological advances in America, the introduction of the concept of interchangeable parts was also linked to the Defense forces. At the time that concerns us, America was waging a war of independence against Britain with France as an uneasy ally. America would not be able to produce all the weapons it would need, nor maintain them during war, if their production were not designed to have parts which would fit regardless of who had made them. Until then a front end charged musket consisted of a barrel fitted onto a wooden gun handle. Despite requiring such diverse knowledge as mastered by metallurgists and carpenters, muskets were produced by artisans, wood carved to fit the barrel. If one part broke in the battlefield, most likely both had to be discarded. America did not then have the capacity to bear such levels of waste.

While Ambassador in France, Thomas Jefferson saw the possibility of freeing America of the dependence in European firearms if they could be produced in America using gunsmith's Honoré Blanc's production system through parts with allowable tolerances in their differences. Blanc's offer was met with only lukewarm receptiveness in Europe, resisted by the apprentice system that would look down on anything less than perfect, partly to defend its own turf.

Unable to persuade Blanc to move to America, Jefferson succeeded in attracting Eli Whitney to Blanc's idea (Meyer, 2006: 74). In 1798, after an impressive display to the US Congress, Eli Whitney secured a contract from the US government to produce ten thousand firearms which, nonetheless, were delivered only a decade later.[1]

---

[1] Eli Whitney had already come up with a solution for sifting cotton fibers from its seed, a feat which rendered Southern America the prime World supplier of cotton. http://web.mit.edu/invent/iow/whitney.html, accessed on July 9, 2010.

The American military did not succeed then in the effort of mass production through interchangeable parts, but the idea of standardizing production to achieve mass production did and from there it would be picked up by the private sector.

Eli Terry saw, in 1806, that interchangeable parts would allow matching tools to the stage of production gearing unskilled workers into mass production (Bourne, 1996: 45). This idea was applied to the making of sewing machines in 1850 and to the production of watches in the 1890s, before Henry Ford would apply it to car manufacturing at the Piquette plant in 1906 (Weiss, 2003: 60). This is why, already in 19th century Europe, manufacturing based on interchangeable parts became to be known as the American System of Manufacture.

Standardizing, however, required precise measurements and those were provided by Carl Edward Johansson, a Swedish machinist who spent some time in America but returned to Sweden to find employment at Eskiltsuna, in the Swedish government's arsenal industry. There, when following-up on a contract to manufacture Mauser rifles in Sweden, he developed the gauges which became internationally known as the Jo Blocs. These allowed different producers to make according to precise specifications, without which there could be no standardization. Johansson eventually also opened shop in America and teamed up with Ford to secure the standardization of components for the Ford model A (Hounshell, 1984).

Perhaps ironically, the French turned to America during World War I to mass produce their most effective 75 mm recoil gun. Their recoil weapon dismissed the need to aim again after being fired. This allowed the French gun to outperform a German weapon by four to one. Hard-pressed by the presence of Germans at their gates, the French could not afford the long apprentice-based manufacturing lead times to produce their weapon at home, and a delegation visited the US with the purpose of seeking a supplier.

The renowned Dodge brothers, of the automobile industry, took the French army contract and started delivering the 75mm recoil weapon only six months later. After the war, French general Foch visited the Michigan Dodge plant in gratitude for its contribution to the war effort. He was surprised to learn that the speedy delivery of the sophisticated French weapon was accomplished by workers with only a couple of weeks of training, but working with parts produced to precise specifications (Weiss, 2003: 61).

This is how, interchangeable parts, originally a French idea to mass produce firearms, made a beachhead in America, after a few interactions between Europe and America, to generate the American System of Manufacture.

INTERCHANGEABLE PARTS IS AT THE ROOT OF HRM

During the late 19th century, whether in America, Germany, or the UK, the main concern was to manage access and effective use of capital (Cornelius, 2001: 7). Emerging markets find themselves now in a similar predicament, capital usually being their most scarce resource. Nonetheless, industrialization in the leading countries was allowing not only the increase of productivity but also company size, including the number of employees, and effective coordination was becoming an issue.

During the early 20th century, increasing company size and the same perspective which brought us interchangeable parts—complex systems could be broken down into simple components—would give place to two streams of thought. One focused on the rise of bureaucracies and the other on what came to be known as American Scientific Management.

On the management of bureaucracies, where Max Weber is among the most noteworthy,[2] he argued that these were legal institutions with authority hierarchies where formal rules were applied impersonally by career-oriented paid managers who created routines, oversaw the administration, and decision making, including the selection and management of workers. Standardization of procedures made the strength of bureaucracies, including corporate ones (Hamilton, 1991: 92). This approach fitted naturally to the idea of segmentation of complex systems into its components, very much like interchangeable parts did. Weber's ideas were brought over to Harvard University by Talcott Parsons, who had become acquainted with them at Heidelberg during his PhD training.

Given the times, and the locus—in or around Harvard's Business School—it is not surprising that American Scientific Management, as purported by Frederick Taylor, relied on the same, decomposition of the complex into its parts. Production, according to what became known as Taylorism, relied on goals which could be broken down into simpler tasks to be carried out repetitively by workers motivated primarily by wages and which would be supervised by managers who would control the workflow (Taylor, 1911). This approach also led to studying the best ways to accomplish tasks in the shortest time under set conditions, suggesting benchmarks against which individual worker performance could be compared (Neff, 2006: 50).

Both ideas, management of bureaucracies and Taylorism, also helped to understand and manage the production line which decreased costs

---

[2] Talcott Parsons, at Harvard University since 1927, became America's most eminent disseminator of Max Weber's approach.

and increased company size, which in turn became associated with Henry Ford and was referred to as Fordism.[3]

These ideas did not happen in a social vacuum. African American migrations to the industrialized Northern America, which also meant the urbanization of African Americans, had started in the 1890s but accelerated during the second decade of the 20th century (Wintz, 2000). In the six decades that spanned from the California Gold Rush to the American Scientific Management, the country had put on a leash the worst of its underlying divisiveness through the Civil War, people had migrated from the East to the West, and from the South to the North. America was now a country united in its mobility. The Communist Revolution took place in Russia with considerable impact in Europe and to some extent in America as well. This was expressed in increased unionism and revolt against the alienation of workers in the production line, while countries were simultaneously encumbered with the demobilization of soldiers after World War I.

Nonetheless, whether more or less resisted, the paradigm of breaking complex systems into components, which would render interchangeable parts on one side and repetitive work on the other, would render workers substitutable in that they would be required to perform simple tasks that required little training for. This pattern is at the core of the beginning of corporate management of a mobile workforce in America.

There may be a Northern "trans-atlantic gap" in Human Resource Management. This gap might reflect American entrepreneurialism, seeking less interference from the government (Kochan and Dyer, 1995), than Human Resource Management in Europe, politically more inclined to welfare capitalism (Brewster, 1995: 286). However, from the perspective of this paper, the conditions which give place to those differences between America and Europe are dwarfed by those which characterize the differences between the same two and those prevailing in emerging markets. This is why I will continue to make references to American Scientific Management and its Human Resource Management dimension, ignoring, for the time being, the Northern "trans-atlantic gap."

Criticism of Fordism and Taylorism, particularly in the 1920s, would trigger the Human Relations perspective on workforce management, focused on a more humane stance, and associated with Elton Mayo,

---

[3] Not surprisingly, since the perspective of people was that of cogs in a machine, Henry Ford is credited with having said: "Why is it that every time I need a pair of hands, I get a human being as well?" http://gmj.gallup.com/content/124214/driving-engagement-focusing-strengths.aspx#2. Accessed on July 13, 2010.

besides, Kurt Lewin at Cornell, MIT and Duke, and Eric Trist at the Tavistock Institute (Milner, 2002: 47). This was not sufficient to neutralize the strong production-oriented rationale underlying the social process, which automated production and tended to make the individual a de-skilled contributor appended to the machine. Such simplified tasks would be easy to describe, thus the job description, and to be filled by de-skilled workers whose work profiles were undifferentiated; thus the reduction of workers to interchangeable parts too. Overall, a production system based on interchangeable parts would now extend to people. These, perhaps even children, would seek to develop simple skills which would snuggly fit into well-defined slots in a production line.[4]

THE MEANING OF INTERCHANGEABLE PARTS FOR THE FABRIC OF SOCIETY

The workers I am speaking of, could not be so mobile if they were bound by strong family ties or webs of loyalty among friends which locked them to a place, including a workplace. Nor would they be so alike and interchangeable if in order to be effective in teamwork the workers had to know their colleagues to develop the trust and knowledge that teamwork is built on.

Any foreigner will be surprised at the ease with which Americans move from city to city in search of jobs or education. Businesses even responded with uniquely American solutions like U-Haul or Ryders, supplying trucks that enable Americans to move their belongings in a low-cost do-it-yourself way, renting a truck at origin and dropping it at the destination.[5]

People find work at destinations but they also find it is unhealthy, as testified by the writers of *Work in America*: "the most oppressive features of work seem to be avoidable: constant supervision and coercion, lack of variety, monotony meaningless tasks and isolation" (O'Toole, 1973: 13). Fear is rampant and innovation is a likely casualty (Behrens, 2010). Less than half of the white collar workers would choose the same work they were doing while this share dropped to 24 percent among blue collar workers (O'Toole, 1973: 30).

---

[4] "I want to take these boys, teach them to make small parts, instruct them in the operation of machines..." Henry Ford as reported in "Henry Ford has two objects in life" as interviewed by the *New York Times*, July 8, 1917, Page 72. http://0800alfredo.posterous.com/henry-ford-has-two-objects-in-life. Posted on July 13, 2010.

[5] http://www.uhaul.com/ and http://www.ryder.com/index.shtml?disp=us. Accessed on July 13, 2010.

Work in America, as per the authors of that volume, is something people do, not because they like it but because they have to. Work is the adult person's ultimate connection to society. But it is the nature of the connection which one should be looking at, and in modern America the person is either not connected to work, and suffers the economic penalties of it, plus the lack of benefit in meaningful activities, or is connected to a work the individual does not like (Khan, 1972: 179).

To the frustration that emanates from work in America, one must add the deprivation of its citizens from the nurturing function of family and similar kinship ties to handle the frustration and eventual defeat that may overcome the individual in its interaction with the corporate bureaucratic organization (Sussman, 1972: 134–35).

Perhaps decades of migrations and appendages to machines corroded precisely the sense of belonging which ties people to a place and to each other. Bleak as this may sound this is the picture that Putnam (2000) alludes to in claiming that Americans are "Bowling Alone." In his book, Putnam argues that Americans have increasingly become less attached from family, friends, and neighbors. Yet Putnam is not alone in decrying the increasing American loneliness, Cherlin (2009) argues that as Americans hop from job to job and from city to city; the ideal of self-fulfillment tears apart marriages and allows for faster entrance into romantic relationships, more so than couples in Europe, Japan, Australia, and New Zealand.

The increased loneliness, or isolation, is not only decried by social scientists but also illustrated by artists like Charles Chaplin in *Modern Times* (1936) where Chaplin tries to keep up with the speed of production lines and only finds respite in a homeless woman.[6] Seven decades later the subject of loneliness is still recalled by Paul Haggis (2004) in his three Oscar award film *Crash* where he has Graham (played by Don Cheadle) saying: "… In L.A., nobody touches you. We're always behind this metal and glass. I think we miss that touch so much, that we crash into each other, just so we can feel something." Or, in the same film, having Jean Cabot (played by Sandra Bullock) after falling down stairs and having no one but her maid to take her to hospital, she embraces her Mexican maid telling her that she is her best friend.[7]

The issue of paid friendship services comes up again in Alejandro González Iñárritu's (2006) Oscar winning *Babel* when Richard Jones (played by Brad Pitt) phones home from abroad and asks his Mexican maid to stay over and look after the couple's small children because his wife (played by Kate Blanchett) suffered a near-fatal accident and cannot return

---

[6] http://www.imdb.com/title/tt0027977/. Accessed on July 10, 2010.

[7] http://www.imdb.com/title/tt0375679/. Accessed on July 10, 2010.

when expected.[8] The underlying message is that there was no family or friends to phone in for that sort of help, not even during an emergency.

What these social scientists and artists are pointing to is lonely people who rely on the economically disenfranchised (a homeless woman in *Modern Times*, or illegal immigrants in *Crash* or *Babel*) to provide for the care that was once found among their families and friends they have estranged themselves from, but also people who have been so radically cut-out of their web or relationships, of their identity as regarding to a place, that they can fit anywhere, be it jobs or even romantic relationships.[9] In addition, for solace in deprivation, these modern Americans turn to Mexicans.

WHY AMERICAN HRM FITS POORLY IN COLLECTIVIST SOCIETIES

To manage Americans, scientific management has developed Human Resource Management techniques that suit individuals detached from their environment. From recruitment and selection techniques relying on profiling to fit job descriptions, to 360 degrees surveys to evaluating individual performances, to ritualized feedback procedures and health benefits which exclude the extended family the worker may live with. America is indeed exceptional; to the point its people management techniques may not fit as well in different societies.

Elsewhere I have argued in which ways Americans are different from Latin Americans, and why they will continue to be different in any time horizon that matters to business (Behrens, 2009). Those arguments find support in more recent data, showing how more collectivist-oriented societies like the Indian, Chinese, and Brazilian ones engage more intensely in Internet-based social media than the American one (Piskorski and McCall, 2010). In this paper, to bring the message closer to India, I will only refer to the differences in the stages of urbanization between America and Brazil, because rural people bring with them values which stress the role of social networks, and because the spatial distribution of India's population of India is still one of small villages, wherein, over 60 percent of the population still lives in small villages; but the migration to cities may move seven times as many Indians, as it moved Brazilians, and it is expected to happen in half the time span (Sanyal, 2010: 227).

---

[8] http://www.imdb.com/title/tt0449467/. Accessed on July 10, 2010.

[9] This may be why it was only in America that Antonucci et al. (2001: 663) did not find any relationship between the network structure and widowhood or illness of late adults.

In Brazil, between 1940 and 1996, the Brazilian population grew from 41 million to 156 million. The share of urban population grew from 31 percent to 78 percent when approximately 55 million people moved from the rural areas to the urban ones. At the turn of the last century, Brazilian cities were small, so much so that the share of population living in cities with up to 100 thousand inhabitants was 31 percent, with as many as 12 percent of households living in towns smaller than 20 thousand inhabitants (Camarano and Beltrão, 2000: 14–15). In small Brazilian cities, even in those as large as 100 thousand, one can expect most activities to revolve around agriculture or animal husbandry, therefore still rural at their base. Even in larger cities so recently urbanized, one expects people's ties and values to remain close to the family's recent rural origins. The more recently urbanized remain more intensely bound to family and place and will need to overcome greater emotional barriers to move elsewhere and still hope to fit in—very different from America, as India is.

But the modern tools of American Scientific Management, developed for, say, an urban 1979 Northern America (74 percent), cannot be equally fitting for Latin America whose faster and therefore more recent urbanization reached, in 2000, only 61 percent, or to Asia's 27 percent (McLean and Kromkowski, 1991). Indeed, Latin America's high urbanization rate is an exception and a very recent one at that (UNO, 2003: 30). Furthermore, while urbanization may be defined bureaucratically, the urban experience or the marginalized poor in the shantytowns of Latin America, be they "favelas" in Brazil, "villas miseria" in Argentina, "barrios" in Venezuela, or "tugurios" in Colombia, have little in common with the search of freedom and opportunities that characterized the initial impulse of urbanization in America. Still, those marginalized populations may only be the expression of informal solutions to the extension of the social space of the migrants like those referred to by Joseph Wood (2001: 162) regarding the peasants of Mexico's Oaxaca, who have extended into the cities their outlook of the world which no longer allows them to secure a living in their preferred traditional home styles, though they still preserve their Oaxcan identity and values in the larger cities.

Peasants, when acting collectively, as teams enlisted in insurrections, were extremely effective in all peasant insurrections in Latin America, from Argentina to Mexico. They were recruited as teams, whole families and neighbors who would know each other so well that any pretension would be short lived. They were teams before they entered into the 19th century insurrections, they were guided by a leader with a vision who had to communicate it, who had to recruit at the lowest possible cost, who had to assess performance and promote, or even ensure the logistics as the column advanced. All these insurrections, from Rosas in Argentina to Pancho Villa's and Zapata's in Mexico, were extraordinarily effective organizations, because their members were teams before they were enlisted (Behrens, 2010b). In fact, all this was recent enough to be at the root of Latin America's recent urbanization and at the poor way that Latin Americans respond to American styled work incentives and people management techniques developed for the socially disenfranchised American.

There may be a lesson in this. Latin Americans may be as effective as Americans when working in teams, provided they are hired as teams and not as individuals from the market to fit job descriptions, when they will take longer to perform as well. Because Latin Americans have been brought up in more cohesive social environments they will need longer to trust and blend and work with strangers. This is why Samba schools in Rio are so effective, delivering a World Class parade year in and year out, on the day agreed to, with no meaningful pay to its members: because Samba schools are made by families and neighbors. Furthermore, Latin Americans may respond differently from Americans to a leader's style, preferring the more paternalistic style over the transactional one (Behrens, 2009).

When it is not possible to hire whole teams corporations should hire internally and if externally, first by internal referrals, thus ensuring a faster induction of the hired. External hiring, by the standard procedure of matching profiles to job descriptions, should probably be the instrument of last resort, not the first, as in America.

There are some interesting cases to bring to the fore, which have not yet made it to the textbooks.

At Autolatina, a fomer joint venture by Ford and Volkswagen in Brazil, after dismissing about half of its 70,000 work force, eventually matters turned around and hiring was back on the agenda. The managers asked their best workers if they had people to recommend, then issued each good worker with a numbered token and had a draw, selecting the amount of tokens roughly equal to the number of new people Autolatina wanted to hire. Besides, Autolatina told the good remaining workers that they would be responsible for the quality of the people they recommended. This is how Autolatina rewarded their most engaged workers and extended their attitude by allowing them to select and sponsor the new hires, which also resulted in a faster induction process.[10]

---

[10] Interview with Fernando Pérez, former VP of Autolatina, on February 22, 2010.

Sudamtex, is the name of prominent textile industries in Uruguay and Venezuela and is owned by the same holding company (Johnson, 2010).[11] In Uruguay Sudamtex had just fewer than two thousand employees and approximately double that amount in Venezuela. The shareholders thought it would be a good idea to bring over from Uruguay some 35 workers to share their knowledge with their Venezuelan colleagues. The Uruguayans did not fit well in the Venezuelan unit and Sudamtex Venezuela could have sent the Uruguayans back. Instead, Sudamtex decided to entrust the whole Venezuelan denim area to the Uruguayans, who, as a team, performed well and their performance even enticed some healthy competition among partner areas of Sudamtex entirely peopled by Venezuelans. Again, teams that exist prior to induction perform better than individuals put together in an American styled managerial environment.

Surely one could find many more examples of teamwork whose effectiveness derives not so much from the managerial technique applied but from the web of loyalties nurtured on the ground. Could Mumbai's meal delivery system through the dabawallas be as effective if they were not all originally neighbors from Pune?[12]

What we need to devise are systems that build on the shared heritage of people of a collectivist orientation, where people prefer to work with whom they know than with strangers; where people go to work to have fun and make friends as well as producing; where people suspend judgment in exchange for protection for them and their families, where people do as they are told to, and consequently dislike being held individually accountable for carrying out orders; where people are more inclined to collaborate than compete; where people cannot wait for long performance-evaluation cycles but prefer instant gratifications and quick reprimands to late rewards and long-lasting anxieties. The list could go on, but it suffices to point into the direction we should be going: research to elicit how people like to be managed, what metrics to measure it when possible and management techniques that reflect those traditions. Until then, smiles at work, and innovation, will be rare and contained, and productivity low. Fortunately, Indians have triggered a change. Their corporate leaders

---

[11] Interview with Ken Johnson, majority shareholder of the holding company, in São Paulo, on June 30, 2010.

[12] Pune is a district about four train hours away from Mumbai. Under five thousand dabbawallas distribute up to two hundred thousand homemade meals per day to workers throughout Mumbai and return the empty containers back to their homes for replenishment for the next day. Communal pride on the work well done underpins the effectiveness of the system which was awarded a six sigma ranking by Forbes.

have broadened their sense of purpose to encompass the whole set of stake-holders, and have developed a global outlook firmly grounded in their domestic beliefs and ways (Singh and Bhandarker, 2010). This change is calling the attention of America, in that the latter is seeking inspiration in Indian management (Capelli et al., 2010). Hopefully one shall see Indian leadership and people management spilling over to other countries of a similar collectivist orientation.

REFERENCES

Antonucci et al. (2001) "Widowhood and Illness: A Comparison of Social Network Characteristics in France, Germany, Japan, and the United States," *Psychology and Aging*, 16(4): 655–665.

Behrens, Alfredo (2009) *Culture and Management in the Americas*. Stanford University Press.

———. (2010) "When in Doubt, Keep Your Mouth Shut." Available online at http://0800alfredo.posterous.com/when-in-doubt-keep-your-mouth-shut (last accessed July 13, 2010).

———. (2010b) Shooting Heroes to Reward Cowards.

Bourne, Roussell (1996) *Invention in America*. Fulcrum Publishers.

Brewster, C. (1995) "HRM: the European Dimension," in J. Storey (ed.), *Human Resource Management, a Critical Text*. Baltimore and London: Routlege, London.

Camarano, Ana Amélia and Beltrão, Kaizô Iwakami. 2000 Distribuição Espacial da População Brasileira: Mudanças na Segunda Metade deste Século. IPEA TD 766. Rio de Janeiro, Novembro de 2000. ISSN 1415–4765.

Capelli, Peter, Habir Singh, Jitendra Singh, and Michael Useem (2010) "The India Way: Lessons for the U.S.," *The Academy of Management Perspectives*, 24(2).

Cherlin, Andrew J. (2009) *The Marriage-Go-Round, the State of Marriage and the Family in America Today*. Alfred Knopf.

Chiang, Flora and Thomas Birtch (2007) "The Transferability of Management Practices: Examining Cross-national Differences in Reward Preferences," *Human Relations*, 60: 1293–1330.

Cornelius, Neraline (2001) *Human Resource Management: A Managerial Perspective*. Cengage: Learning EMEA.

Galanaki, Eleanna and Nancy Papalexandris (2007) "Internationalization as a Determining Factor of HRM Outsourcing," *Journal of Human Resource Management*, 18(8): 1557–1567.

Gamble, Jos (2010) "Transferring Organizational Practices and the Dynamics of Hybridization: Japanese Retail Multinationals in China," *Journal of Management Studies*, 47(4): 705–732.

Hamilton, Peter (1991) *Max Weber: Critical Assessments of Leading Sociologists*. Taylor & Francis.

Hounshell, D.A. (1984) *From the American System to Mass Production 1800–1932. The Development of Manufacturing Technology in the United States*. The John Hopkins University Press.

Khan, Robert L. (1972) "The Meaning of Work, Interpretations and Proposals for Measurement," in Campbell Angus and Philip E. Converse (eds), *The Human Meaning of Social Change*. Russell Sage Foundation.

Kochan, T. and L. Dyer (1995) "HRM: An American View," in J. Storey (ed.), *Human Resource Management: A Critical Text*. London: Routledge.

McLean, George F. and John Kromkowski (1991) "Urbanization and Values," Volume 5. Published by CRVP, 1991 ISBN1565180119, 9781565180116.

Meyer, David (2006) *Networked Machinists: High-technology Industries in Antebellum America*. Johns Hopkins Press.

Milner, John B. (2002) *Organizational Behavior: Foundations, Theories, and Analyses*. Oxford University Press.

Myloni, B., W.W. Harzing, and H. Mirza (2004) "Human Resource Management in Greece. Have the Colors of Culture Faded Away?," *International Journal of Cross Cultural Management*, 4(1): 59–76.

Neff, Walter F. (2006) *Work and Human Behavior*. 3rd edition by Transaction Publishers.

O'Toole, J. (1973) *Work in America*. Report of a Special Task Force to the Secretary of Health, Education, and Welfare. http://www.eric.ed.gov:80/ERICWebPortal/detail?accno=ED070738

Piskorski, Mikolaj Jan and Tommy McCall. (2010) Mapping the Social Internet, Harvard Business Review, July–August, 2010. http://hbr.org/2010/07/vision-statement-mapping-the-social-internet/ar/1

Pudelko, Markus and Anne Will Harzing. (2007) "Country-of-Origin, Localization, or Dominance Effect? An Empirical Investigation of HRM Practices in Foreign Subsidiaries," *Human Resource Management*, 46(40): 535–559.

Sanyal, Sanjeev (2010) "Reimagining Urban India," in T.N. Ninan (ed.), *India 2010*. New Delhi: Business Standard Books.

Singh, Pritam and Asha Bhandarker (2010) *In Search of Change Maestros*. New Delhi: Sage Publication.

Stciner, Dirk D. and Stephen W.G. Gillialand (1996) "Fairness Reaction to Personnel Selection Techniques in France and the United States," *Journal of Applied Psychology*, 81(2): 34–141.

Stciner, Dirk, D. Gilliland, and W.G. Stephen (1996) "Fairness Reactions to Personnel Selection Techniques in France and the United States," *Journal of Applied Psychology*, 81(2): 34–141.

Sussman, Marvin B. (1972) "Family Kinship and Bureaucracy," in Campbell Angus and Converse, Philip E. (eds), *The Human Meaning of Social Change*. Russell Sage Foundation.

Putnam, Robert D. (2000) *Bowling Alone: The Collapse and Revival of American Community*. New York: Simon and Schuster.

Taylor, Frederick W. (1911) *The Principles of Scientific Management*. New York: Harper Bros.

Tungli, Zsuzsanna and Mary Peiperl. (2009) "Expatriate Practices in German, Japanese, U.K. and U.S. Multinational Companies: a Comparative Survey of Changes," *Human Resource Management*, 48(1): 153–171.

United Nations (2004) *World Urbanization Prospects: the 2003 Revision. Volume 237 of Department for Economic and Social Affairs: ST/ESA/SER.A*. United Nations. Population Division.

Weiss. H. Eugene (2003) *Chrysler, Ford, Durant, and Sloan: Founding Giants of the American Automotive Industry*. McFarland.

Wintz, Cary (2000) *Black Culture and the Harlem Renaissance*. Texas: A&M University Press.

Wood, Joseph (1991) "Urban Space as a Region of Encounter," in George F. McLean and John Kromkowski (eds.), *Urbanization and Values Volume 5*. CRVP.

16

Twin-born Antipodes: Leadership and Management as Methods of Organizational Rule

Armen E. Petrosyan

The problem of leadership and its part in organizational life has till now been one of the most knotty matters. In early 1970s, R. Stogdill wrote that there were almost as much definitions of leadership, as those who tried to define this concept (Stogdill, 1974: 259). More than three decades elapsed since then and the number of definitions have only grown while the rapport between them has become progressively less. And nowadays voices are heard that the nature of managers and leaders is quite a moot idea and there are no coherent viewpoints on what they have to do and what makes them act in such a way.

So, G. Salaman is of the opinion that a clear vision of the nature of leadership will never appear because "such definitions arise not from organizational or technical requirements (which are themselves the product of manager's theory of organization), but from the shifting ways in which over time these functions are variously conceptualized. The manager, as much as the worker, is a product of history" (Salaman, 2004: 58). It comes out that all is relative. Today people look at management and leadership from one standpoint but under other conditions their ideas will change. And this kind of attitude is irrespective of the nature of organizations and their "technical requirements". Should one wonder that definitions of leadership not only proliferate but are, for the most part, also very distant from the real activity of organizations?

Such a state of affairs is hardly tolerable in science. And, obviously, it is time to elucidate on this point. What is the nature of leadership? How does it correlate to management? What places they take within organizations and how interact at ruling people? The present paper will focus on answering these questions.

A MERE MANAGERIAL FUNCTION?

When treating leadership many bring it to one of the management functions. Indeed, manager influences his subordinates, motivates them, mobilizes and directs to achieving the formulated and implicit objectives. Under such conditions, it is hard to do without some leader behavior. Just owing to it manages "kindles" the workers and obtains essential outcomes where the circumstances seem to impede his efforts. However it is easy to notice that such leader forms of acting, though being often vitally important for the successful management, go out of its proper framework.

What is a function? It is the task the system is destined for and what is accomplished in the course of its activity. As regards management, its mission consists in ensuring the organizational goals' attainment. A manager sets objectives, organizes the work directed to their fulfillment, and controls its course and results. In its turn, leadership has to inspire and enlist the diligence of workers. A leader "attunes" and inclines them to do all their best to promote the common business.

Thus, leadership is only one of the means supporting the functions of management, along with many others (the special knowledge, the ability to grasp the situation, the skills of handling technical devices, and so on). True, the role of leadership in management processes is so considerable that it acquires inevitably a heightened status. But it doesn't mean that leadership ceases to be a tool of manager and becomes an end in itself.

It is common knowledge that not all managers are leaders. Sometimes they say about a manager: "He's a good worker, competent and skilled. But he isn't leader." Does it mean that such a manager is a grotty one? Not a bit. To some extent, he can fulfill his tasks quite well without distinct leader behavior. Certainly, it is nearly always desired but not necessary at the lowest and, especially, middle levels of management.

Undoubtedly, the significance of leader behavior is increased as the manager goes up to the top of the organization. And it becomes an obvious necessity for many executives. However, even this case is not so simple. There are a host of organizations having subordinate or stable goals (e.g., a daughter enterprise producing components and spares for its parent or the survey office of a governor, destined to attend on his administration). Even their first persons can easily do without any charisma.

Likewise, not all leaders are managers. The most convincing example is a preacher conducting huge crowds but, in the same time, not trying to obtain further insight into the life order of his followers. Jesus Christ, as the Gospels say, felt the burden of routine and became angry when his disciples turned to him for utilitarian wants. He didn't aspire for the power nor had a need for managing his followers in the ordinary sense. He wasn't going to set their mind to fulfill some specific tasks or to distribute among them current duties. Nor had they been supervised by him. Jesus didn't appreciate their conduct in a permanent order as well as reward or punish them.

True, Christ, if to take on and to trust the words of Scripture, had been able to sate a crowd with a few loaves but he looked reproachful at those who thought of worldly rather than of divine things. And only after his death and ascension there appeared a need to put in order the affairs of his followers' community, for it acquired some property structure and a hierarchy of authorities. One might say the same about other preachers—John the Baptist, Buddha, Mahatma Gandhi, etc.

So, what a function of management is leadership, if it being inherent to the activity of many non-managers, nevertheless passes a sizable part of managers by? And why does it differ so much from their other functions?

Can one imagine a manager—even of the lowest rank (such as foreman or head of a small office)—who doesn't, though badly and lubberly, set objectives, find ways and means of achieving them, coordinate workers' activity, and monitor it? Scarcely ever. But, if so, for what reason do we put in a series of planning, organization, and control a mythical "directing" (leading) function?

AN ALTER EGO OF MANAGEMENT?

The clear realization of the unfitness of such a treatment of leadership brought, last time, to a new current. A number of authors acquired firm conviction that they need to distinguish between management and leadership as different activities. They say that these concepts are certainly interrelated but represent quite independent phenomena.

Many are inclined to belief that this tradition of contrasting leaders with managers had been laid by A. Zaleznik. According to him, a leader is an artist who squeezes his way into organizational jungles with the help of creation and intuition, whereas, a manager simply solves problems guided by rationality and control (Zaleznik, 1977: 67–78). True, it is recognized that management and leadership can be concentrated in the same person. However, such a situation is neither unique nor surprising. A financier often lives in harmony, inside himself, along with a merchant, designer with an engineer, and so on.

Sometimes the watershed is seen in that "leaders create and articulate vision" while "managers ensure it is put into practice" (Syrett and Hoggs, 1992: 5). The others emphasize the dynamical aspect of the subject. In their opinion, management "produces a degree of predictability and order" whereas leadership creates "change, often to a dramatic degree" (Conger, 1992: 20). It means that managers don't relate immediately to leadership as well as leaders stay apart from management. Their interplay resembles the relations between a designer developing projects and a technologist elaborating the prerequisites and opportunities for their implementation.

Moreover, this opposition is brought to the logical end where a leader appears as a catalyst focused on strategy while a manager becomes a simple performer. In A. Bryman's words, the latter is an "operator," or a "technician" concerned with the "here-and-now of operational goal attainment" (Bryman, 1986: 6). Otherwise, leaders establish what to do and managers do what is established.

W.G. Bennis and J. Goldsmith go further. According to them, "there is a profound difference—a chasm—between leaders and managers. A good manager does things right. A leader does the right things. Doing the right things implies a goal, a direction, an objective, a vision, a dream, a path, a reach." Management relates to the efficiency and leadership to the effectiveness. The first is associated with the "How" while the second with the "What" and "Why." Managers concern themselves with "systems, controls, procedures, policies, and structures. Leadership is about trust—about people" which means "innovating and initiating." Thus, "leadership is creative, adaptive, and agile." It "looks at the horizon, not just the bottom line" (Bennis and Goldsmith, 1997: 4).

Nevertheless, despite of such rigid, categorical, and, in the same time, far-reaching conclusions, no serious reasons are brought to support them and—what is much more important—no distinct criteria's are adduced. How to differ managers from leaders? The question remains unanswered. Clearly, one can, if desired, consider such criteria's; the "How," "What," and "Why" as well as the opposition of the concepts "efficiency" and "effectiveness." But, unluckily, these criteria's are even more blurry than what is compared with them.

Indeed, the efficiency is associated with the right performance (how to do) and the effectiveness with the right setting of objectives (what and why to do). It means that a leader formulates a task whereas a manager accomplishes it. However, we got used to thinking that the objective setting is one of the basal functions of management as a part of the planning (Drucker, 1999: 400). But here it is committed to the leaders.

A manager turned into a performer looks rather strange. His chief care is how to achieve the goal preset. Is it reasonable or well-founded?—such a question exceeds the bounds of his competence.

The picture is quite clear. But it has, in fact, nothing new. The figures are simply renamed. A manager is called a leader and the performer, a manager.

More explicit is the position of J.P. Kotter. As he states:

> Leadership is different from management, but not for the reason most people think. Leadership isn't mystical and mysterious. It has nothing to do with having charisma or other exotic personality traits. It's not the province of

a chosen few. Nor is leadership necessarily better than management or a replacement for it; rather leadership and management are two distinctive and complementary activities. Both are necessary for success in an increasingly complex and volatile business environment.

Besides, he suggests a relatively distinct criteria for distinguishing between managers and leaders. In his opinion, a manager ensures the goals to be achieved and is provided with authorities for such a function, whereas a leader, by forecasting the future, "grasps" and formulates strategic guidelines for the organization. The task of a manager consists in staff recruiting and appointing, while a leader should provide it with a common vision and prospects of development, preparing to future changes. While "management is about coping with complexity, leadership by contrast, is about coping with change" (Kotter, 1990: 103–104). A manager controls the subordinates and accounts for the outcomes they get. And as for the leader, he mobilizes and inspires the workers, awaking them to act with increasing output.

At that, the key difference of leader from manager is reduced to that the workers follow of their own free will. A leader has no warrant to reward or to punish them. Nevertheless, they entrust themselves to the leader, accepting his demands. As regards the manager, he rests upon a formal authority. It is just this power that gives him to force subordinates to accomplish the objectives set.

This picture of interrelations of management and leadership seems, by first sight, to be a well-shaped and sound one. In essence, the management functions are split into two components. The first embraces the technical side of it (problem-solving, planning, budgeting, staffing, controlling, etc.) and the second deals with personal one (motivating, inspiring, directing, aligning people to a shared objective). However, it begins to resemble a nonsense as soon as the criteria suggested finds some application.

Indeed, if management is a technical aspect and leadership a personal one, does it mean that managers don't play, in their activity, any interpersonal role? Is a manager an insensitive robot, some technical shuttle scurrying about the administrative machine or does he communicate with his subordinates too? Does a manager only issue directives or does he also discuss the decisions with the workers? And a leader—is he somehow gotten involved with the technical proceedings or merely hovers over the organization and declares his precepts from the height?

Can one at all structurally differentiate the technical and interpersonal parts of the management? Doesn't it resemble the attempts to separate the soul from the body? After all, the interpersonal is only a component of the administrative systems and, having lost it, they will cease to work.

Thus, Kotter make an ordinary logical error. One structural element of a system is opposed not to another element but to that system as a whole. As a consequent, the system itself is reduced to a structural element's status.

FORMAL AND INFORMAL LEADERSHIP

Another opposition—between formal leaders and informal ones—is also quite queer. Having recognized managers as formal leaders, should one agree that they enjoy, predominantly, no moral authority, aren't held in respect and don't influence their people? Or, may be, informal leaders of an organization don't at all need for some official power?

What is moral leadership? It interprets people to themselves, suggesting some respect and trust. The followers go after him not because he can award or punish them. They believe him to be a right person whose word and proceedings don't disagree. The people have no doubt that the leader knows where it must be gone, and is willing sincerely to wend his way along with followers, not keeping a separate side-track for himself.

In any organization, managers are endowed with certain authorities over the subordinates but not because they as persons, who without official power are worth nothing, and not only because this power is necessary means of influencing workers. If a manager doesn't have some distinctly defined authorities, a chaos emerges within the sphere of his responsibility. The organization loses its hierarchical structure and turn into a primitive association of "free shots."

But can one say that a manager is able to be at the head of organization or its any unit, only because he has gotten formal authorities? Certainly, no. Otherwise there would be no bad managers. They need only to acquire wider and stronger authorities and even the most useless of them would succeed. However, such events don't occur.

But the affairs in an organization would be getting on worse by far if one of the workers has obtained high moral authority and trust while he doesn't possess any official power. All his colleagues are willing to follow him anywhere by his first call. He has only to suggest something—that becomes at once unquestionable for others. Can one consider this situation as a good fit for the organization? Surely, no. It is a bomb of delayed action.

What does the manager of such an organization feel as a "formal leader"? His status is entirely lowered. He can do nothing against his unofficial competitor. The organization's official head should either ingratiate him with the latter or cease to fulfill his own duties. In fact, both cases turn into chaos, although, nominally, the hierarchical structure of the organization is still kept. Thereby, it does not make sense to demand something from the official person for, in reality, he has nothing to manage. In the same time, the informal leader who practically rules the people has nothing to count for.

The unofficial leadership in organizations is acceptable only to a limited extent. As soon as it threatens the status and the authorities of formal management such a "guerrilla" must be blocked. Clearly, the question isn't of draconian measures suppressing the wills of persons involved. However, apathetic attitude to such a situation inevitably brings one to disorganization.

On opposing leader to manager, Kotter substitutes their proper interrelations for the collision of formal and informal leaders. He considers a leader as an official and a manager as an unofficial one. But informal leaders in organizations are not endowed with some particular status. In a sense, they are "anomalies", deviations from the "normal" organizational structure. That's why they cannot be regarded as authorized persons.

Naturally, it would be foolish to overlook and ignore the informal leaders. Furthermore, it is inadmissible to suppress or burn them out. After all, an unofficial structure appears not on someone's whim but as an organization's reaction to the task to be fulfilled. And if the official structure doesn't cope with the requirements of the situation then the organizational system is spontaneously attuned, compensating the defects of the initial project.

Thus, if the informal leader stays within certain limits he can be of essential benefit for the organization, filling up the derelictions of official channels of information and influence. However it is not a reason for turning all on its head and raising him over the formal one. Even though such a case exists anywhere it means only that a "revolutionary situation" takes place—a dual power (the presence of an alternative manager) is in hand. And this circumstance is fraught with serious consequences for the organization.

If the cause of the diarchy consists, wherein the manager is too weak, then he must be discharged without delay. And if, in addition, the informal leader is strong enough to rule the people he should be appointed to the place freed. In any case, it is unacceptable to allow an informal leader to rise to his actual status (the potential of influencing the workers) up to the level of the formal one.

True, in organizations the official and unofficial leaderships often coincide, that is the manager organically unites within himself the necessary skills of administering and the leader traits. This is good because in this case the challenge to the management hierarchy is radically reduced. Nevertheless even such a manager subjects the informal acting to formal one. He uses his charisma, authority, and influence to achieve the organizational goals. Otherwise, when the informal acting begins to prevail and he expresses the willingness to give up the organization's interests to the strengthening of his own personal popularity as well as the respect and trust on the part of the subordinates; the formal leader becomes perhaps yet more dangerous than the informal one capable to plunge it into a state of dual power.

Anyway, Kotter splits the manager's figure into two parts. He picks out from it a leader's "self" that, being a component of the manager's personality—at that is not always necessary—turns out a separate entity acquiring an independent existence, along with the parent's "body." Naturally, his mind falls apart too. Therefore, the qualities required for successful management get distributed among two figures instead of a single one.

Does it mean that a leader and manager are mutually exclusive figures? In Kotter's opinion, certainly no. They act side by side in the same organization and further its mission by common efforts. He maintains that "the smart companies value both kinds of people and work hard to make them part of the team." Moreover, in principle, these qualities permit of a combination within a single person. According to Kotter, organizations "can begin to groom their top people to provide both" (Kotter, 1992: 16–17). Nevertheless it is hard to chance upon this sort of examples. Obviously, they are not observable.

In this connection, a legal question arises. Why organizations really don't attempt to cross the manager's and leader's figures? The answer is rather limpid. When the leader's self gets independence from the manager's but, at that, doesn't quit his body an inevitable clash emerges between them. It is nothing else than a "professional schizophrenia." As a consequence, it tears to pieces also the managerial work. And the single way to avoid such a "sickness" is to settle this "untethered" leader's self back into the manager's mind. Only in this way one could return to a reasonable conception of leadership as a constituent part of the managerial practice.

RULE IN ORGANIZATIONS

Managers use specified, quantitatively defined, and temporally anchored goals, usually named objectives, to discipline the activity of workers and bring it in some limits. It allows them to impart some distinctiveness to the actions and create an opportunity of checking up and correcting the outcomes.

Workers perform the task because it corresponds, ultimately, to their interests. They strive to attain the objectives for only in such a way their own wants can be satisfied. Manager has to stimulate subordinates to get them acting. They should be persuaded that there is an undoubted connection between their efforts and personal goals realization. Otherwise the organizational objectives scarcely will be attained.

To set going the mechanism of feedback manager must use the factors of rewards and punishment. That allows him to consolidate "right" actions and cut off "wrong" ones. But it requires testing results obtained, monitoring trends of the activity, correcting them when necessary, and sometimes even revising the objectives. Taken together, that constitutes the system of control introduced into the organization's body.

In leadership, on the contrary, the emphasis is placed on "vague" visions, not so much presetting the orientation and character of followers' activity as inducing to it. They are dreams by nature rather than aims to be achieved.

The movement along visions conforms to wants and hopes of followers. That's why they don't need any additional incentives. Their motives immediately appear in the visions and methods of securing them.

Hence, leader doesn't have to resort to measures of coercion. Followers themselves apprehend the necessary action as just what is desired. Since they aspire to visions, seeing them as their own ones, external tool of spurring them up is not required.

People will manifest an extreme self-devotion anyway; at least the sincere ones. That's why just demonstration of fidelity to vision and of vivid examples of "right" behavior turns out to be the leader's chief priority. Being learnt by followers they become a framework of activity and inner "quasi-control" mechanism baring deviations and keeping efforts within admissible bounds.

But, in the same time, management and leadership are not fully independent and mutually indifferent forces. They have many intimately connecting threads that make them very close and even kinder to each other. The point is that a more general human potency is expressed in them. It is called a rule and embraces all the manifestations of guiding and influencing people for the purpose of reaching the results intended, through their hands.

The rule means any exercise of authority, control, or domination. It implies heading individuals and collectives in the broadest sense of the word, including all the instances concerned with the relations of power and subjection. The mechanism of ruling consists of three basic components—goals, driving forces, and feedback. But, naturally, it cannot be uniform and undifferentiated. It is aimed at various or even opposite targets. Hence, the forms taken by the rule must not be identical. The same refers also to the methods applied. They comply with the objects to be ruled as well as with the forms of ruling.

The human groups subjected to rule are divided into two extremely broad categories: formal, officially established and strongly arranged, organizations and informal ones that not necessarily develop spontaneously but, in any case, don't acquire some distinctive branchy structure and, in the same time, retain a sufficient freedom of interactions between their members.

Formal organization can be defined as a union of people whose participation is conditioned by their personal interests. There are officially established functional roles (positions) and vertically integrated (hierarchical) structure, strictly formulated regulatives, and authorities and responsibilities of separate members there. The inducement to work is based on individual motivation and stimulation and the activity itself is subjected to regular and systematical evaluation and modification according to explicitly expressed common (organizational) goals.

Something directly opposite is informal organization (association). It represents a union of people who are encouraged by their aspirations and beliefs. The positions of members are uniform here and the interactions between them, predominantly, horizontal (equal in rights). The inducement to activity arises from common attitudes and unity of expectations what ensures collective inspiration, and the appraisal of activity proceeds from its correspondence to adopted standards (models) of behavior.

Clearly, these two kinds of organizations by no means exhaust all their varieties. They constitute only two poles between which lies a whole chain of diverse intermediate (transitional) forms. However, although they are not something quite different from these poles but combine—in some proportions—features of each of them.

THE FORMS OF ORGANIZATIONAL RULE

Naturally, it would be very strange to suppose that so diverse, if not to say—opposite, people's unions are to be ruled in the same manner. To the contrary, the forms and methods of rule, applied to them, have to differ essentially when striving to achieve the manifold goals intended. No wonder that the mankind over its long history worked out and successfully employed them even without going deeply into their nature and peculiarities.

Even a cursory examination allows to notice that the chief thing in informal unions is to determinate the directions of movement, develop the policy complied with them, and preset some "reasonable" examples of behavior ensuring advancement towards the desired future. As regards formal ones they—just because of goals to be more specified and well defined—provide for a sophisticated mechanism of attachment to them of personal interests of separate members and their stimulation and of permanent control of their activity and non-admission of current and, especially, final results to go out of established limits. That is quite another form of rule that prefers feeling the pulse of an organization's everyday life instead of having a bird's-eye view of it.

The first mode of rule is called "governance." Its meaning comes from "to give direction" or "to set an example". Not in vain one of the archaic but having reached us meanings of the word consists in "moral conduct or behavior." In a contemporary context "to govern" means "to exercise of authority over" or "to perform functions for a political unit." That is to say, it is a question not of power within a specified organizational structure but of authorities regarding some sufficient uniform mass beyond that structure (for instance, of a state body with respect to people or of a municipality with respect to population of the territory).

Governors set directions of further development, work out a political tack, and establish the order circumscribing the citizens' freedom of actions but don't interfere in their private life, set them objectives, and evaluate every step. In short, they don't grasp people by the hand unless the latter break the law. The opposite state of affairs is possible only in totalitarian societies that turn, in fact, into formal organizations. That is an intolerable extremity, on one hand, to be avoided and, on the other hand, *in corpore* (in full measure) unrealizable.

The second form of rule is peculiar to formal organizations. It is known as administration and more concerned with the conduct of everyday affairs and the solution of specified problems. The policy making—if pertaining to it at all—is a secondary task here, going beyond its focus.

That is quite natural. After all, there exists in formal organizations officially established persistent goals, strict rules of behavior, and highly developed division of labor. They rigorously constrain the arbitrariness and spontaneous actions of administrator, and the question of policy or strategic re-orientation arises only at deep-lunged torques when a previous "formalization" of activity (goals, structures, and rules) not merely doesn't favor to achieve much success but rather play a role of "strait-jacket" binding administrators' initiative as well as workers themselves.

It doesn't mean that formal organizations content themselves with administration whereas informal ones know nothing else but governance.

So, a president governs his state. But, for it, he resorts to services of the staff which, being a part of the state machinery, represents a formal organization requiring some inner rule. And the latter is carried out in the form of administration.

On the other hand, even in corporations—typical examples of formal organizations—there are elements that don't immediately concern their inner structure and tower over it. For instance, Boards of Directors or Review boards pertain to them. They don't take part in the current activity of organizations and have no right to impact on decisions of their managers and even ordinary workers. Nevertheless such organs are very influential. They establish long-term goals, adopt strategies of development, and sometimes make appointments to top positions. Like organs govern corporations but not administer them. Their function is as if taken out of the organizational boundaries—not to break the unity of administration.

Therefore, governance, as well as administration, is peculiar to both formal and informal organizations. The only difference is what places they take there and what are their roles. The function of administration in informal associations as well as of governance in formal organizations is secondary. It recedes into the background. But its significance is not merely subservient. As administration becomes the chief form of rule in the inside of authority bodies (institutions) so governance turns out the main way of exercise of influence in the "external" (taken out) bodies of formal organizations.

But if administration and governance pertain to diverse unions of people and are of principally different natures they must, evidently, employ different methods conforming to their tasks as much as possible. Such instruments of execution of rule are management and leadership. The first relates to administration and the second to governance. A manager expresses goals in the form of specified objectives complying with interests of the organization, inclines workers—through securing their personal interests and offering them attractive incentives—to join efforts and together fulfill actions intended, and sets going the machinery of control to ensure their appropriateness and opportuneness. As to a leader, he transforms his own goal into a dream of followers, excites in them some inner desire to strive after it (inspiration as driving force), and "exemplifies" the due behavior (embodiment of "right" conduct as a special mechanism of feedback) and thereby as if automates the "control" over adherents' activity. That allows him to secure both their self-devotion and yearning for unity of actions (Table 16.1).

TABLE 16.1: The Grading of Rule

Elements of rule	Kinds and descriptions	
Objects	*Formal organization*	*Informal association*
	People's union, participation in which is determined by their personal interests, with officially established functional roles (positions) and vertically integrated (hierarchical) structure as well as authorities and responsibilities of separate members. The inducement to activity is based on individual motivation and stimulation. Workers' performance is subjected to systematical evaluation, correction and modification according to explicitly formulated common (organizational) goals	People' union, participation in which is determined by aspirations and beliefs, with uniform positions of separate members and predominantly horizontal (equal in rights) interactions between them. The inducement to activity is based on collective inspiration (common attitudes and a unity of expectations). The evaluation of adherents' performance is usually of non-systematic and unofficial nature and made according to adopted standards (patterns) of behavior
Forms	*Administration*	*Governance*
	The rule concerned with conduct of everyday affairs and specified problems solution. It implies designation of the substance of activity, the structure and functions of organization, its staff and specified regulatives of behavior	The execution of power, carrying-out of functions of authorities. It includes designation of the directions of development, working-out of political tack, establishment of general laws (regulations) constraining the freedom of actions of separate members
Methods	*Management*	*Leadership*
	Setting objectives conforming to organizational interests, inclining workers—through "engaging" their personal interests and offering attractive stimuli—to join efforts and carry out together the actions intended as well as starting up the mechanism of control and feedback	Transformation of goal (vision) into followers' dream, exciting in them an inner desire to fulfill it, and "automation" of control over their activity through "exemplifying" the due behavior (proffering patterns to stick to) and, thereby, ensuring adherents' self-devotion and unity of actions

Does it mean that leadership and management are incompatible, or where one of them is applied the other has no place? Differently, can they be combined and used in the same associations of people and even by the same person?

SCOPES AND LIMITS OF THE RULE METHODS

It must be admitted that formal and informal organizations are only some idealized models. And although most people's unions, in any event, contain both kinds of features they do not necessarily pertain to one of them in pure form but imply also various—sometimes quite significant—"admixtures" of the opposed mode. But even more important is that the substantial part of associations has a transitional nature. The rule in them represents some mix of governance and administration and, naturally, requires a combination of management and leadership.

An obvious example of such organizations is the case of military units. On one hand, they represent, surely, formal organizations with explicit hierarchical structure and crystallized functional roles. Under normal conditions, the rule is based here on personal interests of the members (especially in professional army, in contrast with call-up one), and feedback is provided for—owing to strict mechanisms of control, reward, and punishment. And this circumstance turns every unit head into a manager. But, on the other hand, as soon as a military unit gets into the situation for the sake of which it is created, that is, it begins to conduct combat operations, little things remain from the "normal" procedures of rule. The more intense the operations become, the higher is the strain and the less definite are their consequences and the harder it is to maintain the standard (administrative) order of activity. The ability to govern people is brought to the foreground and leader qualities turn out more and more valuable.

While, under usual peace conditions, unit heads influence their people; first through securing their personal interests (salary, career development, etc.), in extreme situations such a method of rule is practically useless. The point is not only that they have very little time for realizing it and responding conformably. The aspiration for implementation of interests clashes with other powerful motives of personality (for instance, striving to save life and health or avoid overloads). Under such circumstances, the inspiration of people is much more effective. It needs to suggest them attitudes inducing unconditional willingness to accomplish hard and dangerous tasks. Although a commander has the right to demand his subordinates to execute his order and, if necessary, to impose some penalty upon them, it is much more preferable when they understand its sense and implications and strive to fulfill operations required as well as possible. That's why in a battlefield the inspiration and "exemplification" (embodiment of "right" behavior) practically displace all other means of influencing people.

Certainly, the qualities managers and leaders need are far from being always combined in a person. Many outstanding leaders turn out worthless managers, as well as, sometimes excellent managers don't possess leader traits. But other cases when they join these qualities are also known. For instance, H. Ford, was such a person. If we have to take the name of one of our contemporaries, one could name W. Gates. They both not merely succeeded in creating new—large and promising—organizations but also systematically advanced towards top achievements.

Moreover, both the groups of qualities are peculiar to many people. The question is only about their amount and proportions. That's why it is not worth to put insurmountable bounds between them. Not rare are situations when a manager has to turn into a leader or vice versa, where a leader is obliged to function as a manager.

In principle, if all the people's organizations operate under standard and invariable conditions their heads predominantly wouldn't have need to combine such opposite qualities; both managers and leaders would get by with their "toolkits" and not resort to the "alien" armory. But, unfortunately, the situation doesn't remain regular. For instance, the structure of a formal organization is eroded and old rules constrain the freedom of maneuvers and keep back the initiatives of people. When such attendant circumstances begin to dominate, ordinary tools inevitably fail. To bring a situation under control, a manager has nothing else to do than resort to leader's methods of influencing people.

Leadership and management not merely differ from each other; they represent quite diverse and, in a certain sense, even opposite ways of rule. True, both have almost the same destination—influencing people and attaining the results designed, through their own efforts. But instruments used are very dissimilar. That's why indefatigable yearning for leadership in formal organizations (enterprises, institutions, public bodies, and so on) that gets now a great vim looks rather funny. Thus, the Conference Board of Canada reported early in this century that more than 70 percent of Canadian chief executives saw building leader capability, as their most important business priority (Leadership, 2001). They neglect the simple truth that leadership in such organizations can be applied only in a limited scope and under certain conditions which should be regarded as anomaly rather than rule.

The hypertrophied picture of scope and possibilities of leadership is so widespread that many consider it incontestable. Nevertheless it is no more than all the rage of unsteady fashion that, no wonder, meets some resistance—sometimes in form of an opposite extremity. In such cases, not only merely merits of leadership are put in doubt; the leadership itself is depicted as an ersatz mechanism of impacting on workers that threatens organizations with degradation and degeneration.

So, G. Gemmill and J. Oakley affirm that leadership is nothing but an "alienating social myth" that, rather than empowering organizations, deskills employees and creates an excessive dependency of workers. "The leadership myth," they state, "functions as a social defense whose central aim is to repress uncomfortable needs, emotions, and witnesses that emerge when people attempt to work together" (Gemmill, 1992: 123). It is assumed that dependency on the leader figure offers them a sense of meaning, direction, and purpose.

However, such critics of leadership cannot be admitted correct. They would have some reasons if leadership doesn't play an autonomous role. But it is not the case.

Besides leadership is the chief means of impacting on people in associations, from time to time it comes to foreground in formal organizations. Clearly, the latter event occurs not so often and lasts not too long. Nevertheless these rare and short periods get paramount importance for they are connected with critical situations determining the probability of the organization's survival or passage into a qualitatively other state. Of course, no one can disregard so important a factor and, having named it "alienating myth," repudiate the penetration into its nature.

More temperate is the approach of J. Gosling and H. Mintzberg who also express natural discontent with the idolization of leadership. They mordantly notice that leadership today nearly devoured management. "Most of us", they say, "have become so enamored of 'leadership' that 'management' has been pushed into the background. Nobody aspires to be a good manager anymore; everybody wants to be great leader." Certainly one must agree with them that this is a dangerous trend eroding the very foundations of formal organizations. But, unfortunately, Gosling and Mintzberg see threats only where "the separation of management from leadership" occurs. In their opinion, "just as management without leadership encourages an uninspired style which deadens activities, leadership without management encourages a disconnected style, which promotes hubris" (Gosling and Mintzberg, 2003: 54–55). Hence, the problem merely consists in that instead managers not possessing leader qualities, can emerge leaders not able to administrate, what is a transition from one extreme to another.

Meanwhile, leaders without manager arsenal are not that bad as it might seem at first glance. They also can be demanded by practice; for instance, in informal associations dealing with ordinary conditions (especially at higher levels). Their role doesn't yield in importance to that played, under like circumstances, by managers in formal organizations.

The chief peril lies in another thing. Turning one and all managers into leaders not only eliminates them, actually, as class but also abolishes management as an independent "trade." A manager transmutes into a double-headed creature whose heads not merely look at opposite ends but, having sent him conflicting impulses, tears to pieces his everyday activity. As a result, instead of a high professional we get a professional schizophrenic that doesn't know what to prefer. As Bouridan's ass he rushes about between two haystacks, doomed to starvation.

Formal organizations acting, in the main, under normal circumstances require just management, not leadership. The situation changes as conditions of activity go beyond the habitual scope. Then, the role of leadership becomes more salient. And it reaches apogee when the environment grows chaotized and extremely uncertain. But if leader features penetrate manager's activity in an ordinary situation, and "leaderization" of him occurs it brings to destruction of stationary mechanisms of administration.

INSTEAD OF CONCLUSION: OPPOSITE BUT COMPLEMENTARY

The divergence of the forms and methods of rule had begun very early in the human history. The memory of it had been retained in old legends adverting to the origins of the society.

In the Roman mythology, a special place was taken by Janus, the God of all entrances and exits, baring and unbarring (from the Latin word "ianua"—door, gate). He had two faces looking at the opposite ends, and, so, Romans considered him to know the past as well as the future. His name was mentioned the first when addressing to the gods; they called Janus the "God of gods" and the "good creator."

In "Fasti," Ovid's poem, Janus states that the ancients named him Chaos since he was from the old matter (me Chaos antique nam sum res prisca vocabant). From the shapeless mass resembling a lump (globus et sine imagine moles) he turned into a god and the keeper of the order who revolve the axis of the world. Janus proclaims: And as a small sign of the previous chaotic state Janus head's front and back still looked just the same. No wonder that he was regarded as the first ruler of the Latium (rex latinorum).

It is quite natural to surmise that Janus' two faces correspond to the modes of rule whereof one is administration and the other governance. Not in vain Romans appealed to him in such a way:

> Dexter ades ducibus, quorum secura labore
>   otia terra ferax, otia pontus agit:
> Dexter ades patribusque tuis populoque Quirini
>   Et resera nutu candida templa tuo (Ovid, 1909: 3–4).
> (Justly treat the chiefs whose toil ensures
>   Peace to the fruitful earth, peace to the sea.
> Justly treat the Roman people's elite
>   And by thy nod unbar the white temples).

One of Janus' faces looks inwards (larem) and is addressed to the chiefs (ducibus). It symbolizes management. The other face is turned outwards—to the nobility and the class of patricians whose mission consists in leading people. Originally, both the faces were only the different sides of rule as a single whole. But later—as the forms of activity were differentiated, and the division of "ruling labor" deepened—every face got an independent sense.

The differentiation of leadership and management has been occurring from the very beginnings of rule. As soon as administration and governance had been crystallized they began to act, in a certain extent, by not glancing back at the counterpart. However, when one of them didn't cope with the task, it remained nothing but to remember the second and to resort to its help. That's why although management and leadership are real antipodes they represent complementary forces which cannot be fully disjoined. It is not a question of separate heads but two faces of a single one. And subject to the function executed (administration or governance). Janus turns to it the one or the other of his faces.

REFERENCES

Bennis, W.G. and J. Goldsmith (1997) *Learning to Lead: A Workbook on Becoming a Leader.* Reading (MA): Perseus.

Bryman, A. (1986) *Leadership and Organization.* London: Routledge.

Conger, J.A. (1992) *Learning to Lead: The Art of Transforming Managers into Leaders.* San Francisco (CA): Jossey-Bass.

Drucker, P.F. (1999) *Management: Tasks, Responsibilities, Practices.* New York: HarperCollins.

Gemmill, G. and J. Oakley (1992) "Leadership: an Alienating Social Myth," *Human Relations*, 45(2): 113–129.

Gosling, J. and H. Mintzberg (2003) "The Five Minds of Manager," *Harvard Business Review*, 81(11): 54–63.

Kotter, J.P. (1990) *A Force for Change: How the Leadership Differs from Management.* New York: Free Press.

———. (1992) "What Leaders Really Do," in M. Syrett and C. Hogg (eds), *Frontiers of leadership: An Essential Reader,* pp. 16–24. Cambridge (MA): Blackwell.

Leadership for tomorrow: A challenge for business today. 2001. Ottawa: Author.

Ovid. (1909) *The Fasti of Ovid.* London: Macmillan.

Salaman, G. (2004) "Competences of Managers, Competences of Leaders," in G. Storey (ed.), *Leadership in Organizations: Current Issues and Key Trends,* pp. 58–78. Abingdon.

Stogdill, R.M. (1974) *Handbook of Leadership: A Survey of Theory and Research.* New York: Free Press.

Syrett, M. and C. Hogg (1992) *Frontiers of Leadership: An Essential Reader.* Cambridge (MA): Blackwell.

Zaleznik, A. (1977) "Managers and Leaders: Are They different?," *Harvard Business Review,* 55(3): 67–78.

Part II

DIALOGS WITH CHANGE MASTERS

I

Bharti Airtel: From Best to Next

Dialog with Manoj Kohli, CEO (International)
and Joint MD, Bharti Airtel Ltd

Interviewer: *The landscape of business is undergoing a phase of great uncertainty and tumultuous transformation. In your view what are some of the emerging trends that would characterize the business world in the next orbit?*

Manoj Kohli: At present the world is undergoing a major metamorphosis. The most important change that is taking place is that the entire global economic balance is getting re-organized. I can safely predict that by 2020, China, India and Africa would be the new axis of dominant economies supplanting the existing axis of US, Europe, and Japan. Indeed it will be harking back to the era thousands of years ago when China and India were the land of proverbial wealth and immense treasure.

In this transformation, China is playing a very important role. It has been growing at a dizzy rate of around 10–12 percent for more than 15 years now. Even though the growth rate might have slowed down to a single digit, its exports might have come down a notch or two below and its manufacturing facilities might have been impacted by the recent recession, but China has now risen to become the second biggest economy in the world. Africa on the other hand is fast becoming a land of immense promise. Its population growth rate has been higher than that of China and India and it is estimated that by 2040 Africa will have around two billion people, much ahead of China with 1.4 billion and India with 1.6 billion people. Actually as an economy, Africa might just turn out to be bigger than India and China.

As far as India is concerned, it has a very different nature of growth, compared to China and Africa.

The Indian growth story has been primarily powered by Indian entrepreneurs. It is true that the Government of India has catalyzed this growth with its well-crafted, well-calculated, well-paced and well-measured strategy of deregulation, privatization, and liberalization. It is actually this that saved India from sliding into the abyss of recession. Today, the Indian economy has proved to be far more robust and far better protected from the vagaries of external threats.

India also has a more sustainable growth trajectory than any other country. Today, there are 300 million people in India who are below the poverty line. But if India continues to grow, as it is now, at a steady 8 percent plus GDP in the next decade, all these 300 million people will come above the poverty line. Then, all of a sudden India will have an additional 300 million people consuming soaps, shampoos, biscuits, ice creams, mobile phones, and consuming all the non-consumer durables such as television, refrigerators, scooters, cars etc. Obviously this will not happen in one stroke. But every year there will be 20–30 million customers who will be added to the economy. India with this market is thus poised to have a transformative impact on the contours of the global economy.

More importantly, India will play the pivotal role of crafting and providing new business models for the world. Today 80 percent of the population in Asia, Africa, and even Latin America belong to the middle and lower economic strata and are therefore in need of products and services that are more affordable. This is what the companies belonging to the western world would find difficult to provide, given that they are used to providing rich, luxurious, and, of course, high quality products. On the other hand, India has developed a business model that is configured to provide products at an affordable price but without compromising quality. In a country where people belonging to the lower strata of society earn just 1–2 dollars a day, the sachet strategy is the only selling strategy that will work the best. I think in mobile sector for example we have proven this point. The FMCG sector has also proven this point. The sachet strategy comprises of examples like the one-wash shampoo, one-day recharge coupons for mobile phones etc. For the poor people this works best. They get to use a good quality product and service like shampoos and mobile recharge only when they have the necessary earning to support their purchase. So the day they have decent earnings, they purchase the shampoo, and on the day they don't have sufficient earnings, they will postpone their purchase. Thus, the sachet strategy gives them huge flexibility for buying when they need or when they have income and for not buying when they don't have the income. So actually C.K Prahlad's book, *The Fortune at the Bottom of the Pyramid* is coming out to be true in these economies. Now western companies have been unable to exploit this fortune. This is because their business model is heavy, high cost and thus meant only for the upper strata of the society. On the other hand our business model is tailor made more for the middle and lower end of the society. And I think it is this business model which will survive in the long run.

It is already relevant in Asia, Africa and Latin America and will, in the future, also be appropriate in Europe, America and Japan as these countries become more conservative and more saving oriented and would start going in for products and services which are more affordable—the sachet kind of product and services—and which will give them one day consumption or a week's consumption rather than a month's consumption. I think there is a common population of may be four billion people out of six billion people across the world who will be benefited from this business models. All this will herald a sea change in the business world.

One of the foremost reasons why there would be such an impact is because the Indian business model which is customized to cater to even the lower end of society would provide the biggest opportunities for Indian companies. Already a lot of companies, whether multinational or indigenous, but who know the Indian consumer very well, like Unilever, ITC, Nestle and many others are also trying to do many of these things. As such the Indian companies being innovative, low cost, affordable and uniqueare greatly poised to grow to the next orbit. Whether it is mobile phones, small cars like Maruti and Nano, soaps and shampoos, or every small pack which you see, India is the only country which is leading the world. From here we are sending out the small pack philosophy across the world.

Interviewer: *What are the few factors that have propelled Corporate India to play its defining role in the global economy?*

Manoj Kohli: Obviously all this has happened because of some critical enabling factors.

Firstly, Corporate India has immensely benefited from the insistence on indigenization by the Government of India. Take for example, the automotive industry where the Government of India insisted that 90–95 percent of the components whether it's Honda, Toyota, or Suzuki should be made in India. Now initially there was a lot of pain for the companies. But in a matter of just 10 years, some great firms have mushroomed in different parts of India—Chennai, Pune, Gurgaon—who make components not only for Indian auto companies, but also for Japanese, American, and European companies. They export components all over the world. And these components are of the highest quality—six sigma, no defects, no rejection—and that too at rock bottom prices.

Secondly, India has also benefitted from the IT revolution. Indians may be poor but they are also endowed with remarkable minds and a quest for learning. If one goes to small towns and villages, and I go there regularly, and asks small children of 10–15 yrs of age, as to what do you want to become, you will find them saying that they want to learn computers and become a programmer or a systems engineer or just anything connected with IT and ITES. IT has now revolutionalized the mind space of common Indian citizens wherever they are, whoever they are, and whatever they do. This revolution actually has taken India far ahead of several other countries. This is because the future is the software revolution and not hardware and industrial revolution, and this revolution is led by the mind, by intellect, by IT capability and not just by money or by factories. The way things are going I can affirm that in a matter of another 5–10 years, India's IT capability will become a fantastic domain of knowledge for the country. It is available not only for Indian companies like Infosys, Wipro, HCL etc, but also for international companies like IBM which has over 100 thousand employees in India. This is fantastic. An American company, the largest company of the world has 1 lakh employees in India. They are fully leveraging the mind of young Indian engineers in IT. Clearly, it means that the IT capability of India will actually grow by leaps and bounds in the next decade. That will make India much more powerful than what it is today. China is now trying to catch up both on the English language as well as IT. But believe me, this will not be easy. This is because IT requires a different mindset, in contrast to manufacturing, to excel. In manufacturing, one just has to be engineering oriented and precision oriented. IT is different. It is more people oriented and requires a sophisticated amalgamation of technology, process, and people. I think our companies like TCS, Wipro, and Infosys have managed this process extremely well.

Thirdly, I think the Telecom revolution of India, has been a fantastic catalyst for the country. Today we have 650 million customers, the second market in the world after China. And we cover 4,50,000 villages out of total 6,00,000 villages. Villages have been transformed; people are fully connected to the world. These are villages which don't have roads, bridges, no buses, no trains, no connectivity, but they have mobile connectivity. It clearly means that they can connect to the world. If they have a child in Dubai they can talk with the child and vice versa. Along with the mobile revolution, there is the entertainment revolution. Televisions, especially through satellite, have reached the villages. Today, anybody residing in a village is connected to the world through a mobile phone; they are also connected to the world through a color television, and can see the world and the place where his or her child is working. He is now also exposed to the good things in life. As a result, his consumption habits have changed. Till yesterday he was not a consumer, but now is the moment when his consumption habits are changing and going up. Today he has indeed become an emerging consumer.

Finally, it is the demographic profile of India; I think we have the largest youth population in the world of 550 million and we are among the youngest populations in the world. America is ageing, Europe is ageing, Japan has already aged and China is also not that young anymore. Indeed by 2050, India will have the youngest population in the world. This clearly means that India will have the largest number of producers, the largest number of consumers, and the majority of them will be young. This demographic advantage would make India don the mantle of leadership in the business world.

Interviewer: *The way you have powerfully contextualized the business landscape in the next orbit, it seems that the future belongs to India. What else or what more, in your mind, should the Indian Government do in order to accelerate India's march towards leadership in the next orbit?*

Manoj Kohli: I feel the biggest weakness in India is the yawning infrastructure gap especially in areas which are the life lines of the economy: roads, airports, ports etc. India cannot play the role of a dominant economic power unless and until there is appropriate infrastructural development to support its growth.

After infrastructure, the next two priorities are education and health care. The education sector, in particular, begs for immediate intervention. Every year there are billions of dollars spent by Indian boys and girls going outside to the US, UK, Australia, and Singapore for higher education. This is despite the fact that our higher education is good, our teachers are good and our theories, and learning pedagogy are quite modern and sound. But I think it can become better if the education sector gets the right investment. The quality of schools, building, classrooms, and laboratories are not good. Nor are our teachers paid very well, whereby, the teaching profession has very limited ability to attract the very best talent. If this sector improves, billions of dollars of leakage, which is happening today by students who go abroad will stop happening and all this billions of dollars will stay in this country. Here I am not stating that the government should get into education, health care etc or that they should leave them for the private sector. It is true that private sector has brought about fantastic efficiencies wherever they have gone. In Telecom, the entry of the private sector has created unbelievable efficiencies. An STD call which earlier used to cost Rs 24 per minute now costs just 50 paisa per minute. Similar trends are also visible in education and healthcare. In health care a very positive trend is getting increasingly visible. Already millions of people from South-east Asia, Africa, Middle-East and now even from Europe, and America are coming to India enamored by the high quality of health care and surgeries at quite a low cost. If this is done we can have much higher growth in the coming years.

Interviewer: *What about corruption? You have been reading Economic times and Times of India and almost daily in the front page there is one or other story of scam.*

Manoj Kohli: Yes, corruption is a big leakage in India. But I think now things are changing. Well, if development economists say that out of every 1 rupee spent on development, only 16 paisa is reaching the right people, then it means 84 paisa is going somewhere else and obviously it is going into the wrong hands. So the scale of corruption is humungous. And if we are really able to wipe this scourge out from our system, our growth will be far greater and faster than what it is now. But this cannot be done by the government alone or only by the respective industry. It requires a collaborative effort of the government and the industry. What we need are better practices and more transparent practices. A case in point was the recent 3G auctions where everyone in the world knew every day, every minute what was happening. Today CII, FICCI, and other industry associations are helping the government and are working shoulder to shoulder to curb the menace. More than all these efforts, I think we need to have very strong compliance measures as well as a strong consequence management for corruption, whenever it is discovered irrespective of whosoever is involved. Symbolic punishments are very important for everyone to see, especially for the children to see. Indeed, children should feel that that anyone who is on the side of corruption is actually punished in the country. I think such consequence management would definitely ensure that in the coming days corruption will go down.

Interviewer: *What are the few things that corporations should do in order to excel in the next orbit?*

Manoj Kohli: I believe that a corporation's role in making India play the dominant power in the global economy is no less than that of the Government's. It can do this by focusing a lot more on skill building, capability building, and culture building for generating out of box thinking, creativity, ideation, and innovation. Making new business models, making new products and services which the western world could not make is crucial for Indian corporations. This is the unique strength of Indian corporations, and this needs to be nurtured and fostered by the Indian companies through building a culture of openness, experimentation, and thus of innovation. Investing in making the firms innovative will, I think, yield fantastic returns in the long run.

Interviewer: *So, Innovation should be a company's mantra?*

Manoj Kohli: Innovation should be the only mantra for Indian corporations because that is how we will be able to outpace the western world.

Interviewer: *And with an entrepreneurial mind we have got that basic DNA?*

Manoj Kohli: Exactly. The western world in the last decade or two is getting fatigued. It has stopped innovating and has become scared. Scared because of the feeling that its power is going down and its wealth is declining. Except for few companies such as Apple or Google, almost 80–90 percent of the existing companies have become defensive. This situation provides a great opportunity for Indian companies to become more innovative, to become bigger and global.

Interviewer: *Your company is a trend setter and has emerged from nowhere to becoming a great giant. What is the basic DNA of your company? What has been your unique strategy for differentiation and competitive excellence?*

Manoj Kohli: You know we started in 1995. As of now we are just 15 years old, still a teenager company. Now when we started we had two things, two soft things, which many other large companies didn't have. We did not have capital, technology or even a brand. But we had the entrepreneurial ability of the group. In the Bharti Group, we encourage all our professionals to be entrepreneurial and that's what we called PE, Professional Entrepreneur. All professionals own this company and run it as if they are the owners of the company. I think this fact is a big and critical difference between Bharti and any other established large company. Large companies are typically bureaucratic and hierarchical. Over there, people do not feel they are the owners of the company. Hence mistakes are an anathema, entrepreneurial spirit negligible and innovation is absent in such large companies.

The second big thing about our company is employee passion. Through open culture, motivational techniques and other mechanisms for encouraging positive energy, we have inculcated amongst our employees the passion to win in the market and to win every day in the market.

The third big thing about our company is its brand and the way we have nurtured it. Today our brand is number one in India, bigger than Nokia, Coke, Pepsi and many other global brands. This has been only because we have made this brand come close to the hearts of 1.2 billion Indians. And that's a very big achievement for a brand which is just 15 years old. In 1995, there was nothing called Airtel; in 2010, this brand has already made its first foray towards becoming a global brand. By the end of it, Airtel will be launched in another 16 countries in Africa marking the becoming of the Indian consumer brand into a truly global brand.

The fourth big DNA is our unique business model. No telecom corporation in the world has this business model. We have outsourced our network, outsourced IT, and outsourced our call center and many other services, our entire distribution and even our tower companies. This is the way we have built our company and our business that will soon cover 200 million customers. This has been possible only due to our partner eco system, who like Erickson, Nokia and IBM are the very best in the world in their domain and who have supported us in our business and our growth.

The fifth DNA of our company is our insatiable hunger for growth and that too by all the time doing something new. Our portfolio has changed drastically in the last five years. Geographically, we have expanded into Bangladesh, Sri Lanka and now sixteen countries in Africa. Today we have satellite television as a product which telecom companies normally do not have. We have got into media in a big way: Satellite TV, IPTV, Internet, 3G, and BWA. Indeed as of today our aspiration is to become a life style company, a life style brand and not just a telecom company. We want to become a company which gives its consumers telecom, internet and media, fully aware that the maximum time an Indian consumer or a global consumer spends is in front of these three screens: mobile screen, PC or a lap top screen, and the television screen. We want that all these three screens should be Airtel screens. So that is the simple strategy we have. We are fast converting this strategy into a business success. All this requires a huge flexibility of mind and a lot of speed. A case in point is our launch of the satellite TV. We did not have any technology, and neither did we have any media experience. But today we are leading the country in the market share of satellite TV. This is because we know the customer. We smell the customer. We know what the customer needs in terms of technology, content etc and we are all the time geared to provide this to our customers.

So these are the five major factors which takes up a lot of time, a lot of courage to develop and which now constitutes the DNA of the company.

Interviewer: *What do you think needs to be done so as to preserve and perpetuate this wherewithal of success? And what are the new things you plan to do in order to succeed in the next orbit?*

Manoj Kohli: I think the biggest thing about the sustainability of culture is that our leaders have to continue to be bold, brave and boundary less.

Our leaders must be encouraged to take brave and courageous decisions in which they have full confidence and conviction. They know the customers, they know the employees, and they smell opportunity and I think that is the biggest factor behind sustainability.

At the same time we are faced with two of our biggest enemies. First is arrogance. We can't be arrogant that we are leaders in our business and that we have achieved success and that now nobody can compete with us. Second is complacency. We can easily become very complacent. So arrogance and complacency, these are the two biggest enemies which we have to continuously push back, and we are trying to do it every day.

If the next orbit for the company is the global orbit, then we would like to be a global leader of the telecom, internet and media industries. We have taken our first step in 16 countries of Africa and are planning to have 100 million customers in Africa by 2012 and may be another 200 million customers by 2015. By 2015, we would be the second largest company in the world. And beyond 2015, I am sure there will be the next orbit of going beyond. This dream is critical to us. I think we not only have that dream, we also have that passion, commitment, patience, and dedication to achieve that dream. We also have the requisite flexibility so that we are able to adjust with speed and nimbleness to changes—in market, customer preferences, technology, regulation etc—around us. We have an appropriate culture that promotes optimization, professionalism, and entrepreneurial excellence. And above all, we have a partner eco system that supports us to achieve our dream.

Interviewer: *You said that you have a partner eco-system, which I think was one of the DNA you talked about. How do you make them share your dream, your vision, and your commitment to excellence?*

Manoj Kohli: Our business partners are an integral part of our family. They are in there in every meeting, in the strategy sessions, and in every review. They are just like our own employees. We do not differentiate between them and us. In the same meeting we have ten employees and five partners. So actually there is no difference. So partners are never made to feel that they are outside the company. They are indeed inside the company.

Interviewer: *So its all co-creation?*

Manoj Kohli: Yes. It is a co-creation of dreams. Say for instance, we had this dream, this vision for Africa and all our partners are sitting next to us. It is not my dream anymore, it is our dream together.

Interviewer: *Today you go to any company and they talk about co-partnership and building that eco-system. However, there are very few companies which have successfully actualized the strategy the way you have done. Can you share with us one or two unique nuances which you have introduced in the co-partnership or the way you have managed your ecology of partner eco system.*

Manoj Kohli: I think the biggest thing about the partner eco system of Bharti Airtel is that we are not arrogant. Telecom companies all over the world want to do everything themselves, they want to network themselves, they want to do IT, and run call centers all by themselves. However we decided differently. On December 6, 2002, we decided that we will do what we are good at and we will not do what we are not good at. This decision became the core principle which subsequently defined our business, our strategy, and our success and now even our entity as a company. Thus, we decided if we are not good at running a network and Ericson is better than us, then Ericson will run our network. Similarly, if IBM is better than us in IT, IBM will look after IT. After all we were not an IT company. If a specialist call center companies like Mmphasis are better than us in running a call centre, then they will run the call centers for us. So we decided to forge partnerships based upon domain and domain expertise.

We also identified what we were good at. We brainstormed, we discussed and we came to the conclusion that we were good at five things: *(a)* market management: we have great understanding of the market and we know the customers; *(b)* people management: we know our employees; *(c)* brand building: we know how to build a brand; *(d)* regulatory management: we are close to the government and we help them evolve new policies and *(e)* financing: we know how to raise money, the billions of dollars required to be in the business. So we decided that these are the five things we will do. Everything else that we cannot do, we will only supervise. And thus our network, distribution, passive infrastructure, technology, and call centers are all in the hands of our partners.

Globally, this is not the business model and when we made the change in 2003, telecom companies all over the world were shocked. They said this is blasphemous and against the rules of the game and that this is destined to be a failure. But till then nobody had tried. We said, why don't we try, maybe we will succeed or maybe we will not. And then we tried and we succeeded.

So I think we understood very clearly what we are good at and what we are not good at and this understanding demands a lot of humility. At that time it was our humility. Today it is our strength. It has made our partners, Ericson, Nokia, IBM, Mmphasis become an integral part of our family. They are there in all the reviews, all meetings, all the workshops, and all the discussions. They are part of the celebrations of the company; and they also go through similar tough times with the company just like any family member. So it is a "kutumb", a kind of community, interwoven by trust, and faith. And this is the biggest foundation of our success.

Interviewer: *What are some of the things that you do and your experience in terms of the design of the organization, systems and processes and especially people processes that has not only differentiated your organization and given it a competitive edge but also can be a source of great learning for the Indian Business.*

Manoj Kohli: In terms of organization structure, we have very permeable boundaries, probably boundary less. We are very flexible. That's our vision; bold, brave and boundary less. We are all the time multi-tasking and simultaneously working on different platforms. We help our partners to work very well together. They know this is Bharti and they are working with Bharti. We have to work hand in hand. There is no other way. In this system, there is no place for lone rangers in the company. In the company we discourage people who are non-team workers. And we also discourage partners who do not work as a team. So they know that there is no other way; there is only one way—that of partnership and teamwork.

Then there are several people processes which are simply unique to Bharti. There are open houses or town halls which are very unique. Our town halls are extremely open and candid where all type of questions from professional to personal are asked. And they are all answered. All the seniors and everybody from the organization are there. The Chairman of our group, Sunil Bharti Mittal is also there. In the last two months I have travelled to sixteen countries in Africa twice and every time I visit a town hall people say that this is good, this is bad, Manoj do this, don't do this. And instantly we get ideas and we pick some of them. We take instant decisions, and right in front of them. Our people thus develop tremendous confidence in us.

Then is our vision. It is sacrosanct. It is everywhere. In Airtel we believe that vision is not for the notice boards. Instead it is for my day to day decision making. Every day we refer to some part of our vision, benchmark our decisions and then we go ahead. Vision actually is our daily check list.

Interviewer: *Your business requires a convergence of both technology and market. While you have stated that your company is great in understanding* *the market and the customer, but what about the technology? Who tracks the technology?*

Manoj Kohli: We have very good technologists in the company. More than that, we have great technology partners like Ericson, Nokia, IBM etc. working with us. These technology partners keep on updating us every three months about the trends in the technology division. Let us understand we are not a technology company. Indeed, we don't want to be. This is because we don't understand technology that well. But we understand the consumer and nobody can beat us in that. More importantly, we pride in our ability to convert the given technology into very easy convenient services for the consumers. So this is what we do, our partners understand the needs of consumers from us and after which our partners convert/adapt the technology to cater to the convenience of the consumers. Take for instance the launch of easy charge—the electronic recharge for prepaid services. Many years back there used to be paper coupons and then we changed paper coupons to electronic. As of today, Bihar provides the highest electronic recharges of India. Now strictly speaking it should be the lowest. But, because we have made the electronic recharge so simple, so convenient that even an illiterate retailer or shopkeeper or illiterate consumer in villages and small towns in Bihar can use it without any discomfort. He loves to use it. And this is not just technology. Rather, it is all about how to convert technology into an easy and convenient tool to customer. That's our job in Airtel.

Interviewer: *You have been a very well known HR person in this country. What is your message to the HR professionals? What are 3–4 things that they must do, what do they lack and what should they do more etc.*

Manoj Kohli: I think HR is a great function and I learnt a lot when I was in HR for 8–9 years. I have few things to say to the HR professionals in this movement towards excellence in the next orbit of business.

Firstly, the biggest transformation which HR should bring within the community is the business orientation. I don't think even today HR is oriented towards business. It is more oriented towards itself. HR is not for the sake of HR. HR is for the sake of the future. HR is for the sake of dreams and visions. In several companies the involvement of the HR is very low in the day to day business. They talk only about increments, salary administration etc. Whereas, in our company, HR is in the centre of the business. All these outsourcing, all these changes, the new business models I talked about has HR at the centre.

Secondly, HR must now think about learning and development in a fundamentally different way. For example, functional training, that old and hackneyed kind of training, training methods and program cannot work. This is because the future is not going to be like that. The future today is much more dynamic, more cross functional and therefore in need of people with attitude and skills appropriate to multi-tasking. So HR has to innovate the developmental paradigm. Knowledge and skill development have to be more innovative, more practice oriented, more simulation oriented, so that people are enabled to perform much more on the job.

Another thing which HR has to do now, which is different from the past, is career planning in a different way. Today youngsters are impatient, they want a jump and by the time they are 30, they also want to become the boss. Obviously they can't become a boss at that young age. And if they do, sooner or later they will be frustrated because there will be nowhere to grow from 30–60. So career planning needs to be done, very judiciously, in a very well planned and deliberate way. They must design each and every stage of a person's career. What will the person do at this stage of their career, how long should they stay there etc. What will be their learning at that stage? What after that? Everything has to be systematically planned. Unfortunately in lots of organizations, career planning is done in a very ad hoc fashion. That is the precisely the reason that there are lot of burnouts happening now, people are either becoming senior leaders very fast and they don't know what to do after that or they don't achieve their goals too fast and hence they become frustrated and they overwork and burnout. So today I think careers are built in a very ad hoc way. Some good careers are built because of good luck, not because of very systematic interventions. So these are the three-four ideas which HR professionals should try to inculcate in their function.

2

Towards Transformation:
K.R. Kamath's Oddysey

Dialog with K.R. Kamath, CMD, Punjab National Bank

Interviewer: *India is amongst few of the economies that has since recent times been rapidly growing. If one looks at India's strength and weaknesses, how well do you think India is positioned to play an important role in the next orbit?*

K.R. Kamath: I think we are in a tremendously advantageous position in certain areas. Despite the global meltdown, our financial system has remained rock steady. Even though during the time of recession, the regulators and the Government took what we had initially thought were retrograde steps of putting liberalization in the back burner, the fact of the matter is that it is these steps which proved to be our saviors. It actually boosted our confidence in our financial system and has given rise to the belief that we are capable of handling any situation that comes our way. This belief in itself has tremendous positive implications.

The second advantage which India enjoys is the age profile of its population. The Indian population today has greater number of youths as compared to other age groups and other countries. The youths have their own energy and will provide tremendous strength to the country.

The third is that the government has been continuously focusing on what is required for the youth in terms of their physical and intellectual infrastructure. It has recently taken quite a few initiatives like setting up roads and ports and erecting power plants. All these things sooner or later will build the capability for the future take off.

So putting all these things together I am sure that at the growth rate of around 9 percent as against the growth rate in developed economies of around 4 percent, sooner or later the country will be poised to move to the next orbit.

Interviewer: *Do you think there is anything else or anything more that should be done in order to enable India to transit and succeed in the next orbit?*

K.R. Kamath: One of the most worrisome issues that need to be addressed is that in India we have a rather skewed pattern of development with almost

60–70 percent of the population out of the process of development. It is reflected in the fact that today more than 60 percent of eligible people do not use banking facilities. So an effort is required to bring them into the banking fold. In our own small ways, we tried the kiosk model but have just realized that the regulatory requirement mandates that we have to also man these units. So from the banking side, I would say that providing banking facilities to the unbanked and bringing them into the mainstream development process becomes a very critical need, if India has to succeed in the next orbit.

Interviewer: *The recent RBI guidelines and policies are directed towards relaxing the controls and thus paving the way for the entry of new banks and increase in competition. What is your take on these developments?*

K.R. Kamath: I think competition has been good for the banking sector in India. Indeed until 1991, all banks looked the same, did the same things, and provided the same products and similar services, and standards of service. It was all based upon the belief that customers have no choice, they will go nowhere. But with the entry of the new generation private sector banks, the entire banking service got redefined. The private sector banks started setting the benchmarks. They had no legacies to worry about. They started with new technologies and new products and services and they offered the best of things to the customers. Then the public sector banks did not keep quiet. They came back with force and within no time. Today, we public sector banks are now contemporary and comparable to any private sector bank, in terms of products and services. And with the collapse of finance majors and run on some banks abroad during the recent meltdown, Indian public sector banks are now looked upon as more secure and safe by our customers. On an overall basis, competition has led to some desirable consequences; it has brought the best out of the people and ultimately the final customer has benefitted. So I think we must look forward to the entry of new banks. I feel banking services in India will once again get redefined.

Interviewer: *Another trend in the banking and the financial sector has been the movement towards consolidation. Even the Government of India at times has talked about merger and consolidation of public sector banks. How do you see this trend in India?*

K.R. Kamath: I would say consolidation of banks and its operations is inevitable. It has to happen. But the moot question is when. Earlier also we have talked about consolidation. But since 20th December, 2009 we have been talking about it rather differently. Today the consolidation is not any more being thought about as a forced merger of two sinking banks. Instead, consolidation is being taken to mean a merger or getting together of two equally powerful and performing banks. However, this also requires a proper climate, a conducive environment politically and economically and above all a felt need by both the parties that they may find the going difficult if they don't come together. That sort of situation is not prevailing in the country nor is that feeling being felt by the banks. There is a good reason for that. For, if more than 65 percent of the Indian population is still outside the pale of banking, then everybody, however small he may be, will be right in feeling that he has a role in the development of the economy and he can also have a share of the cake. So there is a reason and there is an opportunity for everybody to coexist. It is only when political and economic conditions change domestically, and international operations becomes a serious and big business for domestic banks, then probably some banks will start feeling the need to come together. Then yes we will come together.

Interviewer: *Given that the economy has changed and the landscape of business globally is also changing, what impact will it have on the banking business, especially in terms of the product features, in terms of service delivery mechanisms and the other wherewithal for success?*

K.R. Kamath: We are an integral part of the global economy today. We can no longer remain isolated and say this will only happen in India or whatever happens elsewhere will not happen to us. So as more and more international companies come into India and start their operations, they will also start demanding services from Indian banks. These services must match what they get in their home countries, both in terms of size and in terms of quality. Similarly, some of our Indian companies are going in a big way to international markets and have stated operating there. It is quite natural that they would expect some of the Indian Banks to follow them and support them in their ventures outside.

The second is the age profile of the country. With more and more of the youth coming into the incoming generating bracket, their requirements will be quite diverse. Indeed very few of this generation's customers would be aware of the location of the branch, given that they are prone to operating their account through internet or through ATM. How do you service such a customer? How do you meet their expectations? It is these customers with whom we will be dealing and who will set the road map for change in the banking sector in the future.

Interviewer: *What do you think will be the profile of the branches, the zones and the corporate office in the emerging business landscape?*

K.R. Kamath: Some time ago people started talking about branchless banking, in the belief that branch units will have no role to play because the new generation customer will never come to the bank. But this proved wrong because ultimately somewhere the Indian customer likes to see the face of the bank. To that extent, branches will have an important role to play. However, the number of branches that will be opened will not be as much as what used to be in the past. The role of the central offices is also now an issue. The PSU banks were at one point of time on a four tier system. Now we have moved to the three tier system. This three tier system is yet to stabilize in the full way. The reason being that in the four tier system, after the branch, there was a region which focused on the development and the zone which focused on the control. Today, both these activities are merged into the middle tier, which is called the circle. In this system, there is an inbuilt conflict of interest, that is, whenever you concentrate more on the development, you lose focus on the control and when you focus on control, you have less time to look after development. Now in the present three tier system, the third tier is to stabilize in the full way so that it concomitantly focuses on both the areas: of development, as well as, the control. In the public sector banks, I would say that, the circle offices will play a crucial role. In PNB today, we have in all 5,000 branches. We obviously cannot run these branches directly from the head office or the branch without there being a middle layer. So the role of the middle layer is critical because it has to disseminate what is happening, and what is the thinking in the corporate level to the ultimate unit levels. The head office probably will undergo changes. More and more departments will start looking after functional areas like retail, assets, SMEs, etc. The head office will play the role of strategist and the control functions will rest more with the middle layer who will now look after administration.

Interviewer: *If we have to put the Indian corporate to the next orbit what are some of the concerns according to you that can constrain them from being successful. .*

K.R. Kamath: It is wrong to think of the Indian corporate as a single monolithic entity; rather there are different types of corporate organizations. The big corporates are already moving towards the next orbit mainly due to their well-developed radar system, vision, capability, and professionalized management. On the other hand, the middle level corporates lack the critical mass, a clear compelling reason, and capability to move to the next orbit. So even if these companies had become global and had ample opportunities to acquire companies abroad due to the global melt-down, they were unable to take advantage of it. For, they had very restricted capabilities to handle an international company. I think professionaliz-ing these companies, a lot of whom are individual driven, and bringing international standards in them is very critical, if the middle range Indian companies wish to move to the next orbit.

Interviewer: *Let us now talk about your experience as a CMD in Allahabad Bank and its transformation.*

K.R. Kamath: Let me give you a little bit of background on my career so that you will have a sense of perspective.

It was after putting in about 29 years service in the Corporation Bank that I moved as an ED to the Bank of India. Very soon I realized that this is a totally different ball game. It was then that I thought that when you reach this level or the board level position, you do not have to perform. You need to make others perform. That is your challenge. This is possible only when you carry the team with yourself. Now how do you do this? For, when you reach this level, there is always a gap that is created between you and the rank and the file. And this gap is there and nobody can deny it. So what you have to do is to develop approachability and accessibility to the staff. I think that sends a very strong signal. I remember when I was moving from the Corporation Bank to the Bank of India, during my send off function in Corporation Bank, the representatives of the officer's organization remarked that, "Sir, you have been successful, because you are accessible. So keep the door of your heart and also of your cabin open for everybody." So next day, when I came to Bank of India, I said I will not close the door of my cabin. My doors were kept open, so that anybody can walk in. This was something unbelievable for the people that the ED is keeping his door open. I said "Anybody can walk in with their problem and I will try my best to get it resolved." Now this very fact gave a feeling to the people that we have an ED who can be approached anytime. Now once this sort of a feeling is created you will find lesser number of people will come to you with their problems. Because they start feeling that there is always somebody who will solve my problem if it goes beyond my control. So the very fact that you are available to your staff instills a confidence in them and enables them to perform. This was exactly what I put in place when I joined the Bank of India.

The second thing is that it was a very apt time for me to enter the bank. Bank of India was celebrating the centenary year. We had a centenary vision for the bank. So what we did was that we developed a placard to keep on the table of every employee saying that this is our vision and this will be achieved. One slogan I had been using right from the Corporation Bank days was "together we can, together we will." I had started using this slogan when I was heading the cash department of Corporation Bank. It helped me tremendously to bring my team together and also to make my team develop the confidence that we can do. "Together we can" demonstrates the confidence level of the team and "together we will" shows the determination of the team. Now the slogan I adopted showed that the Centenary Vision is not something out of our reach and that we can do it. This slogan became very popular in Bank of India. People started to believe that we should forget our differences, join hands and work in one direction. The chairman was also very much involved in this. So both of us travelled to different locations of the bank, addressed the staff members, and propagated this theme.

The third thing that I did in Bank of India was that I tried to streamline the HR system and policies. This is because I believed that HR policies should often get tweaked in tune with our requirements and our environment. This is the only way the credibility of these policies can be built and sustained. So we worked on the policies and we brought out such clear and transparent policies that made performance the cornerstone of reward and promotions. People slowly started realizing that they do not need godfathers anymore for their career progression in Bank of India. Anybody and everybody who will perform will get duly recognized. That brought tremendous confidence in the whole process in the bank. These are the few things which took me closer to the rank and file. Once the rank and file starts identifying themselves with you, I think probably you then create some kind of a mass movement. This is what helped me to create a place for myself in Bank of India.

Now with this success I moved to Allahabad bank. There were a few posers that were hurled at me at that point of time. People said that you are going to the East! Nothing can change in the East. East will remain a lethargic East. Things cannot move.

The first thing I did was that I started moving around, going to different locations of the Allahabad Bank, talking to various people at different levels in the hierarchy, talking to customers etc. So very soon, I started asking my zonal managers as to why they did not implement single windows, especially when they know how useful it is to the customers. Very soon, I got wind of some silent responses challenging me to first try it out in Kolkata and then to exhort others. So I got a message that if you have to change anything in this bank, you have to first experiment it in Kolkata and prove it and then only others will do it or even be told to do so.

I then called for a staff meeting and this was about one and a half months of my joining Allahabad Bank as the CMD. On September 18, 2008, I addressed the entire staff numbering more than 1,000 in the city of Kolkata and I made a few points. I said that for a person, who starts his career in banking, becoming chairman of the bank is the ultimate goal and I have achieved it. I have nothing more to go beyond this. So I don't have to prove anything, I don't have to achieve anything. Had I anything more to achieve, I will surely work for it. But then I had no personal milestone to achieve, no personal agenda to meet. I said that you know, people always keep on saying, "Sir, we are with you to achieve your goal...we are with you to achieve your vision." Then I told these people that your chairman is a blind person. He does not have a vision. If you people having worked in this bank for 30–35 years could not develop a vision for the organization, how do you expect a chairman of one and a half months to develop a vision for the organization? You are in a way placing the whole control into the wrong hands. Instead, it is you who should have a vision for this organization and the chairman should have full capabilities to implement that vision and to actualize your vision. So I related a small anecdote saying that when you sit in a car, who will decide where the car will go? Should the passenger decide? Or should it be the driver? The answer is as obvious as daylight. It must be the passenger who should decide. Then I said now think you are the passenger and I am the driver of the car. You will tell me where you want to go. I have got a license to drive your tram and I have got a license to drive your aero plane. So whatever you want, I will do. In case all of us in this meeting now collectively decide to enjoy our life, I will enjoy my life as I have achieved everything that I wanted.

Next day in the morning, I directed my circle head to immediately start implementing single window systems in the main branch and let us see what will happen? Later in that day, around six to seven union leaders came and said we have come to meet you. They said that we have implemented single window system room in the main branch and we are here to work with you. Whatever you want to achieve by this, we are with you. That was a paradigm busting event in Allahabad Bank.

Then again in one investors meet, I went along with my ED. I asked them why the Allahabad Bank prices are not finding the fair value. The investor responded that this is because it is an East based bank and that it cannot change. So I came back with this problem to my union leaders and staff members and I asked them that is it true that the East cannot change? Then I told them that the Allahabad Bank used to have a different work culture. It had originated in Allahabad and was run by the British even up to 1969. As such there is a British culture in the bank which has been now overlaid by the Kolkata work culture. Once again people reiterated that we are willing to change and are willing to work with you on this. I started moving across the length and breadth of the Bank. Everywhere I had the same message. Indeed wherever I talked to people, I talked to them about how they can help the bank to change rather stating that I want to bring this change in Allahabad Bank, that this is my vision for the bank and that you must cooperate and after some time when my words would die down, start accusing the staff for not cooperating. I think this is a very negative way of bringing about change. Accordingly, I started talking to the people asking them how at their own level, of being a peon or a clerk or a subordinate staff they can change the image of the Allahabad Bank. This had a cataclysmic effect. People soon started realizing that I was one amongst them and I was talking to them in their language and about what they were doing in their every day work life. Eventually they all started identifying themselves with me and in one word they all stated that we are in a position to work with you.

I started focusing on customer service in a big way. We started bringing out a newsletter called "Customer Voice." Normally when one gets a complaint it is never direct, as in where the basis is, but is filtered through various hierarchical levels after which we bring it up in the staff meeting and without naming the person discuss it and conclude by saying that is not an acceptable thing. We decided that this is not the way we want customer complaints to come up and be addressed. So we decided to publish the customer complaint as it comes giving the branch name and the name of the staff member as it is. This had a salutary effect. Soon everybody came to know who was doing what wrong and in which branch. This created an evolution towards better customer service in the bank. We followed this up with an organization wide training program called "Jagriti" or "awareness" on customer services and 20,000 employees of the bank starting from the Chairman to the subordinate staff were made to undergo this. It had its own spin off. All of a sudden several subordinate staff members, who were earlier never exposed to any training, started feeling that the organization today finds me to be a very important and crucial component of itself. Simultaneously we started working on other areas of business like the stock price. We started meeting investors, talking to them and in just a short span of time, our share price catapulted from 37 to more than 200. All this helped people to regain their lost confidence.

There is another thing which happened. It was something unique for which I would be wrong to claim the sole credit. In the long history of around 130 years of Allahabad Bank only one person from the bank became the Chairman and not a single person rose to the position of an ED. Others could go only up to the level of GM after which they would retire. During my small tenure of 15 months, we saw three people becoming ED. Then the bank felt that we have got the same capability, which other banks have. Once they gained this confidence, the rest is now history.

Interviewer: *What about your current tenure as CMD in Punjab National Bank. What has been your experience?*

K.R. Kamath: PNB as compared to Allahabad Bank is a mammoth organization. As a result when I came over here, a lot of my friends told me that in PNB, people have a different way of looking at things and therefore that your strategy may not work over here. I started wondering whether this is really true. So, when I came to PNB, I said the same thing that I had earlier stated at Allahabad Bank. That for me, it cannot get bigger than this. I have now become the Chairman of one of the biggest nationalized banks and that I have nothing more to achieve. But then having come over here, I definitely would like to add value to this bank. However, it depends upon you. I have a language of communication which is soft, mild, collaborative, and hugely supportive. I would always like to speak in my language first, but the purpose of communication is that each party should understand what the other party has in mind. In case you show me signals that you don't understand my language, I will be forced to learn your language. The choice is yours.

Then I started doing the same set of things as I had done in my earlier stints: making myself accessible to people and responsive to their needs. I shared my mobile number and said that if anybody finds any issue which is bothering him, he can send me an SMS and if I am in the country you will receive my response by the end of the day. In case you want to talk to me, you can leave a missed call on my mobile and if you have something to tell me you can send me an e-mail. It will always receive my attention. Soon people found out that this was true and that the chairman does respond to all genuine cases. As cases started getting redressed, people began to have faith in the system and reliance on the internal processes rather than on external pressures for getting solutions to their problems. This process got a further fillip due to our review of the promotion process. We advanced the promotion process in time, made it transparent and reviewed each case. So the promotions to the higher level happened in the first three months of my joining PNB. Overall, the communication process, the accessibility, the responsiveness of the management to people and their problems and the transparency of the promotion process made people have faith in the organization and its management.

Then of course, we took some bold administrative steps. In PNB, there was the concept of field GMs which had only been partially implemented. We took up this concept, redefined the role of the field GMs, and implemented it right through the bank. According to this system, the GM was now the extended arm of the management available to the circle officers for the business development. The role of the field general manager was only business related work for which they were answerable to the CMD; for all administrative work the circle officer was responsible. As of now we are stabilizing this system and the processes. But this has already given positive signals to the people.

Interviewer: *What is your dream for PNB?*

K.R. Kamath: PNB is in an enviable position. Financially, it is the benchmark for the industry. Last quarter our Net interest margin was 3.94 percent, our cost to income ratio was something like 39.5 percent, capital investment was 14 percent and CASA 40 percent. The challenge is to sustain this growth and ensure that it is always above that of the nearest competitors. This is my dream for PNB. In this regard, I must admit I have been fortunate. When I came to this bank, there was already a vision document called Vision 2013, which after thorough deliberations of the Board has now been put in place. The Vision document clearly outlines what will happen to this bank over the next five years, starting from 2008, how it will happen and who will do what. So a chairman need not look for any thing beyond this. All he has to do is to implement this document and do the good work. This came very handy to me. I started meeting people and telling them, "Look this is your vision and not my vision, because the document was adopted before I came, and that you need to know this and implement this." The only thing that I added was my slogan, "together we can and together we win" which again generated a similar response in this bank. You must understand that PNB is distinct from all PSUs banks and all nationalized banks. The only Public Sector bank ahead of us is the State Bank of India and it is quite ahead of us in terms of balance sheet size, to even think of competing with. What we compete on is our financial strengths and effectiveness on financial parameters. It is this which we would like to consolidate and maintain.

Interviewer: *You have worked as a leader and you have also worked with many leaders. What are your views on leadership?*

K.R. Kamath: I think leadership is all about making your team feel that you are one amongst them. This makes your people feel that they are all working together and creates a synergy that is just tremendous. On the other hand, if you keep a distance and you say that I am your leader, then people will keep their distance from you and will follow you. So the best thing for a leader is to become one among the team and say that I may be a little ahead amongst you, otherwise all of us equal.

When I talk to my staff members, I usually say that we are a like a cricket team. Each one in the team has a role to play. I am a captain by virtue of the decision of somebody else. I am here to work with you, play with you. There is always somebody who will feel that he is on the boundary line and has a limited role to play. I am deliberately using this metaphor of boundary line because in banks we do post people at different places and at distant places which is not at all liked by the person posted there. Indeed such a person feels highly de-motivated, for they start believing what worse could happen to them than this. This is when I tell them that you know you are on the boundary line; if you make a mistake, it will cost the team four runs and if somebody here at the centre makes a mistake, he is only giving up one run. Your being at the boundary line may be not because of your choice. But because of my compulsion, because I have to post somebody to the boundary line, you are there. However your role is very critical, because you have four runs to save whereas somebody else can save only one run. Now people understand this. The example and the imagery works. People start appreciating the importance of whatever they are doing, the role that they are playing regardless of wherever they are playing that role: at the head office or on the boundary line. So I think a leader's role is to tell a person how important is he for the team and how critical is his role in the organization. The same is true for the subordinate staff that is passing the cheque. If he is made to feel that his passing the cheque in time is so critical for the completion of customer services and that he has an important role to play, he will no longer feel that he is a class IV employee who has got no role to play in people coming and going from the bank. So I affirm that leadership is all about telling people that you are one amongst them and is the process of taking others along with you.

Interviewer: *Leadership is typically backed by some values. What are some of the values that underlies your leadership?*

K.R. Kamath: I attach a lot of importance to few value systems.

Firstly, means and end are intertwined. I always say that the end is very important. But the means to the end is equally important, because it is the ethical values that keep us intact. If in our anxiety to reach the end we do not look at the means then probably we lose a lot as we go along.

Secondly, is transparency. When you are at the top, every one looks at you. In fact, in the bank we say that there are one lakh eyes looking at us.

In this context, if you say something, and you act differently, people will not believe you. Because people are interested in what you talk and are interested in how you act.

Third, is the sincerity. A lot of times we say that we want to do this and we want to do that and after some time we forget. As a result people start doubting one's sincerity. So transparency and the sincerity have to go together. So that people feel that, Yes! He is very transparent and he is sincere in achieving what he wants. Now this sends a very strong signal.

The fourth value system is hard work. I think there is one *shloka* from the Gita which manifests my value system: "don't look at what comes, what is your reward. But do your work sincerely and leave the rest to god." I have followed this dictum in my personal life and God has always rewarded me, more than probably, what I deserve. So every time it happens, it reinforces my faith in this.

Interviewer: *One last question, about your message to the HR Community.*

K.R. Kamath: I think today HR is all encompassing. If you ask any CEO or any team leader they will always assert that HR has to be one of his foremost areas of performance and focus. This is because even if you are at the level of the CEO, you have to get things done and if you want to get the things done, then you have to get it done only through your people. This can happen only when a system is created, an eco system is created where people feel very happy to work with you. Thus, HR is very critical for the top management and because of this the CEO should have sufficient time for HR. For, once the top management understands HR and its importance, others in the organization follow. The result of this is that everyone in the organization tries to create an environment that is conducive for performance.

Interviewer: *What are the issues and challenges facing the HR professionals?*

K.R. Kamath: I would say that sometimes, people feel that HR is a subject, like any theoretical subject. I feel that HR is a practice. It is not subject matter which is to be taught or which is supposed to be lectured. It is an issue which is to be practiced. So once you practice HR, I think things fall in place. If you preach HR and then you don't practice, then you create a gap which is visible to everybody. Most of the time, I always try to distinguish between two concepts which are normally mistaken for each other.

Personnel administration and HR are two different things, but normally people confuse them as the same and use it synonymously. This is not correct. HR is substantially bigger than personal administration. The problem is when it comes to preaching, we preach HR but when it comes to practice, we practice personnel administration. And that creates all the problems—for the HR professionals, for the way others in the organization looks at them, for the performance of the organization, and the organization itself.

3

Towards Cutting Edge Competitiveness:
Issues and Challenges for Indian Managers

*Dialog with Santrupt Misra,
Director, Group H.R. & CEO, Carbon Black Business,
Aditya Birla Group*

Interviewer: *How do you see the landscape of business today? What according to you are some of the notable trends affecting the context of the business organizations?*

Dr Santrupt Misra: Well the most notable feature of the business landscape today is the unprecedented economic and financial uncertainty. This is the world where even though the western capitalist economy is not that dominant anymore, the countries in North America and Europe still enjoy almost unrivalled purchasing power. Then are the emerging economies in the BRIC countries and even though they seem to be attractive investment options, there is a great degree of uncertainty attached to make investors cautious and investments a highly risky proposition. The anxiety gets heightened when you watch the stock exchanges in both India and other countries especially in South America which in the short run is giving such high returns that there seems to be no point in doing long-term economic activity. To add to the uncertainty has been the fluctuations in currency and oil prices which have made the economy unpredictable for countries, corporates, and consumers. Both small and large events in any part of the world are having consequences in other parts of the world in multiple ways; some direct and a lot of them indirect. The volatility and unpredictability has been such that it can defy and defeat any plan.

Then are other issues that both individually and together are fast complicating the business environment today. First as an aspect of world economy and the business trend that is emerging as the biggest challenge, is the whole crisis of trust: between neighbors, towards proponents of Islam, within the European union, for institutional mechanisms like the judiciary and parliament, for banks and financial majors, and with regard to governance of corporates and the integrity of CEOs. All this has heightened the difficulty in decision making and in creating organizational architecture, processes, communication and information systems and the mechanisms of check and balances. In such an atmosphere marked by lack of trust, it has become almost an insurmountable challenge to inspire confidence amongst investors, employees, customers, and business partners.

Then is the complexity in the corporate world. On the one side there are some large global companies which are marching forward, others that are folding up and still others like BHP that is trying to become bigger. At the same time there are companies originating from emerging economics that have started to go all over the world. Amidst all these activities of the large scale organizations, one can discern hectic activities of small and medium enterprises that are fast becoming engines of economic recovery. They are the ones that have started to drive production and services, employment and consumption. Entrepreneurship, especially Social Entrepreneurship, which was once a Silicon Valley phenomenon, is fast becoming a phenomenon in business schools in India. Today India has become a hot bed of entrepreneurial activities. And this includes both for-profit small entrepreneurial ventures and ventures that are social, non-governmental, and not-for-profit. These trends are also impacting each other in a world where connectivity and interdependence is becoming stronger and stronger.

And then there is this new, mad scramble for natural resources by companies all over the world. Indeed, natural resources are fast becoming a new genre of competition. It is no longer a competition for market share and customer. It is an unusual competition which has customers at the backend. In my view, competition for market share and customers will seem to be far feeble as compared to the nature and ferocity of competition that will be there for natural resources. In India, there is an added problem related to land, how do you acquire land, how do you compensate those ousted from their land, how do you compensate the erstwhile land owners and make them a meaningful partner in economic development? I think all these issues have created a very complex environment for all of us.

Interviewer: *In this era of uncertainty and complexity, what do you think are the strengths and weaknesses of Indian companies?*

Dr Santrupt Misra: I think the strength of the Indian companies has been that Indian companies are reasonably cost conscious and frugal. Indian companies do not believe in wastefulness. They have so far shown a great amount of business maturity in terms of absorbing emerging trends and modern management practices whether it is a technology called ERP, telecommunication, data processing, outsourcing, corporate governance practices, etc. Indian corporations have not remained insular. They have always looked at the world. They have tried to learn from them. In sum, the resilience of Indian corporates to adopt, adapt, and meaningfully use the emerging trends of the environment into its working processes has been its biggest strength.

Indian corporation's other strength has been that it has always hired well qualified management personnel and has invested well in its human resources. They have also been able to innovate to compete at one level effectively in their own market and also in the other markets.

The fundamental weakness of Indian companies perhaps is the absence of too many Indian managers with experience of working in the global arena or of working in countries outside India. The second weakness is that because of low investment in R & D, no fundamentally big brand or products has come out of India. Despite the success of idlis, dosas, vada paos, India has not been able to create a McDonald. Despite the long history of Ayurveda and the availability of untold wealth of roots and fruits in Himalayas and the Ayurvedic therapy tradition of Kerala and others, India has not been truly able to globalize or avail the opportunity. Thus Indian companies' ability to brand, package, present India or India's products etc as a great marketable product or brand or service has not been very strong. IT and ITES may have succeeded at one level but the success of IT and ITES has not been so much premised on high brand and high end solutions but on low costs. How to go up the technology scale to create value added products, value added services, technological solutions which are not cheap, but are innovative, generated out of insights into cross or interdisciplinary science and technology or whatever is now the biggest challenge for Indian corporate organizations.

Another weakness of Indian corporations has been that Indian corporations often try to behave like Indian corporation everywhere rather than as global corporations. Presence in multiple geographies does not automatically mean globalization. It is a mindset. It is a way of doing things.

Interviewer: *Can you elaborate upon this.*

Dr Santrupt Misra: Well it goes like this. Just because a company is present in 20 countries does not make it a global company. To be global, a company needs to globalize its employee profile, create a global supply chain and weave suppliers from multiple countries with manufacturers and assemblers and customers in multiple countries. It has to think about customers globally and supplies and suppliers globally. Aligning systems to move knowledge and best practices swiftly from one part to the other,

I think all of that is a part of globalization. Effectively competing in every market is part of globalization. Thinking of everything in a larger scale is globalization. Now these are something that Indian managers will have to do more and learn more.

Interviewer: *Do you see any opportunities for Indian corporates in the present situation.*

Dr Santrupt Misra: There are tremendous opportunities. The very fact that India has an economy which is strong and growing provides possibilities for companies to become profitable, generate surplus and invest elsewhere. This surplus can be even used to buy companies abroad especially in the west where the economies have become weak and that too relatively cheaply. These acquisitions would provide companies with tremendous opportunities to gain access to high end products, technology, know-how and market.

The success of IT can be perhaps replicated and should give Indian companies confidence to be able to do high quality work. This does not necessarily mean doing it at a low cost, but at an appropriate cost. This high quality work can be then leveraged into other sectors. As more and more people have started to move around perhaps because of globalization, it has opened up tremendous opportunities for Indian tourism and Indian tourist companies. Indian corporations have this opportunity to leverage the tremendous brain power or English language its employees have. Further, in so much as India is emerging as the low cost hub of R & D, it has a perfect opportunity to leverage that and become a bedrock of high quality research and innovation at least internally. This necessarily does not mean premising innovations on low cost. I think India needs to shift from a mind set of everything low cost to a mindset of cost value creation which means to create a value at an appropriate cost and price them in such a way that people are ready to pay.

What it means is that there are generic opportunities and there are sector by sector opportunities that India can exploit and avail of. Provided India and Indian companies play their cards smartly.

Interviewer: *It is at times stated that the next millennium is India's. What do you have to say on that? Do you really believe in this?*

Dr Santrupt Misra: This is something that has been well and truly hyped. With 24 hours news channel, media, too many magazines, too many newspapers, it is today easy to hype up something in the short run. This hype is difficult to believe. While we talk about the next millennium being

India's millennium, let us not forget the data and reality. The reality is in terms of rampant poverty, poor infrastructure, inadequate health care, and economic developments premised on inequity and regional disparity that leads to various social strife's in all its multiple manifestations, whether it is religious, caste and even territorial strife. Indeed whether the next millennium is India's millennium depends on how effectively India is able to address problems that are very specific, unique and internal to itself. I am not cynical to believe that it is not possible. But I also do not believe in the hype that just by talking about it, writing articles in the magazines, discussing on the TV, it will become India's millennium. Is there a strong opportunity? I am sure there is. But there are enormous and humungous internal challenges and necessities to create constructive agendas internally, include different sections of the society, and prioritize and align them to a larger economic agenda. It is only then perhaps we can say truly that the next millennium belongs to India.

Incidentally, I do not understand what does India's millennium actually mean. If 50 percent of the Fortune 500 companies would have CEOs from India, would that make it India's millennium? If India becomes the fastest growing economy, gets a seat in the Security Council, goes up in the competitiveness index or the transparency index, will that qualify India to call the next millennium its own? This is important because the next millennium can be India's only when the millennium is defined in terms of specific goals and targets, there is resource allocation towards it, people are assigned to work towards its achievement and there is a monitoring and measurement of progress. There must be certain trajectory lines and parameters on which we want to India to be before we can call it India's millennium. Otherwise it is a lot like what used to happen when all of us were children and used to write essays like "What will I do when I become the Prime Minister of India" or "What is my ambition in life." These assignments were considered good because it made the child develop imagination. But it is not good for an adult to not be specific, practical and articulate about where we have to go and how. What are the milestones and destination or even what are the millennium goals?

Interviewer: *There are basically two points people have been making as to why the next millennium will be India's. One relates to India being a hub for low cost manufacturing on which you have already reflected and the second relates to the young demographic profile of India and that few decades from now India will have a population that will be the youngest in the world.*

Dr Santrupt Misra: So what if India has the largest population or for that matter the youngest population in the world? It is ludicrous to talk about it as a strength when a vast majority of that population is illiterate, badly educated, and in any case without the necessary skills to be employed or gainfully employed or to create a productive economic output. Moreover, that India's population is young is not a product of any of our great intervention or policies. We happen to be young. The real transformation of that youth into something meaningful has to come through education, healthcare, employment, training, and availability of technical institutions, where they can get employable skills. We do have an opportunity. But we would be wasting it. That the next millennium will be India's depends upon whether India has got the ingredients or the enablers of success.

Interviewer: *If you have to really sum up, what are the interventions required to make India seize this historic moment?*

Dr Santrupt Misra: There are many things. One is creating access to educational institutions, doing demand simulation, opening up of the education sector to private enterprises and freeing education from government regulations. This will ensure that the quality flows in and automatically education will flourish. Second, is to reform our regulations so that the opening of small or medium scale enterprises, operating it and thriving in it becomes easier so that any honest person wanting to make a livelihood out of a small scale enterprise can do that easily, quickly and run his business smoothly. Third is by creating enablers of business such as infrastructure and support services like the roads, highways, ports which means the entire transport and transit sector, health care etc will keep this product economy supported adequately. A focus on these three to four areas will remove restrictions and obstructions to economic activity and create a situation where it will actually flourish. This will increase government revenue and profits which can be then ploughed back into creating and strengthening the social sector. So I think we need to enlarge the size of economic activity to be able to benefit at the social level. Just by pumping money into the social sector without enlarging the economic activity will lead us nowhere. The two has to go hand-in-hand.

Interviewer: *What about the interventions which Indian organizations have to make if they have to transit and flourish in the next orbit?*

Dr Santrupt Misra: It will entirely depend on the sector and the competitive sets Indian corporates are operating in. So it is very hard to generally prescribe a few things. But if one were to do so, then it will involve interventions that would create organizations which would *(a)* be ethical and value based; *(b)* continuously invest in employee learning and re-learning; *(c)* invests in research, technology and development; *(d)* not be rigid, but flexible to be able to respond, adapt and avail of opportunities and the market; *(e)* be sensitive to issues of sustainability, not just sustainability of themselves, but sustainability of the society, the ecology, and the communities around; *(f)* conserve natural resources; and finally *(g)* continuously rebalances its priorities so as to incorporate emerging issues and challenges and thus have the capability to be flexible and adaptive.

Interviewer: *Can you illustrate this last point about rebalancing?*

Dr Santrupt Misra: Well, take for example, you have made investments in Mexico and suddenly there is an oil spill. You will have to quickly change that priority. How do you do that? Your organization must be geared towards beings able to do that, find and have other opportunity elsewhere and move there quickly. Organizations must be able to change its strategy to respond to the crisis and must do this realignment faster. This problem will persist for one year. I have taken much longer. Can I turnaround faster. Take another example. A certain product fails in the market. But then I invested in a manufacturing capacity which is so large that even if my product is failing, my fixed costs remain very high and I am unable to change anything. So it all boils down to how do I architecture the organization, its cost structure, its organization design, process, and others that are so flexible that it can respond to a crisis fast and avail of the opportunity even faster.

This last point is important because very often we are bothered about responding to the crisis fast. But we are not bothered about availing of the opportunity faster. But then opportunities come and go like a flash. The challenge is how you keep your organization's antenna up. How can you despite being a global company become aware of local sensitivities and changing realities and be able to make those quick moves into these markets in as reflexive a manner as the moving of the hand automatically and quickly to the foot where the mosquito has just bitten. It is that speed of response. From the bite to the brain and to the hand movement. In any organization, the corporate headquarters is the brain. The antenna of the organization quickly gives a signal to the brain which immediately responds to tell you that here is an opportunity and you move to seize that opportunity. Today opportunity windows have become short and will be far shorter, going forward. I find that on risk management and crisis management there is lot of effort and lot of elaborate processes. But organizations have to think whether it has a well designed structure and systems to respond to opportunities that have much shorter window and time for action.

Interviewer: *So, in terms of strategy, you are looking for an organization that is able to scan, to seize these opportunities and respond to it as fast as possible and be agile and nimble about it.*

Dr Santrupt Misra: Yes. Also remember during the good old days the entrepreneurs would send someone as far as 10,000 kms to South Africa. And whenever that person operating 10,000 kms away was required to take a decision, he would take it on the ground rather than wait for more than three months for the message to go and the response to come. I wonder whether Email and SMSs has brought about greater centralization or decentralization. But one thing is for sure, today for global organizations how do you create in a globally connected world enough entrepreneurial empowerment that people can do things on the ground faster is a great challenge.

Interviewer: *As far as the positioning of the Indian companies is concerned, being low cost is one end and we have talked about it. But the real issue is how can Indian corporates move up the value chain, in order to take advantages of the opportunities that are there? What should Indian companies do?*

Dr Santrupt Misra: Well I think, one thing that companies must increasingly realize that it cannot do everything by itself anymore. So it has to create an eco-system, a network of relationships which it can leverage and draw upon to bring necessary expertise to skills, technology, architecture and other wherewithal for effective functioning and success. So the monolithic organizations of the past that were self contained and could do everything themselves, perhaps is no more relevant. Today, organizations needs to think more in terms of how can it manage a network of relationships and connectivity that it can draw upon in the short term rather than trying to create everything in-house by itself. It should be in a position where it is the nucleus that is surrounded by a partner eco system and has the ability to quickly plug and play with any combination that it wants. In such a situation, organizations would need to have the capabilities *(a)* to create a large and flexible enough network, *(b)* to be flexible and effectively plug and play in response to opportunities and *(c)* to effectively manage social relationships and an economic distribution system or reward and incentive system, which can bring the eco-system together and make the partner organizations successful.

Now the classical definition of positioning called low cost, high value and all of that will vanish because, this eco-system will enable an organization to play at any level it wants and with different combinations just like the keyless combination locks or hotel chains that operate on different segments simultaneously. This is because the market will be so complex and market opportunities will be at such levels that an organization which does not have the capability to play at different levels at different points in time and flexibility to quickly vacate and move from segment to segments will not be able to survive. The Bottom of the Pyramid suddenly did not come alive because C.K. Prahalad wrote about it. The bottom of the pyramid always existed there. That is when he saw it there. Similarly there are other segments in market that are existing and are waiting to be seen. It already exists. But do you have the capability to see it? Your network must be able to sense that you know market segments, that you have market relationships, that you have the ability to create that position, and that you have the flexibility to re-configure to service that market. So, the question is, do you as an organization have the ability to make quick choices and get in there, get into something or come out of something? This does not mean that you have to be everywhere and everything to everybody. The question is do you have the capability to make those choices?

Interviewer: *So in this situation, where organizations have to think more in terms of the eco-system, what will be the role of entrepreneurship and innovations? Will it be based upon network relationships or will it be more home grown?*

Dr Santrupt Misra: Well, entrepreneurship by definition has to be something that organizations create on their own. But its expansion, its relevance to many other things would depend on the relationships it has. The world of business is becoming increasingly interdependent, relationship centric, and this is becoming all pervasive. The growth of social networking sites like Facebook or Linkedin is a manifestation of the growing importance of relationships and the role of relationships in our existence, both social and economic.

Interviewer: *We will now talk about the some of the things that is much more nearer home to HR. If you look at HR interventions, what are the few key interventions that is required to enable business to succeed and thrive in the next orbit.*

Dr Santrupt Misra: In a complex business situation today, it will be wrong to talk about just HR interventions. Instead one should talk about interventions. In an intervention, there may be an HR component, a commercial component, or a technology component. It is the presence of this totality that makes it an intervention.

Say for instance, Top Team effectiveness. A new sector opens up called telecom or insurance. The top twenty people of your company that you have found are people that have come from different companies and different sectors. This top team of 20 people now needs to be highly effective in work relations. For it is their effectiveness, which will set the tone of the company. Now that is not just a function of only HR intervention. It also a question of asking, what kind of business model are they familiar with? For, it is that familiarity that has built their capacity or incapacity. Or what kind of issues these people in their previous career have handled, how much of what they handled was dependent upon certain technological solutions that were available or what kind of supply chain enabled their success, what kind of decision making system and reporting environment they operated in or what kind of MIS was available to them and how. Today, when we have to talk about top team effectiveness, we need to work on all of these pieces. Just going on an outbound, having a campfire in the night and singing "we are the world," that kind of touchy, feely HR intervention will not make the top team effective. Instead, they need to discuss about what technology solutions they are familiar with, what technology solutions we need. And then the HR has to worry about how they can all be able to make a contribution to making the decision choice collectively. So the interventions have to be technological, and behavioral and somehow more in terms of business context and business models. A shared mindset will be created out of this, which will eventually lead to team effectiveness.

So I would say that we should not think about pure HR interventions anymore. This is the reason why HR interventions fail, because HR leaders lead interventions purely as HR interventions. I reiterate we have to create multi-disciplinary interventions. It is like treatment of any cancer where multiple therapies are brought together. Increasingly the role of HR should be that of a facilitator who is able to bring multiple interventions together, creating a whole that is synergistically aligned. My appeal to most of the HR leaders will be to identify the non-HR elements of their interventions and weave them equally well into other parts of the so-called HR interventions thereby creating a more effective intervention.

Let me give one more example. We talk about performance management. Everybody talks about performance management intervention. Now how do you use performance management as an intervention?

Performance management is not about giving appraisal feedback. In fact, performance management is about goal setting, which in turn leads to understanding of the businesses value drivers and the competitive landscape. Then is performance measurement which involves issues of financial measurement, non-financial measurement, complex subjects like EVA and CVA. So today if any one wants to use performance management as a way of improving organizational effectiveness and thinks that it is all about the boss and subordinate discussion over performance without any understanding of your EVA, CVA, goal setting, business value drivers others, competitive landscape, regulatory environment, then I think that person is limiting the idea of performance management as an intervention. This is precisely the reason why I think HR interventions have not succeeded very well. And partially it is because of the failure on the part of HR leaders.

Interviewer: *Any experience that you may have and would like to share in this regard?*

Dr Santrupt Misra: Well, we have done many interventions. Say for example, in retail business which we recently built, we brought the senior leadership together a couple of times. In the retail business, people have been drawn from all over the place. So when we said we want to build the top team effectiveness, the first thing that we did was to bring everybody to the same level of knowledge and understanding as to what retail is and what the business is all about. The second thing was to understand what are we trying to achieve and how. Then what is the scale of our ambition, which part of retail business, what we want to retail and why and which end of the market all had to be understood the same way. Also what are we trying to achieve and how are exercises in resource acquisition, mobilization, allocation, and optimization to be carried out. What capabilities are needed and what supports the success at the store level and distribution centre level. Sometimes bringing people together to a common level of understanding about a business and its value driver itself works out to be an intervention. The challenge is how you bring people onto the same platform of understanding. That's what we kind of tried in retail. We took up issues related to marketing, branding, financial analysis, information systems and people processes in retail. Only when we brought all these elements together that we were able to create a team with a shared perception and that we believe would unleash a shared energy to achieve something. What intervention is this? I for one cannot say that this was a pure HR intervention.

Interviewer: *What are the competencies which an HR professional should have in order to succeed in the present business and corporate environment?*

Dr Santrupt Misra: It's a very tough question and it is a tough question for very different reasons. Answer to this question depends on several things. First we should recognize that the competencies vary with different stages of your career. The competencies required at the first stage of your career are much different from what you would require at the mature end of your career. So different stages of one's career requires different HR competencies. Second, the nature & size of the business changes the mix of competencies that is required. Third, the nature and size of the organization also changes the mix of the HR competencies required.

Let me start with the last one, giving an example to you. If I am in a privately held large corporation, how to work at the board level, helping the board or its nominating committee to identify successor to the next CEO, successor to senior leaders, determining compensation, helping the remuneration structure etc are competencies that are most required. But if you are in a large listed company having a strong active board and the board functions in a regulatory environment, the competencies that would be expected from the HR would be different. Again the nature and size of your business also affects your competencies. Are you in an organization that is in the global business or local business, service business, manufacturing business, multiple product business, single product business? These are some of the questions that need to be answered for determining what are the competencies required of an HR professional. The third is the nature of your organization. Are you are a kind of a paternalistic organization, are you a professional organization, listed, privately held, non-listed etc. Thus the dimension, the business, the organization and the career stage all affects the required competencies.

Interviewer: *What are the few competencies that you can think about at different career stages?*

Dr Santrupt Misra: You see at the junior level, the HR person should be good in three to four areas. He should be good in his functional skills at this level, know the statutory requirements, know how the pay roll is processed and its tax implications. So at the junior level he must have competencies in three buckets: functional, business and interpersonal. As you grow to the middle level, more general management abilities are required. For example, the business abilities become more general management abilities. How to make decisions, how to integrate decisions, how to sell decisions, how to gather points of view, and create a picture. Whereas, at the senior level, how to connect the external environment forces and cull out the implications of it for your organization and con-nect it to the strategy of the organization—are also important. How to integrate the business needs of the organization and the demands of the environment becomes important in creating the HR strategy. So HR strategy building is a capability which is not needed at the lower level in the organization. At the senior level, this is what is needed. Besides, a lot more of influencing skills are required at the senior level than at the lower level, where good communication and presentation skills would be just good enough requirements. So I think the senior level requires competencies related to ideation, integration, external representation, persuasion, and influencing.

At the generic level, what is important for the HR people is, apart from understanding the context of business, to believe in their ability to make a difference. They need to have self-confidence in their body of knowledge and must be able to assert why this body of knowledge is relevant and useful for making a difference to the organization. But all this depends upon the extent to which the HR professional has the pas-sion to want to make the difference. Otherwise they will be unable to add any value. Indeed it is this passion that will ensure that they have the right motivation, courage, and perseverance to overcome the resistance and cynicism towards what they do. However, the credibility, accept-ance and success of the HR functionary would depend upon this critical fact whether their arguments and interventions are arising from the per-spective of narrow functional specialization or from the larger business.

In sum, I think the quest for HR competencies is a complex and interesting one. To try to reduce it to a common minimum of four to five competencies is perhaps a very risk prone approach. But this is not to say that you cannot start somewhere. You need to start somewhere. Basically it is important that at the junior level, the fundamental and functional concepts must be absolutely clear in the mind. At the middle level, integration and decision making are more important and at the senior level, it is the ability to bring the external perspective and making it relevant in the context of a business strategy and to create a workable HR strategy that becomes the most important.

Interviewer: *There are few HR people who are playing a very active role at the board level. You have been one of them. Again a very few HR people have become a CEO, you are also one of them. What do you think are the factors that have restricted the HR people from becoming the CEO?*

Dr Santrupt Misra: I think perhaps historically more brighter people went into finance and marketing as compared to those who came into

HR and therefore they scored over the HR people in the race to become the CEO. Secondly, Marketing, Finance or Operations as a function has had a more direct impact on business. Being closer to business they were able to get greater opportunities to move up. On the other hand, HR never was close and never tried to be close. Third is and this is the most important, I want to emphasize on that, nobody deliberately kept the HR people out of the CEO role. May be many of the HR people did not want to be the CEO. They were happy being called HR people. It is just like many high quality professors do not want to be Deans and Vice Chancellors of the University in India and abroad, or like many of the finest lawyers who do not want to become judges of the court, finest of the surgeons who do not want to become the deans of medical colleges. I think, in every profession, there are some people who take pride in their profession, who believe that being in the profession is more honorable and being acknowledged as an expert is more fulfilling than anything else. So I think there is a professional pride which did not drive many HR people into wanting to become a CEO. I also think that we should also not think that becoming CEOs is of a far greater value than becoming an outstanding HR head. I do not think, we should make that mistake. India at this moment needs high quality and highly capable HR heads as it needs high quality and highly capable CEOs. It is this myth that also made a lot of good engineers from IITs and other places to enter civil services or to do an MBA because somewhere they started believing that being a technocrat they cannot get the same societal recognition or monetary value etc. than what they can get by becoming a general manager. Unless and until we try to bust that myth or create organization's processes where a functionalist or a technocrat is made as valuable as a CEO, we would be unnecessarily emphasizing the importance of CEO or becoming a CEO. I personally would much rather be a top-class HR head than a failed CEO. If I can be a very successful CEO and an equally successful HR head that is well and good. But if I have to make a choice, I would prefer to be an outstanding functional professional. So I think we should not create the image in people's mind that becoming a CEO is a greater sign of success than becoming a well acknowledged highly capable HR head or a marketing head or a finance head.

Interviewer: *So are you saying that there is no competency gap over here?*

Dr Santrupt Misra: I don't think I am saying that. I am not saying that several HR head do not have a competency gap in becoming a CEO. These are two issues which should not be confused. The point that I am making is akin to saying which is better to be a Christian or to be a Hindu.

Now both the routes lead us to God almighty. It is a matter of birth, choice, and faith. Similarly, is the question, which is better: to be a CEO or highly respected HR head. I think it's your personal choice. If you feel you are capable of being a CEO and you want to be a CEO, you must try by all means to become one. But if you do not have the capability to be a CEO and you aspire to be one, then that is not the right thing to do. If you do not want to be there, do not go there. Thirdly just because you are an outstanding HR head, you must also recognize that you may not make an outstanding CEO. The two things are very different. And therefore even if you get an opportunity and you become a CEO, chances are very high that you will not succeed there. You should also not feel bad about it either because all you have done is that you had some sense that you have some capability, you got an opportunity to try it out, you tried it out and probably either you did not enjoy or you did not enjoy it doing it too much or there were elements to it which you did not enjoy and therefore you did not succeed. You can still come back and be able to be a good HR head. Nothing takes that capability away from you.

So I think it is all about the paradigm of success and failure we create in people's mind. The way we create a value hierarchy of jobs. People start aspiring for one job while being in the other. We need to move away from that. This is one of the tragedies of our education system, where society does not value different professions for what they bring into it. That is why in the West, I don't think people hesitate to say, I am a carpenter or a plumber. Because if you do excellent work in plumbing and carpentering, you also have a great living and you are in demand. I think in India, we need to remove this false hierarchy and create that sense of pride in whatever we are doing.

Interviewer: *But if we have to ask you one mantra or two mantras that can make an aspiring HR head to succeed in a CEO position, what would they be?*

Dr Santrupt Misra: First is a general interest in other aspects of the business viz. marketing, finance, operations, HR and more importantly the interconnectivity and interaction between and amongst them. What creates value? Do you really enjoy juggling many things in the year at the same time; do you enjoy interaction with customers; the pressure of delivering quarterly results, handling crisis and various other things that comes in the course of doing business. So do you enjoy certain things and do you know what these things are? If you invest yourself in knowing those things and you enjoy the kind of challenges that comes with it, then you can succeed. But if you neither enjoy, nor do you invest in doing things and you just aspire to be there, then this becomes a disastrous combination.

Nevertheless, I want to reiterate, not everybody must necessarily aspire to be a CEO. Being acknowledged in your profession as a high quality professional in HR in itself is a great recognition, once you think about it. If you don't have pride in your own profession, then trying to seek salvation by migrating to the CEO role is just escapism. But if it comes along your way, and you are fortunate enough and you think you are capable for it, then always try your hand. Then success and failure does not matter. Not everybody succeeds with everything. Just as this is true in films. Many people who can do comedy are not able to do serious drama. Similarly, those who do serious role cannot do comedy. But that does not make people who are in a comic role less relevant than an action hero or a romantic hero. It is a different meaning in life and we need to understand that.

Interviewer: *What is your message to the young HR professionals?*

Dr Santrupt Misra: Well, I think basically four things: know yourself well, know your subject well, know your business well, and know the world very well. This is because success lies in the effective integration of this four. How well I know myself, my subject, my company or my business. How well do I understand what is going on in the world? If you neglect any one of these four, I am not sure whether you will get any success. I cannot be an insular HR person who knows nothing about what's happening in the world. Just being focused on my business, on my function and myself will not work. If I am the one who focuses only on my function, my company, what's happening at the world, but I am not able to see myself, then I won't succeed. And if I don't know my own function then there is just no point in my existence, even if I know my business, the world, and myself. And finally, if I don't know my business, my function has no context. It cannot contribute to anything. My whole knowledge of myself, my function and the world is useless. I am irrelevant. So I think we need to understand. These four aspects are very integrally connected and HR professionals must invest in knowing all the four very well. This is my message.

4

March towards the Next Horizon: Lessons in Capability Building in Maruti

Dialog with S.Y. Siddiqui, Managing Executive Officer—Administration (HR, Finance, IT, Company Law and Legal), Maruti Suzuki India Ltd.

Interviewer: *It is said that the landscape of business is undergoing a tectonic shift and the context of business therefore would be radically different if not totally new. In order to survive and excel in this environment, organizations in India would have to be different in terms of their structural configuration, strategic positioning, systems, and processes. What according to you are the few important things that organizations must do in order to succeed in business in the next orbit?*

S.Y. Siddiqui: In my understanding the organizations will have to take into consideration the twin facts, one that they are now operating in a global business scenario and the second that the external business environment is really volatile, complex, and very much different from whatever they have experienced till now. It therefore becomes necessary for each corporate to prepare itself strategically for the next orbit. This preparation relates to breaking out of the comfort zone in terms of their business strategy, business plans, organization structure, systems and processes, leadership and people policies so that they are better able to grapple with the new methods of doing business in rather challenging circumstances. Say for instance in the automotive sector, there is no company that can actually control the kind of competition which it is going to face in the future or make a claim that any specific domain or territory will be entirely dominated by a particular product or a particular business. In that sense, perhaps the kind of preparation which is required, is to take into consideration that there will be intense competition, there will be excellent product offerings and there will be a kind of congestion. The business strategy should be such that it provides for a proactive and aggressive stand with regard to routes to and realization of business growth and business success. It is now also incumbent upon companies to have a business strategy that has both Plan A and Plan B so that they do not get surprised in the face of volatility of the sector. Finally, they will also have to shed this basic approach of operating on a short term or immediate term basis and look at concrete strategy from the long term perspective. It is also important that companies must prepare for this kind of challenging times well in advance, when the going is good and everything is going fine. Indeed, the recent recession has shown two things: that firms which were mature, consistent and prepared during tough times to deal with volatile, complex and uncertain external business environment and that firms had responded with a middle to long-term perspective recovered better and gained handsomely.

Interviewer: *What were some of the ways in which Maruti Suzuki India Limited prepared for the challenges?*

S.Y. Siddiqui: We in Maruti began our preparation starting from 2004 onwards. That was the time when we took the decision to change the product design, in the sense that we took a call to design products which were aimed at a younger customer profile in India. The whole thought was that the kind of cars which Maruti was famous for may or may not have much potential going forward, in view of our understanding that over the next five to seven years most of the demand will be from the younger population of customers looking to buy cars. In 2005, a major change was introduced by Maruti when we introduced a contemporary design in "Swift."

Another thing that we did was that we started decentralizing our sales and marketing department. We created four zonal offices cutting across the length and breadth of our country. To support them we increased the number of regional offices from 8 to 16. This restructuring was not as easy as it seems. For people at the head quarter level were quite habituated to having a fairly high power of decision making and exercising it down the line. After the restructuring, they had to delegate and pass on that decision making power to the zonal heads and to the regional heads. But over the last few years, this particular restructuring gave us a tremendous competitive edge. This was also the time when the competition had intensified in the domestic automobile industry sector.

We also took a strong initiative with regards to developing a leadership pipeline in collaboration with MDI, Gurgaon and more specifically with Dr. Pritam Singh and Dr. Asha Bhandarker. It was in 2004 that the top management decided to develop a 4–5 year plan for broad basing the leadership layer of senior people at Maruti. The idea was that if we succeed in developing the leadership engine in Maruti over the next 4–5 years, then when the company would be growing aggressively and would be requiring people with the right leadership capability, we would not be dependent on external hiring. We will be able to provide our own in-house high potential candidates absolutely ready to take on higher responsibilities.

Today, all the 10–12 people in the managing executive officer kind of roles at the board level in Maruti Suzuki are in-house talent. This to a great extent validates the entire preparatory strategy move which was launched in collaboration with MDI, Gurgaon for the leadership development process including assessing people on leadership potential, providing developmental plans, supporting them with 360 degree exercise and then ultimately making them ready when the time came for the company to broad base the leadership layer.

In 2005, we did something more. In the restructuring exercise that we had carried out, we developed an altogether new group in the sales and marketing organization to deal with corporate and institutional sales. A team of almost 50 young professionals were constituted out of the blue in 2005 to provide for a focused approach towards corporate and institutionalized sales. At the same time, there was also a strong thinking that in about five years time the urban sector will be so congested and so competitive, that Maruti will have to expand into the rural market, if it wanted to create additional volumes. This proactive thinking helped us to create two teams within the sales and marketing division viz. corporate and institutional sales team and the rural marketing team. In 2003–04, rural sales was just two percent of the total volumes of Maruti; today it is roughly about 16 percent of the total volumes of our company. We were able to comfortably tide over the economic slowdown. Our proactive move had given the Maruti a very big competitive edge.

Interviewer: *Such a startling growth from 2 to 16 percent in the span of 6-7 years has been because of sales of the same kind of product or have you developed new products to cater to the rural market?.*

S.Y. Siddiqui: Our approach to the rural market was all about reaching out to them and providing the rural customer with a current product range itself. In that sense we did not get into designing a specific vehicle for the rural population. Therefore, perhaps if we look at a current portfolio of 13 models, the product range became extremely handy and the penetration and reach of the Maruti to the rural segment emerged as a big differentiator. More importantly, since rural sales do not depend upon a financial enabler, the transactions were typically in cash. So during the economic slowdown in our country when the financial institutions got the biggest jolt and urban sales got affected very badly, Maruti Suzuki, because of its complete reach and the penetration into the rural segment was able to cash in on this rural sales.

Thus the basic idea which I can share out of the Maruti experiences is that those companies who will prepare for a tough time and especially when the going is good, will perhaps have a better balance of performance and business growth.

Interviewer: *Apart from preparing well during the good times, what are the other things that organizations need to do in order to succeed in the next orbit.*

S.Y. Siddiqui: I will talk about few posers which has become critical for firms to consider in this context.

First, are we prepared to break our comfort zones and look at and explore new methods of doing business?

Second, are we capable of challenging the status quo? Most companies are very busy in doing things which they have been doing for many years and have been successful in doing those. But today there is no guarantee that what worked for the last ten years will work the same way in this changing business environment.

Third, and this is related to the first two principles, are we driving innovation and change in our organization? It is a very natural phenomenon that most of the organizations and most of the people with the kind of experience which they carry will be prone to resisting change. Typically, in such organizations there is a slogan for innovation but in actual reality in terms of systems and processes and the culture of the organization, such innovation and innovativeness is completely missing. It is because of this that innovation needs to be top driven and must be institutionalized in the very manner people think and do business. We in Maruti have harvested the benefit of it. In the last financial year, employee's suggestions and Kaizen process led to more than 1,00,000 suggestions and savings in excess of ₹173 crore. This was due to the institutionalized approach involving training people, nurturing people, empowering people and then letting them think for the company, and encouraging small, incremental piece meal improvements.

In this context, perhaps, I will recommend a simple thought for organization leaders to introspect. This is to examine for the current financial year 2010–11 the following: *(a)* how many projects which they are dealing with are based upon their current expertise, current knowledge base, current specialization, current performance level, and successes; *(b)* how much time will they be spending on projects which are in the adjacent space, which are new, but related to their core competencies, but which the company has not done before; *(c)* how many projects are totally out of box, totally new and may not be even related to their core competencies. I believe that innovation is all about challenging the status quo, exploring the opportunity share, and making driving of innovation a perspective to evaluate projects and products that are part of a organization's work culture. This is the kind of preparation that is required for transition and success in the next orbit.

At the same time each company must also look at its talent base. A transition to the next orbit crucially hinges upon capability building processes where more than acquiring talent, perhaps it is critical to nurture talent. Therefore, the first challenge is to develop the capability of people within the organization. Second, is to link this capability with the new business order so that the talent pipeline is aligned to the business needs. This means that traditional training, technical training and training for the sake of training, and man-days are no more relevant.

This capability building must be complemented with high people engagement practices. HR must now be directed towards bringing in an engagement perspective rather than merely looking at employee satisfaction level in all its processes, practices, and activities. This would entail examining the job content and its fit with the capability of the person, job excitement, empowerment, and internal communication systems for bringing about involvement, ownership, and commitment. A right combination of capability and commitment is very critical for this journey to the next orbit. For, competitive edge in the post internet era of work can no longer be achieved because of tangible factors like cost, technology, product features, core competencies, but because of intangibles like speed, customer responsiveness, employee capability, and employee commitment.

Interviewer: *If in order to succeed, organizations must be fast, innovative, engaged with its employees, customer centric and competing from the inside out, then what is role of HR in facilitating this excellence?*

S.Y. Siddiqui: In my view, HR must align with business strategy. Indeed, over the past few years this perspective has been building up—that HR should play the role of a business enabler and business partner, instead of just being a support function. HR investments should lead to measurable, and value add to business and its performance. To a great extent, it will also be expected of HR functions to bring in this fine balance between employee aspirations and demands of the business. This perspective notwithstanding, there are many corporate organizations where HR remains an isolated identity and where HR professionals religiously specialize in leave and salary administration, hiring people and arranging separation formalities, and periodically undertaking employee satisfaction surveys. I think there has to be a major shift in the basic understanding of the HR function.

In this regard I do not think simply benchmarking the company's HR practices and blindly cutting and pasting benchmark practices into a company is going to pay any dividend. We have to move from benchmarking of best practices to looking at what works best in a business sector, in relevance to a specific business strategy, in the context of the maturity and work culture of a given organization and in tune with the local social structure of a given geographic region where the business is located. The erstwhile model of conventional HR separate from business and struggling for its identity must be jettisoned. Obviously, this co-partnership between business and HR will redefine the basic competencies for a HR professional.

Interviewer: *What are the basic competencies HR professionals now need to have in order to play their role in enabling their organizations to transit into the next orbit?*

S.Y. Siddiqui: Firstly, I think HR will have to look at developing its own professional identity, not a kind of identity which gets straight away influenced by top management or the diktat from the business managers. When we talk about this professional identity there has to be some kind of linkage between the specific competencies required for leadership, domain knowledge in HR and the capability to influence business in the best possible manner.

Secondly, the risk taking ability of HR professionals to a great extent will have to be redefined and revisited. This is very much linked with developing his professional identity. It involves an ability to say something which is not pleasant, to say something which is different, to challenge the status quo, to explore untapped areas and also to have the courage of re-defining organization, redefining systems and processes, and redefining policies.

Finally, when in this dynamic, volatile, ever-changing business environment nothing can be static irrespective of whether it is HR or any business, HR professionals must have the capability to introspect, to look at things from the audit perspective and from the innovation perspective.

Interviewer: *Yours has been an eventful journey in the HR profession. What were some of the challenges you faced and how did you deal with them. How did it prepare you for the position you are holding today in Maruti that of Managing Executive Officer of HR, Finance and Legal.*

S.Y. Siddiqui: It is important to talk about some of the key challenges of Maruti which I faced as a HR professional. An HR professional is expected to bring in a lot of change and one big change was that at the time when I joined in 2003, Maruti had just turned into a private sector company with Suzuki Motor Corporation of Japan as the majority equity partner and owner. This would possibly be a drastic transformation for a company which for 20 years was under the government and boasted of a very successful business performance record. From the people's perspective there was a huge challenge in changing from a public sector culture to a private sector culture. I thought one of the best ways is to first inculcate few principles before attempting to bring about any change.

The first principle was that the change will have to be top driven. The second principle was that the change must be owned by the business heads in Maruti and therefore it should not be a HR driven change alone. Third was that since internal communication process held the key to any change effort, people must be explained the need, process and objectives of change. This in turn will lead to involvement and commitment in the change process. The fourth principle was that we may have to create on the way champions all across the company to drive this change. The last principle was that the change should be a gradual process best spread over three years rather than being a sudden jerk overnight, thereby, unsettling people and unsettling the organization.

In that context, I think , it is also important to mention the significant contribution that came in from MDI Gurgaon, and where we engaged Dr Pritam Singh and Dr Asha Bhandarker to provide a blue print for the road map. Then we started identifying specific areas for this change. Here we realized that the most important challenge was the need to change the mindset of the people to be a part of the private sector entity. We thus launched training and development program for the entire organization right from shop floor workmen to all supervisors, experienced middle management and the top management, including the MD and the CEO. We also decided that this training will be both in-house and external. This was followed by programs on leadership development. Finally we started talking about 360 degree feedbacks. But this met with opposition more due to the fear of the senior management that if juniors started evaluating them, it will generate some kind of backlash. We kept our implementation in abeyance for another five months.

Interviewer: *Why did you go in for 360 feedbacsk? What was the emergency?*

S.Y. Siddiqui: I think to a great extent, evolving the leadership layer to become more effective with the changing time and specifically in tune with the expectation of generation "Y" required people to unlearn some of the experiences and create space for relearning some new concepts.

So the 360 degree feedback was to show the mirror to the employee and to put them on development paths.

In any case our initiative in 2006 became a highly successful initiative. The response rate in terms of juniors giving feedback to the superior was to the tune of almost 89 percent. This was followed by creating individual development plans for each of the superior. Here again IDPs for senior management was developed in collaboration with Dr Pritam Singh and Dr Asha Bhandarker from MDI Gurgaon. The collaboration with MDI Gurgaon in creating the IDP spread over 3–5 years brought in continuity, consistency, and accountability in our investments in creating and strengthening the leadership layer in Maruti.

We then started working on the third perspective: development of the Maruti team concept. Till 2003–04 perhaps each division, each functional area worked as a silo and thought that it was Maruti. The need of the hour was to evolve an identity for the Maruti Suzuki team and then for job role purposes define organizational departments and divisions. This was followed by creating cross–functional teams and putting them into training programs directed towards improving their team work. Today, when we look at Maruti, we look at only the Maruti Suzuki team. All others are blurred. It is a boundary less kind of organization.

Interviewer: *What role did HR play in all this cultural change?*

S.Y. Siddiqui: In order to enable HR to play a fruitful role in the entire change and transformation process in Maruti, we did two things. First, we exposed our HR team to some of the globalized HR policies, system, and processes. Second, we sought to make HR, a shared responsibility in the organization with all senior managers and leadership teams owning HR. Keeping this in mind, we decentralized the HR function and embedded it in different divisions and functions. So now we have a plant HR, Engineering HR, Commercial HR etc., with each of them partnering with business. HR innovation and audit now involves taking up each and every policy and practice, refining it and redefining it with the involvement of the people and in keeping with the demands of the changing business environment. We have been updating and formulating new policies but today there is one big difference: these policies are not defined or articulated by HRs alone. They are defined together with all our business colleagues in a process which we call HR initiative development team. This is the team which takes a call on what is relevant for our business and what is relevant to our people and then a new policy takes birth in Maruti.

Another significant change that has happened in Maruti is that during the monopolistic era and until 2003, Maruti's focus was just on how to produce and produce. So the real image of HR was confined to managing a factory, managing unions, managing negotiations and managing conflicts. But as the business became global and competitive, HR was completely restructured and redefined to realign with the business demands. That was a huge change. At the Board level, a significant new initiative which we call as the HR think tank was also created. The partnership of HR with business is now truly forged in Maruti.

Interviewer: *How easy was it for you to make this shift?*

S.Y. Siddiqui: I started with the basic educational back ground, specializing in personnel management and HR at the post graduate level and starting my career with Escorts. But along the way, I think one realization came in very strongly that keeping an isolated HR identity will become a very tough challenge in this changing business environment and therefore there is no other option, but to look at fastening the alignment with the business where HR can become a value add and where HR can perhaps create a business impact. This realization to a great extent accentuated the need to know subjects and concepts based upon the strategic integration of HR and business. One cannot keep on talking on HR without understanding the nuances of business itself.

Since the last four to five years I have moved more consciously towards the business role and to a great extent the credit goes to the Board of Directors and the top management in Maruti, that they gave this opportunity for me to express my capability in business. So I started by aligning business strategy with HR and now I also manage business. Today in my new role I am expected to manage human resources, finance, IT, and the company secretarial and legal functions of Maruti. More than just a strategic role, it is more a management role. Whatever be it, the principle remains the same: the capability to learn, to unlearn, and to relearn, and so on.

Interviewer: *What is your message for the young HR professionals?*

S.Y. Siddiqui: I think to a great extent, my one message which I always try to share with people is that HR should be a really genuine and passionate responsibility. HR is not related to the power of decision making and neither is it related to competing with business managers. HR I think should be more of a catalyst and an enabler for creating this excellent work environment, where employees are highly engaged, are inspired to perform, and are enabled to add value to business performance and business growth.

5

Towards HR's Integration with Business

Dialog with Arvind Agrawal, President—Corporate Development and Group HR, RPG Group

Interviewer: *What according to you are some of the salient features of the context of business today?*

Arvind Agrawal: As far as the landscape which is unfolding in front of us is concerned, I think I can summarize it in one word, and that is "globalization." There is globalization in all aspects of life and business today. Anything can be sold anywhere in the world. So customers are global, suppliers are global, market places have become global. You can source anything from anywhere in the world. Till yesterday, the purchase people or the sourcing people, used to look at what is available in the neighboring vicinity and even 1,000 kms was considered distant enough by them. Today, people are looking at sourcing things from anywhere in the world, provided it gives them comparative, and greater still, competitive advantages. The same is the matter in the case of talent acquisition where companies are hiring talents wherever it is available, regardless of the person's nationality. Finance means global finance, with foreign institutional investment and foreign direct investment coming to India. It may come and go very fast, but the fact is that whether it's borrowing of money from the banks or whether it's the shareholding, finance has become global in all respects. In this globalised context, the benchmarks such as that of quality, features, price, customer requirements, productivity, and even outputs have become global. The parameters for companies will now be compared with the best of the world and it has to meet that.

So now with all the benchmarks having moved to being global, the challenge for corporate leaders is move the business similarly and that too at globally defined and accepted standards. Now this has imposed a huge pressure on the business leader who is already under demands arising from the uncertainty, velocity, and complexity of the business. It can be gauged by this simple example that a couple of decades ago, time lag between a letter received through surface mail and response to it would take about a week at the earliest. So for a week if one did not hear anything, one would assume perhaps that the response is still on the way. Today if you have received an email, you are required to respond within 24 hours lest you don't want to receive a reminder telling you that an email has been sent and that you must have had read it by now and that a reply is awaited. So the velocity of the business has compounded. As a result of this an executive is supposed to go around with a blackberry, periodically check the mails and respond to it regardless of whether he is with family or on an holiday. The speed at which the business is now conducted has accentuated. The standard of the business has changed and the demands on the business from all stakeholders have multiplied. The business leaders thus have no alternative but to become very demanding.

In that canvas, if you have to look at HR, who is also a business partner, then naturally the delivery of HR professional, in terms of the value the HR professional is adding to the business, comes under scrutiny. Is the HR professional helping the business by making the business more customer friendly? Is he helping the business by improving productivity or reducing cost by reducing attrition levels? All these questions are also the requirement of the business. Now when you look at this from the HR point of view, you need to ask this pertinent question, whether whatever I am doing, is adding any value to the business. Quite often, I have sat through presentations by HR professionals in which they speak in a rather self adulatory way about the new things that have introduced in HR: 360 degree feedback, engagement survey, training program, the new method of inducting people, etc. Undoubtedly, all this is good HR stuff. The problem is that the HR professionals in these presentations have nothing to say about how the proposed change will affect or help the business. This is especially when today business requires that right from the start to finish, everything has to be seen in the context of business objectives and the differences it can make. If the productivity has to be raised from a level A to level B and there is a gap, how can HR help fill up the gap? If the cost has to be reduced from one particular level to another level, how can HR help reduce the cost? How does HR help that cause? So HR today is required to become a problem solving business partner. By problem solving I mean, HR has to analyze the business gap in terms of the goals and targets which business leaders are pursuing. He has to look at what are the key issues, identify the causes, take corrective actions and thus close the gap between adverse reality and expectations. This is the fundamental shift which is required today. Earlier it was enough for the HR to do nice things and get respect. Today a contemporary HR professional has to bring in new practices, solve problems and overall be a business partner to gain just an acceptance.

Interviewer: *In this globalized world what are the few things that is required for an Indian organization to be a leader or at least be a global player. If you have to audit India's capabilities, what are the strengths and weaknesses of India and Indian organizations?*

Arvind Agrawal: I will start with talking about India's strength. I think in India, the people who are very innovative can always find newer ways of getting the job done. So we don't feel overly constrained, even if there are seemingly intractable problems. So there is this enterprise that makes us in some way or the other to get on top of the difficult situation. This is definitely a major strength of the people in India. Secondly, we have a large number of educated people, who may not be necessarily capable. But the fact is that we have a vast pool of educated manpower. Thirdly and there is no doubt of this, is the consumption power of a huge market today. Fourth, is the presence of an institutional mechanism, be it the government, the judiciary, stock market, banking or the regulatory framework. The presence of such institutions has been very conducive to doing business. Fifthly, a lot of Indian educated class, which constitutes the corporate work force, speaks in English and that is our major strength. I experienced this problem, to know what I am talking about. We have recently acquired SAE Towers and in that company the manufacturing is in Mexico and Brazil. Out of the 800 people, there will probably be just only 20 people who speak English. The balance do not have English speaking capabilities and that is a big constraint for them and for us too. So while they can excel in their own environment, they cannot connect globally. The advantage that India has is obvious. Sixth is the growth rate of Indian economy, which is again a major strength, because the increase in economic activity will have an overall positive impact. Finally we have an entrepreneurial streak and a class who are growth and investment oriented. While this is not a new phenomena and a continuation of something that has been there for the last 100 years, it has in its wake, established some of the finest institutions in India.

If you look at weaknesses, first is that our large population itself is a major weakness in many ways. The country faces gargantuan challenges in matters related to education, health, food, shelter, and the basic necessities of life. Secondly, our education system is not sufficiently vocational or technically oriented. There is therefore a shortage in the country of people in every vocation. If you need a driver, you cannot even easily find them in a country that produces millions of cars and trucks. The same is true of mason, painters and even a machinist. Every conceivable vocation you think about, we have a gap, which is what we as a nation need to address. Moreover, while we have huge manpower, the employability of this manpower perhaps is not as great as we would like it to be. So this is a major weakness, unemployablilty of our educated people. They are educated people, but they are not employed. Today our factories talk about shortage of labor. Even basic labor is in short supply, despite the kind of population India has.

The third gap relates to our labor legislation. It does not give the Indian corporate the kind of freedom which we witness around the world. Today the cost of labor in proportion to the output of labor is increasing, thus putting our labor cost advantage under great threat. Today places like Vietnam has an average wage of around five to seven thousand rupees a month. In India, in most of the factories, you would not be able to get any labor at this rate. In fact, in good companies, the wages of workers may range from easily from 25–50,000 rupees per month. So cost wise, India is becoming non-competitive. Unless the productivity rises to justify the level of wages, it is a weakness which needs to be overcome.

Infrastructure is another major weakness. This is one sector where the country as a whole took inexplicably a lot of time to wake up. The quality of roads, sanitation and hygiene system, medical facilities are awfully behind times and a huge lag. But it is the lack of quantity and quality in the vocational system that has exacerbated the matters.

Interviewer: *So is the quality of the education a real issue?*

Arvind Agrawal: Yes, quality and perhaps the nature of education and in particular what is being taught are real issues. It is not that there is no vocational education. The problem is that a lot of people are outside the net of vocational education and do not have the wherewithal that will be meaningful for their livelihood. So this is a gap. Where industry suffers is that you don't have that many people whom you could employ. I can cite our experience over here. We have found out that in retail business, if we recruit a 10th class pass person and sufficiently train him, they become a very first class asset in the retail store and very soon are ready to take on the mantle of being a store manager. But then this also shows the institutional weaknesses in our educational system. It is a different matter that this is one of the issues on which the business leaders now depend upon the HR person to find solutions, so that the business does not suffer because of lack of manpower or its unavailability when it is required or the skill gap between the need and the availability. So developing a manpower supply chain is one of the areas for which the business people depend upon HR managers.

There is a connected problem as well. That of high attrition. I believe high attrition is only because of skill shortage. High attrition rate adds to the cost. That cost ultimately makes Indian companies less competitive in a global sense and less competitive than our counterparts. This is the reason why there is now a growing trend of recruiting talent from abroad. The global talent is more dependable and stable. For when you hire a person on a five year contract, you know that this person is here for five years. But when you hire an Indian native for five years, you are not guaranteed that this person will remain for five years. He or she is in such big demand that you turn your head and the person is gone. So it's an interconnected problem which is challenging Indian companies in its ability to compete with the global players.

Interviewer: *What role should company play in order to close the skill gap?*

Arvind Agrawal: At a company level, we have to start where people are and accept the kind and level of education they come with. What we can do at our end is to identify the entry points in our companies where people can be inducted and trained like the example I cited in retail business. Now retail at the store level does not require a graduate. Yet because graduates are available, we have temptation to hire graduates when just class 10th is good enough. Then when you hire a person with just a class 10th qualification in three months with proper training and development, this person acquires the capability to become not only competent but also a store coordinator and store manager over a short period of time. This requires a lot of hard work from HR managers and many HR people shy away from it. But business appreciates. Then there is this example of our Chennai branch. Here the HR manager had the responsibility for about 1,500 people. She had an attrition level of around 20 percent which meant that she had to constantly find 300 persons through the entire year. Her solution was simple. She had batches of 25–30 trainees coming right out of the school every fortnight. So she had in a way set up a process by which trained manpower will be available. This model was replicated in 20 such centers across the country to make sure that trained manpower was available to retail business for its growth.

In a way it is true that HR by trying to breach the gap between the skills that people have and the competencies that we required does play the role of a finishing school. I think this is one of the strategic roles of HR. The creation of manpower supply chain not only takes care of the attrition rate in a context of skill shortage, it also keeps the cost low for the business, provides the basis for the steady growth of the business, and makes HR a business partner instead of being an ornamental entity in the organization.

Interviewer: *You have been a CEO of an organization previously. How do other line functions such as production or marketing or finance view and talk about HR?*

Arvind Agrawal: You know we hear both kinds of things. On the positive side, whenever a HR person has risen to the occasion and challenge of the business, they have earned great appreciation. For example, both in retail business as also in life sciences, we in the last three months added the sales force by about 50 percent, something the line managers had not imagined in the wildest of their dreams. The HR team earned many plaudits from them. And these were HR professionals who had come out from the business school just two years ago and were extremely young.

On the other hand, you also get remarks from the line managers that HR people live in their own world. They like to talk big things. Often time they have no idea how their concepts or activities or propositions will connect with or benefit the business. Above all, the line people have started to feel, more frequently now than earlier, that the HR people cannot be depended upon or trusted to deliver anymore given that they seem to be pre-occupied in figuring out their own career and are prone to change jobs at the drop of their hats. You will be surprised to know the attrition level in HR is more than in any other function, partly because there is so much demand for HR professionals and partly because the HR person is getting swayed by the lucrative opportunities dangled before them rather than remaining firm with the commitment to do some thing and make a difference in a place he has he/she has chosen to be in or to his/her profession. I have seen people who have absolutely high level of capabilities, but within 18 months or two years time they decide to leave, giving the profession a really bad name. From the line manager's perspective, HR professionals are seen as people, who cannot be relied upon, cannot be trusted to deliver on their promises; something that they in marketing or in production or in finance are made to do. Just think, the HR professionals talk about commitment and all before others and do not think twice before displaying their lack of it. HR people have to show commitment to their profession, to the organization's agenda, and to their own professional ethics. The line people do that, the HR people also need to do that and this is not difficult. This would require HR professionals to display certain values. You have to honor your commitments and only then will you be counted upon. I have seen so many good HR professionals who have this commitment and who honor their commitments. I was this morning talking to one of my colleagues, who is an HR professional, and he was making a point that currently there is a paradigm that unless you change your job every two years, you cannot advance in your career. I asked that person a counter question. I said can you name a single professional who has really succeeded and has moved to the top of the organization in his profession at least by changing jobs every two years. He could not name a single person. Well to be honest, in my decades of industrial experience, I have not come across any successful people who has changed job every two years and who has succeeded. A typically successful professional is the one who has stayed in the business for five, ten years and fifteen years. This is the kind of patience and commitment required to succeed. Only then are you able to make a difference.

This is the kind of commitment which is required if HR needs to be a credible profession. Otherwise HR runs the risk of being called a function with double standards: who demand this commitment from others and do not practice it ourselves. The problem is exacerbated by the fact that there are no role models in the country where a person in any profession would have succeeded by changing jobs every two years or every one year. And yet people are chasing this model. This is the reality that we have to drive home. This is the paradigm shift which we need to bring about in the country. However, this can be facilitated if we have a large pool of better and high caliber professionals. This will ensure that there will not be so much demand and so much chasing of accomplished professionals and therefore hopefully there will be lesser temptations and then perhaps there will be greater stability. We have seen this phenomenon in the years of recession. When there was a recession, automatically people became more stable, demand for professionals came down and the attrition level had dropped.

Interviewer: *Today there is a rat race or madness about compensation. What can the HR people do at the industry level to curb and end this evil?*

Arvind Agrawal: I think the first step has to be initiated by management institutes. I think couple of years ago, there was a serious objection which students took at their salaries being brought up in the newspaper and that was a major breach of privacy; but today institutes are more careful to give away the salary figures of their students. Then I keep talking to people in the press, that when you talk about MBAs, why do you only talk about the salaries, which institute has got what salaries? Why don't you talk about the kind of jobs which people are getting, the shifts that could be taking place from one industry to another or from sector to another sector in terms of jobs and profiles? Why do you only have a pre-occupation with the salary? This is also very unique about the management profession as such. Because if you look at the websites of other technical or higher education there are no other programs which talks about salaries. This is true about the legal profession, medical profession, engineering profession, etc. Nobody is so pre occupied with salaries as the management professionals. So management institutes are the only institute which in their website will talk about average salaries of their graduating batch. I think this pre-occupation needs to change. I think we need to get down to the more substantive things rather than only talking about the remuneration. But then it seems that today salary is seen as an index of success, as also an index of Indian ethos. Today if you go to a village, your relatives and others want to know how much salary you are earning. Somehow it has become our national pre-occupation to measure people's success by salaries. Hopefully education and maturity will change this over a period of time.

But after saying that, I must also say that now the salaries have gone up pretty high to a degree where it is becoming non-competitive at the global level. Today remuneration level has reached a point which perhaps our competence and output does not justify. Today if you are hiring a Vice-President for let's say manufacturing, you typically have to pay up say about a crore of rupees in a year. A crore of rupees means close to about US \$25000. For US \$25000 you can very well hire a person from anywhere in the world including US, who will have 25 years of experience and have all the domain knowledge that you would be looking for. This is the competition which an Indian talent is going to face sooner than later. I am already beginning to see this shift. There are many industry captains who are advocating bringing in global talent. For, they will do the job at no additional cost in a much more dependable manner.

Therefore I am of the opinion that salaries should be reduced. Like everything else, if as a professional we are earning global salaries, then that is great, but we must make sure that our competence, output, and reliability should also be of global levels. That's the gap which we need to fill out and I believe as an HR professional, we have a role to help our people make that advancement.

Interviewer: *If you have to recommend four to five suggestions to young HR professionals so that they can advance in their chosen profession what would those be?*

Arvind Agrawal: First, I would say is that, try and understand the business that you are supporting and in particular the key drivers of that business. What are the key anxieties, which the business leader has in that business, etc? Second, then think as an HR person what can you contribute to mitigate some of these anxieties. When you do that you are seen as adding value and it gets you a lot of respect. The third thing, I would say is that, whatever you believe you can contribute, be dependable enough to make sure that it is delivered. You must ensure that you don't get swayed by phone calls from head hunters with alternate job opportunities and can stay committed. You will be respected and you will definitely go up in your career over a period of time. More importantly you will make a name for yourself for the difference that you have made. Fourth, is the personal sense of credibility and value that you bring, in terms of how one deals with the others, in the organization. What kind of respect you give to everybody else also matters. Just because you have a higher education does not mean you are superior. You must appreciate that everybody who is in that organization is there because they have certain values which they bring to the organization. Quite often we miss this point and we believe just because we have the luxury of higher and may be better education, we are superior. The fact is that we are not superior and we contribute as much as everybody else. So that humility to accept that others are as great as you is very fundamental to your getting accepted.

Interviewer: *How can HR and HR professionals become more relevant in terms of competencies that would be required?*

Arvind Agrawal: A HR person must understand the business of the organization. He must know what kind of goals the business leaders are pursuing. He must understand what are the global standards of productivity and quality, the segment of customers being targeted and the amount of returns which are being given to the shareholders. As the business leaders seek to bridge the gap between global standards and organizational achievements, the HR professional needs to see what he can bring to the table to help business leaders in their endeavor. That is the reason why the ability to understand the business is the first and the foremost competency which HR professionals require in order to succeed in the next orbit.

The second competency is the ability to see the connection between the business problem and their deliverables. After all what does a HR person deliver? He hires people, develops people, formulates and implements policies which help people be productive or more productive. Now if one looks at all these deliverables, then the ability to see the connections between all this and the level of productivity, which is one of the abiding concerns of all line managers, is important. Herein, lies the challenge, that if a business leader is having productivity as a major anxiety, then the HR person must seek to solve the problem. What is causing that drop in productivity? Is it because of lack of motivation, lack of skills, lack of the right kind of environment in the organization or an absence of the right kind of technology which is available to the individual? Now if it is lack of technology, then obviously it is not the HR's problem. Then technology people have to deal with that. But if it is any of the others, such as lack of motivational environment because of absence of appropriate policies, skills and system of rewards and punishments and HR systems and practices, then HR must be able see the connection, isolate the cause and its interrelationship with others and come up with solutions. An HR professional would then be required to develop those skills through training and development programs, change or modify policies and systems that were found to be de-motivating and create other interventions to boost the deliverables. HR can make a difference by closing the competency gap and by creating an environment which is conducive for performance.

This is what I would call the harder part of the HR competencies.

On the softer side, a HR person needs to make sure that he has a basic commitment and lives up to the values which he believes in and which the organization subscribes to. These values could be customer orientation, respect for individual, integrity, and passion for excellence. The second part of the soft skills, I would say would be the ability to relate with people and the ability to observe the dynamics within groups and the organization. Thirdly, the HR person must have the capability to influence the group dynamics. This is extremely important because the authority lies mostly with the line managers and the HR person has to rely on his personality and influencing abilities to get the work done.

But the key to all this and acceptance, dependability, reliability, and credibility lies in the extent to which the HR is immersed in the business and in the issues and challenges that people in the line function and the organization faces. Immersion is the key.

6

Cultural Routes to Excellence:
The LG Experience

Dialog with Yasho Verma, COO, LG Electronics, India

Interviewer: *According to you what are the few trends that are emerging in the landscape of business and in the architecture of organizations in the world and in India?*

Dr Yasho Verma: I very strongly believe that business is no more business. It is war, either you win or you lose. Over the past few years we have seen some interesting developments. We were always given to understand that giants take over dwarfs. But now it is dwarfs who are taking over the giants. Tata steel having a global market share of less than double digits took over Corus which had more than 20% of market share. Arcelor's take over by Mittal is now a pretty well documented experience. Similar was the leasing of Electrolux brand, which few years ago was number one in consumer durables in Europe to a small company in India called Videocon. So any organization which is more flexible, which can dance faster and which can move quicker is the winner. This is the challenge for the global organizations, for the CEOs, and for the HR.

Now coming back to some of the trends in the corporate world, I will give one example. IBM had its PC division which was making losses and hence got sold off to a Chinese company called Lenovo. Today, the CEO and Chairman of Lenovo is from one country, COO is from another country, CFO from another continent and CTO from still another continent. Earlier we used to say that a certain company is an Indian company, is a European company etc. But in this case we do not know anymore whether it is a Chinese company or a global company. A bigger question is what values or whose values should it have. Ideally, it should have global industrial values to match the global competition. This is a very big challenge. I will give another example. There used to be a comic serial in Disney Channel called the Higglytown heroes. Every week it used to come out with an episode. The writers of the serial were separated by almost 1,000 km from each other. The editors, animators, and script writers were from all over the world in Los Angeles, San Francisco, Bangalore, Tokyo, and Shanghai. And all their work used to be coordinated on a minute-to-minute basis so that in a week, a full half an hour episode comes out. It posed a huge challenge to all the conventional notions of organizational design. This is the new global organizational structure. What would be the implications of this structure on the concept of leadership, communication, and all the human processes? Another emerging trend is in the context of change management. WPP is amongst the largest advertisement company's in the world. They decided that now we should have an open culture and the first thing they did was they broke all the walls whereupon everyone started to work in a hall. This was a new way of how to manifest change: show it physically. The example of Jack Welch and the way he turned around GE is well known. But when he retired, he chose his successor, Jeff Immelt who was known to be quite different from him in terms of his thought process and style of working. This we were told, and I was in Cottonville, USA at that time, was because Jack Welch was convinced that if GE was to have any future, than it had to break free from its past and that can happen only if the CEO was absolutely different from him.

Interviewer: *What should organizations do if it has to survive and move to the next orbit of performance? And what should be the role of HR in that process?*

Dr Yasho Verma: Now when I stated that business is no more business and that it is war, then it must be understood that war is not won or lost because of equipment, weaponry, and logistics. The most important thing is passion, commitment to the cause, commitment to the purpose, and excellence. Those who lose they get killed and this is what is now happening to the organizations. In this process of building a culture of excellence, the role of HR is extremely crucial. For, it is because of them that a culture is created and passion is generated. But if change has to happen then HR must be at the centre stage and be a part of the mainstream, talking in the language of business which those who run the business can understand. If they are dealing with manufacturing, they should talk in their language, they should not talk in their HR jargons. In case, they do so and people in other divisions do not understand their language, HR would never be in the mainstream and would be marginalized in the change program. Just because HR is not there does not mean change in the organization will not happen. The only thing that will happen would be that the HR would also be reduced to playing a peripheral role in the organization.

The second element which is very important for any organization to succeed is innovation. Innovation requires humility. The greatest regret that Einstein had was that because of his arrogance he did not accept the importance of quantum physics and therefore could not work on it. Innovation also requires passion and dedication. If HR professionals of today think they will work 9 to 5, five days a week and have a fantastic work life and at the end of the day be very innovative and excel in the career, then they are living in a fools' paradise. I don't think these two things go together. We cannot say I will innovate from 9 to 5, five days a week and I am committed to it. I think this commitment has to be lived with, it has to be imbibed. In LG we promote innovation differently. Our R &D people produce innovation only because we create conditions in which people are put together as a team in a room with all facilities, all medium of entertainments, and where they can just dream and think innovations and work on it. Innovation has to be lived in. So innovative excellence, I think, has to be lived with and it has to be imbibed. The challenge for the HR is how to create that passion and how to create that culture.

Thirdly, organizations can succeed in the next orbit only when they have the capability to execute their strategy. Indeed, it is not good enough to just create a strategy. Execution is more important. It is this that makes us go ahead even though the strategy is imitated—in the world without barriers and boundaries, this is faster than ever before. Indeed innovations can be copied but the spirit of innovation is well nigh impossible to copy. This is the reason why even when our employees were poached by our competitors in the belief that they will similarly innovate for the new company, innovations over there did not happen. I think one of the most important characteristic in an organization is its culture. And culture is not about strategizing but an outcome of strategy execution. There is this interesting piece in the book called "Winning" by Jack Welch where he states that he did not spend so much time strategizing that before the train starts from the station, you know your competitor is already there. Indeed it was all intuitive. The moment we felt that it would work, we used to go out and implement it. It is true that there were times when he realized that the strategy pursued was wrong, but then unless and until one executes the strategy one will never know and the moment we came to know that there was a flaw we would tweak our strategy. Execution was always the focus for Jack Welch.

Then is the ability of the organization to manage change especially the one that is innovative and that hits at the base of vested interests. I will give you one example. Three years back in LG India we decided that we will now have a different way of selling and marketing. We called it the GTM method (Go to Market method.). I was made the sponsor of that change. Now GTM basically believes in bringing science into the art of selling. It proposed that there should be a scientific basis of selling. For example, if you were giving trade discount in India, it is called a scheme; now you were required to provide scientific basis to that scheme. Now, business, as I said, is also war; it is a power game in which whether you will win or lose in negotiations depends upon the power of your brand. But you can win in the long run only when there is a win-win relationship with other stakeholders' viz. the trade partner and the customer. That was the basis on which we decided we will have GTM. However, initially our sales people rejected it. They were called, they were told what the concept is, they were explained and they said it cannot happen. If there is a powerful trade partner, let us say X and he gets 30 percent of the scheme, then why will he settle for 25 percent of the scheme. There was another reason why the sales personnel opposed it. Every month the sales team had a target. So at the beginning of the month and when there used to be trade discounts he would dump the product, and then by the month end he would try to meet the shortfall in target achievement by dumping even more by giving the trade partner some more discount.

This thing had to change. I believe we succeeded in bringing about the change only because we did certain essential things. Let me state them.

I think change happened only because we communicated it 20–25 times—continuously, persistently, and consistently. This has to be communicated differently in different situations but as long as communication is happening, it helps to break down the resistance.

Secondly, change in the values of the organization has also to be repeatedly communicated because the success of LG, especially in the past three years, had given rise to a lot of arrogance amongst the marketing and sales team about their selling strategy for LG India. They were so blinded by their success, they could not see that the market dynamics were changing and buyers' behavior was also changing. Earlier consumers used to buy products during festivals, marriages, and other joyous occasions. But now people buy products whenever they have the money, festivals, and auspicious times notwithstanding. The purchase of consumer has become flat over the year. This was what GTM was all about.

Then change management also requires a short-term usage of force to overcome resistance and to show the viability of the alternative proposed. I will give an example. Three years back, we had adopted a strategy: premium marketing and low price selling. After some time, our market shares became high, reach became wider, and extraction higher but all at the cost of our premium branding. So we intervened. For instance, around 20 percent of my sale happens during the Diwali festival. In 2007, we resolved that we will not give any gifts. This was the decision we took at the top management level. All the sales and marketing people said we cannot sell without a gift. We also said we will not give discounts on price and in about a year, we came out with good products and increased our prices which was higher by 10–12 percent, as compared to the nearest premium brand product of the competitor. Till just three days before Diwali, our billing was around ₹200 crore, whereas, a year back it was ₹1,000 crore. We knew that the dealers were not accepting the change, they were not even willing to sell our products and our sales people were not even pushing the sales. At that time I was heading HR, my CEO was in Korea and my Sales and Marketing Head was also in Korea. This is when my CEO called me from Korea and instructed me to ensure that the sales teams push the products down the channel. So I called the sales team and told them in so many words as to why they have to push and what will happen if they do not. The stick worked. In a single day we clocked record sales of about ₹300 crore. We eventually broke the previous year record of sales during the Diwali time. So without giving gifts, making the prices 10–12 percent higher, the myth of the sales people—that it is gifts and lower prices that makes your brand sell— were totally shattered. Indeed our prices were even 15 percent higher than that of Sony and we started enjoying 45 percent market share as against 32 percent of Sony, in 2007. This example is to understand that at times the classical way of making change accepted works. But this can only be for a short while. After that if the concept is useful and once people see that it is delivering better, they will embrace the change wholeheartedly.

This also showed the viability of the GTM and the science behind it. The science was that you have to study the consumer continuously rather than study the trade partner and believe the colored feedback they give. For any organization, the moment of truth of their product or services is the customer. And his expectations has to be met and exceeded at every moment of time right from brand shops, ambience of the environment, knowledge of the counter staff and advisors, installation, after sales service and all. The time had totally changed, so the strategy also had to change. But change is very difficult. Besides, there is no one particular way that the whole organization will change because the culture from department to department is different. So different teams have to be handled in a different way; different individuals have to be handled in different way.

Interviewer: *You wrote a book called "Passion: The Untold Story of LG Electronics India." How did you change the culture, how did you build passion in an organization?*

Dr Yasho Verma: Changing the culture of an organization is extremely difficult. But then there are some things that we did to build the passion in LG India and I will share it with you.

When we started LG in India, I remember it was a green field project. We used to work for 14–18 hours a day in a green field project where it was a very normal thing to work for about 2–3 hours. We established 18 branches in three months. Our closest competitor did the same thing in two and a half years. They did it about two years before us. There were two global consultants who came to study the Indian market before LG started its operations in India. They had predicted that if LG starts in 1997, they will be able to make profit for the first time only in the year 2005, and that they will have a turnover of about ₹1000–1500 crore in the year 2005. We started in 1997. In 1997, we broke even in the first year and we had a turnover of ₹225 crore. In 1998, it was ₹500 crore and this year we will be around ₹19,000 crore. I think where the consultants made their biggest mistake was that they filled up all the attributes and the parameters in their own business model and forgot three factors which are the most critical things: people, passion, and the processes. The excellence of people, the creation of passion, and excellence of processes were the factors that made LG India the game changer.

I'll give examples of a couple of things that we did in LG to create passion and to create excellence. LG had decided that in India, the local people will run Indian operations and as such two persons, VP, Human Resources and Head, Sales and Marketing will be Indians. The manufacturing and finance person will be FSE (Foreign Service Executives) meaning a person coming from the home country. The job of the FSE will be to coordinate with Korea and to set the processes for manufacturing, quality, and accounting. However, the day-to-day decisions will be taken by the locally recruited General Managers. This is how it started and we started to work in May from a half complete office in Badarpur without any AC. I remember we used to take three sets of shirts and two sets of change clothes because there was no AC. We had just fans, sweat, spare clothes, and our passion. And we worked. The passion that we had was because we were empowered. I have a very strong belief that if people get truly empowered and have the power of taking decisions which can influence the area of working, they become more passionate and engaged. I also believe that the most important way of training people is by giving them power and holding them accountable.

Another interesting incident was when we started we recruited people from lot of our competitors. We had wanted quick results and so we took people who can just come and from next day start delivering. Now the biggest challenge which we had initially in 1997 was that we did not have an LG culture. So if some employees had come from BPL, Onida, Videocon or for that matter any other company, their thought process and their way of working would differ from the other. To make matters worse, each thought that their's was the best way to do things. As a result conflicts started in the organization. India itself has so many cultures and then there was another element of the FSEs and Indians. So, cultural conflicts and then the value conflicts became rampant. Things became very political in the organization. It was during this time that my CEO advised me that the best way to stop people from politics and conflicts is by increasing their targets by 150 percent more. They will be so much involved in doing their job that half of the conflicts will go down. Let me tell you this worked. Everyone got involved in work. There was another thing that we did. Earlier, whenever we had to take decisions we would get into differences arising from the clash between BPL's way of doing things, Onida's way of doing things etc. We decided that we will take decisions by consensus. This resulted in a lot of lobbying and politicking. Once again the CEO gave me a practical solution. He said wherever there will be two human beings, there will be politics. So just go ahead and take very quick decisions. It will reduce the element of politics because once the decision is there and it is being executed, everyone goes back to implement it. So he said take an issue and set a deadline that this issue will have to be decided in 24 hours. After the lapse of this time, if the decision is not taken, the authority will decide. It also does not matter whether it is a good decision or a bad decision, because one can always go back and fix the bad decision based upon the feedback.

In order to improve team work we introduced trekking. This trekking was carried out in the Annapurna Mountains in Nepal and it was an extremely tough trek. People were sent in groups and we usually used to send those people who used to bicker a lot with each other. This had a great effect. In a span of just a week, I had teams that were completely bonded with each other. I believe, that if you want a team, create a crisis.

TPI-50 (Total Productivity Innovation-50 percent) was an important mechanism by which a culture of learning and excellence was strengthened in LG. We had TPI-50 for the first seven years. It meant that every person, process, and system had to improve its efficiency by 50 percent in one year's time. After seven years, this TPI-50 was reduced to TPI-30 implying that efficiency now has to be improved by 30 percent. The first time I got my target, I complained. But I achieved it. Next year again I got the target, I again cribbed like everybody else and again I achieved it. An important learning that, I got was that if you think in the same way, you think achieving even 5 percent improvement in efficiency is impossible. On the other hand, if you change your thought process, a 50 percent improvement is easily possible. We in LG have given an example of this. Give a challenge, set the focus for people, give them a direction and leave them free to decide. I think this was the crux for changing the culture. I remember after seven years or eight years, the CEO started making a statement in the press and other forums that he never believed in it earlier but now he does, that the most important thing in our organization is not its product, not its marketing, not its brand, but it is its culture. If you take any multinational like LG or any other, we have tremendous similarity in terms of our R & D, brand, and quality of people. The differentiator is just one: culture. That is the reason why one company has a market share of 30 percent and another has 18 percent.

I will give you another example of how we the built the culture of passion in LG. In 2004, four journalists from Forbes had come to us and said that we have identified LG India and we want to write an article. They studied LG for about one month. At the end, when they come out with the results and conclusion, they wrote a two page article in that magazine. The head line was "How LG conquered India? And they had only two points. They said, that firstly the passion of LG Employees is so high that they have changed everything and secondly, that we had changed the payment terms of trade partners. The conclusion, that in LG, people felt that we can change anything came from the passion that they had and this passion came from the empowerment, accountability, and training offered. We had this super 8 training in which the focus was on mindset change and this was the toughest training people can have like playing with snakes, running for 4–5 hours, sit ups 150 times for girls and doing unimaginable things like piercing a potato with straws etc. Another thing that we did was, we harnessed the energies of people by creating slogans which people were to shout at different occasions.

The result of creating this culture of excellence and this passion was that LG electronics in India grew on an average by 40 percent CAGR. In some months we even grew by even 80 percent and that was on a base of 10,000 crore. This year alone we would grow by almost 35 percent on the base of ₹19,000 crore.

Now for the first 10 years we created a culture and at that time work was everything. Then we realized that now we have to slow down, otherwise people will soon start burning out. So five years back we decided to have Sundays off. Under no conditions anybody whether in the factory or office would work on Sundays. I also created a position in the branch, of an HR mentor, whose job was now to coordinate and ensure that branches do not work on Sunday. Despite that I saw that people in their sales report mentioned some heavy sales on Sunday. I asked how could this be possible and confronted the branch managers. They assured me that nobody comes to the branch on Sunday and so people might be working from home and that when they called the staff on phone on Sunday, they were all there in their homes. Now I struck upon an idea. I told the branch manager next time you talk to these people at their homes on Sundays ensure that you also talk to their wife or children. So I announced the rule that from now on if my HR person was not able to talk to the wife or child of an employee on a Sunday, we would deduct two days salary of that person. In another four weeks, the sales went down to zero. And I know that after six months or eight months my HR people were the most popular people in the family of the sales people.

One learning that can be drawn from the above illustration is that change should not only be simple and small but even its execution should be done in the simplest way. Many a time change does not come through papers; because everyone is the boss in his own department and he thinks he knows the HR the best. Rather it has to come through in a strategic way and after that once the change has been brought, then it is the usefulness of the system that ensures its sustenance. The policy if it is useful will continue. But if it is not useful, you cannot continue it for long.

In a company which has nine regions and 49 branches all over India, how do you ensure that people when they are empowered to take decisions at different levels do not take erratic and mutually contradictory decisions. This is where the role of values becomes very important. The values should be identified. They should be put in a very simple and practical manner. Just saying that quality is the most important thing has no meaning. For manufacturing, quality should be in terms of usage of line, productivity, manpower etc. and even stopping the production line if you see a defect or an anomaly and rewarding a person for that. This is the only way people understand that quality is important for the organization. So the values must be communicated in the way people understand and the way it affects them.

Another thing that we did to communicate our values was through our vision statement. Unlike other places, we did not have a long prose on our vision. We decided that our vision should be short and measurable. We said LG should be no. 1. What does this no.1 mean? It means 35 percent market share; 5 percent profit and 80 percent top of the mind. This is the definition of being no.1 and this will be known to everybody and will be of meaning to everybody; only then they will know what no.1 is. Otherwise no.1 has no meaning. No.1 in HR means what should be the attrition rate in the company; how much should the engagement be etc.

We then used the performance appraisal system to ensure that organizational norms and values are accepted, the same way right across the organization. Sales personnel in LG were never worried about costs as much as they were worried about targets. They were all empowered, they had their own scheme budget, their own marketing budget and they used to decide. You also cannot take such decisions centrally and unilaterally. What we did was, we fixed certain things: your profits should be this much, scheme percentage should be this much, or your sale should have at least five percent contribution from premium products, 20 percent from middle line products and so on. This changed the attitude of the people.

To sum it up, values, communication of values, and performance parameters have to be very specific rather than general and focused on target population rather than on an entire organization. This was my learning. Finally, culture building happens only because of leadership. How the leadership conducts itself, is extremely crucial. I have always felt that in any organization where the HR processes, systems, interventions are very strong or very weak, 60–70 percent credit or discredit should be given to the CEO. An HR person, if he is very competent, can create interventions, he can try to create ownership but unless there is overt and covert blessing and backing of the CEO, he can never succeed. I believe that if an organization is very strong in HR, it is to some extent because of the HR professionals but to a larger extent it is because of the CEO.

Interviewer: *How could you do it? You don't get the CEO of your choice.*

Dr Yasho Verma: I will give you an example. I have seen my friend working in a group company where there were three brothers and he was very useful. All three brothers had different styles of managing. The elder brother was very humanistic in nature but not the person who believed in systems, processes etc. The second gentleman, the owner of his business, was very professional. The third one was a very young person, very immature and he was interested only in two to three things. So this friend of mine, whose intention was to professionalize the HR system, used to interact with the three brothers differently. He used to be professional with the second brother and humanistic with the first. As a result he became a confidante of the eldest brother and was able to push through all HR policies, strategies and interventions through the second brother. There is another friend of mine who worked with a CEO who was shrewd, ruthless, and who believed in short term. His belief was that if you survive today, you will survive tomorrow, you survive day after. He had no belief in HR. But soon he discovered that the HR person was well-versed in business and he started trusting him and his HR interventions. So in sum, if an HR person wants that there is ownership of his interventions, he should be seen as adding value in short-term and in the CEO's core things one way or the other. Only then can you get the confidence of your CEO.

Interviewer: *You made a powerful statement that in order to be global and transnational, the top management in such companies should also be truly global, heterogeneous, and diverse. Would this not be a big challenge? These people do not belong to you, they have their cultural biases and prejudices and they are also successful. So how can HR create that convergence?*

Dr Yasho Verma: I was talking to Dr. C.K. Prahalad. He had to come to LG to conduct training for us two to three years back. He was recounting his experience of consulting with a top organization and its globalization strategy. He said this company decided that in the first step, the local subsidiary will be headed by a local person. In the second step, the best, irrespective of his nationality, will be posted in any place and can head any operations. Secondly they decided that irrespective of their mother tongue, everybody was now to communicate in English. For the first few months everybody got secretaries who knew English. But sooner than later they had to learn. In LG, we have a top management which has been drawn from different parts of the world. Thus the CHO, CTO, CMO, CIO who are all at the level of CXOs, are from different countries. This diversity has thrown up great challenges, almost bordering on the point of being jingoistic. But this is overcome by the bigger realization that whenever any company becomes global and they do not get the best skilled person for different functions, they will not be able to survive properly. So one part of the problem was cultural. The other part is at the level of processes especially the assimilation process which assumes greater importance in a product, brand, and a technology dependent company. Then is the HR policy especially in terms of salary and compensation. This should be uniform. For, unless and until it is so, it will not be easy to transfer people from one place to another. So there has to be a global process in this matter. Finally, the global process must have flexibility and breadth to absorb local elements. Indeed, unless and until the global process is local and flexible, it cannot be strong and will not yield excellence.

Interviewer: *What do you think are some essential competencies which HR professionals must have if they are to enable their organization to move and succeed in the next orbit.*

Dr Yasho Verma: In the 1980s, I read an article which prophesized that the span of control of the boss will go up to be between 20–40 people rather than 6–8 people that we had studied in MBA schools. You can understand that I have about 25 people reporting to me and each of them have businesses in which they handle hundreds and thousands of crore. In any case, if a person reaches this position at the age of 40 and assuming that ideally he would have had joined the organization at the age of 25 and would have been transferred every two years, then he would have the experience of around seven to eight jobs. Out of these he would have a good knowledge of two to three jobs, and the other jobs he can just appreciate, provided these jobs have not become obsolete. For the rest and all other things he would have no knowledge. So what should be the attribute of such a manager? First, he should be a very good listener. Second, he should use his intuition, perception, and his impression to listen, sift, and absorb different suggestions. Third, he should have a very strategic mind. Fourth, he should have competencies to execute. And finally he should have perseverance.

As far as a HR manager is concerned, I think the following attributes and competencies are most imperative.

First, the people in HR should know the business day in and day out. If the organization is having meetings to discuss weekly manufacturing figures, weekly defects, weekly sales, weekly collection of money, the HR must be aware of the problems the business is facing. The figures should be on their finger tips.

Second, HR should know the language in which these different departments whether it is manufacturing or sales converse in.

Third, HR people should go directly to the people and talk to them. Emails must be barred for HR. I think the biggest threat to HR is their increasing proclivity to interact through mails. In the process in most of the organization, HR has lost its personal touch.

Fourth, HR must have perseverance. They should not leave a matter unattended for long. In LG, the line people complain that HR people have become like warriors. They come and they sit in my room for hours while I attend to my other matters, and then go back only when the decision is taken. Secondly, the line people also confess that even though they know that the HR person does not add value to their department, the very fact that they are there, they start talking about the problem and have a listener and a sympathizer and a sounding board and then have a solution.

Fifth, HR must respect personal matters and keep things confidential. When you are dealing with emotions of people, it should not be leaked. It also should not be politically used by HR to influence people, especially those who have shared their emotions with you. So HR should not become political. They should also refrain from giving value judgments on an issue.

Finally, HR must know the mindsets of the employees they are handling. I will give you two examples. In TATA steel, where I had worked earlier, we were told that if you have to know the workers go and have food with them in their village and in their houses. In LG, I have used the same concept, although in a much more simple and improvised form. We have created two systems. The first is of family ambassador and the second is of line guardianship. In the Line Guardianship system, every HR person has about 20 workers and some white collared people. Every 10 days they have to meet and talk on some issue either during tea time or at some other time. The objective is to know, understand, and appreciate the thought process of the employees. The second concept was that HR persons were to be family ambassadors for some workers and white collared employees. They are required to visit the family twice a year. They had the budget, they took gifts for the family and they would spend an evening with that family. With this we have the thinking of the entire family with regard to the LG, their personal and professional problems, and other general issues. Now it is important, that if somebody created an issue or left the organization and my HR coordinator who was his line guardian or family ambassador was not able to predict three months in advance, then I think that person has failed in discharging his duties. This for me is a matter of accountability too. For it is your job as an HR person to know the mindset of your employees, to analyze it, and respond to it. So these are some of the qualities which are very important for a HR manager.

Interviewer: *What are some of the problem with the HR people?*

Dr Yasho Verma: I think for the HR professionals, the biggest problem is that they interact on mails, they use HR jargon which nobody understands, they do not understand the business, they are not in the mainstream and yet they want power.

7

Kaleidoscope of Leadership: The Ageless Mantra

Dialog with Pritam Singh, Padam Shri and Professor of Eminence, Management Development Institute, Gurgaon

Interviewer: *Of late you have been talking about "towards the next orbit"; what do you mean by this?*

Dr Pritam Singh: The business world today has drastically changed. I will explain this with a couple of analogies. When I was in the USA, the whole business world was like my experience in America…you are driving on the American highway, cruising at the speed of 175 miles per hour. The horizon is very clear. There was no anxiety and no fear. That was the business scenario in that orbit. There was no competition, no anxiety, no fear, no need to introduce, and no need to reinvent. As far as the business scenario today is concerned, it is like driving your car somewhere in Chandni Chowk, full of crowds and a confusing mix of traffic, with everyone trying to get ahead. Then you see the red light and you stop your car. But when you stop the car you see something very peculiar and something very disturbing. That although the other cars around you have also stopped, the honking continues. This honking symbolizes the noise in the business world today. Then as the signal turns green and you start driving your big car, suddenly from nowhere a small car comes and dents your big car and despite all your efforts to catch it, the small car races away and loses itself in the crowd. I am using the words, small car and big car, symbolically. Today the smaller players like smaller cars are denting bigger players, the bigger cars. So L.N. Mittal dented Arcelor, Kumar Mangalam Birla dented Novelis, Sunil Bharti Mittal dented Zain in Africa, and Tata acquired Corus etc. This is the peculiarity of the business scenario today. It is the smaller players who are acquiring the bigger players. Indeed it seems that ideas are bigger than size in the corporate world. The challenge today is not that bigger players do not have any future, but that if the bigger players want to survive in this Darwinian dance then they cannot rely on their size anymore. They need to have the characteristics of the small players, characteristics in terms of being lean, nimble, quick, agile, and responsive.

Another facet of the business world relates to the importance and criticality of managing constituency. Today, the success of the corporate and leadership in the corporate world is all about being in tune with their constituency, being immersed in them and managing, and nurturing them. I will explain this with another analogy. Today I straddle three generations: as a son, father and grandfather. I still remember when I was a child, I was rather curious and had a very inquiring mind. At that age, whenever I used to ask my father any question it was based upon the presumption that he was a reservoir of knowledge and wisdom, which he definitely was, and that "daddy knows everything." After some years, I got married and by this time the electronic era had begun. A household was known by the number and variety of electronic gadgets it had. Now I had another streak in me and this was to dabble with things, with electronic gadgets. True to all dabblers I would know how to open up and dismantle the electronic gadgets but had a very limited ability of putting things back together. It was because of this nature, I must have had spoilt almost half a dozen gadgets in my house. But I was never short of trying. One day when I was involved in all this, I overheard my younger son, who was talking to my wife, say something very interesting, "Mom, you would be glad to know that even daddy knows how to operate these gadgets…" So I saw one drastic shift: from "daddy knows everything" to "even daddy knows." The thinking of the constituency has changed. But the millennium child is a different child altogether. And I soon found out. One day I was sitting with my grandson who is based in America. Somehow, my daughter had made him believe that I was a very wise man and that if he had anything to discuss, then I would be just the right person to talk to. So he was talking to me and then he asked me a question to which I did not have any answer. As such I asked him why don't you ask your father this question. Surely he will have the answer for you. Pat came the reply, "But he (daddy) doesn't know anything." That day life turned a different circle. From "daddy knows everything" to "even daddy knows" and now "daddy knows nothing", the constituency revealed a tectonic shift in terms of its mindset and behavior. It is this constituency, people extremely different from you and with a mindset that questions, that doubts and that is configured differently in terms of its attitudes and values that now has to be managed, made to understand and believe, and nurtured to explore, perform and realize.

Now if you put all the three things together, a business world full of noise, small fish swallowing the big fish and the millennial constituency, the organizations and also the individuals, the leaders must have the capability to move from one orbit to another orbit, from one horizon to another horizon and connect them all together. Unless and until they have both simultaneity and the ability to integrate, I don't think that they will be able to survive.

"Towards the next orbit", is not about making money, not about being prosperous or necessarily about winning. Instead it is a matter of survival. It is this which is on stake. There is this famous rule of the jungle where both the deer and the tiger when they get up early in the morning ask themselves a question: "How can I run faster than the other?" And then they practice, they adapt, and prepare to run faster than the other. For if they don't, one would be killed and the other would die of hunger. This is the reality, the new context for the organizations and leaders today. If the organizations and leaders do not move to the next orbit, they will not be able to survive long. "Towards the next orbit" is not a slogan, it's a mindset a way of life.

Interviewer: *What are the other facets and nuances of business in the next orbit?*

Dr Pritam Singh: The contors of business earlier was characterized by "Vertical Integration." It was a very time tested business model which espoused that everything in the business world should be vertically integrated. As per this dictum, if you are into steel, then you must have mines, you must have the power-plant and you should actually have the steel-making unit. Even in the telecom sector, the diktat of vertical integration ran across all companies. And then Airtel came up with a new organizational architecture. Today companies are moving from vertical integration to virtual integration. Companies are saying, "We should do what we are best at and where we are not the best in, we should outsource." So this outsourcing model has become a way of life in the business world. The business model has now changed. This model is also not easy to manage. For now instead of managing just your organization, you now have to manage your entire partner ecosystem. Virtual integration involves many players none of which belong to you; yet each one of them is an inextricable part of your family.

Another thing which I find today is that when people join an organization, they don't join for their life time. The concept of life-long employment has become a myth that belongs to a different era now. The concept of loyalty to the organization now is a phenomenon of the past. This is a paradigm buster. Commitment must now be seen in terms of not time but what value people are contributing. It is not anymore important to talk about retaining people, it is more important to create a situation, a culture where an individual is motivated and enabled to give his best to the organization. That is now the new reality.

Linked to the above phenomena is the emergence of a nomadic class of employees. These are employees who would not like to work in just one organization, they would rather be associated with four to five of them at the same time. This is the new consulting class, the idea giving class who work with multiple organizations. The concept of loyalty becomes even more tenuous and the notion of commitment has been transformed to mean being transient and ephemeral.

Fourthly, the way the whole organization used to think about strategy and strategic positioning has undergone drastic revision. Earlier the norm was to operate on a mass scale; then it became differentiating by doing mass scale customization. Today something very interesting has started to happen. Companies have started to realize that people don't buy the product anymore, but rather, people buy identities. Now strategy, positioning, and marketing have to be directed towards individual customization. The companies which are marketing identity will survive. Those companies which are marketing products are fated to die sooner or later. Companies are no more in the product business, instead they are into the business of lifestyle. They are the only ones who will survive and who can win now.

Above all, the very nature of competition has changed in the new orbit. It is no more just fierce. It is different. It is a war of a different kind. Earlier people in the battlefield were aware of who was their enemy, which territory or domain was at stake, which battle to fight and which not to, and from where the arrows and the bullets will come. Today the contours of competition are such where one does not know which terrain is he trying to capture, who is his enemy and from where the bullet will come. The only thing that you can be convinced about is that some fellow, sitting somewhere in his garage is manufacturing the bullet that will be shot at you. From where the shooting will come, from where the bullet will come, it's very difficult to know. The world has become a global minefield. We now need a totally different kind of organization. An organization that is like a radar, that has an alert antenna, that is like the warrior prince, Arjuna, who was capable of shooting enemies with the sound of the words. That is the kind of organization that is needed today, drastically revised, drastically re-modeled and fully aligned with the emerging realities.

Interviewer: *You are unarguably the foremost thinker and trainer on leadership in the country now. What do you think has been the impact of the changing reality on leadership especially in terms of both theory and practice? What kind of leadership do you think we require in this orbit?*

Dr Pritam Singh: Well, I think that one basic paradigm that has been firmly put in place in these turbulent and concept defying times is that of constituency. While it has been a much researched concept in electoral politics and political science, it has not been talked about in the arena of leadership. I think in the present day reality, constructs like stakeholders, hold limited relevance. This is because, great organizations and great leaders have realized their greatness only because of the way they have nurtured their constituencies. Much like what happens in electoral politics, those who nurture their constituency repeatedly win, and those who don't, they sooner or later go out of circulation.

Mahatma Gandhi is the primeval example of somebody who understood this concept well and used it to telling advantage. Even before he launched the non-cooperation movement, Gandhi went around India to understand his constituency. This is what the good kings in the earlier times used to do: move around in their kingdom in disguise. The underlying paradigm remained the same: "let me try and understand my constituency." Today this constituency for a lot of leaders has become global in nature. Therefore, today a leader must have global vision, global wisdom, and a global strategy. They must understand whatever is happening in not only their own business, but also in their own country along with what is happening in other businesses in the other corners of the world. Leaders must have a global perspective and a capability to understanding global nuances and global contours of the business. Jack Welch, Larry Basidy, Ratan Tata, Kumar Mangalam Birla, K. V. Kamath etc, all those leaders whom we talk about in our classroom and who have been celebrated, have been reputed to have a tremendous sensibility to understand about the globe. Indeed if business has become global, then you must have a global perspective. Earlier organizations were capable of surviving without even thinking about the globe. Today, organizations which are unable to influence the globe would struggle to survive. When I met Kumar Mangalam Birla, he said that "he saw the world as a business arena..." He didn't see India as a business arena. And his famous statement was that "when I'm not allowed to do business in India, I can do my business in Philippines, Thailand and Egypt" and that's how Aditya Birla Group became a global company. The same strategy was also used by Ratan Tata.

There is another aspect of leadership on which I have a slightly different opinion than those who have been writing about leadership. Leaders should and are supposed to be strategic thinkers and the formulation goes that they should spend 90 percent of their time in strategic thinking and the rest in others. In my experience, as both an academic leader and a consultant-trainer-researcher who has worked with around 400 CEOs in India and the world, I have found that great leaders have been those who have the remarkable ability to connect the horizon with the ground reality, always connect. They have the ability to at once fly 40,000 ft. above and walk effortlessly on the ground. This they are able to do because they do not only think about the strategy but also its execution. They believe that strategy is not strategic formulation. It is not just about crafting strategy. It is about execution as well. Indeed, I believe it is more about implementation. Everyone wants to dream, everyone wants to be a leader, everyone wants to have the market share, but it is those who are capable of implementing, converting their dreams into action, who win in the corporate world. I think there is this instance in Mahabharata where Dhristrashtra asked Sanjaya, "Who is going to win in the great war?" And Sanjaya answered, "It's the Pandavas who are going to win...because Pandavas have got Krishna and they have got Arjuna; the perfect amalgamation of thought and action." I personally feel that this division of thought and action, between thought-leaders and action-leaders needs to be re-examined if one wants execution, speed and excellence. Great corporate leaders are someone like A.M. Naik who is as much a shop floor man, as he is capable of flying at a height of 40,000 ft. Similar is the case with K.V. Kamath or for that matter Sajjan Jindal who would go right inside the plant and start instructing people to do this or that.

I believe in India it is even more important to have this amalgamation. For, Indians want to see their leader in the battlefields. We have this great need... "the king must be visible." This is the reason why I think in the Indian context, what people have been talking about as the shepherd leadership or war general leadership or servant leadership alone and in isolation will not work. In the Indian context, leadership is all about leading from the front like a general in the war, leading from behind like a shepherd leader and also serving your constituency like the servant leader. A symbiosis of all three is the only way leadership can be defined. Thought must be integrated and manifested in action. This is the new gestalt of leadership which nobody had earlier talked and written about. It is holistic and complete.

Today if a leader has to survive, grow, excel and win, he must have the capability of out-of-box thinking and creativity. This does not mean that all leaders in order to succeed must be out-of-box thinkers or entrepreneurial innovators. They may not be so and this is perfectly fine. But they must under all circumstances create a culture of entrepreneurial innovation. It is for this reason alone that empowerment becomes important or empowerment for innovation becomes important. In the context of the Indian society which has been extremely hierarchical, control centric, centralizing and restrictive, empowerment would be frame breaking, and initially disruptive too. But in the long run this is the only way innovations will happen;

only way organizations would become innovative and succeed in the next orbit. Indian leaders have just no way out but to learn to empower, to decentralize, to facilitate and to enable. In my forthcoming book on Change Maestros in which I have interviewed the seven leaders who have defined business in India, each one of them is celebrated for being empowering. Empowering has been the mantra. Empowering for what? Empowering with the accountability for innovating, performing, and excelling. In all the writings on good leaders and bad leaders and toxic and non-toxic leaders, the thing that differentiates them is their ability to trust, to delegate, to empower, to enable, and to achieve.

The fourth essential trait the leader should have is the capability to see opportunities in everything. The one thing that differentiates the great leaders from the non-great leaders is that the great leaders see opportunities in the problems. For them, if there is a problem there is an opportunity. So that's why the great leaders are always ready to confront problems. There have been several times we have seen in our leadership development workshops—that it is stretched targets that makes people become innovative, collaborative and achieving. Just like henna which gives better color on the palm only when it is grounded, leaders also become better when they undergo periodic trials of fire. These are the times when the leader displays an opportunity sensing mind. Indeed, those who are great leaders have this unique competency.

The fifth point about leadership is that there is a need to understand that "there is a man behind the gun." It is important to appreciate the importance, criticality for the functioning and outcome of the organization of even the lowest functionary in the organization. In steel plants at different moments of time the trolley man is more important than the plant manager. Seen thus leadership is not about the power of mind. The western world has talked about the power of mind. I find that leadership is more about the power of the soul. If there is a leadership crisis in the world, it is not because we have not used the power of the mind. Intellectually people have become sharper, have more information and more data and yet there is a crisis. This is because we have not incorporated the power of the soul in our concepts of management and leadership. And I think that there is a need to integrate the soul and mind especially when human beings are, in all mythologies, in all religions, an integral part of God and have the same element of divinity. It is only with soul force that the leader can motivate others to realize their immense potentiality, to contribute and to excel. This does not mean that a leader must ask a bird to run and a rabbit to fly. A leader must perceive the potential and talent idiosyncratic to a person. This is the only way a leader can be a mentor, a coach and a shaper.

Another thing which I could see about the leadership and that is extremely important is that all good leaders believe in the proverb of "Satyamev Jayate" …the truth ultimately prevails. Jim Collins in his monumental work has shown that the companies that have survived right through the century had one common fundamental principle and that was all of them were ethical. It is only when you are ethical that you can serve your customers and your people. This is because ethics gives courage. Indeed this is the reason one finds that all the great leaders who have been talked about have been reported to have a soul that is honest, truthful, and ethical.

The last point which I would like to mention is that somewhere the "winning streak like Olympians" is really important for a leader. Leaders are like Olympians who participate in the Olympics to break their records and by the time they reach home, they take a decision that "next time, I am going to break my own record." If you read about all the great leaders, they behave like Olympians. They don't compete with others. They compete with themselves because they want to break their own records. They have a tremendous, restless, insatiable appetite to grow, to win and to keep on winning. Great leaders always create the second curve because they are never satisfied with the curve that they have created and always want to break that curve.

These are some of my reflections about the kind of leaders which we require now to move to the second orbit.

Interviewer: *Almost about 10 years ago, you wrote an article in which you gave the five mantras of leadership. Are these mantras still relevant today? If no, then what modifications would you like to make.*

Dr Pritam Singh: I would like to say that when I wrote, it was mantras to lead, mantras to galvanize, mantras to excel. So let me talk about these five mantras and find out how relevant they are today.

My first mantra was "Himalayan vision creates Himalayan energy." If I think about the Himalayan vision, we can talk about the Himalayan ambition, the oceanic drift. It is very much relevant today. When you think about Sajjan Jindal, he's talking about "romancing with limited resources" he's never satisfied; so I find that dream, vision and mission has its importance. Even though ambition has not been viewed very positively by the psychologists but the burning desire to prove, to contribute, to succeed and to win is extremely important. All the seven leaders whom I interviewed in my book showed the burning desire to make contributions for the organization and for the country. Indeed their patriotism is inextricably linked with the desire to create a winning organization.

The second mantra is that "life begins from death." I think by saying that "life begins from death" symbolically we wanted to communicate that there should be "creative destruction." I think that if you try to read the great deeds of all the seven leaders whom we have interviewed, the great story of Jack Welch, Larry Basidy or of Jeff Immelt, you will find something very interesting that they have been destroying and they have been creating. Today this mantra has become even more very powerful. Because, unless we destroy, we can't create. Creative destruction is now the only way to change, to move forward and to excel.

The third mantra is more individual related. I had said that "life is equal to contribution." I think people don't remember you by your position, the power you have got, or for how much wealth you have people remember you only for what contributions you have made. So that's why, we wrote that the mathematics of life is contribution. So to become a great leader you must contribute something, as people look up to you for the contributions you have made. I think that all the great leaders have made contributions. That is why we say that those who contribute are immortal. If Gandhi is immortal today it's because of his contribution and Gandhi did not occupy any position. The same is true for Lincoln, Jefferson, Churchill, Mandela and all the great leaders whom we revere. Those who live for others, they never die. This is why the constituency concept of leadership, which we talked about as a necessary attribute of a leader in the next orbit, has become extremely important.

Another mantra which we said at that time was "what a leader does, people follow." Even today I think that this mantra is very relevant. Even if the situation has changed now, I feel more intensely about the relevance of the mantras today. This is a different world. In this millennium people have knowledge, people want transparency, people watch you all the time, people are impatient and people desire responsiveness and accountability. So all in all, each of the mantras that we talked about in 1997–98 are still very relevant and very pertinent. Those mantras are even today very common and pertinent.

Interviewer: *Any mantra that you would like to add now to these original mantras?*

Dr Pritam Singh: I would like to say one mantra which weaves all these mantras. This is the super mantra or apex mantra. It is thus: "Leader must have the capability to look beyond, to look around and look within." This is the all encompassing mantra.

Those who are great leaders and would like to move to the next orbit must look for tomorrow; those who look for "tomorrow," they make their "today" but those who look at their "today," they make their "today" but spoil their "tomorrow" and those who look at "yesterday," they spoil their "today" as well as "tomorrow." That is why "looking beyond" is important. Unfolding the future into the present is important. This is what all the great leaders did in the past and this is what the seven leaders I have interviewed for my book also are adept at doing.

The second thing that I find is that great leaders should have the capability to know what is happening around. Happening around means in any arena: politics, economy, society, etc. You must know what is happening around you. For, if you don't look around, you will be unable to identify the person who is manufacturing the bullet to shoot you. While in the long run everyday dies, you will die in the short run itself. So looking around from a business intelligence point of view becomes very important.

And the last point that I want to make is that to be a leader, you must be reflective. You must rewind five minutes before you go to sleep, and think: how has been my day? Have I done something great, have I repeated the same thing which I have been repeating? Is it a repetition of chores, mundane activities or creative activities? So that's why I think that reflection is important. You become a very evolving and flowering human being. You blossom when you meditate andwhen you reflect. So reflection is important. Gandhi was a reflective person. Kumar Mangalam Birla is a very reflective person. I also see that K.V. Kamath is a very reflective person. So reflection is important. You can call it business meditation. You can call it reflection. You can call it thinking.

In sum, these three phrases summarize all the earlier mantras. In order to lead, in order to excel, you must unfold the future into the present, look around and look within. All great leaders do this. And that is precisely the reason why they became great. This is the capability that has to be developed.

Interviewer: *You have talked extensively about your book and we have heard a lot about that book in which you have interviewed the seven corporate giants in India, the great corporate change maestros. What are some of the essential elements of the kaleidoscope of leadership that has emerged in this book?*

Dr Pritam Singh: One has been the "Satyamev Jayate" meaning, the belief and the value that truth shall ultimately triumph. All believed in that.

The second one is a "deep hunger" and being ruthlessly ambitious about business results. They would always keep on moving, relentlessly pursuing and not relaxing. In fact, I remember very well, that Sunil Bharti Mittal had said that when I work for 24 hrs, I relax; my working for 24 hrs is a relaxation exercise.

The third is that they all are highly patriotic. They all said that the 21st century belongs to us and they can be seen to be using their own organizations to create a new India. So perhaps 15 years back when I wrote, no one talked about patriotism, no one said that the 21st century belonged to us. Today they all said that this is our century and we must use our organizations to create a new India. I discerned in all of them a dream, a passion, a burning desire to create a new India, a successful India, an economically super-power India.

Fourthly, all of the leaders were "out-of-the-box" thinkers. You approached them with a problem and they were capable of connecting the dots. They all demonstrated a remarkable capability to sense size, divergent forces, connections, patterns, and all that.

Fifth, all these leaders had a very elephantine memory. They had all the nitty-gritty details of their business on their fingertips. They are all reputed to be a storehouse of information.

They all believed in people power. They said you can imitate technology, imitate processing, imitate culture, imitate vision but you can't imitate people. They live the words, "Give me my own men and I'll build another force."

These were some of the unique nuances on leadership which I could glean while talking to these change masters.

Interviewer: *What is your message to the HR professionals?*

Dr Pritam Singh: I have this basic philosophy, "No philosopher can be a great philosopher without being a great king and no king can be a great king without being a great philosopher." This is also a dictum, an adage expounded by Plato and Chanakya. The biggest problem that I see about HR people is that they have philosopher's mind but not the mindset of a king. They don't understand the king's role or the nuances of the kingdom. They don't understand business or business strategy. So my first message to the HR professional is that they should try to become a philosopher king. This means what? It means they must be able to integrate their HR role with the business.

Second, I feel HR professionals must develop self esteem. They must have a sense of pride in what they are doing and their functions. Chanakya never thought like that. It is a reality that Chandragupta Maurya was a great king only because of Chanakya. Can we become Chanakya? Chanakya was not a philosopher. He was a great king. He had a king's mind along with a philosophical bent of mind. However, most of the time HR has been found to be woefully lacking in their ability to integrate their role with business. That is the precise reason why in many organizations, people from line functions become HR heads. This is because business functionaries, including CEOs, feel, rightfully so, that what is the unique value addition that is done by HR to the organization? If it is recruitment, anybody can do recruitment and if they cannot do, then outsource it; they do training, anyone can provide that too. Professors can provide training, and if they talk about 360^0 performance appraisals, again anyone can do it. One can call people from outside to do that. So they conclude that whatever these HR professionals can do, anyone can do. This is quite unlike the finance or the marketing or the operations who do things, which cannot be done by anybody else. HR professionals must thus ask themselves this question, "What value addition do we bring to the organization? What value addition must we bring to the organization to justify our role? They must ask, "How do I see my role?" You will be shocked to know, I have done a lot of workshops for many companies. Quite strangely I do not see HR people participating in that. It seems that they feel that learning is the responsibility of the line fellows and that it is not their responsibility. So they neither know business nor do they learn business.

And the last point which I would like to say is this. I am taking the liberty of saying this because I belong to this community. I think we live under some kind of intellectual colonialism or American colonialism. We mindlessly hear, read and apply all the American junks that are peddled to us by the marketing geniuses, as the wisdom to think, run and win in business. It is now incumbent that HR people sit together and discuss what new techniques they have been talking about. How long can they import something like 360 degrees appraisal, assessment center, psychometric instruments and apply it unthinkingly in their organizations. What is their contribution in all this? I think it is high time that the HR professionals interact with management schools to know what new things are happening and keep on demanding whether all that can be done in their organization or not. HR must become business oriented.

8

Towards the Next Orbit: Wisdom for HR Professionals

Subir Verma

"It is a perfectly imperfect world"

THE EMERGING BUSINESS LANDSCAPE

The landscape of business is undergoing tectonic shifts of such great magnitude that it has unleashed a repeated tsunami of change for the corporate world. Much of these shifts have been triggered by globalization, now a *fait accompli*. Today the business world is witnessing a homogeneity of consumption choices, with seamless production processes cutting across borders and walls on the back of spatially mobile western based MNCs and TNCs, globally integrated market and financial systems and through the use of technology based information and communication system (Singh and Verma, 2009). The corporate world is indeed at the cusp of a new era, an era which Sirkin et al. (2008) called "globality." This is where business flows in all directions, companies have no centers, nothing is foreign and market presence, supply chain, capital, talent and mindset are all global. Even the benchmarks for performance have become global. Companies are now being evaluated on the extent to which they are able to measure up to the global standards set by the very best for quality, features, price, customer requirements, productivity, and even outputs. It is more challenging, if not intimidating, for fledgling start-ups as they not only have to hit the road running but also have to keep bucking the swirls and eddies of a global world.

The challenge for the corporate world has become even more formidable because of the unprecedented economic and financial uncertainty. One reason for this is the reconfiguration of the global economic balance. The growing tilt towards BRIC countries is matched by the concomitant decline of the earlier rich man's club consisting of North America, West Europe and Japan. Although this has encouraged investments in such economies, the uncertainty attached to these markets as demonstrated by the huge fluctuations in the stock exchanges, has made investments a highly risky proposition. Today money has very few places to go. This uncertainty has been compounded by mind boggling fluctuations in currency and oil prices. Indeed, the volatility and unpredictability of the business environment is of such immense proportions that it can defy and defeat any well laid out plans.

This hyper turbulence has also been aggravated by the growing complexity of the competitive world. So on the one side are some large companies which are trying to cross new frontiers in a borderless and flat world, there are others like BHP which are trying to become even bigger by acquiring other companies and there are still other entrepreneurial firms which are driven to compete on the grace of their idea. And then quite paradoxically there are seemingly dwarf companies like Tatas, Mittals, Videocon, RPG, Airtel etc. which are acquiring giant companies which are bigger in market share and of more worth than they themselves. The challenge today is not that bigger players do not have any future, but that if the bigger players want to survive in this Darwinian dance then they cannot rely on their size anymore. They need to have the characteristics of the small players: agile, lean, nimble, quick, and responsive. And even that is not good enough. For, ideas are the only winners today.

In a world where borders exist no more and which is dotted with companies and their networks, every competitive move and or anything that can affect competition, like a birth of a start-up firm in a garage somewhere in a distant corner of the world, becomes significant enough to set off a chain of events which gathers momentum, size and information overload for the boundary spanners and decision makers in the organization. Indeed business has become war; but of a different kind. Earlier the enemies were known, the allies were obvious, the bone(s) of contention and the weapons to be used were all known. Today a firm does not even know that from where the next attack on its competitive position will come, who will launch it and in what form. The corporate world is fast becoming a global minefield.

As the organizational decision makers, straitjacketed by the heightened ambiguities, seek to enact the environment for strategizing and organizing, they now have to confront the paradigm busting switch in the notions of strategic positioning. Today, firms are discovering that more and more people purchase products and services for its impact on and manifestation of their putative identity rather than for its intrinsic use. The message is loud and clear. It means that those firms who blindly or obstinately continue to market products and services will sooner or later die. So if survival of the firms is all about marketing identity and competing in that, companies cannot be any more just in the product market business. Instead, in the next orbit, companies will have to be in the business of lifestyle if they have to thrive and excel.

Even as organizations respond to the contours of business, their configuration is acquiring new forms. Till very recent times, vertical integration was considered the basis for reaping competitive advantage. But with the espousal of concepts like core competencies, inauguration of the phenomena called outsourcing, virtual integration has now become the new motif of organizational architecture. Creating network and inter-dependencies, managing partner ecosystem's as in Airtel and coordinating between geographically dispersed and culturally diverse work groups in a classic illustration of distributed mind for the Disney cartoon series called Higgly Town Heroes is the new challenge. Virtual integration is actually intimidating, both to create and to manage. This is because it involves many players none of which belong to company; yet each one of them is an inextricable part of the company that is at the nucleus. This is the new global organizational structure. And this has tremendous implications on the concept of leadership, communication, and people processes.

Amidst all this, the notions of work and employment are getting transformed. The idea of life time employment and commitment is now obsolescent. Loyalty has assumed a different meaning altogether. As a new class of nomadic employees who work simultaneously in multiple organizations and belong to the breed of fiercely independent class of idea givers, emerge from the shadows of the consulting class, the meaning of loyalty is becoming increasingly transient. Commitment is not seen anymore in terms of time. Instead it is being increasingly seen in terms of the value which people bring to the table and contribute to the organization. Organizations too no longer talk about retaining people. Instead, organizations are fast realizing that they now need to create a situation and a culture where an individual is motivated and enabled to give his best to the organization as long as he/she is there.

Finally is this inescapable reality for all the organizations that they are operating in a context that is marked by a crisis of trust: between neighbors, towards proponents of religious and ethnic aggregates, amongst establishments that constitutes institutional framework, towards institutions such as banks and financial majors, governance of corporate and the integrity of CEOs. Companies today face almost an insurmountable challenge in inspiring confidence amongst investors, employees, customers and business partners. The traditional way of doing business has come under great challenges. Indeed the call for jettisoning it altogether has become shrill with the demands for more sustainable, equitable and just development models. Being open, transparent, ethical and socially responsible is not only a good business sense. For some, it is business. As an imperative.

All in all, the operating environment for business is now characterized with unprecedented discontinuity as a result of complexities, hyper-turbulence, and ambiguities. Intertwined with political, macro-economic, and social dynamics in their economies, the corporations, and their managers are under humungous pressure to keep pace with rapid technological advances, global competition and new, and at times shifting, government policy initiatives.

THE INDIAN BUSINESS LANDSCAPE: AN AUDIT

Despite all the trials and tribulations that the countries, companies and societies all over the world is facing, India has risen to great heights and is, rather arguably, poised to regain its rightful place of leadership in the comity of nations.

Today the Indian economy has proved to be far more robust and far better protected from the vagaries of external threats. India also has a more sustainable growth trajectory given the fact that as its population increases and gets younger and as the economy continues to grow at 8 percent p.a. in GDP, and this added population comes above the poverty line, it will translate into addition of about 20–30 million young producers and consumers every year into the market This will have a transformative impact on the Indian economy.

More importantly the Indian business model of providing products and services that are low priced, affordable, convenient, and of good quality has proved to be of immense potential in a world where 80 percent of the population in Asia, Africa and Latin America belong to the lower and the middle economic strata. As the companies belonging to the western world are more accustomed to providing rich, luxurious, and, of course, high quality products which are targeted at the rich and moneyed strata of the society, the Indian business model involving a sachet strategy of providing products and services meant for one or limited use is proving to be a handsome winner for the people in the lower income bracket. For the sachet strategy allows them to use a good quality product and service like shampoos and mobile recharge only when they have the necessary earning to support their purchase. It has given people the convenience, flexibility, affordability, without compromising on quality, in purchasing and using products and services. This business model which will benefit more than four billion people out of six billion people across the world today has heralded a sea change in the business world. The good news for the Indian corporate is that India is at the centre of this innovative, low cost, and high quality business model.

The Indian growth story has been primarily powered by Indian entre-preneurs. Indeed the silicon valley phenomena is being duplicated in India with entrepreneurs and social entrepreneurs spawning organizations to provide products and services, targeted at different niches of the market and the different notches of the society. But it is also true that the Government of India has catalyzed this growth with its well crafted, well calculated, well paced and well measured strategy of deregulation, privatization, and liberalization. It is also true that had the government not taken the timely, some say retrograde steps, in putting liberalization in the economic and financial sector on the back burner during the time of the meltdown, India would have slid into the abyss of recession. Corporate India has also benefited immensely from the insistence on indigenization by the Government of India. The mushrooming of some great firms in different parts of India—Chennai, Pune, Gurgaon—who make components not only for Indian auto companies, but also for Japanese, American and European companies, have led to India becoming the centre of auto com-ponents: highest quality—six sigma, no defects, no rejection—and that too at the rock bottom prices. The IT revolution and the telecom revolution have ensured that not only Indians are more well connected, mobile, aware and uninhibited in conducting business with a global frame of reference, but also that the software revolution has provided India with inimitable capability in domain knowledge which is not only being leveraged by IBM that has its largest employee base in India but the rest of the world as they outsource and off shore to be competitive and sustainable.

But whether this millennium will be India's depends upon how well India is able to overcome the four lags: infrastructure, education, health-care, and poverty. Having a demographic advantage and the youngest population in which a large number is not educated enough and even if educated, lacking in employable skills in a society would not only deprive the corporate sector of manpower but also create conditions for skill shortage, high attrition rate and exorbitant salaries thereby undermin-ing the low cost advantage of Indian corporate. As far as the vocational, technical and higher education is concerned, the loss of Indian students to institutions abroad has also created a tremendous leakage of resources from India. While investments by the Government on roads, ports, power, health care and education etc would catalyze development, it will still fall short because of the scale of corruption where 80 percent of investments goes into wrong hands and where there is no compliance and consequence management and bureaucracy whose maze of rules and regulations are enough to drive away the most passionate entrepreneur. Another gap relates to the labor legislation. It does not give the Indian corporate the kind of freedom that is available to corporate elsewhere. Today the cost of labor in proportion to the output of labor is increasing thus putting India's famed labor cost advantage under great threat. So cost wise, India is becoming non competitive and unless and until the productivity rises to justify the level of wages, it will become a weakness which has to be overcome.

TOWARDS THE NEXT ORBIT: ROAD MAP FOR THE CORPORATES

The road map for the Indian corporate organizations is clear. The Indian corporate have certain strengths and certain glaring weaknesses. Indian companies have been traditionally very cost conscious and frugal which not only gives them a cost advantage but also enables them to sustainably provide a business model to the world that is based upon low cost, high value, affordable and convenient product and services. It has also shown over time to be highly flexible and adaptive to environmental and technological changes. Besides, the Indian corporates have demonstrated excellent and highly professional management capability. Given the fact that most of these managers are English speaking, it has also provided impetus to their aspirations of becoming a global player. Indeed it is the absence of adequate number of managers with experience in working in the global arena which is an Indian company's biggest bane. This adds to the reasons that have prevented Indian companies from becoming a global player. Indeed Indian companies have still remained constrained in terms of being local in terms of their supply chain, market, and mindset. Then are the inabilities to brand, package, present their product or services as an innovative and technologically sophisticated value adding product and services which has proved to be a further weakness in the global market. It is for these reasons that despite having their footprints in multiple geographies, Indian firms have continued to operate more as a local and India centric player.

It is in this context that the road map for the Indian corporate for transition and excellence into the next orbit must be seen.

Be perpetually prepared: Firms must be in the state of perpetual preparedness. This means that firms must have the ability to break out of the comfort zone in terms of their business strategy, business plans, organization design, leadership and people processes. This is what Maruti did as they decided to launch a vehicle targeted at the younger segment of the population given the emerging demographic profile of

India, restructured the organization and developed a leadership pipeline in collaboration with MDI Guragon. This apart, the recent recession has shown two things: *(a)* that firms which were mature, consistent and prepared during tough times to deal with volatile, complex and uncertain external business environment and *(b)* that firms which had responded to the environment with a middle to long term perspective recovered better and gained handsomely.

Be flexible: Firms need to be flexible to respond to changes in its domain. They must have the ability to rebalance and reconfigure themselves to avail of the opportunities and respond to the crisis. This would require organizations to have such design architecture and strategic positioning that allows it the flexibility to realign itself in the face of crisis such as the oil spill in Mexico or the product failure in the market. Then again in a classic repudiation of the strategic positioning principles, firms must have the capability to switch segments and operate in plug and play mode to respond to opportunities which typically have short windows and much shorter response time. Firms in their design must have an alert antenna. Boundarylessness has to be both internal and external. For, that will determine the fate of the organization.

Be innovative: The firms have to be innovative. For, they cannot succeed unless and until they outpace the world. However, innovation can happen only when it is institutionalized through systems and processes that can enable them. It requires a professional and entrepreneurial DNA in the company. It must be top driven so that the resistance is overcome. Finally, it requires a culture where people can have the motivation, the passion and the dedication to innovate as seen in the case of LG electronics. Innovation cannot happen in a routine scheme of things. One cannot work from nine to five, five days a week and expect to innovate. It must be lived in. In case of networking organizations like Airtel, it also depends upon the company's humility and the ability to manage its partner eco system. Indeed, as the western world is getting fatigued and defensive, the innovativeness of Indian firms would go a long way in making them bigger and global.

Build capability: A transition to the next orbit crucially hinges upon a firm's capability building process. This requires that talent acquisition has to be done with care and that learning and development of employees has to be linked with businesses, its drivers, and its deliverables. The capability building also has to be complemented with high people engagement practices. This would entail examining the job content and its fit with the capability of the person, creating a culture of empowerment and devising internal communication systems for bringing about involvement, ownership, and commitment. In view of the fact that a competitive edge of a firm cannot just be obtained through tangible factors like cost, technology, product features and core competencies, but because of intangibles like speed, customer responsiveness, employee capability and employee commitment, people and their capabilities is now the crucial arch on which the success of firm in the next orbit rests.

Manage change: The ability of the firm to manage change rather than being caught in its vortex and straitjacketed into inaction is a significant reason why certain firms survive, grow and excel irrespective of time and conditions. Change management is therefore a strategic activity which requires communication, its reiteration through various forums, its manifestation, buttressing and inculcation through appropriate organizational policies, processes and management practices. As in the case of LG electronics, it was by just the way the change was managed that culture for excellence and passion to win was created. The turnaround of Allahabad Bank and the success of the Punjab National Bank under the leadership of K.R. Kamath are the twin odes to the role of leadership in creating the open, transparent process in which people believed in.

Indeed it is only by creating the trust in the organizational processes, the management and the leadership that people can be mobilized and energized to achieve organizational goals. Indeed, unless and until constituencies are managed, there is no way leadership and the organization will succeed.

Manage partner eco system: Finally, in order to win, firms must have a well developed capability to manage partners, relationships and interdependencies. Firms must realize that they cannot do everything by themselves. Airtel for instance made a choice what it was good at and then outsourced the rest to its partners. It thus created an eco-system, a network of relationships which it can leverage and draw upon to bring necessary expertise to skills, technology, architecture and other wherewithal for effective functioning and success. Today, an organization's success depends upon how well it is able to manage its network and how successful it is in creating a community. The resounding success of Airtel is a tribute to its capability in transforming its partners to become co-creators and an inextricable part of the community—sharing in the dreams of Airtel and then striving for its realization.

TOWARDS THE NEXT ORBIT: THE LEADERSHIP IMPERATIVES

Whether organizations move to the next orbit or not and whether they succeed in the next orbit or not, depends crucially upon the nature of leadership. For it is the leadership style of the top management that determines what will be the organization's vision, goals, and strategic objectives, how decisions will be made, how the staff will be mobilized and motivated and how control and coordination will be effected. It is these values that resonate, envelop and permeate the entire organization. If towards the next orbit is not a slogan but a mindset, a way of life, then the role of leadership is critical for organizations.

Manage constituency: The most important attribute of leadership is the ability to understand and manage one's constituency. This constituency does not only comprise of the myriad stakeholders of the organization. Indeed it is a mindset that enables a leader to understand the attitudes, values, aspirations and mindsets of his employees and the partner eco system, and see its connect with the very context of his business. In so much as the context of the business has become global, the leaders are now required to have a global vision, global wisdom, and global strategy. Leaders must now have a global perspective and a capability to understand global nuances and global contours of the business. And all this must happen concomitant to their role of understanding and nurturing the constituency within from where he and his vision get their legitimacy, strength and energy.

Strategy is execution: The second critical attribute of leadership relates to their ability not only to dream and strategize but more importantly to execute and act on the ground. Indeed a leader must be the confluence of a war general that is visible in action in the corporate battlefield, a shepherd who leads and guides actions from behind and a servant who nurtures his constituency and mobilizes them to win. The leader in the next orbit must be a seamless integration of both thought and action leadership. The gestalt of leadership now is a celebration of this holism.

Be entrepreneurial: The leader must now have the capability of being an entrepreneur who seeks opportunity and sees that even in problems and adversities. This in one sense also requires in the leader the capability to think out of the box and to be creative and if that is not the case, create a culture of creativity in the organization. It is this that would unleash entrepreneurship and innovativeness in the organization. Needless to say such a culture is possible only when the leader becomes empowering, facilitating and enabling.

Develop Soul force: Today a leader must have belief in the power of the soul. The power of mind has its own importance especially in an era of information overload. But it is the power of the soul which will determine the functioning and outcome of the organization. For it is only with soul force that the leader can motivate others to realize their immense potentiality, to contribute and to excel. This does not mean that a leader should ask a bird to run and a rabbit to fly. A leader must perceive the potential and talent idiosyncratic to a person and then mentor and shape its realization. This soul force gets its added credibility from the personal ethics of the leader. This is the belief in the power of truth. It is this that makes the leader ethical and courageous.

Ceaselessly raise the bar: Finally the leadership required in the next orbit is all about being an Olympian who has an insatiable hunger for success and glory in which he himself is his competition. Towards the next orbit is all about leaders who have this tremendous, restless, insatiable appetite to grow, to win, and to keep on winning. Great leaders are all about the next curve and the next orbit.

The Mantra of leadership: In sum as Dr Pritam Singh ordained: "a leader must have the capability to look beyond, to look around and look within." He should be capable of unfolding the future into the present. He must be able to hear the sound of the unborn child. He must have the capability of looking around and to know the issues and direction of business. Finally, he must have the capability of reflecting, to evolve and to flower. This is what all great leaders do and this is what all leaders are required to do if they aspire for leadership and greatness.

TOWARDS THE NEXT ORBIT: THE ROLE OF HR

Don't just be HR. Be business: HR must align with business strategy and one can discern this perspective building up over the past few years of HR in a business influencing role rather than as a so-called "support function." To a great extent, it will also be expected of the HR function to bring in a fine balance between employee aspirations and expectations, and demands from the business. But in the reigning firmament of what firms require to do in order to succeed in the next orbit, the role of HR cannot just be recruitment and selection, training and development, salary administration, industrial relations, performance appraisal and reward management and conducting exit interviews. Instead the function of HR is to deliver in the core business as any other function in the organization and thus would have to play the role of business partner. If productivity is the problem that is dogging the business head, then it is the responsibility of the HR professional to find out all the causes that is leading to the drop in the productivity and so long as it is not technological, to devise solutions and strategies for its resolution. HR deliverables therefore are business deliverables. Further, HR investments should lead to measurable value, in order to add to the business and its performance. Indeed there can be no such thing as just an HR intervention. Even an intervention such as that of building a top management team today, as Dr Santrupt Misra talked about, is more a business related intervention involving creating a shared understanding of the common goals and devising processes for decision making and problem solving. Nor can the performance appraisal be anymore shorn off the understanding of financial dimensions of people performance such as EVA and CVA EVA, CVA, goal setting, business value drivers others, competitive landscape, regulatory environment, if they are to be relevant and meaningful. And in a world where employee commitment is transient, employee engagement is necessary for instilling a culture of passion, capability the basis of competitive advantage, innovativeness, the assurance of firm survival and excellence, culture building, performing with due diligence and creating integration vital for consolidation and growth and change management necessary for creating an enabling environment significant for firm's transition to the next curve, then HR is nothing else but strategy. In short, HR cannot be for the sake of HR. HR is for the sake of the future. HR is for the sake of a dream; it is for the sake of a vision.

There are quite a few challenging problems that confront the HR in India and these require solutions that have to be both context specific as well as of global standards. Some of these are the needs for proper manpower supply chain management, learning and development program, for bridging the skill gap; devising employee engagement programs and systematic career planning to combat issues related to attrition, motivation, commitment, and even burnouts; building a culture for passion, excellence and innovation; managing change to better fit the organization with the emerging business landscape and strategic requirements; fashioning team work amongst people sourced from different companies, different operating systems, different countries and cultures, and managing relationships with partner eco system. They all require HR to be at the center. In so much as that the erstwhile model of conventional HR separate from business must be jettisoned.

Be original. Be contextual: In view of these imperatives, where HR cannot be inward looking but oriented towards business, the drivers of business and deliverable required for business, it would be now puerile for HR to blindly cut and paste benchmark practices primarily from abroad and more specifically from America and expect it to pay any dividends. HR in a company can operate only in the context of that company. Indeed HR must transit from benchmarking of best practices to looking at what works best in a business sector, in that company, appropriate to specific business strategy, in the context of the maturity and work culture of a given organization and in tune with the local social structure of a given geographic region where the business is located.

Develop professional identity: It is incumbent upon HR professionals to develop their professional identity and their self esteem. This is an identity which depends upon the relationship which HR has with business and its deliverables and not something that gets easily influenced by top management and the diktats from the business managers. However, this professional identity itself is a function of three specific competencies: leadership, domain knowledge in HR, and capability to influence business. HR must have a self confidence in their body of knowledge and its relevance, and a passion to make a difference. Indeed if this passion is there, motivation, courage and perseverance will all be there to overcome resistance and cynicism. However, the credibility, acceptance, and success of the HR functionary would depend upon this critical fact whether their arguments and interventions are arising from the perspective of narrow functional specialization or from the larger business.

Develop personal credibility: Much of this also depends upon the personal credibility and value that the HR person brings. There are several reasons why the employees in line function have some kind of disparaging views of HR and its functionaries. According to them, the HR people live in their own abstract world and their ideas, propositions, and activities have no connect with their function or benefit to the business. Secondly, they believe that HR cannot be depended upon and use the confidential information they acquire about them for partisan and political purposes. This lack of trust is exacerbated by the so-called double standards practiced by HR professionals. While at the one end they talk about the loyalty and commitment from others, then in a classic instance of forked tongue they leave the company for more lucrative offers elsewhere. HR professionals are thus seen as people, who cannot be relied upon, cannot be trusted to deliver on their promises something that they make the employees in marketing or in production or in finance functions do. All this requires that the HR functionary should know the business day in and day out, to know the figures and the issues relating to the organization or the department or the division, to talk in the language and jargon of that particular department or division to be accepted by the people in the line functions. And then they are required to know their people, to keep information about them confidential, to show commitment to their profession, to the organization's agenda and to their own professional ethics to earn credibility and respect. Only then can HR be a credible profession and a HR professional, a respected, reliable, and dependable partner.

COMPETENCIES FOR HR PROFESSIONALS FOR THE NEXT ORBIT

Although competencies for the HR professional would vary with the dimension, the business, the organization and the career stage of the individual, certain competencies are important at certain levels and also at generic level. At a junior level, the HR professionals need to have the knowledge of their function, of statutory requirements, and tax implications. At a middle level, the skill set would be more of a general management in nature. As such abilities to gather views, integrate viewpoints, make decisions and sell those decisions becomes important. At a higher level, it is the ability to connect with the external environment, understand its demands on the organization and weave it into the strategy of the organization that becomes important. Indeed competencies at the senior level are related to ideation, integration, external representation, persuasion, and influencing.

However, at a more generic level, competencies required of the HR professionals are related to the abilities to:

1. understand the business of the organization and its drivers;
2. understand the connect between business and HR deliverables;
3. understand the role of self in building acceptance, credibility and respect in the organization; and
4. understand employees and their mindset so as to weave a relationship between their aspirations and organizational demand.

All in all, a HR professional must have the mindset of a philosopher king. He should be like Chanakya who was not just a philosopher; he had the mind of the king. He must understand the famous adage "no philosopher can be a great philosopher without being a great king; and no king can be a great king without being a great philosopher." Indeed the only value addition that HR has is towards business. Indeed HR is business. This is their only *raison d'être*.

The only constant is change.

ABOUT THE CHANGE MASTERS

Manoj Kohli
CEO (International) and Joint MD – Bharti Airtel Ltd

Manoj Kohli is the CEO (International) and Joint MD, Bharti Airtel. He heads the International Business Group. He is a Director on the Board of Bharti Airtel. Prior to becoming CEO (International) and Joint MD, he held multiple roles as CEO and Joint MD, President and CEO, and Head of Mobile Services business at Bharti Airtel.

Manoj Kohli started his career in 1979 with DCM Ltd., where he initially led the HR function, followed by leadership positions in the Foods, Chemicals, and Fertilizers businesses and assignments in engineering projects, including Shriram Honda. He left as Vice President, responsible for the Air Conditioning and Refrigeration business unit (now known as Tecumseh & Daikin) after a total stint of 16 years. He subsequently worked at AlliedSignal/Honeywell, where he was Executive Director in charge of its new Industrial Park and operations in India. He joined Escotel, which he led for over five years as Executive Director and CEO, before coming on board at Bharti Airtel.

Manoj Kohli is the Chairman for the Confederation of Indian Industry (CII) National Committee on Telecom and Broadband. He was member of the Board of GSMA in 2008. He has been the Chairman of Cellular Operators Association of India (COAI). He was adjudged "Telecom Man of the Year" and "Telecom Person of the Year" by Media Transasia and Voice & Data respectively. He is a member of the Academic Council of the Faculty of Management Studies and has been awarded the "Best Alumni Award" by SRCC, Delhi University.

He holds degrees in Commerce, Law, and MBA from the Delhi University. Manoj also attended the "Executive Business Program" at the Michigan Business School and the "Advanced Management Program" at the Wharton Business School.

K.R. Kamath
Chairman and Managing Director, Punjab National Bank

K.R. Kamath is a Fellow of the Indian Institute of Banking and Finance. Some of the important positions he has held earlier are: Chairman and Managing Director, Allahabad Bank; Executive Director, Bank of India; and General Manager, Corporation Bank. He is Chairman of the Board of PNB Housing Finance Ltd, PNB Gilts Ltd, PNB International, and PNB Investment Services Ltd. He is a member of the Governing body of Indian Banks Association, Indian Institute of Banking Personnel Selection, NIBM, IIM Lucknow, and Oriental Insurance Company Ltd. He has held Directorship of several organizations such as Indo Zambia Bank, ASREC (India) Ltd, BOI Shareholding Ltd, Bank of India (Tanzania) Ltd, Star Union-Daichi Life Insurance Co., P.T. Bank Swadeshi, Jakarta, Universal Sampo GIC Ltd, and All India Bank Finance Ltd.

Santrupt Misra
Director, Group H.R. and CEO, Carbon Black Business, Aditya Birla Group

Dr Santrupt Misra is a Director on the Aditya Birla Management Corporation Private Limited Board, the apex decision making body of the US $29.2 billion, Aditya Birla Group. He is the CEO of the Group's Carbon Black Business and is also the Director, Human Resources of the Aditya Birla Group. He is on the Board of the Aditya Birla Science & Technology Company Ltd, Alexandria Carbon Black Co SAE, Thai Carbon Black Public Co, Ltd, and the Alexandria Fiber Co, SAE, which are part of the Aditya Birla Group.

In 2009, Dr Misra was inducted on the Global Advisory Board of the Association of Executive Search Consultants (AESC). In 2008, he was conferred with the Fellowship of the National Academy of Human Resources (NAHR), USA. He is also on the Board of the Worldwide ERC (Employee Relocation Council) for the period 2008–10. In 2007, he was elected as a Member of the Society of Fellows of the Aston Business School Society. He is also on the Board of the Xavier Institute of Management, Bhubaneswar and the Board of the Asian Heart Institute and Research Centre Pvt Ltd. He was the President of the National HRD Network from 2002 to 2005.

Dr Misra was has been conferred with various awards and fellowships, some of the most notable are the Eisenhower Fellowship in the year 2000, the "Role Model and Exemplary Leader Award" at Asia's Best Employer Brand Awards 2010, Singapore, the "Outstanding HR Professional of the Year Award" 2010 by The Bombay Management Association, and the "Outstanding HR Chief Award" by the National HRD Network in 2002. The All India Management Association (AIMA) admitted Dr Misra as an AIMA Fellow. *Business Today* identified Dr Misra amongst the "20 Hottest Young Executives" in the year 2002. He has had full-time professional work experience with the J.K. Group, the Tata Institute of Social Sciences, and Unilever, India.

With two post-graduate degrees, in Political Science and in Personnel Management and Industrial Relations, Dr Misra has won four gold medals in his educational career and has stood first in various university exams. He has two PhDs, one from India and the other from the Aston Business School in UK, in Public Administration and Industrial Relations, respectively. He also won a Commonwealth Scholarship in 1990.

S.Y. Siddiqui
Managing Executive Officer—Administration (HR, Finance, IT, Company Law and Legal) Maruti Suzuki India Ltd

S.Y. Siddiqui is responsible for Corporate HR for Suzuki Powertrain (Engine Company) and Suzuki Motorcycles. He is a part time Director on the Board of Suzuki Motorcycles and is a special Invitee on the Board of Suzuki Powertrain India Ltd.

A Post-Graduate in HRM, Mr Siddiqui has a career track of around 30 years in the HR Function of Indian Corporates as well as MNCs such as Escorts Limited, DCM Group—DCM Toyota Limited, DCM Daewoo Motors Limited, DCM Benetton India Limited, and New Holland Tractors India.

Widely traveled abroad, he has handled global and multi-cultural HR issues in highly competitive business environments in India and Europe. He is thus well-versed with global HR policies, systems, and processes. He has the unique experience of working in multicultural environments and deal with people of different nationalities, that is, Indians, Japanese, Koreans, Italians, British, Americans, and others.

Presently he is the Regional President of NHRDN (North) and a Board member of NHRDN (National HRD Network).

Arvind Agrawal
President—Corporate Development and Group HR, RPG Group

Dr Arvind Agrawal has been the President—Corporate Development and Group HR in the RPG Group since 1999. His current respons- ibilities in RPG comprise of HR and TQM. He is an alumnus of IIT (Kharagpur), IIM (Ahmedabad), and IIT (Bombay), from where he completed his PhD in the area of Strategic Leadership.

The first 12 years of his working life was spent in the HR function in companies like Escorts and Modi Xerox. Thereafter, he assumed add- itional responsibilities for TQM in Modi Xerox, which brought him closer to the business environment and issues. The exposure gained in TQM equipped him to take on the role of Corporate Strategy and Marketing at Modi Xerox itself.

During the years 1994 to 1999, Dr Arvind Agrawal was Chief Executive at Escorts, responsible for the two Construction Equipment Business Companies; Escorts JCB, and Escorts Construction Equip- ment Limited.

Dr Agrawal has been active in Management and HR forums in the country. In 1992, he was awarded the National HRD Award. He served as the National President of National HRD Network during the year 2000–02.

Yasho Verma
Chief Operating Officer, LG Electronics India

Dr Yasho Verma is the COO of LG Electronics India from January 2010. His responsibility includes looking after business operations of the company from his earlier role as Director HR and MS for LG India. He joined LGEIL as VP (HR and MS) in 1997. With effect from January 1, 2008 he was elevated as Executive in the LG Global hierarchy. He has been the first Non-Korean to reach this level in the LG Global hierarchy.

Dr Verma is an Engineering Graduate with Post-Graduation in Business Administration and PhD in area of Organizational Behavior from Indian Institute of Technology, Kharagpur. He started his career with TATA Steel in Jamshedpur and worked for around 15 years. He has been with LG Electronics for over 12 years.

He was rated as "HERETIC" by *Business Today* and Gallup and featured on the cover page of *Business Today* in 1997. He has delivered several lectures and has addressed boards of prestigious companies in India and abroad. Some of these companies include ITC, JK Group, and Ispat Group, Bangkok.

He has visited the London Business School, Seoul University, Wharton Management School, and Philadelphia for guest lectures in addition to other premier Management Institutes in India.

He has been conferred the Honorary Fellowship by the All India Management Association for significant contribution towards professional management. He is also member council of the Management of All India Management Association. He is President, Consumer Electronics and Appliances Manufacturers Association (CEAMA) for 2009–11. He has authored *Passion: The Untold Story of LG Electronics*. He is also the Honorary Editor for the *Journal of Projective Psychology* and *Mental Health* by Anchorage USA.

Pritam Singh
Professor, Management Development Institute

Dr Pritam Singh has spent his entire life tirelessly doing what he does best: awakening students, academia, corporate heads and policy makers to raise their excellence to the next level. As the chairman and member of several policy-making committees and bodies of Government of India, he has stamped his perspective on policy issues that surround both management education and corporate management in India. As a consultant, Dr Pritam Singh has done work with more than 200 CEOs in India and abroad.

As an academic administrator, Dr Pritam Singh has an unparalleled record of making significant differences in his roles as Director at IIM Lucknow and MDI Gurgaon, and as Dean at the Administrative Staff College of India, Hyderabad and IIM Bangalore. In the contemporary management world, he is, therefore, known as a Midas touch leader.

A thorough leader with extraordinary insight, Dr Pritam Singh is the author of seven academically reputed books, three of which are award winning. He has also published over 60 research papers in various national and international journals. He is a globally sought after speaker and has addressed various Indian and global audiences in various countries.

His distinguished services were acknowledged by the country when the President of India conferred on him the prestigious "Padam Shri." MIRBIS—the leading global, management school in Moscow, honored him as the "Global Thought Leader" in 2006–07. He was not just the first Indian, but also the first Asian to have walked in this global hall of fame. He has also been the recipient of several prestigious awards, to name a few: Sarvapalli Radhakrishnan Memorial Award: Teacher of Teachers; Lifetime Achievement Award: Vivekananda Foundation; TIE-UP California USA Outstanding Entrepreneur Award; Outstanding CEO: NHRD Award; Best Director Award of Indian Management Schools; and the First AIMA-Kewal Nohria Award for Academic Leadership in Management Education.

ABOUT THE EDITOR AND CONTRIBUTORS

EDITOR

Subir Verma is Fellow (PhD) from IIM, Ahmedabad and M.A. (Gold Medalist) and M.Phil in Political Science from Delhi University. He has more than 16 years of teaching experience and has been a visiting faculty at ESCP-Europe, Paris. He was earlier the Chairman of the flagship MBA program, Chairman of the Corporate Relations and Placements Committee, and Chairman of the EQUIS Accreditation at MDI.

Professor Verma has consulted with top MNCs in India on their Organization Design, Change Management, and Leadership Development. He has also designed and delivered numerous workshops, both in-class and outbound-based experiential learning, on leadership, teamwork, managerial effectiveness, and negotiation skills for the middle and senior level of management of several reputed public and private sector organizations.

Professor Verma has edited two books, viz. *Organizing and Managing in the Era of Globalization* (along with Pritam Singh, 2009) and *Creating Boundaryless HR* (2009), and published several articles in reputed national and international journals. His forthcoming book on *M.K. Gandhi: An Epitome of Leadership* is slated for publication next year. At present, he is engaged in carrying out the AICTE funded research on "Identification and Benchmarking of Best Practices in Organizing and Managing in Corporate India." Professor Verma has presented his research papers in several prestigious international conferences such as of the Academy of Management, World Congress of Sociology, Asia Pacific Researchers in Organization Studies, International Human Resource Management, and the European Group of Organization Studies.

Professor Verma is a recipient of numerous awards and honors, some of which are the Dr Karan Singh Gold Medal, Professor C.J. Chacko Prize, UGC Fellowship, Club Internationale (Paris) Fellowship, and the AICTE Research Grant. He is on the editorial board of the *International Strategic Management Journal*. He is a Board Member of the Asia Pacific Researchers on Organization Studies and Member of the American Academy of Management, International Sociological Association, and the National HRD Network.

CONTRIBUTORS

Shubhabrata Basu is an Assistant Professor of Strategic Management at the Indian Institute of Management (IIM), Indore. He is the founding Chairperson of the one year full time Executive Post-Graduate Program (EPGP) at IIM Indore. He is a Fellow (PhD) in Management (in the Business Policy Area) from IIM Ahmedabad. His research interests include Indian Public Sectors, Organizational Slack, Environmental Discontinuities, Knowledge Evolution and Intellectual Capital, and Innovation Characteristics in Emerging Economies.

Before joining academics, Dr Basu served the Industry and the Civil Administration, in various posts of repute, for about 10 years. He has designed and executed various national and international projects in the Steel and Power Sector. He also served the Government of West Bengal in the capacity of Assistant Labor Commissioner in the Durgapur Region.

His research papers were accepted in various national and international conferences. He has several cases and working papers to his credit. He has professional affiliation to the Institution of Engineers (India), Strategic Management Society, West Bengal Labor Service Association, etc.

Alfredo Behrens, an economist, holds a PhD from the University of Cambridge. He has lectured at or consulted for various institutes and business schools including Princeton University's Woodrow Wilson School; University of California at Berkeley London Business School, etc. Alfredo Behrens has broad experience in advising senior public officials, shareholders and board members of banks and large corporations and universities. He is most active on issues such as leadership, cross-cultural management, and HR-related issues, besides strategic planning focused on the internationalization of companies. He has worked with the private and public sector in America, East and Western Europe, and Southern Africa.

His book *Culture and Management in the Americas* (2009) was selected as the best Brazilian business book of the year. He is currently writing a book on leadership in Latin America: *Shooting Heroes to Reward Cowards: A Sure Path to Organizational Disaster*. Some of the prestigious awards received are the McNamara Fellowship by the World Bank and the Hewlett fellowship by Princeton University.

Asha Bhandarker is the Raman Munjal Chair Professor of Leadership Studies at the Management Development Institute (MDI), Gurgaon. She is a distinguished psychologist and a management thinker. She has published five books and many articles in various national and international journals. Her book *Winning the Corporate Olympiad: Renaissance Paradigm* (co-author Pritam Singh) was awarded the best book award by the Delhi Management Association. Her recent publication is *Shaping Business Leaders: What B Schools Don't Do*. She is a well recognized trainer and consultant closely involved in the corporate sector where she works with the boards and top teams of large companies and banks. She is passionate about the area of leadership studies and teaches and trains in this field. She has also been awarded the best teacher award at MDI. Dr Bhandarker has been a Senior Fulbrighter and a Visiting Professor at Darden School of Business, University of Virginia and at the George Mason University, USA. She has been a visiting fellow at the London Business School.

Shivganesh Bhargava is the senior most professor at the Shailesh J. Mehta School of Management, Indian Institute of Technology, Bombay, India in the area of Organizational Behavior, Human Resource Management and Entrepreneurship. His past teaching and research association has been with the Indian Institute of Management (IIM), Lucknow and IIM, Ahmedabad. He is the recipient of the Emerald Literati Network Award for Excellence (2010), VKRV Rao Award (2003) in Management, MPCOST Young Scientist Award (1988), and ISCA Young Scientist

Award (1986). He has published three books from the SAGE (Response) Publications on *Entrepreneurial Management* (2008), *Developmental Aspects of Entrepreneurship* (2007), and *Transformational Leadership: Value Based Management for Indian Organizations* (2003), one case at the European Case Clearing House, over 40 research papers in international journals and has presented/contributed over 100 papers at international and national conferences/seminars.

Jyotsna Bhatnagar is Associate Professor, HRM and Chairperson, PGHR program at the Management Development Institute, Gurgaon, India. She has a PhD from the Indian Institute of Technology, Delhi. She is the Board Member for Asian Academy of Management and Indian Academy of Management. She recently received the award for the Best Paper for Practical Implications, 2009-Emerald, UK; and the Best Paper Award from the Indian Society of Training and Development World conference, Kolkata, 2000.

Dr Bhatnagar has conducted/designed organizational diagnostic consulting studies and senior level management development program interventions on HR issues of talent management, high performance work systems, employee engagement, human capital development interventions for various public and private sector organizations as well as for the department of the Government of India. She has published around 60 research papers in national and international journals and co-edited two books: *Future of Work* and *Changing Face of People Management in India*.

Soumendu Biswas is an Assistant Professor in the area of Human Resource at the Management Development Institute (MDI), Gurgaon, India. Dr Biswas has a PhD from the Indian Institute of Technology (IIT), Kharagpur in the Area of Industrial/Organizational Psychology. He has published articles in several national and international journals and has also presented papers in several international conferences such as the annual conferences of the Academy of Management, the European Academy of Management, the Asian Academy of Management, the Australia-New Zealand Academy of Management, the American Society of Training and Development, the National Academy of Psychology, and the Indian Council of Social Science Research.

Dr Biswas' research interests include organizational culture, international dimensions of organizational behavior, and multivariate data analysis with particular reference to SEM procedures.

Giovanni Scarso Borioli is Assistant Professor of Operations Management. He teaches Problem Solving and Decision Making at graduate and post-graduate levels. He is an M.Sc. in Engineering and is currently undertaking his doctoral studies at the University College of London. Giovanni spent three years working as Project Manager after which he started his business studies at ESCP Europe, where he participated in the 2006 edition of the GMP (General Manager Program). He is also an active management consultant and he works with international companies in fields such as constructions, pharmaceutical, and energy.

His research interests include the implementation of large-scale change in organizations, particularly the implementation of lean management, evidence-based management, and decision-making support tools. He is also working in the field of sustainability of supply chains and green supply chain management.

Ashita Goswami is currently pursuing her doctoral studies at the Department of Psychology, Michigan University. She is an MA in psychology from Delhi University. She works in the areas of leadership, meaning of work and spirituality.

Arun Kumar Jain is a Professor of Strategy, IM and Corporate Governance at IIM-Lucknow (Noida Campus). He has published more than 100 articles and research based case studies in reputed national and international journals, including HBR. He is advisor to the Government and is on the Board of several statutory and business organizations.

He has taught at leading MBA institutions across the world, including Bradford (UK), Connecticut (USA), and has been a Visiting Professor at leading universities in USA, UK, Greece, France, Germany, and Singapore. Dr Jain has lectured at reputed forums like the Global Corporate Governance Forum, World Bank/IFC, OECD, UNCTAD, and MITI.

Currently he is the Chairman and President of Center for Accelerated Learning, Innovation, and Competitiveness at Germany (on leave) and Affiliated Professor of Strategy, International Business, and Corporate Governance at EM Strasbourg School of Business, Strasbourg.

Deepa Mazumdar is Professor in HRM at the National Institute of Bank Management, Pune, India. She has a PhD in Career Decision-making from the University of Lausanne. She has published articles in reputed journals like *Journal of Social Psychology*, *Journal of Applied Social Psychology*,

Irish Journal of Psychology, Swiss Journal of Psychology and in *Management and Change*.

Her areas of specialization are organizational behavior, leadership, communications, mentoring coaching, and counseling and psychological assessments. She is certified in *(i)* DISC, *(ii)* Culture at Workplace and Competency, *(iii)* Neurolinguistic Programming (NLP), and *(iv)* Emergenetics.

S. Mohan is an alumnus of BITS, Pilani and IIM, Bangalore. He holds a PhD in Management. He underwent training in "Change Management" at Stanford, and attended the Executive Development Program at Kellogg and at Robert H. Smith School of Business, Washington. He has co-authored a book, *The Indian CEO—A Portrait of Excellence* which was released by the Hon. Prime Minister Dr Manmohan Singh in July 2007.

He is a life member of the All India Management Association and served as President of the Bombay Management Association (2008–09). He is also a life member of the Institution of Engineers, India. He has wide corporate experience of handling various functions. He worked with TELCO, Pune; BHEL, Bhopal; and is currently on the Board of Bharat Petroleum Corporation Ltd as Director (HR).

Armen E. Petrosyan is a Professor of Management and Public Administration, North-Western Academy of Public Service, Tver, Russia. He holds a PhD and Grand PhD (of higher level) from the Moscow state Lomonossov University. He has more than 25 years of working for scientific and educational institutions and about 20 years of experience in business consulting and functioning as executive. His main scientific interests include business and management, sociology and politics, philosophy and psychology, logic and methodology, and history of science. He has published numerous books. Some of the latest ones being, *Management: Ideas, Problems, Tests*, 2008; *The Queen of Marketing*, 2007. He has published several articles, the latest being a series of papers on leadership in New Management, such as "The arsenal of leadership: Vision as a vague image"; "The arsenal of leadership"; "Mechanisms of inspiration"; "The arsenal of leadership"; "The embodiment of 'right' behavior".

John Pisapia is a Professor of Leadership Studies at Florida Atlantic University. Dr Pisapia brings over 23 years of management experience as a principal, state commissioner of education, University Department Chair, and Research Director to his academic podium at Florida Atlantic University and his consultancies. He previously held tenured faculty positions at West Virginia University and Virginia Commonwealth University.

His work in strategic thinking and execution has received national and international attention. His book, *The Strategic Leader*, promising a new direction for leading in a globalized world was published in 2009. He has developed two research instruments: The Strategic Thinking Questionnaire (STQ) and the Strategic Leadership Questionnaire (SLQ). He has published articles in the *Leadership Review*, *International Journal of Leadership Education*, *The American Journal of Business Research*, etc.

Kshipra Rustogi is a Research Associate at MDI, Gurgaon in Organizational Behavior Area. She has done her Masters in Psychology (specialization in Organizational Behavior) from the Faculty of Arts, Delhi University. She has one and a half years of work experience. Kshipra Rustogi's areas of interest are leadership, meaning of work, values, and social psychology of virtual communication.

Ajay Singal is a doctoral student, Indian Institute of Management, Lucknow (India).

Pritam Singh is a management professional who has devoted his life to the development of management education in India and abroad. He is currently a Professor of Organizational Behavior at the Management Development Institute (MDI), Gurgaon.

As the Chairman and member of several policy-making committees and bodies of Government of India, Professor Singh has lent his perspective to a number of policy issues surrounding both management education and corporate management in India. As a consultant, he has done work with more than 200 CEO's in India and abroad.

As an academic administrator, Professor Singh has an unparalleled record of making significant differences in his roles as Director at IIM Lucknow and MDI Gurgaon. He has authored seven academically reputed books, three of which are award winning. He has also published over 60 research papers in various national and international journals.

He has been the recipient of the prestigious "Padma Shri." He has also been conferred with many other prestigious management awards and is in the board of over eight Indian blue chip companies that includes Godrej India, Hero Honda, Maruti Suzuki, etc.

Davide Sola is a Professor of Strategy and Management on the London Campus of ESCP Europe. He is a PhD in enterprise economics with a thesis on "Organizational Transformation" from the University of Torino. He has been involved in a number of technology start-ups. He has worked as Head of New Ventures for the Hartley Investment Trust based in London and for McKinsey & Co. in Italy as their Engagement Manager. He has also held the position of Director of ESCP Europe, London campus. Professor Sola is also very active as corporate advisor, supporting the top management of leading enterprises on issues such as new business models, pricing, leveraging economic uncertainty, and strategy at large. He is an economic advisor to the Italian Ministry of Economic Development advising on themes related to growth strategies.

His research interests are in corporate transformation, strategic renewal, entrepreneurship, and applied economics (in particular the application of Austrian principles in the corporate world). He has authored numerous articles, policy papers, book chapters, case studies, and papers presented at international research conferences (Academy of Management, SMS, EIASM, etc.).

Marie Taillard is a Professor of Marketing on the London Campus of ESCP, Europe. She is also Director of the School's Master Program in Marketing and Creativity which she launched in 2010. She has a PhD from the University College, London. She teaches a range of marketing courses across post-graduate and executive education programs. Her research in marketing focuses on the creation of value by consumers and social media. Her background in Linguistics, Social Psychology, and Cognitive Psychology also accounts for her interest in shared intentionality and change management.

Sumati Varma is an Associate Professor in the Department of Commerce and Business, at Sri Aurobindo College (Eve), Delhi University. She has over two decades of teaching experience, is the author of two books and is currently engaged in research in the area of firm internationalization, born global firms and international entrepreneurship. She is also a consultant in higher education with the NCERT and the Institute of Life Long Learning (ILLL), Delhi University.

Ellen Van Velsor is a Senior Fellow at the Center for Creative Leadership headquarters in Greensboro, North Carolina. She has a PhD in Sociology from the University of Florida, and has completed her postdoctoral fellowship at the Center for the Study of Aging and Human Development at Duke University.

Ellen is co-editor of the *Center for Creative Leadership's Handbook of Leadership Development* (1998, 2003, and 2010), and co-author of *Breaking the Glass Ceiling: Can Women Reach the Top of America's Largest Corporations?* (1987 and 1991). She has authored numerous book chapters, articles and reports, including "Leadership Development as a Support to Ethical Action in Organizations" (*Journal of Management Development*, 2008).

Her current research focuses on lessons of experience in Asia and the US and on leadership practices and processes related to corporate social responsibility in global organizations.

Meena Surie Wilson is Senior Enterprise Associate with the Research, Innovation and Product Development group of the Center for Creative Leadership—Asia Pacific, based in Jamshedpur, India. She holds a PhD in adult and organizational development from UNC-Chapel Hill. Meena's most recent assignment as Research Director for the CCL-APAC office in Singapore involved starting up a research unit to advance knowledge about leadership development in countries in Asia. Her research focuses on the power of experience as a catalyst of leadership lessons, and on cross-cultural adaptability as a source of managerial effectiveness. Her latest book is the forthcoming *Developing Tomorrows' Leaders Today: Insights from Corporate India*. She has also contributed chapters in several other books.

In addition, Dr Wilson facilitates assessment, feedback, and coaching modules included in several CCL programs, and contributes to the design and delivery of conference modules and workshops. She has been on the team of the Center's Design and Evaluation group in Greensboro, North Carolina. Her previous work experience includes educational policy analysis for the state of Alaska, program development for public schools in Anchorage, AK, and project work at the Xavier Labor Relations Institute in Jamshedpur, India.

James Wright is the Dean of FIA Business School, and Director of FIA's International Executive MBA program which he started in 1992. He is a Professor of Strategy at the School of Economics, Administration and Accounting, of the University of São Paulo, and heads its Future Studies Program, founded in 1980. He has a PhD in Business Administration from the University of São Paulo. His research interests include technology and business forecasting, strategic planning, cognitive mapping, and computer-aided group decision making.

He has professional business experience in industrial project management in Brazil and Africa, and does extensive consulting work and serves on the Board of Directors in international companies and other organizations. He has received several teaching awards and the prestigious Jabuti Prize 2000 as co-author of a book on Agro-environmental Impacts. He is also the recipient of the Thomas Kuhn Gold Medal awarded by the International Union of Air Pollution Prevention and Environmental Protection and the International Academy of Science, for his contribution to the Floram Project, 1992–95.

INDEX